KINGS, QUEENS AND FALLEN MONARCHIES

KINGS, QUEENS AND FALLEN MONARCHIES

ROYAL DYNASTIES OF INTERWAR EUROPE

ROBERT JAMES STOVE

PEN & SWORD
HISTORY
AN IMPRINT OF PEN & SWORD BOOKS LTD.
YORKSHIRE – PHILADELPHIA

First published in Great Britain in 2024 by
PEN AND SWORD HISTORY
An imprint of
Pen & Sword Books Ltd
Yorkshire – Philadelphia

ISBN 978 1 39903 542 2

A CIP catalogue record for this book is available from the British Library.

Typeset in Times New Roman 9.5/11.5 by
SJmagic DESIGN SERVICES, India.
Printed and bound in the UK by CPI Group (UK) Ltd.

Pen & Sword Books Limited incorporates the imprints of Atlas, Archaeology,
Aviation, Discovery, Family History, Fiction, History, Maritime, Military,
After the Battle, Military Classics, Politics, Select, Transport, True Crime,
Air World, Frontline Publishing, Leo Cooper, Remember When,
Seaforth Publishing, The Praetorian Press, Wharncliffe Local History,
Wharncliffe Transport, Wharncliffe True Crime and White Owl.

For a complete list of Pen & Sword titles please contact
PEN & SWORD BOOKS LIMITED
George House, Units 12 & 13, Beevor Street, Off Pontefract Road,
Barnsley, South Yorkshire, S71 1HN, England
E-mail: enquiries@pen-and-sword.co.uk
Website: www.pen-and-sword.co.uk

or
PEN AND SWORD BOOKS
1950 Lawrence Rd, Havertown, PA 19083, USA
E-mail: uspen-and-sword@casematepublishers.com
Website: www.penandswordbooks.com

Continental States which have already been shaken by revolutions are under constant fear of being shaken again by restorations.

G.K. Chesterton[1]

This war would never have come unless, under American and modernising pressure, we had driven the Habsburgs out of Austria and Hungary and the Hohenzollerns out of Germany. By making these vacuums we gave the opening for the Hitlerite monster to crawl out of its sewer onto the vacant thrones. No doubt these views are very unfashionable.

Winston Churchill[2]

Virtue with a crown on it is a greater enemy to the world revolution than a hundred tyrant Tsars.

V.I. Lenin[3]

It is not religion but revolution that is the opiate of the people.

Simone Weil[4]

1 G.K. Chesterton, 'King George V: "A Patriotic Ruler and a Public Servant"', *Illustrated London News* 188 (25 January 1936), 5049.

2 Churchill to Anthony Eden, 8 April 1945; quoted in Sir Winston Churchill, *The Second World War: Triumph and Tragedy* (New York City: Houghton Mifflin Harcourt, 1948), 750.

3 V.I. Lenin, quoted in Gerard Shelley, *The Speckled Domes: Episodes of an Englishman's Life in Russia* (New York City: C. Scribner's Sons, 1925), 220.

4 Simone Weil, *The Notebooks of Simone Weil* (London: Routledge, 2014), 596.

Contents

In memoriam
SYLVAIN KERSHAW
Translator, connoisseur, and treasured friend, taken from us too soon

'All my life, I have had a certain idea of France.'

Prologue

The movements in Europe which, between the two world wars, aimed to restore the royal and imperial houses forced out of power in 1918 – or, in Portugal's case, eight years earlier – are among the great hidden political narratives of the twentieth century. They acquired media coverage and, often, strategic importance far greater than anyone these days would suppose from the often cursory and dismissive treatment they have received from most historians.

Campaigns to reinstate such dynasties as the Hohenzollerns, the Habsburgs, the Wittelsbachs, the Braganças, and even France's House of Orléans, were taken seriously at the highest governmental and journalistic levels in London and Paris, not to mention the Holy See. Upon the whole phenomenon, this book seeks to shed light. It discusses both the phenomenon's 'soft power' manifestations (the designs of newspaper tycoon Lord Rothermere upon the Hungarian throne for his son, for instance), and the 'hard power' manifestations (the 'Monarchy of the North' in Portugal, 1919; the 1921 attempts at a Habsburg restoration in Budapest; the appearance in Hungary, Bavaria, and post-1931 Spain of 'monarchists without a monarchy'; the coups of inter-war monarchism in Albania and Greece; the championship in Austria of the Habsburg heir, Archduke Otto, as the sole alternative – especially after 1934 – to either communism or the *Anschluss*).

Nothing could be more misleading than to dismiss the relevant monarchist movements as deriving from mere pointless, powerless Ruritarian daydreams. They were nothing of the kind. And certain events in Germany during late 2022 suggest that in European states now republics, monarchism's death has been greatly exaggerated.

This volume includes so much material which even numerous history specialists (whether inside or outside academe) will seldom have known before, that the author's duty to spell out in advance the nature of his approach and the range of his treatment becomes obvious. Here, then – if in these paragraphs I may be permitted a lapse into the first person[1] – is some ancillary explanation of the project. On grounds of space, I have restricted myself both chronologically and geographically.

Chronologically: in several chapters I have needed to furnish some pre-1918 background, and have also needed to discuss events which occurred after 1939. Nevertheless, I have concentrated overwhelmingly upon the inter-war period, confining to an epilogue most of the 'Where are they now?' coverage by which readers can ascertain subsequent developments in the protagonists' careers.

Geographically: I have restricted myself (again, on grounds of space) to continental European nations which, between 1918 and 1939, were sometimes or always republics. Thus, this book includes Portugal, Germany, Austria, Hungary, France, Spain, Greece and Albania; but not Italy, Bulgaria, Yugoslavia, Romania, the Benelux nations, the Scandinavian nations, or Britain. Nor does it venture further east: it includes no coverage of efforts to revive the Ottoman Empire after Atatürk's triumph, or of Pu Yi's 1931 installation by the Japanese as obedient sovereign of Manchukuo.

Attempts to bring back the Romanovs in Russia have likewise been omitted from this survey. Here I hesitated longer before jettisoning coverage of such attempts, but eventually decided to exclude it for two reasons. First, fear of making an already long, dense and unwieldy tome longer, denser and more unwieldy still; second, the absence of wide political support for reinstalled Romanovs, even (or especially) among those Russian leaders who had most cause to loathe and fear Bolshevism. Mikhail Alexeyev, one of the abler White Army generals during Russia's post-1917 civil strife, went so far as to state: 'It is precisely because I knew the monarchy as it really was, that I don't want to have anything more to do with it.'[2] Such was the length and the menace of the shadow which Rasputin had cast over the Russian elite; in any case, Alexeyev died (of natural causes) in 1918, when the military struggle against Lenin had two more years still to rage. Nor did the chief political figures of London and Paris at the time – even that passionate monarchist Churchill – ponder any practical notions of a Romanov-comeback, the way several of them pondered the concepts of facilitating, or at least of refusing to hinder, the return of other dynasties.

Readers who hanker after some Grand Theory of Everything to emerge from the fog of war (whether the war concerned involved monarchists versus republicans, or, particularly in Spain, monarchists versus other monarchists) will hanker in vain. While I would give much to be as talented and commercially successful a historian as Barbara W. Tuchman was, in my own defence I can cite Mrs Tuchman's aversion to what she called 'gallon-jug' historiography:

> I mistrust history in gallon jugs whose purveyors are more concerned with establishing the meaning and purpose of history than with what happened. [...] Corroborative detail is the great corrective. Without it historical narrative and interpretation, both, may slip easily into the invalid. It is a disciplinarian. It forces the historian who uses and respects it to cleave to the truth, or as much as he can find out of the truth. It keeps him from soaring off the ground into theories of his own invention. On those Toynbeean heights the air is stimulating and the view is vast, but people and houses down below are too small to be seen. [...] It is wiser, I believe, to arrive at theory by way of the evidence rather than the other way around, like so many revisionists today. It is more rewarding, in any case, to assemble the facts first and, in the process of arranging them in narrative form, to discover a theory or a historical generalisation emerging of its own accord. This to me is the excitement, the built-in treasure hunt, of writing history.[3]

A.J.P. Taylor offered similar counsel, deadly serious in its intent, for all its characteristically waggish phrasing. 'Of course,' Taylor admitted:

> historians must explore the profound forces. But I am sometimes tempted to think that they talk so much about these profound forces in

order to avoid doing the detailed work. I prefer detail to generalisations: a grave fault no doubt, but at least it helps to redress the balance.[4]

The element of historical causation (according to no less a Marxist theorist than Trotsky, in an unexpected display of letting the cat out of the theoretical bag) 'refracts itself through a natural selection of accidents'.[5] And if this element of contingency is present in most areas of politics, how much more present is it in the saga of inter-war monarchism: where the importance of accident, of individual bravery, of individual poltroonery, is unmistakable. How often, in my book, have the differences between monarchist failure and monarchist success depended on what Othello called 'hair-breadth 'scapes in the imminent deadly breach'! I can only hope that the following chronicle of hair-breadth 'scapes, not to mention of imminent deadly breaches, will arouse interest and will provoke wider thought as to how political authority is won or lost.

Robert James Stove
Melbourne, January 2024

Acknowledgements

All historians, before they can see, must stand on the shoulders of giants, supposing that they can ever stand anywhere or can ever see anything. My debts to chroniclers of the past are conveyed in the source materials of this tome, and sometimes in the body of the main text. Among those who have given me more immediate help during the research and writing processes, I must single out certain individuals in even the briefest and least adequate thank-you note.

My sister, Ms Judith Stove, and my colleague Professor James Franklin, read chapter after chapter. In so doing, they saved me from typographical errors and syntactic ambiguities that I had not myself spotted.

Pen and Sword editor Ms Sarah Beth-Watkins afforded me boundless (though by no means sycophantic) encouragement throughout the authorial process. She made this process, not free from pain – no editor can, nor should, be the mere equivalent of an analgesic – but, it seemed to me, fundamentally worthwhile.

The long-suffering staffers at the State Library of Victoria (Melbourne), the Matheson Library at Monash University (also Melbourne), the National Library of Australia (Canberra), the State Library of New South Wales (Sydney), the library at the University of Auckland, and the Bibliothèque Nationale de France performed heroically. If there is a special place in hell for historians who plagiarise and lie, there must also be a special place in heaven for librarians purely by virtue of their being librarians. No inter-library loan request which I lodged, however irksome and onerous, ever failed to be granted or ever appeared to disconcert these stoic professionals.

Dr Boyd Cathey, Mr David Clarence, Dr David Daintree, Dr Bernard Doherty, Mr Edwin Dyga, Emeritus Professor Paul Gottfried, Mr Pastór de Lasala, Ms Sophie Masson, Emeritus Professor Stanley G. Payne, Mr James Rogerson, Mr Guy Rundle, and Professor Barry Spurr all saw some of this material in draft stage and commented helpfully upon it. Emeritus Professor Payne read my Spanish chapter and his meticulous comments saved me from a number of factual errors and ambiguities in the original version. I am indebted to Mr Rogerson for, in particular, alerting me to C.B. Fry's Balkan monarchical connection. Mr Rundle brought to my notice the claims of John Belushi to be included (notwithstanding his American birth) on the extremely brief list of world-famous Albanians.

The present expression of gratitude must conclude on a note of bitter grief. Mr Sylvain Kershaw, who had read and commented favourably upon the typescript of Chapter IV, died with appalling suddenness during August 2023, while being taken in an ambulance to a Carcassonne hospital. My hope had been to give him a copy of the book which he did so much to encourage. Now that hope is dashed, and I must content myself with dedicating the volume to him as his memorial.

Perfectly at home both in France and in Australia, Sylvain self-effacingly taught me and other provincials more about French history than he ever imagined he was doing. Intellectually and morally fearless, he was irreplaceable. The news of his death called to my mind a phrase from Jean Cocteau's funerary oration for his composer friend Arthur Honegger: 'This is the first time that you have ever caused us sorrow.'

R.J.S.

A Note on Foreign Terminology

Every reader of Aesop's fable 'The Man, the Boy, and the Donkey' appreciates that if one tries to please all, one will infallibly please none. This unforgiving apothegm applies at least as much to foreign nomenclature as to any other topic. Reasons for usages within the following text deserve, then, to be spelt out beforehand.

The general policy has been to employ wherever possible the foreign versions of individuals' names, but to incline towards English words for political job descriptions. Thus, the penultimate Habsburg ruler is in this book called Franz Josef, not Francis Joseph; his successor is called Karl, not Charles; Italy's penultimate monarch is here called Vittorio Emanuele, not Victor Emmanuel; the last Hohenzollern head of state is here called Wilhelm, not William; and Admiral Horthy keeps his original Hungarian given name of Miklós, rather than having it compulsorily Anglicised as 'Nicholas'. The Hohenzollern case is further complicated by the fact that three successive generations of male heirs bore the same given name: Wilhelm II's eldest son was a Wilhelm, and *his* eldest son (killed in the Second World War) was likewise a Wilhelm. With luck, confusion among these namesakes, whenever they share a paragraph, will have been obviated.

Matters differ somewhat concerning offices held. A particular problem occurs when one strives to describe the head of a German government at state level. The literal English translation of the Teutonic original is 'Minister-President', which sounds decidedly awkward. One cannot very well employ 'Governor', the American equivalent, because that noun possesses a wholly different meaning (a fundamentally vice-regal role, in other words) to inhabitants of Australia and much of the Commonwealth. Since the appellation 'Premier' for a state or provincial government's head is universally comprehended in both Australia and Canada, and is easy enough to comprehend elsewhere, 'Premier' seemed the best choice for this volume. (I take comfort from the fact that the usage also appears regularly in the English-language versions of Deutsche Welle transcripts.) Be it noted that Australians and Canadians never use 'Premier' to mean 'Prime Minister'.

Strictly speaking, heads of the Habsburg house should be called 'Kaiser', since that is what they were called in the German language. Unfortunately the word 'Kaiser' is now so inextricably associated with the Hohenzollerns – and with one Hohenzollern above all – that the historian seeking to avoid mix-ups between the two dynasties is obliged to refer to each Habsburg monarch as 'Emperor'.

Latin nations, whether monarchies or republics, enjoy devising for political posts various elaborate descriptions that mean very little to the average Anglo-Saxon reader. For such a reader, the phrase 'Speaker of the Italian Parliament' conveys far more than the literal translation 'President of the Italian Chamber of Deputies', and has therefore been used here. Similarly, 'Prime Minister' has a clear meaning in English; the frequent

Latin equivalent, 'President of the Council of Ministers', means little or nothing (and invites misunderstandings when there exists a separate President of the Republic). The term 'Chancellor' (in German, *Kanzler*) has become common enough in English to be employed here for denoting the post-1918 heads of government in Berlin and Vienna.

As for the names of cities, conventional usages are mostly the ones adopted in this book. 'Lisboa', 'München' and 'Tiranë' have fallen into the lost-cause category for English prose, and in consequence, this book refers to the relevant cities as Lisbon, Munich and Tirana respectively.

R.J.S.

Chapter I

Regicide and Revolution
Portugal

The revolutionaries are those who know when power is lying in the street and when they can pick it up.

Hannah Arendt[1]

It had all happened with such appalling haste, in a few gruesome seconds. Her husband, his spine snapped by a bullet, lay dead against the side of the carriage. Her elder son still breathed, but noisily and convulsively.

By instinct, she hurled herself between the attackers and her younger son, who had been wounded in the arm. In the panic of the moment she reverted to her native French, yelling *'Infâmes! Infâmes!'* at the two men who had struck, and hitting out wildly at the second man with her bouquet of flowers. Her fury failed to deter him. He had leapt onto the carriage's outer step, whereupon the elder son fired four shots at him, and – a fatal mistake – forced himself, with one last agonised effort, to stand up. His attacker tumbled from the step onto the ground, but not before discharging one last bullet which passed right through his victim's skull. The younger son grabbed a handkerchief and frantically, unavailingly, tried to staunch his brother's bleeding.

By now their mother had nothing to lose. She tottered to her feet, screaming for help. Two men and a woman ran to her aid and jumped into the carriage, giving her elder son what little comfort they could. A third man, a soldier – though himself injured by a bullet to the leg – halted the first attacker. Another soldier likewise shot in the direction of the first attacker. By this time both attackers had incurred wounds severe enough to prevent them fleeing, and struggle as they might, they could no longer resist with any force when the police arrested them.

Within half an hour all the mayhem had finished. The elder son, like his father, breathed no more. Amid the commotion, both attackers lost their lives. So did a genuinely innocent bystander, employed in a local jewellery store, and wrongly believed to have taken part in the attack. Two bullets in the head silenced him.

Thus, in central Lisbon's *Praça do Comércio* (Commerce Square) on 1 February 1908, occurred a bloodbath which dealt the fatal blow to Portugal's Bragança monarchical house. The terrified, screaming woman: Queen Amélie d'Orléans, aged 42. Her husband: the 44-year-old Carlos I, who had been Portuguese king since 1889. Her elder son: Luís Felipe, aged 20. Her younger son: Manuel, aged 18 – and now king by default.[2] The innocent bystander in the jeweller's store: Sabino Costa, a self-confessed monarchist. The attackers: Afonso Luís da Costa, store clerk, and Manuel Buíça, schoolteacher. Both belonged to the secret society, of Masonic and post-Napoleon

1

origin, known as the *Carbonária*. Both could boast years of revolutionary intrigue behind them, despite their youth (Costa having been a mere 24, Buíça 31). Both took part in a coup attempt, planned at a Lisbon library, on 28 January. Both had eluded the police on that occasion, unlike several dozen of their confrères.

The regicide, of course, dominated the next day's newspapers on both sides of the Atlantic. Those papers which ran any kind of news reports on their front pages (by no means all, before the Great War, did: many, English journals in particular, devoted their front pages to classified advertising) had ready-made front-page horrors on which their readers could sup full. Typical was the *New York Times'* coverage:

KING OF PORTUGAL AND HIS HEIR ASSASSINATED /
Carlos and the Crown Prince Shot Down in a Street of Lisbon –
Second Son Wounded /
QUEEN'S BRAVERY IS VAIN.[3]

That last banner reveals a public attitude where chivalry, however honoured in the breach, continued to be vital in the observance. An age which could more or less envisage with composure the slaying of kings, presidents, and prime ministers retained a curious squeamishness about queens being caught in crossfire.

The US Senate, two days after the killings, passed a resolution 'that the death by unlawful and inhuman violence of the King and Crown Prince of Portugal is sincerely deplored by the Senate of the United States of America'.[4] Meanwhile in London, Edward VII, shocked to the depths of his being at the massacre (he told his physician, Sir Felix Semon, 'It is horrible – horrible'),[5] gave a practical focus to his grief at the loss of Carlos, whom he viewed not merely as a fellow monarch, but as a friend. On 8 February, he set a precedent by attending, along with Queen Alexandra, a Requiem Mass for the repose of the slain royals' souls. No English sovereign since 1688 had dared appear at a Catholic liturgy. King Edward's decision to do so provoked an outburst from the Protestant Alliance, which proclaimed that it 'viewed with astonishment and distress His Majesty's attendance at a Mass for the dead'.[6] Predictably, the King ignored this sectarian rebuke.

In 1908 Western man had not grown emotionally inured to violence of this sort, even if individual men had. (Rare was the mocker capable of matching for sheer callousness the response of Lenin, who in an article written on 19 February about what he blandly called 'the happening to the King of Portugal', made the prophetic confession: 'we regret one thing – that the Republican movement in Portugal did not settle accounts with all the adventurers in a sufficiently resolute and open manner'.)[7] True, the preceding decade had witnessed the murders of several heads of state: Empress Elisabeth of Austria-Hungary in 1898; Italy's King Umberto I in 1900; America's President William McKinley in 1901; Serbia's King Alexander I and Queen Draga in 1903. It had also witnessed a plot in Madrid which almost succeeded in its purpose, namely, the 1906 bomb-throwing by a Catalan anarchist on the wedding day of Alfonso XIII and English-born Victoria Eugenia (both the intended royal targets survived unscathed, but two dozen spectators perished).[8] Nevertheless, although Umberto had himself said of attempts on his life that 'These are the risks of the job [*Sono gli incerti delle mestiere*]',[9] few really believed him at the time. After 1908, it became much easier to accept his jaunty credo. Therefore, if one wanted to pinpoint the precise cultural moment at which the most bloodstained of all centuries truly began, and at which 'the long nineteenth century' so beloved of modern chroniclers truly finished, one could make a good case for saying that that moment occurred not (as conventionally supposed) in 1914, but six years earlier on that winter's evening in the Portuguese capital.

Characteristically, neither Carlos nor Amélie – returning from a family vacation – had bothered with the adequate security that would be automatic for subsequent rulers. Their carriage remained open to the elements as well as to murderers.

❀ ❀ ❀

When Kaiser Wilhelm II complained to Sir Arthur Henry Hardinge (the British ambassador to Portugal) about King Manuel's faults, Hardinge pointed out that the new monarch:

> was a mere boy who had seen his father killed and his brother mortally
> wounded by revolutionary assassins; that he had not been educated with
> a view to immediate succession to the throne; and that he was completely
> ignorant of what persons in the army and in politics could be trusted.[10]

Then again, Carlos's own training for the throne, while longer than Manuel's, had scarcely been more efficient. Carlos had every motive for believing that his father, Luís I, would enjoy a reasonable compass of years, and that his own princely apprenticeship – which included three short periods as regent between 1883 and 1888, while Luís visited other European nations – would proceed at a tolerably leisured pace. Such dreams proved too optimistic. On 19 October 1889, twelve days before his fifty-first birthday, Luís died at what was then the resort town of Cascais.

The 26-year-old Carlos inherited his father's preoccupation with oceanography, and added to it a passion for painting and drawing.[11] None of these gifts conduced to statesmanship; and even if they had done, the newly enthroned Carlos would still have struggled to cope with two problems that would have challenged the combined endowments of Richelieu and Metternich to solve. For neither problem can he be blamed. Both involved foreign policy, and occurred within a year of his accession.

First (15 November 1889) came the coup deposing Emperor Pedro II, the head of the Braganças' Brazilian branch.[12] Wholly unexpected outside Brazil itself, this coup followed the May 1888 decision – a decision signed into law by Princess Isabel in her father's absence, though with his support – to abolish chattel slavery, which Brazil alone among Western nations still kept, and which the nation's increasingly vocal republican movement sought to retain.[13] Rather than stand his ground when the coup leaders arrested his Prime Minister, Afonso Celso de Assis Figuiredo, the Emperor shuffled off quietly into exile, Isabel and the imperial children accompanying him to Europe in what turned out to be a perpetual banishment. The implications for Pedro's Portuguese relatives were ominous indeed. If so intelligent, versatile and conscientious a sovereign as the Brazilian Emperor (who survived his deposition by little more than two years, dying in the Hotel Bedford in Paris) could be forced from his throne – unable even to bequeath his empire to his offspring thanks to a well-organised landowning clique – it augured ill for the survival powers of less-gifted monarchs, particularly monarchs bound to Pedro through ties of blood.

3

Still less capable of being worked out by anyone of Carlos's ascertained faculties was the crisis involving Portugal's role in the Scramble for Africa. Over a ten-year period (1869–79), the colonial administrator Alexandre de Serpa Pinto had led three expeditions into the heart of southern Africa, as a consequence of which successive Portuguese administrations claimed control of a trans-continental band of territory, extending from Angola in the west to Mozambique in the east. *Mapa cor-de-rosa,* 'the rose-coloured map':[14] so the Portuguese themselves described the relevant area. Though the *Mapa cor-de-rosa* endured after the Congo Conference, held at Berlin during 1884 and 1885 with Bismarck in charge, Portugal's rulers never foresaw what actually took place: the threatening of their African territories – not by Bismarck's Germany, but by their nation's oldest friend, Britain. Portugal and England had been sworn allies ever since the 1386 Treaty of Windsor, but against the ambitions of Cecil Rhodes, and the state of de facto political blackmail which Rhodes levied against Lord Salisbury's Conservative government, mere half-millennium-old pacts of friendship availed nothing. Salisbury issued an ultimatum in January 1890, commanding that Portuguese soldiers abandon the territories of Shire-Nyasa (now Malawi) and Matabeleland and Mashonaland (both of which are now part of Zimbabwe). The 'Mr Petre' mentioned in the ultimatum was George Glynn Petre, British minister in Lisbon from 1884 to 1893, while the 'governor of Mozambique' was Serpa Pinto himself.

> What Her Majesty's Government require and insist upon is the following: that telegraphic instructions shall be sent to the governor of Mozambique at once to the effect that all and any Portuguese military forces which are actually on the Shire or in the Makololo or in the Mashona territory are to be withdrawn. Her Majesty's Government considers that without this the assurances given by the Portuguese Government are illusory. Mr Petre is compelled by his instruction to leave Lisbon at once with all the members of his legation unless a satisfactory answer to this foregoing intimation is received by him, in the course of this evening, and Her Majesty's ship Enchantress is now at Vigo waiting for his orders.[15]

Probably not one Englishman in five thousand knew or cared about the ultimatum, which went beyond what Rhodes wanted. Within Portugal, by contrast, it left a wound that stayed raw for a generation. Diplomat Sir George Young, seeking to put the best possible gloss on Britain's actions, nonetheless conceded the scale of the harm which the ultimatum had done to Portuguese *amour-propre*. Writing in 1917, Young observed:

> It mattered little that the motive of our government was possibly not careless contempt for all comity or even courtesy towards a weaker nation, but a wish to prevent the often preposterous imperial pretensions of Portugal from prejudicing its international position and its further internal prosperity. The effect on the Portuguese people was just the same even though the slap in the face may have been well meant … The new mood was one of grim determination so to set its house in order at home as to secure respect abroad; and incidentally, as England was too strong to retaliate upon, to make reprisals against the English party in Portugal, that is to say, the Crown.[16]

Regarding the ultimatum, an English colonel, F.C.C. Egerton, expressed himself much more sharply than Young:

> [I]t came from an ally, an ally to whom Portugal had always been faithful, without counting the cost to herself. It is hard to find any justification for it. Effective occupation was laid down as the *sine qua non* of Portuguese sovereignty: but our own occupation, for some considerable time, consisted of no more than making agreements with native chiefs and hoisting the Union Jack. Only a year before the ultimatum, Lord Salisbury, speaking about Nyasaland in the House of Lords, declared, 'The region is not British territory and is not under British protection.' On another occasion he said, 'We have not raised the British flag in Nyasaland; it is not British territory.' The whole affair was an unfortunate application of the immoral principle that might is right.[17]

Republican sentiment, hitherto marginal even after the Brazilian empire had ended (though since 1878 there could be found one openly republican deputy in Portugal's national legislature, the Cortes), now flared into life. In the north-western city of Oporto, a specifically republican uprising erupted on the last day of January 1891; and while within a week Oporto had been pacified, advocates of a republic had tasted blood. Those inspired by the resulting confusion included one politically naïve insurgent who disarmingly announced at his trial that while he did not understand what the word 'republic' actually meant, 'it could not help but be a holy thing'.[18]

Among leading republican agitators, one participant in the Oporto rebellion, the professor and dramatist Teófilo Braga – 'arch-druid of positivism and prolix historian of Portuguese literature',[19] one chronicler called him – proclaimed that 'the four main causes of the country's decadence were the Inquisition, the Jesuits, the Braganças and the English alliance'.[20] By 1891, the first of these targets was no more than cheap rhetoric (Portugal's Inquisition had been abolished seventy years earlier); the other three did arguably constitute barriers to national progress. Individual republican politicians henceforth secured Cortes membership with increasing frequency, three of them being elected in 1892, four in 1906, and seven in 1908.[21] While they had limited national impact at a time when a mere 1 per cent of the population possessed the right to vote for anybody,[22] they promised trouble for Carlos quite transcending their small numbers. They had the signal advantage of knowing what they supported and what they opposed.

As much could no longer be said of the monarchist parliamentary mainstream. Since the early 1870s it had functioned on the principle of what the Portuguese themselves called *rotativismo,* according to which the two main political parties took turns in forming government. These parties were, respectively, the *Regeneradores* (broadly centre-Right) and the *Progressistas* (broadly centre-Left), though as an editorial in London's *Times* tartly noted, in practice they 'neither regenerated nor made progress'.[23] (A similar system prevailed at the time in Spain, where it was called *el turno pacífico,* but Spanish politics had a complicating factor absent from the Portuguese state: passionate separatist campaigns, notably in Catalonia and the Basque lands.)[24] Explicitly traditionalist monarchism had been discredited in Portugal ever since its failure in the 1828–34 civil war,[25] a failure that both anticipated and paralleled the repeated defeats of Spain's Carlist monarchical candidates, in that both countries witnessed 'the enthronement of that branch of the Royal House which was forced to look to the Left for support'.[26] When Carlos sadly described Portugal as 'a monarchy without monarchists [*uma monarquia sem monárquicos*]',[27] he exaggerated his plight, but not – as events proved – by very much. It hardly helped the royal cause that the most eloquent, colourful and popular among monarchist spokesmen – Mousinho de Albuquerque, former governor of Mozambique – committed suicide in 1902, 'with a revolver bullet in a cab'.[28]

Under Luís, *rotativismo* had more or less worked; and an unusually vigorous politician, the *Regeneradores'* Fontes Pereira de Melo, served, in total, twelve years as Prime Minister. After Fontes' death in 1887, no such success or strength attended the system. Nor did Cortes members display modes of behaviour likely to inspire faith (whether felt by King Carlos or by anyone else) in their judgement:

> The Cortes functioned poorly. Meetings were turbulent and sometimes violent; personalities prevailed over ideas; governments rarely got the opportunity to execute their programs; election results were often disputed; there was heavy absenteeism among deputies [...] When one party decided to leave office, whatever the reason – a lost vote in parliament, an incident or scandal, tired leadership, or lack of royal confidence in the leadership or program – the king dismissed the premier and nominated a new one from the other major party. This new government was then 'granted' dissolution of parliament, elections were held, presided over, and invariably controlled by the newly appointed government. Because elections were rigged, this government was bound to receive a majority in the new parliament.[29]

Between 1889 and 1907 eleven general elections occurred – two of them in 1906 alone – and the same few politicians, mostly undistinguished in all eyes save their own, occupied the Prime Minister's office again and again, on a 'get in, get rich, get out' basis. None of this would have mattered overmuch if the nation's economic fundamentals had been sound enough to counterbalance foreign-policy reverses. They were not. Twice, in 1892 and again in 1902, Portugal was officially declared bankrupt.[30]

By 1906 standards of Cortes decorum (rarely high) had sunk to unprecedented lows. During November of that year, the youngest, most articulate, and most celebrated among republican spokesmen, Afonso Costa, told his fellow deputies that 'for many fewer crimes than those perpetrated by Dom Carlos I there rolled on the scaffold, in France, the head of Louis XVI [*Por multo menos crimes do que os practicados por D. Carlos I rolou no cadafalso, em França, a cabeça de Luís XVI*]'.[31] This utterance caused Costa to be banned from the legislature for a month, but he otherwise suffered no punishment. Outside the Cortes, republican abuse could be, if anything, even more personalised. Guerra Junqueiro, a radical poet offended by the King's corpulence, vociferated: 'The tyranny of Dom Carlos derives from that most obese animal: from the pig. Yes, we are the slaves of an increasingly fat, near-sighted tyrant [*A tirania do sr. D. Carlos procede de feras mais obesas: do porco. Sim, nós somos os escravos dum tirano de engorda e de vista baixa*].'[32]

More and more, confronted with insults such as Costa's and Junqueiro's, Carlos pined for a strong man, a Bismarck, who could cut through Gordian knots of governance. He thought he had found such a Bismarck in the person of João Franco, a career administrator (born in 1855, and therefore the King's senior by eight years) who, while still in his thirties, had demonstrated marked journalistic and business aptitude.

Of curiously Oriental mien, with his narrow eyes and high cheekbones[33] so pronounced in surviving photographs, Franco – no relation to the much better-known Spanish dictator – specialised in managing humdrum institutions like customs departments. A Cortes member from 1884, he held the ministries of education, public works, and (most notably) finance for various *Regenerador* cabinets during the 1890s. Upon falling out in 1901 with *Regenerador* leader Ernesto Hintze Ribeiro, about the best of an uninspired prime ministerial bunch, Franco formed his own party, the *Partido Regenerador Liberal*. Since everyone in the Cortes knew Franco to be free from personal corruption, he made a formidable antagonist, particularly when it came to the national tobacco monopoly, a lucrative and more-or-less legal instance of what later ages would call rent-seeking.

Hintze Ribeiro took sufficient fright at *Partido Regenerador Liberal* and *Progressista* censures to beg, during early 1906, that Carlos prorogue the Cortes and grant Hintze Ribeiro himself dictatorial powers. This Carlos refused to do, saying: 'Woe betide those who can only rule in such a manner.'[34] That this refusal sprang more from distrust of Hintze Ribeiro than from unswerving royal allegiance to constitutionalism is suggested by the fact that when Franco sought similarly authoritarian powers from the King, he obtained them, though admittedly not at once. Both Franco and Carlos initially wanted to reach a *modus vivendi* with their Cortes opponents. After Franco became Prime Minister in May 1906, he worked with rather than against the Cortes. His cabinet settled the tobacco issue, strengthened existing laws against left-wing political agitation, and came nearer than any of its predecessors to balancing the national budget. The reciprocal tolerance was brief.

When Costa and other Republican deputies made impassioned protests against Franco's high-handedness the following November, fully expecting the usual gentle-tap-on-the-wrist treatment from the authorities, they found to their astonishment that Franco was fully determined to expel them from the legislature. This he did – and moreover, the King backed him up. His dynamism also found other outlets, culminating in his April 1907 closure of the Cortes *sine die*:

> He proceeded to deprive the state parasites of all imaginary posts so infamously monopolised by them. The corruption was such that a gentleman named Minister of Portugal in China had for two years drawn £2,400 a year without ever leaving Lisbon. Even ladies were found to be receiving public money, which had for years been paid to them for the imaginary task of searching female travellers as they passed through the customs-houses! [...] He [Franco] presumed that no good could be expected from submitting any further questions to a vehemently distracted Parliament, and he assumed dictatorship, which he proclaimed in a most unconstitutional way. The Cortes [was] dissolved, and Franco announced, through the *Diario Illustrado,* the organ of his party, that the bills which had been debated but not passed would nevertheless receive the force of law.[35]

7

Carlos defended the coup in a discussion at Cascais with a French journalist (Joseph Galtier) for a Paris daily (*Le Temps*). At this stage – Kaiser Wilhelm's efforts aside – the entire concept of a monarch giving a newspaper interview remained novel, and the unaccustomed opportunities for self-revelation disconcerted Carlos himself enough to provoke him into outspokenness that he seldom otherwise showed: 'When the elections have given us a big majority and when normality has been re-established, the remedy which I judged indispensable to an extraordinary situation will cease to be necessary [*Quand les élections nous auront donné une grande majorité et que la normalité sera rétablie, le remède que j'ai jugé indispensable à une situation extraordinaire cessera d'être nécessaire*].'[36]

But how long could Franco's rule continue? For all his success in vanquishing the Cortes, his political enemies still had their own Lisbon-based newspapers, via which they raked him fore and aft. In a country where the great bulk of the population still could not read – statistics usually given for Portugal at this period show a national illiteracy rate of at least 75 per cent[37] – the impact of such yellow journalism on the emotions of those who *could* read was automatically disproportionate. Any dictatorship later in the twentieth century (not least Dr Salazar's reign, between 1932 and 1968, in Portugal itself) would have imposed thoroughgoing press censors without a second thought. Franco would now and then declare sanctions against the newspapers representing, *inter alia*, the *Regenerador* and *Progressista* parties,[38] but enforcement of these sanctions remained haphazard.

Besides, while the King continued to favour Franco, Queen Amélie – a stronger personality altogether – harboured great misgivings about him. The kindest thing she could find to say on the topic (November 1907) was 'Franco is in the right, but he has no tact.'[39] Subsequently she likened Franco to 'a rough, awkward architect, who, seeing cracks in a house, sticks in his pick-axe to strengthen it, and brings it all down'.[40] Carlos himself fretted so much over the future that he planned a visit to Brazil, hoping thereby to draw on still-powerful monarchist sentiment in that land, after the manner of British Prime Minister George Canning, who had stated long previously: 'I called the New World into existence, to redress the balance of the old.'[41] Whether this scheme would have worked (and indubitably it warranted an attempt), we shall never be able to resolve. The killings of 1 February 1908 aborted all hopes in that direction.

As regards those killings, one puzzle, above all others, remains. It has been conjectured,[42] although it cannot be confirmed, that the murderers adopted regicide as a fall-back position and that their original choice of target had been Franco. Later, certain monarchists would allege that Franco suspected something of the kind, and that in the days before the shootings 'he changed his dwellings every night'.[43] Why, then, did he give to the King, to the Queen, and to their sons the all-clear before they made their disastrous journey?[44] No one doubted his monarchist credentials. The idea of him having secretly wanted to save his own skin by sacrificing that of the Braganças clashes with everything we know about him. Incompetence on an epic scale is far likelier. Against the hypothesis of Franco as the *Carbonária*'s intended victim must further be set the much greater publicity value for the *Carbonária* itself in eliminating a king and a prince, instead of a mere politician.

Once the immediate shock of the killings had subsided, Queen Amélie and King Manuel told Franco to his face that they no longer wished him to continue in office. They withdrew his commission, although Manuel had originally wished to keep him on.[45] Franco fled both the capital and the country, taking refuge in Genoa; and while he lived another twenty-one years, some of which he spent in exchanging letters with Manuel,[46] he never again enjoyed political sway. Charles Maurras, most blistering of French polemicists, pursued the disgraced Franco in print:

> Whereas Stambouloff [Bulgarian Prime Minister 1887–1894], who made Bulgaria, whereas Cavour, who made a united Italy, whereas Bismarck, whereas Cánovas [Antonio Cánovas de Castillo, Spanish Prime Minister six times between 1874 and 1897] or so many other of those contemporary dictators backed, like M. Franco, by thrones, have succeeded in an exemplary way, because in an exemplary way they obeyed the law of real things, M. Franco has failed. Through the fault of the dictatorship? By no means: through his fault [*Où Stambouloff, qui fit la Bulgarie, où Cavour qui fit l'Italie Une, où Bismarck, où Cánovas ou tant d'autres de ces dictateurs contemporains adossés, comme M. Franco, à des trônes, ont exemplairement réussi, parce qu'ils ont exemplairement obéi à la loi des choses, M. Franco a échoué. Par la faute de la dictature? Nullement: par sa faute*].[47]

It was the most dramatic downfall of any European statesman since the famous day in 1890 when Kaiser Wilhelm had dismissed Bismarck, 'dropping the pilot'. The move would have made perfect sense if any other monarchist in recent Portuguese politics had demonstrated levels of industry and talent akin to, or even half as notable as, Franco's own. Alas for the Braganças, by 1908 political initiative and enterprise had largely become the republicans' own preserve. In the acidic words of a 1960 historian, Caetano Beirão: '[The regicide] presented the nation with a dilemma: either to govern energetically or abandon everything to the criminals. The Palace and the politicians chose the second alternative.'[48]

The Duchess of Palmela, a prominent well-wisher of the ousted politician, sought to condole with him: 'What a misfortune, João Franco! I, who placed so much hope in you … It's the end of the monarchy, isn't it?'[49] She spoke better than she knew (or than she ever would know, since by the end of 1909 she herself had died). Swiftly the murderers' own graves became objects of pilgrimage. As for the slain king and prince, we are told that 'only one newspaper had a black border [on 2 February] – it was the organ of Senhor Franco, the Dictator'.[50]

Young Manuel sadly told hearers at his first council of state that 'I am without knowledge or experience, and I place myself in your hands, counting on your patriotism and wisdom.'[51] As a candid statement of fact, this admission had its merits; as an affirmation of political realism, let alone as a rallying-cry to waverers, its virtues were less conspicuous. At least there could be no doubt of Manuel's conscientiousness. 'His days,' we are told, 'were occupied with audiences, desk work and the necessary recreation for his health. This routine rarely allowed him to retire to his bedchamber before two or three o'clock in the morning.'[52]

There followed an amnesty for political prisoners, the abrogation of such press censorship as Franco had imposed, and a return to the short-lived cabinets of pre-1906 days. Rarely did a prime minister stay in office for more than five months. The main difference from the pre-1906 Cortes situation lay in the fact that *rotativismo* no longer flourished. Cabinet ministers increasingly eschewed party affiliation. Hintze Ribeiro had died four months after Franco shut down the Cortes; and when another *Regenerador* leader, Francisco António da Veiga Beirão, emerged, he proved much less steadfast. The *Partido Regenerador Liberal* pretty much collapsed with its founder's overthrow. Having had sixty-five seats in the previous legislature, it was reduced in 1908 to three seats.[53]

Prominent irritations of Manuel's existence included another prominent *Regenerador*, Júlio de Vilhena, who did his utmost to thwart successive cabinet governments while refusing to lead one himself. As one commentator acerbically put it, 'With monarchists like Vilhena, Manuel really did not need any republican opposition.'[54] In the meantime, while the monarchist legislators talked, the republicans acted. More and more of the capital's newspapers openly favoured junking the crown. A republican protest march through the streets of Lisbon on 2 August 1909 attracted a crowd of no fewer than 50,000 persons: this on the testimony of Queen Amélie herself, who can scarcely be accused of a desire to overstate the numbers concerned.[55] The preceding April, a three-day republican conference at Setúbal, to the south of Lisbon, had demonstrated that whatever disagreements the republican leaders might have among themselves mattered little or nothing in the face of their determination to organise a coup.

To a remarkable extent the republican leadership had a socially homogeneous nature. In its ranks, the army was not particularly well represented, but the navy was. Even more numerous within the leadership than sailors were journalists, lawyers, physicians and professors. All the chief republicans had long been active in Freemasonry, which in Portugal at this stage usually presupposed militant anti-Catholicism (though after 1917 this would change, and though Carlos himself is said to have felt occasional Masonic sympathies,[56] as Emperor Pedro unquestionably had done);[57] a large minority had joined the *Carbonária;* an outright majority looked for their philosophical inspiration to France, above all to Jacobin France, and subscribed to the positivist doctrines of Auguste Comte, which offered a scientifically propelled 'religion of humanity'. (Portugal had had a Socialist Party since 1875, but it wielded far less influence than its French, German and Scandinavian counterparts, and it stood largely aloof from national republicanism. Marxism had even less impact on the republicans, while Anarchism enjoyed nothing like the following in Portugal that it had won in Spain.) The University of Coimbra grew especially receptive to republican efforts, and one of the older republicans, Manuel de Arriaga, became the campus's rector. In this role 'he is said to have declared that in Portugal there was not room for both science and the Almighty, and that he preferred the elimination of the latter'.[58]

During June 1910 the *Regenerador* cabinet, which since the preceding December Veiga Beirão had ineffectually led, collapsed amid a banking scandal. When Veiga Beirão resigned, Manuel appointed to the prime ministry another *Regenerador* politician, albeit one with clean hands: António Teixeira de Sousa. By this stage, as one 1911 commentator noted, 'The time had arrived when the dullest and the most bigoted mind had to perceive that monarchical Portugal had seen a writing on the wall that was not hard to decipher.'[59] Lisbon itself had gone republican without the smallest ambiguity. At the Cortes election of 5 April 1908, when it might have been expected that monarchists would be benefiting from electoral sympathy over the regicide, the total republican vote for Lisbon constituencies had been 13,074 (as against 10,982 for the total monarchist vote there).[60] The next general election – 28 August 1910 – increased the number of republican-held Cortes seats to fourteen, all except four of these being within Lisbon itself. Queen Amélie, shrewder than her son, dreaded using the telephone for fear that *Carbonária* members could eavesdrop on her private talk.[61] Only an incitement to ultimate republican agitation was lacking still.

On 3 October that incitement happened, with the shooting of a republican deputy, the psychiatrist Miguel Bombarda, by one of his more deranged patients. No evidence emerged to show that Bombarda's killer operated from political motives. Yet it suited the republicans to insist that the murderer had acted with monarchist foreknowledge, given the vital part Bombarda had played in fomenting the propaganda war against the palace; and they swung into action, having infiltrated several army units.

At first their manoeuvres seemed premature. Authorities differ with one another as to how many troops the King had at his disposal in Lisbon, but they agree on the disparity between the monarchist and the republican forces. Historian Douglas L. Wheeler gives the figures of 3,500 soldiers for the monarchists and a lowly 450 for the republicans.[62] One of the most forthright and committed republicans in the navy, Admiral Carlos Cândido dos Reis, made the error of believing reports (which turned out to be false) that the republicans had launched their drive too soon and had been conquered. Overcome by despair, he shot himself. Meanwhile, Henrique Mitchell de Paiva Couceiro, a veteran of Mozambique and Angola, received the mystifying order from his commanding officer that his column was to retreat, even after it had dispersed rebels gathered at Lisbon's Rotunda Square. Paiva Couceiro and his allies learned the following day why this instruction had occurred, and at once the mystery ended. The directive had come from General António Carvalhal, soon to re-emerge in the republican high command.

King Manuel, playing host at the time to the understandably bewildered Brazilian President Hermes da Fonseca, had been as efficaciously imprisoned inside the Palace of Necessidades as if he had been locked in Lisbon's deepest dungeon. The army units still faithful to the monarchy had no chance of freeing him, because the railroad tracks connecting the provinces to Lisbon had been sabotaged, and the main governmental telephone lines had been cut dead. Somehow the King managed to discover a line that still worked, and with that, he reached Teixeira de Sousa's office. Moved to an abnormal toughness by the urgency of the situation, and appreciating the significance of Paiva Couceiro's forces for any hopes of monarchist victory, he instructed the Prime Minister to summon those forces. Already naval mutineers had taken command of two cruisers, the *Adamastor* and the *São Rafael*, which were bombarding the palace. Teixeira de Sousa, a broken reed whom certain monarchists accused of being a conscious traitor, could counsel only flight: preferably to Cintra, where Queen Amélie and Carlos's mother Queen Maria Pia both remained.

By the morning of the 5th, the monarchists were finished. At eleven o'clock, the republicans formally proclaimed a 'Provisional Government of the Republic', with Braga as its president, with Costa as its Justice Minister, and – not least critical – with Dr Bombarda and Admiral Cândido dos Reis as its accredited martyrs. Portents, in terms of twentieth-century European absolutist rule, abounded for those (Lenin and Hitler included) able to descry them.

11

The leading republicans had established, in the most dramatic possible style, the almost complete meaninglessness of such ill-defined liberal notions as 'people power' and 'the consent of the governed' when confronted with a militant minority; a minority, furthermore, which had acquired the technological skill to strike at the heart of mass transit and mass communications networks. Against those weapons, mere numerical superiority on the monarchists' part became not merely ineffective but a handicap. (Teixeira de Sousa, refraining from joining the new cabinet, equally refrained from censuring it.) Altogether the *Cinco de Outubro*, as the Portuguese came to call the revolution, constituted an expensive lesson in terms of blood, toil, tears and sweat – not least for the approximately fifty persons who lost their lives in the melee – but a lesson not easily absorbed through gentler methods.

When the result had become unmistakable, Manuel fell into suicidal despair, telling those around him: 'All of you may go if you like. For my part, since the Constitution assigns me no role except to let myself be killed, I will try to fulfil my part decently.'[63] Unable to achieve even this outcome, the hapless King (soon to acquire the retrospective nickname *O Desventurado*, 'The Unfortunate'), his uncle Afonso, his mother and his grandmother boarded the yacht *Amalia IV*, originally intending to head for Oporto; yet while at sea they ill-advisedly abandoned this plan. Finally they disembarked at Gibraltar. Never would Manuel see Portugal again.

Following the near-incredible news of Portugal's republican coup which greeted telegraph operators in Europe's capitals late on 5 October 1910, came the still stranger tidings of the republican leaders proclaiming their all-inclusive altruism. The television age takes these protestations so much for granted – in our epoch, almost every more-or-less neat transfer of national power from government to government is accompanied by the winners' tributes to the losers' sportsmanship, and vice versa – that we are apt to forget how historically novel a thing this syndrome is. Paris's revolutionists in 1830 did not waste valuable administrative time sympathising with the defeated and exiled Charles X, nor the same city's revolutionists eighteen years later with the likewise defeated and exiled Louis-Philippe, nor twenty-two years after that with the fallen Napoleon III and Empress Eugènie. 'To the victor, the spoils': the struggles of post-1789 Continental Europe had firmly established that particular doctrine, across the ideological spectrum. And if the spoils involved 10,000 corpses inside seven days, as in the 'Bloody Week [*Semaine Sanglante*]' which notoriously followed the Paris Commune's May 1871 suppression, then they involved 10,000 corpses inside seven days.[64]

Régime change in Portugal proved very different. It was almost as if the wire-service bulletins bore the dateline 'Garden of Eden', such was their evocation of all-purpose goodwill. They implied an innocence so prelapsarian that, on re-reading them in the early twenty-first century (to quote a witticism once uttered, in a very different context, by an Australian book-reviewer), 'you can see the apple leave Eve's hand and re-attach itself to the tree of knowledge'.[65]

'The struggle is over! Now there are no enemies! Today all Portuguese, exchanging fraternal embraces, will collaborate in the work for the regeneration of the fatherland! There are no more enemies now! There are only brothers!'[66] This enraptured pledge came from Admiral Machado Santos, who – not yet 36 years old – had risen to become the republicans' de facto chief of staff: less through any particular desire for the position, than through displaying a competence and improvisatory dash which obtained for him the position by default. From another and much older republican, the journalist and lawyer Augusto Manuel Alves da Veiga, then in his early sixties, came an equally sanguine but more sober edict: 'The Portuguese Republic has before it a great mission to carry out – to create a new fatherland, to build a modern people.'[67]

Braga, as interim President, temporarily combined in his person the functions of that office and that of the Prime Ministry. A widespread hope arose that some solid, adequately broad-based coalition could stay in power if the 67-year-old Braga remained in charge of it, with his extreme austerity of life. Reluctant to incur the expense of vehicular transportation, Braga preferred to walk to and from appointments; sometimes he even repaired his own clothes.[68] The aforementioned Coimbra professor Arriaga became Braga's Minister of the Interior. Bernardino Machado was another professor whose signal influence and expertise as an agronomist were somehow considered to qualify him for the Foreign Affairs portfolio. Most influential of all in the cabinet, and most obviously portentous in his function, remained Afonso Costa, whose overseeing of the judicature included responsibility for religious assemblies, a responsibility summed up in the bland title 'Ministry of Justice and Cults'.

As might have been expected, the euphoria concomitant upon liberation did not long forestall managerial niceties. Portuguese wallets abruptly ceased to contain any coin known as the *real*, let alone the large silver coin known as the *milreis*. 'The "rey" part of its name [having] proved irritating to Republican sensibilities',[69] the main currency unit became the escudo, this change to an obviously non-monarchical word being formally enforced in May 1911. Before that date, Portugal had acquired a new national anthem (*A Portuguesa*, its tune being the work of the recently deceased German-trained composer and painter Alfredo Keil) and a new flag. Shortly afterward its language acquired a new spelling system, with fewer diacriticals and fewer traces of foreign orthography than the old. Roads and government buildings which, prior to October 1910, bore the ignominy of Bragança-related nomenclature now had their names changed in homage to those two revolutionists who had already been given a spectacular public funeral: Dr Bombarda and Admiral Cândido dos Reis. Bliss was it in that dawn to be alive, but to be dead was very heaven.

By definition, the dead could seldom suffer overmuch for outspokenness against the new régime. Living Portuguese found it harder to avoid the risk which such outspokenness carried. On the fourth-last day of December 1910, well before any elections occurred, the country acquired a Law for the Defence of the Republic (*Lei de Defesa da República*) which criminalised, among other things, any spoken or written utterance that 'offended' the President or the cabinet.[70] This enterprising sanction against what, one hundred years later, would come to be called 'hate speech' seems to have marked the very first – and by no means the last – occasion in a First World country under which public statements of political dissent were banned, not because they had a good chance of threatening a ruler's physical health, but because they had a good chance of hurting his feelings.

To 'spread false rumours with the purpose of alarming the public spirit, or susceptible of causing injury to the State, public credit or social safety ['... *espalhem boato falso, destinado a alarmar o espírito público, ou susceptível de causar prejuízo*

13

ao Estado, ao crédito público, ou à segurança social]'[71] became likewise punishable by imprisonment, there having been doubtless envisaged a judiciary of omniscient solons who could adjudicate upon how a rumour's intentionally conceived falsehood would be ascertained, or upon what injury the State remained forever 'susceptible' to, versus what injury could be inflicted on the State without more than fleeting damage. More specific crimes which now carried jail sentences included conniving at a monarchist restoration. When election day for the Cortes dawned on 28 May 1911, the success of the incumbent party, the PRP (*Partido Republicano Português*), had been already guaranteed by its explicit prohibition of monarchists – and indeed of republicans known to be practising Catholics – from seeking Cortes seats. Even then, the PRP managed to gain a mere 97.9 per cent of the votes cast,[72] which suggested vast depths of oppositionist depravity among the remaining 2.1 per cent.

Braga, incidentally, did not stay around for long after the results were in. On 4 September, he resigned, his vision having become so impaired that reading even big print was a struggle for him. Arriaga (less of a fire-breather by this time than he had been before) took over Braga's role, and Portugal acquired the very first of its many ex-presidents.[73]

Among all the leading cabinet ministers, Foreign Minister Machado had the most difficult job. The difficulty was his misfortune, rather than his fault. In pre-1914 (and to a large extent pre-1939) Europe, the profession of diplomacy enjoyed a reverence, a glamour, a direct political muscle, which subsequent ages were to find almost beyond belief. A British, French, German, Austrian, or Russian ambassador, indeed a Spanish, Greek, or Italian ambassador – however unimportant the land to which he was temporarily accredited – would often possess all the advantages, and none of the disadvantages, appertaining to an Oriental despot. The phrase 'Concert of Europe' expressed not a mere pious wish but a discernible, if humanly imperfect, reality. (This reality was, at times, extended to include even Americans. Many a Connecticut Yankee in 1910, unable to reach King Arthur's court, longed to be presented at Kaiser Wilhelm's, Emperor Franz Josef's, Tsar Nicholas's, or George V's.) Diplomatic protocol still obviously, profoundly, *mattered*. And no aspect of it mattered more than the extent to which a government could obtain, for itself, open recognition by other governments.

Portugal's new breed of republican philosopher-kings accordingly discovered that such recognition was annoyingly slow to arrive. By New Year's Eve it had come from Argentina and Brazil, but from no other power.[74] Even the United States, the world's most obvious non-Swiss model for republican rule, deliberately made Braga wait. Its plenipotentiary in Lisbon, Henry T. Gage, was actually brought home to Washington on 19 November 1910, in order to indicate American displeasure with the turn of Portuguese events. William Howard Taft, in the White House since March 1909 was, by temperament and by conscious endeavour, perhaps the least Jeffersonian president who has ever lived. When Taft's representative in Madrid (Henry Clay Ide, a former governor of the Philippines, and thus perhaps not the most obvious candidate for winning Spanish hearts and minds) discussed American attitudes to the Lisbon situation, he contented himself with a bromide about 'benevolent expectancy'.[75] Only on 11 May 1911 did Washington explicitly recognise the PRP as Portugal's legitimate administration.[76] France refused to do so till 25 August. Britain, Germany, Austria and Spain held out till 11 September.[77]

No actual enthusiasm for the recognition characterised the relevant officials in London, Berlin, Vienna, Paris or Madrid. They provided it in a spirit of reluctantly countenancing what they thought to be inevitable. In Paris and Madrid, above all, the emphasis fell on 'reluctantly'. France's President Raymond Poincaré, on the way back home from a state visit to Spain's capital, 'could not be induced to return to Paris via Lisbon'.[78] Poincaré, unsentimental even by Gallic political standards, would have been much more obliging – and so would Western Europe's other rulers have been – if the PRP had condescended to distance itself, in a formal sense, from the regicide. It did not, and, for whatever reason, scorned even to attempt doing so.

Spain went much further than Poincaré's purely negative expression of disapproval. Ever since Spain lost its sixty-year control of Portugal in December 1640, it has been a recurring dream of numerous Spanish leaders to get such control back, when such leaders have nothing better to do; and it has been a recurring nightmare of Portuguese that this dream will be fulfilled. (As a British onlooker during the 1910 coup noted: 'Spaniards look down on the Portuguese – the Portuguese absolutely hate the Spaniards.')[79] Neither right-wing sympathies nor left-wing sympathies preclude this expansionist aspiration. It was longed for by King Philip V in the eighteenth century and by Madrid's Jacobins in the early nineteenth. The Spanish Popular Front broadcast it in 1936–39;[80] the aged General Franco seriously entertained it in April 1974.[81] But in 1911 it had a better chance of success than on most other occasions before or later. Among all those horrified by Manuel's overthrow, none felt greater unease – or had a shrewder insight into the coup's worrying connotations for his own survival – than Alfonso XIII, Spain's monarch from the day of his birth in 1886.[82]

Alfonso's man in Lisbon was the 47-year-old Rodrigo Saavedra y Vinent, the second Marques de Villalobar; and of Villalobar it may be said that, in a richly crowded field, he ranks among the most amazing officials whom even Spain has ever produced. He did not bestride the world like a colossus; in fact, he did not bestride anything because he had been born without any legs. His feet protruded directly from his torso. *The New Yorker*'s Alexander Woollcott gave further details:

> His head was hairless and he had only one hand he could let anyone see. The other he carried, whenever possible, thrust into the bosom of his coat. It was, they say, a kind of cloven claw.
>
> I do not know by what heavy and intricate contrivance Villalobar raised himself to the stature of other men and managed a kind of locomotion. It was serviceable enough, however to carry him to the ends of the earth, and his will lent him seven-league boots. Furthermore, it was so deceptive to one who did not see him move that when first he appeared at court in Madrid, a fledgling diplomat already booked for some minor post in Washington, a great lady – some say the Queen Mother [Maria Cristina], but I do not believe that part of the legend – turned quickly when she heard his name and told him how as a girl she had visited his part of Spain and how she had always wondered whatever became of the Villalobar monster. It seems she had heard curious countryside tales of a monster born to the Villalobar line, just such a one as shadowed

[Scotland's] Glamis Castle in those days and shadows it today. Such a fascinating story, my dear Marquis. Quite gave one the creeps. One heard it everywhere. Had the creature died? Or been killed? Or what?

'Madame', said young Villalobar, with a malicious smile twisting the rich curve of his lips, 'I am that monster,' and, bowing low, he shuffled away, leaving her to wish she had never been born.[83]

Keeping Villalobar in Lisbon was King Alfonso's idea of secret diplomacy. But nothing secret, or automatically discreditable, marked the Spanish sovereign's anxiety over the Portuguese situation. It arose from three motives.

First and most obvious was October 1910's affront to monarchical solidarity in Europe as a whole. Second, the more immediate threat to Alfonso's own position, since the year before the Portuguese coup, Catalonia had been riven by the 'Tragic Week' of July-August 1909, where separatist and anti-Catholic insurrection had been crushed only after the death toll had reached 150, and had come close to bringing the Spanish monarchy down. Third – a factor almost always overlooked by historians – Alfonso's sense of personal guilt. For in the spring of 1910 Queen Amélie had actually visited Madrid, and had begged Spain's Prime Minister José Canalejas to authorise military aid on the Braganças' behalf.[84] Canalejas dared not do so without his master's permission; this permission Alfonso had refused to grant, and now Alfonso found himself faced with the consequences of his refusal. During early October 1910, with the final result in Lisbon not yet clear, Amélie had transmitted similar supplications to Canalejas, but again to no avail.

Intensifying both the leading Portuguese monarchists' anger and Alfonso's deep disquiet was the perfidy by which the capital had turned republican in the first place, '[f]our-fifths of the nation,' military historian Sir Charles Oman reported, 'being profoundly uninterested in Lisbon politics'.[85] The monarchists thought it bad enough that Britain had refused to intervene on Manuel's behalf, as several Braganças (not, it seems clear, the despondent Manuel himself) believed that she would.[86] They found much more galling the treachery on the home front. Marshal Manuel Gomes da Costa, committed to monarchism before he eventually made his peace with the republic, emphatically stated in his 1930 memoirs that one regiment, deployed in the Rotunda, would have made the rebels flee ['*Que o general com um regimento so que fosse, atacasse a Rotunda*'].[87] General Paiva Couceiro, on the basis of his own experience, concurred. The conviction fails to take into account Manuel's own lack of leadership ability, or the extent to which 'his nerve had been shattered for good'[88] by the regicide. Yet it accords with what Oman, visiting Portugal before the coup as part of his researches into Napoleonic battlefields, noticed when dealing with General Raposo Botelho, Manuel's last War Minister:

He [Raposo Botelho] had never heard a shot fired in war – but no more had any of the rest of the rest of the officers of the Portuguese Army ... he was elderly and a little invalidish – the last person in the world suited to deal with a sudden insurrection.[89]

Whatever capacity existed within the monarchist ranks for initiative and daring lay with the officers known as 'the Africans', so called because, despite having been usually Portuguese-born, they had spent most of their careers in Angola, Mozambique or both. The melancholic and eventually self-destructive Mousinho de Albuquerque (who on returning to Lisbon had served as private tutor to Prince Luís Felipe) belonged to this group. Paiva Couceiro was the group's most flamboyant exemplar. In him, the derring-do natural to almost any late-nineteenth-century colonial administrator's circumstances strengthened a purely individual aggression. While stationed during 1895 in Mozambique's capital (Lourenço Marques, as Maputo was known till 1976), he had taken offence at the behaviour of three journalists – one American and two British – who jeered at Portugal itself. Rather than merely criticising them, as the average proconsul would have done, he publicly thrashed them. His over-reaction earned him a purely pro-forma reprimand from his civilian superior, António José Enes, but made him extremely popular with most of his compatriots as one who would stand no nonsense. The republicans would quickly and lengthily rue the day they underestimated his tenacious courage.

Or, for that matter, Villalobar's zeal for action. 'Give me one shot, give me one shot, and I'll restore the monarchy in Portugal [*Dêem-me um tiro, dêem-me um tiro, que implanto a Monarquia em Portugal*]!' Spain's deformed ambassador uttered this singular challenge not in the hushed purlieus of a bureaucratic office, but 'in a loud voice [*em alta voz*]' at Lisbon's own Martinho café.[90]

A first attempt at a monarchist restoration, with Paiva Couceiro himself in charge of it, came in October 1911. By this time, the Republic's leaders had already made themselves thoroughly hated even among sectors of Lisbon's own populace. Francisco Manuel Homem Christo, a recognised anticlerical, soured on the coup before it was a month in the past:

> The disorganisation of Portuguese society [under Manuel II] was very great. Is that disorganisation now going to end? [...] The regiments were not led against the King by officers. They were debauched by revolutionists. It was the work of anarchy.[91]

Efforts led by Afonso Costa to indict ex-Prime-Minister Franco for treason were pronounced unlawful by the five judges in Portugal's Court of Appeal, which refused to declare criminal any of Franco's behaviour while in office. Costa greeted this defiance by dismissing one of the judges and packing the other four off to Goa.[92] This arrogance received little coverage in foreign lands. Not so Costa's obsessive, internationally discussed, determination to humiliate the Church. The 'Law of Separation' which the government proclaimed on 20 April 1911 had been his handiwork, in which he overruled more restrained colleagues. It ratified decrees which Costa had first formulated late the previous year, including the confiscation of church properties; the expulsion of the Jesuits from the country; the dissolution of all other religious orders; imprisonment for public wearing of religious attire by priests and nuns; the secularisation of schooling; the legality of divorce; and the prohibition of church marriages. Four Portuguese bishops who complained about the results found themselves exiled. France had passed similarly intended laws less than a decade earlier, but with more loopholes, and with less protest abroad.

Costa gloatingly announced that 'within two generations [of the April 1911 law], Catholic religion will have been annihilated in Portugal'.[93] To aid this outcome, he created a tame Catholicism of his own, which accorded to its members worldly benefits of which real Catholics had no hope. By this means he revived an approach which had well served the Jacobins of revolutionary France and would be subsequently successful for communist régimes after the Second World War (most notoriously in mainland China's post-1949 'Patriotic Church'). A hostile Irish visitor to the capital noted:

> There are now in Portugal several hundred Catholic clergymen living openly with women, to the scandal of such old-fashioned parishioners as still retain some faint reminiscence of the Faith. Those clergymen have broken with Rome, but are paid and recognised by the State.[94]

The results annoyed Protestants as well as Catholics. Sir Arthur Hardinge, himself a Protestant, warned that Britain would keep on refusing to accord the Republic official recognition unless British Catholic teaching orders resident on Portuguese territory were left safe. Only after the Republic's spokesmen promised to abide by this agreement was recognition granted.

In these circumstances, Paiva Couceiro could be forgiven for thinking that the monarchists' hour had struck, particularly when Spain's monarch agreed with him. It is still not entirely clear how much practical succour – as opposed to cost-free verbal assurances – King Alfonso then gave, although a recent study[95] furnishes some details. (That he and Paiva Couceiro maintained regular written contact, before and after the military campaign led by the latter, is beyond dispute.) Crossing the border from Spain into the north-eastern province of Trás-os-Montes on 4 October, Paiva Couceiro wanted to turn to the monarchists' advantage the administrative and cultural gulf between Lisbon and the rest of Portugal. He maintained that if he could establish a foothold in the north, where the Republic aroused little enthusiasm and much distaste among the locals, conquering the south would be easier. In fact his troops held out for only three days before army units loyal to the new Prime Minister, João Chagas (backed by President Arriaga mainly in order to keep Costa out), prevailed. According to one commentator, the monarchist troops were ludicrously under-supplied and had only enough ammunition to last them half an hour.[96]

Whatever help Spain supplied directly to Paiva Couceiro, it proved inadequate. Shifting the balance still more in Chagas's favour was the apathy shown toward Paiva Couceiro by most northerners, whose monarchist allegiance involved fond memories of early-nineteenth-century throne-and-altar traditionalism – the creed embodied by King Miguel in the 1830s before his final defeat – and who regarded poor ineffective Manuel as little better than a republican figurehead. Then again, Alfonso XIII's own fondness for playing double-games, through a low boredom threshold much more than through malice, needs to be remembered. Anglo-Portuguese ties remained so strong, and Alfonso's own Anglophilia so great, that he dreaded the showdown with Britain which a thoroughgoing Spanish destabilisation project against the Portuguese Republic would have involved. As one biographer noted in 1963, regarding Alfonso's congenital impatience:

> [H]e would have done better to have more effectively disguised his contempt for many of those with whom he was brought into contact,

but the suffering of fools – and knaves – gladly is not an easily acquired accomplishment, quite apart from the fact that it was very alien to his temperament.[97]

Even these handicaps to the monarchist cause would not have doomed it outright, but for the extreme caution of Manuel himself. One caustic British commentator summed him up in three words: 'amiable but spineless'.[98] That harsh judgement could be easily arrived at with hindsight. He did not always strike others as so frail. The young Churchill admitted, in a letter to his new wife Clementine, that he had found Manuel unexpectedly vivacious and determined:

> brimful of life and spirits [...] He is extremely clever and accomplished. We became great friends. He told me much about his views of Portugal and his hopes of returning soon by a coup d'état.[99]

Grasping the unlikelihood of monarchist success without at least the pretence of cooperation between Manuel and the traditionalists – the 'Miguelists', as the latter were known, their leader being the 58-year-old Duke Miguel, the son of former King Miguel – Paiva Couceiro, who had returned to Spain after his setback, helped to arrange, and was present at, a formal rapprochement. This rapprochement, the Pact of Dover, was signed in London by Manuel and by Duke Miguel on 30 December 1911 and rendered public the following month. Through it, Manuel proclaimed Duke Miguel and his descendants to be legitimate heirs to the Portuguese throne, thereby reversing what had been the ruling house's policy since 1834. Duke Miguel, in return, acknowledged Manuel as the rightful sovereign.

In June 1912, an Oporto-based tribunal had condemned Paiva Couceiro, *in absentia*, to ten years' banishment. The latter showed his unconcern for this sentence by organising yet another incursion, once again entering Trás-os-Montes (on 8 July) from his Spanish base.[100] He now led more than 500 soldiers – Miguelists among them this time[101] – as opposed to approximately 270 republican troops in the area.[102] The latter had as their military commander General António Ribeiro de Carvalho, and the nearest city, Chaves, had as its administrator 31-year-old António Granjo, who would later play an important part in national politics. (Prime Minister for two short terms, Granjo would eventually fall victim to an October 1921 blood-letting by ultra-leftists; others murdered in Lisbon that same night included Machado Santos.) Soon Paiva Couceiro's men captured Chaves' customs-house, from which they flew the monarchist flag. Ribeiro de Carvalho and Granjo had to call for reinforcements, and these played the crucial part.

Artillery fired by republicans from the hill of Alto de Forca proved lethal to the aims of the monarchists, who once again lacked enough ammunition. By sunset all was over, with thirty monarchists dead, with most of the survivors thoroughly disheartened, and with Spain having once again failed to give decisive assistance. Paiva Couceiro himself put it thus: 'it was the army of Lilliput in the palm of the republican Gulliver's hand'.[103] Lisbon confirmed the original ten-year exile sentence against him.

Further damage to the monarchists' hopes came with the Great War. Manuel's Anglophilia, if anything, surpassed Alfonso XIII's. Ensconced in comfortable expatriation at Twickenham, approximately fourteen kilometres south-west of central London, he collected second-hand books with ardour (eventually he would produce an entire three-volume treatise on the subject, *Livros Antigos Portuguezes 1489–1600*), and found other consolations for exile.

The chief among these consolations had already been a part of his life in Lisbon: Gaby Deslys, the Marseille-born, scandal-generating actress and dancer whom he met in Paris during 1909, and upon whom he lavished a pearl necklace worth, even at the time, US$70,000. (This sum of money in American dollars was the equivalent of £14,400 in 1909; 115 years later, the equivalent figure in sterling would be no less than £1.92 million.) Gaby's surname had originally been Caire, but Deslys ('of the lilies' in French) had far more public appeal, and so she adopted it. Routinely affronting censors in Boston and London through the provocativeness of her dance steps (of which the 'Gaby Glide' became the best-known) and the skimpiness of her costume, she attracted, in addition, the wrath of John P. Maud, Anglican Bishop of Kensington, who protested against the immodesty of her stage attire. Unfazed, she told reporters assembled to bid her farewell at Dover on her way back to the Continent: 'Tell your bishops, I love them – but they show too much leg!'[104] Diverting enough to readers in retrospect; perhaps less diverting to those royalists back home who had lost their fortunes, and in some cases lost family members, for the sake of the cause.

On one point, at least, Manuel and the republicans were united: both supported the British military effort from August 1914 onward. (A more cynical and resilient refugee could have used this shared war aim to extract political leverage from the republicans on his own behalf; not Manuel.) It had been agreed in both London and Lisbon that the 1386 Treaty of Windsor bound nations, not dynasties, and therefore it remained valid despite the Braganças' overthrow. Especially worrying to the PRP were Germany's designs on Portugal's African territories, designs which the Royal Navy alone seemed capable of obstructing. As one historian summarised the matter:

> With the war certain to spread to part of Africa, Portugal felt great anxiety about the colonies. Teixeira Gomes, the minister in London, sounded the Foreign Office concerning British protection for Angola and Mozambique. Sir Edward Grey immediately guaranteed protection if necessary, but otherwise declared England would be satisfied if Portugal took no military action for the present and merely refrained from proclaiming neutrality.[105]

But that last confident estimate presupposed that hostilities would 'all be over by Christmas'. When 1915 passed without the slightest prospect of an Allied victory, Lisbon acceded to the British Foreign Secretary's request that the seventy-two warships berthed in Portuguese harbours be seized. Grey knew, Bernardino Machado (now Portugal's president) knew, and Afonso Costa (now Prime Minister) knew, that such seizure amounted to a *casus belli*; but the thing was done. Consequently, both Germany and Austria-Hungary declared war on Portugal in March 1916.

From the first, the action spelled disaster. Not for a century had soldiers from Portugal served in a wider European conflict. When members of the Portuguese Expeditionary

Corps eventually got to the Western Front during early 1917, it became obvious that they were badly trained, badly equipped, and deficient in morale. Amid the prevailing near-stalemate, these shortcomings could be overlooked. Not so after the Battle of the Lys River in April 1918, during Ludendorff's Spring Offensive – *Kaiserschlacht* ('the Emperors' Battle'), the Central Powers called it – which resulted in 7,000 Portuguese casualties in one day. Clearly this could not continue. And by this time Portugal had a boss resolved to ensure that it would not continue: Sidónio Pais, comparatively youthful (45), active, versatile, with a powerful mind and an eloquent tongue.

Pais, as has been succinctly observed, 'seemed to many what Manuel II might have been but was not'.[106] He embodied the monarchical theory, without those numerous hostages to fortune which the pliant Manuel had given in monarchical practice. Academically exceptional, a mathematics professor at the University of Coimbra before entering public life (Dr Salazar was economics professor at the same campus prior to embarking on politics), Pais had approved of the republic's establishment, had served Lisbon as ambassador to Berlin for four years, and had even become a Freemason; but after 1916 he decided he had had enough of the prevailing Costa-dominated Cortes intrigue, and he realised that no Portuguese government could keep on harassing Catholicism forever. The national atmosphere of late 1917 having a decidedly apocalyptic character in any case – the sequence of Marian visions at Fátima being much the most renowned and dramatic manifestation of this character – it proved an ideal time for Pais to strike. Which, on 7 December, he did. He led a coup of his own that deposed Costa, neutralised the Costa faction of the PRP, and benefited from the endorsement of Machado Santos, who became Interior Minister.

Monarchists took abundant heart at Pais's emergence, more especially those monarchists who formed the nucleus of the movement known as *Integralismo Lusitano*. Established at the University of Coimbra in the year the Great War began, and dominated from the outset by the short-lived intellectual António Sardinha, *Integralismo Lusitano* owed a great deal to the philosophy of Charles Maurras and of *Action Française* in general. Its support of Duke Miguel, if necessary against the weakness of Manuel, accorded with Maurrassian doctrine. Happy to have gained *Integralismo Lusitano*'s approval, Pais appointed some of the group's members to his staff. But the group needed him more than he needed it, and the very month which had witnessed the Lys River disaster also witnessed Pais's election to the presidential office.

Even those with the greatest reason to resent Pais acknowledged his skill in winning over crowds. There existed in Portugal an opening for populist demagogy, and Pais exploited it, aided rather than hindered by his speaking voice, which retained the distinctive timbre of the north-west where he had been born.[107] His first-hand knowledge of Germany led ill-wishers to suppose he would be Kaiser Wilhelm's puppet; but this expectation he also thwarted. Domestic affairs interested him much more than foreign affairs could do. As president he scrapped the most severe of the Costa-derived laws against Catholicism, lifted most of the existing constitutional restrictions upon adult male suffrage, permitted monarchists to run for public office, signed a concordat with the Vatican, and overhauled army administration in order that no more Lys-type fiascos could occur. He seemed spurred on by a presentiment of how little time he would ever have to rule. 'Chain-smoking, coffee-drinking, with little or no sleep for long periods',[108] he possessed no formal party mechanism to minimise the personalist burdens of his office, even after Armistice Day had at last arrived, to rejoicing in Lisbon's streets.

What the wrath of Costa's still-potent machine could not achieve by way of eliminating Pais, a solitary ideologue could. On 14 December, at Lisbon's Rossio train station, whence he had gone in the hope of travelling to Oporto and winning over monarchists based there, Pais was gunned down. His killer, José Júlio da Costa (no relation of Afonso Costa and unconnected with him), saw himself as a sacrificial victim and surrendered to police without protest. Disappointingly for his explicit hopes of martyrdom, Portugal had outlawed capital punishment.

Pais's death terminated the last monarchist hopes of a republican friend at court. Or, to be more precise, of a politically powerful republican friend at court: since Pais's successor as president, Admiral João do Canto e Castro, favoured monarchism but dared not actively champion it. A more immediate threat to Canto e Castro than monarchist sentiment came from left-wing rebels, angry with the caution of new Prime Minister João Tamagnini Barbosa. These rebels, accusing Tamagnini Barbosa of having betrayed the republican revolution, took control of Santarém (approximately sixty-seven kilometres to Lisbon's north-east) on 8 January 1919. They surrendered to government artillery only a week later, by which time a dozen of them had perished. Paiva Couceiro could hardly believe his good luck: if Lisbon had that amount of trouble suppressing extremists in the republican camp, what might monarchists not achieve?

Thus it was that on 19 January in Oporto, Paiva Couceiro spurned the cautious border-crossing of his earlier attempts and audaciously proclaimed to the world that the Monarchy of the North – *Monarquia do Norte* – had begun.[109] He now benefited not only from *Integralismo Lusitano* backing (Sardinha actually enlisted in the monarchist ranks) but from the active support of a much more experienced fellow 'African', João de Almeida, who, two days before Christmas 1918, had used the threat of a monarchist uprising within Lisbon by units loyal to him, to force Tamagnini Barbosa into purging left-wingers from the cabinet. Another important figure aligning himself with Paiva Couceiro was a former Cortes member, Aires de Ornelas, who acted as a go-between when it came to liaising with Manuel himself. City council after city council in the north welcomed the royalists, and flew the Monarchy of the North's blue-and-white flag: Viana do Castelo, Braga, Guimarães, Villa Real, Viseu, even Chaves, scene of the 1912 débâcle.[110] Tamagnini Barbosa declared a state of emergency, allowing left-wing prisoners out of jail, on condition that they helped to defend the republic.

In Lisbon itself over the following week, the result was something of a draw. Monarchist troops in the capital's Monsanto region had surrendered by the evening of the 24th, thanks largely to a rag-tag force of volunteers mobilised by the government. A total of thirty-nine persons perished in the battle.[111] The price for the surrender was a high one; three days later, Tamagnini Barbosa resigned. Canto e Castro chose as the next Prime Minister José Relvas, a farmer who had been Minister for Finance under President Braga, and who subsequently was ambassador to Spain. The panic felt in official circles at Paiva Couceiro's successes can be gleaned from the fact that Relvas also served as his own Interior Minister, rather than entrusting that post to a possible rival. Relvas entrusted other cabinet jobs to three Sidonists – as Pais's supporters were called – and, in a path-breaking decision born of coalitionist need, to a Socialist Party member.

By this stage the republicans rather than the monarchists suffered acutely from ammunition shortages, because the civilians who had been entrusted with weapons for the Monsanto combat were showing themselves decidedly reluctant to give those weapons up. A future Prime Minister, Francisco Cunha Leal, who was demonstrating his own skill at Costa-style oratorical outbursts against the government, demanded to know why action against the monarchists was not being taken much more vigorously. 'Real civil war',[112] in his own large-hearted phrase, required far greater boldness. Meanwhile a basic question preoccupied monarchists and republicans alike. What would Manuel do?

The answer to this question astonished all concerned, though in view of the ex-sovereign's previous behaviour, it perhaps should not have caused surprise. Manuel himself not only had no intention of being 'the king [who] comes into his own again'; he expressed, via telegram,[113] outright horror at the Monarchy of the North's very existence. From his Twickenham redoubt, he called it 'a crime which was committed against all my instructions and orders [*um crime que se cometeu contra todas as minhas instruções e ordens]'.[114] The government, not least through fear of Cunha Leal's tongue-lashings, acquired new confidence. Monarchist-controlled centres such as Águeda, Estarreja, and Oliveira de Azeméis were won over to the republic. José Maria Ferreira Sarmento Pimentel, a republican commander since the heady days of 1910, suffered from influenza but had no intention of being incapacitated thereby. In early February 1919 he simply arose from his Oporto hospital bed, discovered to his relief that sections of the local military still wanted to keep a republic (even if Paiva Couceiro had imposed on them the new name of *Guarda Real*), and rallied them.

On the 13th, the Monarchy of the North went down fighting – but still, it went down at a cost of a further 150 lives. Manuel's own refusal to countenance it had enabled Alfonso XIII to feel understandably justified in not sponsoring it either – openly or, as far as can be ascertained, even covertly. At a time when diplomatic recognition by Madrid would have been an immeasurable fillip to Paiva Couceiro's hopes – it is hard to know how strife-torn Lisbon could conceivably have held out against an Oporto-Madrid alliance – Spain calculatingly withheld such recognition.[115] (Villalobar could no longer affect the outcome. He had been transferred to Brussels, where he laboured frantically but unsuccessfully to save Edith Cavell from execution in 1915.) Manuel, in his eagerness to disown the Monarchy of the North, took the opportunity to jibe at his more successful Spanish counterpart, saying:

> Paiva Couceiro incurred the greatest responsibility of the last century ...
> Do not be surprised that they say that Paiva Couceiro has been well received in that country ... he has been a plaything in the hands of the Spanish government, interested in our internal disorder [*Paiva Couceiro incorreu na maior responsabilidade politica do último século ... Não se admiraria que lhe dissessem que Paiva Couceiro foi bem recebido nesse país ... ele tem sido um joguete nas mãos dos governos espanhóis, interessados na nossa desordem interna]*.[116]

This time the government wanted to set an example to all remaining monarchists. It would permit no mere brief and fundamentally pleasurable vacations abroad for Paiva Couceiro himself, as his previous sentences had ended up becoming. In December 1920, a military tribunal sentenced him to twenty-five years' exile.

Sardinha and his fellow *Integralismo Lusitano* activists abandoned the whole concept of sacrificing everything for a Bragança restoration. They preferred to concentrate upon defending the rights of Catholicism itself, given that Costa was lastingly sidelined (in Paris) and given that no later prime minister could bring himself to undo all of Pais's concessions to the Church.

At an April 1922 conference with Duke Miguel in Paris, Manuel conceded to the Miguelists their dynastic demands. By 1922 it had become obvious that Manuel and his German-born wife, Augusta Victoria of Hohenzollern, were most unlikely to have children of their own. Duke Miguel, on the other hand, had a son: Duarte Nuno, then aged 15. Manuel confirmed that if Duke Miguel predeceased him, and assuming that he himself remained childless, then Duarte Nuno would be the recognised head of the Bragança clan. There remained no real amity, as opposed to a reluctant truce, between Manuel's adherents and Miguel's. For Miguel, Manuel remained the treacherous liberal, which in Miguelist eyes he had always been. The mutual aversion separating both monarchist camps continued past Miguel's own death in 1927.

Gaby Deslys had long since gone from Manuel's life. Influenza, unable to impede Sarmento Pimentel, dealt much more cruelly with her. She came down with a throat infection that could have been cured, but at the cost of leaving her beautiful neck scarred. This disfigurement she refused to allow surgeons to perform. In February 1920, not yet 39, she passed away.

As for Manuel, Francis McCullagh had scathingly written back in 1914: 'Portugal has had Constitutionalism too soon; she has had the Republic too soon; and the Monarchy should not try to return too soon. Of course a monarchy is not essential; a reactionary Republic like the present Chinese Republic would probably suit Portugal better.'[117] When, after 1926, it became incontestable that any stable non-monarchical government in Portugal would be either headed de facto or headed *de jure* by the still young, but intimidatingly ambitious, Salazar, the former king publicly declared his approval of the new dispensation. On 2 July 1932, a day after he visited Wimbledon to watch the tennis championships, he unexpectedly died at Twickenham. The cause of his death was given as 'acute oedema of the glottis';[118] foul play was ruled out, though some monarchists believed that a Carbonária assassin had struck.

Within four days Salazar achieved the Prime Minister's office which he had so long craved, and his first official acts included granting to the former sovereign a state funeral. Those closest to Salazar – including his last Foreign Minister, Franco Nogueira – credited him with lifelong monarchist attitudes.[119] It is true that he tended to avoid using the word 'republic' in official documents (which usually called General Óscar Carmona – President from 1926 – 'Head of the State', instead of 'President of the Portuguese Republic').[120] But he had steered clear of active support for Paiva Couceiro, and once in power he vetoed the amnesty which Couceiro had been given before his quarter-century sentence had finished. (Not till 1939 was the monarchist veteran, by then with only five more years to live, permitted to return to Portugal.) A 1932 observation of Salazar's includes this rather dismissive assessment of the Braganças' future:

> In the younger generations, the attitude which seems to predominate is that of indifference to the problem [of monarchism versus republicanism], a belief that many other problems must take precedence over that of the form which government should assume, intellectual and political questions which today must come first. So long as this attitude prevails, the monarchist principle has lost its energising power.[121]

When cabinet ministers or other officials occasionally urged Salazar to give Duarte Nuno a political role, he always rebuffed them, even though Carmona's death in office (1951), and the absence of an obvious presidential candidate to take Carmona's place, provided monarchists with an opening. At times Salazar sought to remind his audience of his fluency in three languages: Portuguese, French and Passive-Aggressive.

> *It is as well not to leave men chained to corpses!* [italics in original] [...] The royalist problem embarrasses and embitters the progress of all governments in Portugal, and more especially those of the Right. This problem must be disposed of in a straightforward way, avoiding all those manifestations and declarations which could possibly give it a chance of a fresh life at the first opportunity. I obviously cannot ask men whose political education has been in the direction of another ideal to abandon their principles, to bind themselves to the government and come out in the street to cheer the Republic. I should be the first to have my doubts about certain people who two days after their conversion should be claiming to be more republican than the old republicans themselves. No, what I ask of our royalists – or, perhaps I should put it, what I advise them to do – is that, if and when they enter our public life, they shall put aside any false or even dangerous notion that their coalition in the present government is any step towards realisation of their aspirations. The national life itself is beset at the moment with problems of enormous importance, and questions of this or that regime are in comparison quite in the background, trifling, and almost absurd. Let us get to work, then, with real facts and not with dreams or fantasies.[122]

How sensitive Salazar could become on the whole monarchist issue long after Manuel's demise[123] emerges from the following account:

> On 12 November [1935], a small and apparently innocuous notice in the English newspaper, the *Daily Telegraph*, advised that 'the pretender to the throne' of Portugal, Dom Duarte Nuno de Bragança, on a visit to London, had been received in Buckingham Palace by the royal family, and would lunch with the ambassador of Portugal.
> It was known that the ambassador Rui Ulrich was a monarchist. Immediately, the news item gave rise to comments in Lisbon and a request, to the ambassador for clarification, signed by the Minister [Foreign

Minister Armindo Monteiro] himself. In the meantime, however, the rumour spread that Salazar was conspiring with the English to restore the monarchy and the republicans requested the intervention of General Carmona. On the nineteenth, the Minister agreed with the ambassador on the text of a communication that would put an end to the question, explaining that all that had happened was a lunch between friends, of which the Minister for Foreign Affairs had been completely unaware. However, in the Council of Ministers of 22 November, Carmona, responding to a question from Salazar, pronounced in favour of the dismissal of the ambassador. To communicate this decision Rui Ulrich was called to Lisbon. He was offered in compensation, the embassy in Madrid, which he refused, as he did not want to go to another post 'as an ambassador in disgrace'. A replacement was suggested – Alberto Oliveira, attached to the Vatican as Minister Plenipotentiary. At that time the only Portuguese delegations with the rank of embassy were Madrid, London and Rio de Janeiro.

In addition to illustrating the intensity of rivalry between monarchists and republicans and the role of arbiter Carmona still played at this time, the episode also had some repercussions both for the reputation and for the political position of the Minister. Indeed, on their return from London, Ulrich and his wife Veva de Lima, threw themselves body and soul into a bitter campaign against the Government, and in particular against Monteiro. Subsequently, when Monteiro was nominated as ambassador to London, Ulrich himself insinuated publicly that his dismissal was owing to intrigues by the Minister, who coveted his [Ulrich's] position. That does not seem to have been the case. But in the small world of Lisbon at this time, it was inevitable that the intrigue provoked some damage.[124]

Not damage to Salazar, though, in the upshot. Another Francis McCullagh passage furnishes a bleak epitaph for Manuel 'The Unfortunate':

[H]e [Manuel] went to Gibraltar, awaiting a 'call' to come back. If Napoleon in Elba had waited for a 'call' from France he would never again have entered the Tuileries. Kings must in these matters take a certain amount of initiative and risk.[125]

Chapter II

Hohenzollerns, Wittelsbachs, and the Men Who Jailed Hitler
Germany

> He [Hitler] may have been the most popular revolutionary leader in the history of the modern world. The emphasis is on the word *popular,* because Hitler belongs to the democratic, not the aristocratic, age of history. [...] He showed respect for some of the old things; but a conservative he was not, and a reactionary not at all.
>
> John Lukacs, Hungarian-American historian
> and survivor of Hitler's slave labour system[1]

The question was one which no Prussian drill-sergeant's manual, however comprehensive, and no expertise in Clausewitz, however conscientiously acquired, could answer. Yet to elements of the German High Command during the first days of November 1918, the question persisted: when military defeat is inescapable, how do you persuade your Supreme War Lord – His Imperial and Royal Majesty Kaiser Wilhelm II, head of the House of Hohenzollern, by the grace of God Emperor of Germany and King of Prussia since 1888 – to kill himself?

At the High Command's headquarters in Spa, occupied Belgium, someone had raised the issue. It is not clear who; the likeliest candidate is the outspoken, ruthlessly commonsensical General Wilhelm Groener, who during October had succeeded Erich Ludendorff as Quartermaster-General.[2] Telephones were constantly shrilling, telegrams constantly arriving, with news from the home front, all of it bad. On 7 November, in Brunswick (Braunschweig), Cologne, Darmstadt, Düsseldorf, Frankfurt-am-Main, Lauenburg, Leipzig, Magdeburg, Oldenburg, Osnabrück and Stuttgart, exuberant workers' councils took over municipal administrations.[3] At Kiel, the sailors were mutinying. Bavaria, likewise on the 7th, went so far as to slough its own royal dynasty. King Ludwig III simply fled his Munich palace and made what he supposed would be a short-term home in Salzburg's Anif Castle. In his place the local socialists under journalist Kurt Eisner had proclaimed a republic. With pardonable exaggeration and with an understandable amazement at his own good fortune, Eisner gloated: 'The Wittelsbachs ruled over Bavaria for seven hundred years. I got rid of them in seven hours with seven men.'[4]

But perhaps (thus ran the increasingly desperate theorising) a successful blow could be struck for national honour if the Supreme War Lord himself went to the front and made one glorious, suicidal charge into oblivion. Field-Marshal Paul von Hindenburg wanted none of it. What, he asked, if the Kaiser remained alive only to be captured by the Allies? Or, worse still, by revolutionists within his own ranks?

As for the Kaiser himself, the very idea – when he learned of it – revolted him. His post-war memoirs, ghost-written in much of their wording but authentically naïve in their sentiments (and in their frequent resort to the third person), explained the mixture of religious and military considerations that made him refuse a hero's apotheosis:

> Some say the Emperor should have gone to some regiment at the front, hurled himself with it upon the enemy, and sought death in one last attack. That, however, would not only have rendered impossible the armistice, ardently desired by the nation, concerning which the commission sent from Berlin to General Foch was already negotiating, but would also have meant the useless sacrifice of the lives of many soldiers – of some of the very best and most faithful, in fact. […]
>
> Still others say the Emperor should have killed himself. That was made impossible by my firm Christian beliefs. And would not people have exclaimed: 'How cowardly! Now he shirks all responsibilities by committing suicide!' This alternative was also eliminated because I had to consider how to be of help and use to my people and my country in the evil time that was to be foreseen.[5]

Nor could Wilhelm, supposing he had acted on the recommendation to do away with himself, have felt any confidence that his counsellors would adhere to this recommendation after giving it. Already, in 1915, Admiral Tirpitz (notwithstanding the oath of loyalty to the Kaiser which he and all his fellows had sworn) seriously considered having Wilhelm certified by doctors as unfit to rule.[6] During November 1914 Wilhelm had admitted to Prince Max von Baden, who would become his last Chancellor, how little authority he retained: 'The General Staff tells me nothing and never asks my advice. If people in Germany think I am the Supreme Commander, they are grossly mistaken. I drink tea, saw wood, and go for walks.'[7]

Might abdication bring the war to an end and secure adequate peace terms for Germany, even if hastening the Kaiser's ascent to Valhalla could not? It is a measure of the monarchical impulse's continuing strength at the time that initially the concept of deposing the monarch seemed to most politicians and soldiers fantastical. As British historian John Terraine observed: 'In Germany, not even the Social Democrats desired the end of the Empire; only the extreme Left looked towards that goal. The High Command, the Officer Corps, and the large body of conservative opinion that supported them, all viewed such thoughts with horror.'[8]

Few European republics (Bavaria aside) existed before Armistice Day. And fewer still gave outsiders the impression of being durable. Not all the Baltic states had yet become independent. Finland, for most of 1918, had been torn by civil war, which killed more than 1 per cent of the country's whole population. (So scared were the victorious Finnish conservatives of further strife from local Bolsheviks that they actually offered to make the Kaiser's brother-in-law, Friedrich Karl, Finland's king. Germany's surrender aborted that scheme before Friedrich Karl could visit his kingdom.) Habsburg territories, however war-exhausted, remained officially intact until early November. Poland's continued autonomy in 1918 looked improbable: the 'Miracle on the Vistula' which guaranteed short-term Polish safety from Soviet aggression would not occur for another two years. The USSR itself inspired more and more alarm, and not merely within those countries with which it shared borders, such as the short-lived Ukrainian National Republic, which the Red Army would soon overthrow. That left four republics in Europe: France, Portugal, Switzerland and the micronation of San Marino. The French and Portuguese examples, with their seemingly incessant turnover of cabinets (except on the rare occasions when a Poincaré or a Clemenceau could make the French system work despite itself), inspired little trust in the exportability of republicanism elsewhere.

When the notion of the Kaiser giving up the throne was first mooted, Groener firmly opposed it. So, understandably enough, did the Kaiser. Prussia's Interior Minister, Wilhelm Arnold Drews, urged his sovereign on 1 November to abdicate. The Kaiser, in a private description of the meeting written two days later, chewed out Drews with spirit and (when not indulging his racial as well as social prejudices) considerable predictive shrewdness:

> I said, 'How comes it that you, a Prussian official, one of my subjects who have taken an oath of allegiance to me, have the insolence and effrontery to appear before me with a request like this?' You should just have seen how that took the wind out of his sails. It was the last thing he expected, he made a deep bow on the spot. 'Very well, then, supposing I did,' I said. 'What do you suppose would happen next, you, an administrative official? My sons have assured me that none of them will take my place. So the whole house of H [Hohenzollern] would go along with me.' You should have seen the fright that gave him, it again was the last thing he'd expected. He and the whole of that smart government in Berlin. 'And who would then take on the regency for a twelve-year-old child? My grandson? The Imperial Chancellor [Prince Max] perhaps? I gather from Munich that they haven't the least intention of recognising him down there. So what would happen?' 'Chaos,' he said, making another bow. You see, you only have to question such muddle-heads, and go on questioning them for all their confusion and empty-headedness to become obvious. 'All right then,' I said, 'let me tell you the form chaos would take. I abdicate. All the dynasties fall along with me, the army is left leaderless, the front-line troops disband and stream over the Rhine. The disaffected gang up together, hang, murder and plunder – assisted by the enemy. That is why I have no intention of abdicating. The King of Prussia cannot betray Germany. I have no intention of quitting the throne because of a few hundred Jews and a thousand workmen. Tell that to your masters in Berlin!' When he was going, I called the Field-Marshal [Hindenburg] and First Quartermaster-General [Groener]. Hindenburg told him the same thing bluntly and then Groener [...] he went for Drews like a wild-cat, he fairly gave it to him. [...] Now I may have ruled well or badly, that's not the point at the moment, most of it was of course bad! But I have lived for sixty years and spent thirty of them on the throne. There is one thing you must allow me, experience![9]

At such fraught times and amid such shouting matches, mere unglamorous stolidity became a pearl beyond measure. Max von Baden, coping as best as he could with a bout of that misnamed 'Spanish flu', which within two years would kill more people than the Great War had, had concluded that the only way of propitiating Woodrow Wilson, and of making his Fourteen Points (spelt out by Wilson to the US Congress in the preceding January) the basis for peace, was to deprive the Kaiser of his crown. Accordingly, the Chancellor asked one of the leading Social Democrats in the Reichstag, Friedrich Ebert: 'If I go to Spa and obtain the abdication of the Kaiser, can I count on your support in the fight against social revolution?' Ebert, an erstwhile saddle-maker incapable of happy talk, assured Prince Max: 'I don't want social revolution. I hate it like sin.'[10] Ebert's own fidelity to the Reich was indisputable: two of his sons had fallen in the war.

In the end Prince Max, rather than personally obtaining the abdication, pre-empted it. He simply announced to the world, without having notified the individual most closely involved (or Hindenburg), that the Kaiser's reign had finished. Only by this drastic means, he believed – the leading Social Democrats shared his belief – could the extreme Spartacist Left, under demagogues like Karl Liebknecht, be thwarted. 'A revolutionary gesture,' as Ebert put it, 'is necessary to forestall the revolution.'[11] On the Reichstag's steps, fellow Social Democrat and future Chancellor Philipp Scheidemann, similarly bent on thwarting the pro-Liebknecht crowds, showed himself to the crowds and announced (to the naturally cautious Ebert's displeasure) that Germany had turned republican.

With what rage the Kaiser greeted these tidings, on learning of them two hours later, may be imagined. At first, he insisted upon the face-saving scruple that, even if the Empire had ended, he could cling to power as King of Prussia. Groener had ceased to think that such legalistic half-measures remained viable:

> 'Sire, you no longer have an army. The army will march home in peace and order under its leaders and commanding generals, but not under the command of Your Majesty, for it no longer stands behind Your Majesty.'

> The Emperor turned upon Groener, his eyes blazing with anger. 'Excellency, I shall require that statement from you in black and white, signed by all my generals, that the Army no longer stands behind its Commander-in-Chief. Have they not taken the military oath to me?'

> 'In circumstances like these, Sire, oaths are but words,' replied Groener sadly.[12]

Insufficiently emphasised in most literature on the Kaiser's downfall is the strength of his fear that he – and, more alarming still, his loved ones – would end up like the Romanovs. Ebert and Scheidemann were decent patriots, but then so had been Alexander Kerensky, the hapless Prime Minister of Russia – and look what had happened to *his* hopes of keeping control. Already in Berlin, the Imperial Palace had been stormed by Liebknecht and his followers, who had hung from its balcony a red blanket, until Scheidemann's counterstroke forced them to retreat. Preying on the Kaiser's mind was the fact that in July his first love, Elisabeth, Princess of Hesse ('Ella'), who had married Russia's Grand Duke Sergei – himself assassinated in 1905 – had been thrown into an abandoned mineshaft with five other grand dukes by her Bolshevik captors. These gentlemen then flung two hand-grenades down the shaft before sealing the entrance with heavy blocks of timber. The Kaiser can hardly be blamed for dreading that Liebknecht and company intended a similar fate for the Hohenzollerns.

Hindenburg helped to ensure otherwise. If the Emperor could escape to neutral Holland, the Field-Marshal thought, the worst civil unrest at home could be dampened down. While a republic might have become unavoidable, regicide was not. So it proved. In The Hague, Queen Wilhelmina appears to have been informed by one of her own generals who had visited Spa about what was planned. She and the Prime Minister of the Netherlands, Charles Ruijs de Beerenbrouck, granted sanctuary to Wilhelm and his household. The first accommodation for them on Dutch soil was Amerongen Castle, owned by a Dutch aristocrat of part-English lineage, Count Godard Bentinck. Two days afterwards, Prince Max having handed the Chancellorship to Ebert, the war was over. In 1914, H.G. Wells had issued a book about the conflict's early stages, over-optimistically called *The War That Will End War*.

❀ ❀ ❀

A 1977 biographer of Wilhelm II wrote of the six months following Germany's surrender: 'The fatherland had become like a lunatic asylum left in charge of the patients.'[13] This was no mere glib wisdom after the event. At the time in Berlin, Ben Hecht – then representing New York's *Daily News* – cabled to his boss Henry Justin Smith: 'Germany is having a nervous breakdown. There is nothing sane to report.'[14]

Lemmings are widely, though erroneously, said to destroy themselves en masse by jumping over cliffs. A similar profound collective willingness to end it all gripped Germany's twenty-one other kings, princes and dukes during the weeks immediately before December 1918. In no case did furious popular demand (even of the limited sort manifesting itself in Bavaria) force them to abdicate. In few cases did popular agitation against them exist at all. None of the monarchs in question fired so much as a pea-shooter in his own defence. All can be acquitted of being physical cowards. Rather, the Kaiser's escape had simply turned these sovereigns' mental universe upside down, as if somehow gravity had ceased to operate. (Ludendorff would refer to the Hohenzollerns' downfall, not as a mere change of government, but as 'the collapse of the world'.)[15]

Earliest of the evacuees was the Duke of Braunschweig, who had stepped down on 9 November; the last sovereign to hold out, Wilhelm II of Württemberg, resigned on 30 November. King Wilhelm made a token complaint about his departure; namely, that because his palace belonged to him as an individual rather than to the state, the socialist republicans lacked the statutory right to fly a red flag from it. This complaint being duly registered, he went without fuss,[16] after he and the Grand Duke of Baden had received from their respective states' new republican administrations 'what amounted to votes of thanks'.[17] Saxony's king, Friedrich August III, responded to the question of whether he was prepared to abdicate with the sheepish words 'Oh well, I suppose I'd better.'[18] Another of Friedrich August's remarks to the local republicans implies greater brio, and one hopes that it is authentic: he is said to have told them, in his ripest Saxon dialect, *'Nu da mach doch eiern Drägg alleene!'* Roughly translatable as 'Now you can take care of this crap by yourselves!'[19]

But if the Fatherland had indeed become a lunatic asylum, Munich resembled its locked ward. Bavarian Premier[20] Kurt Eisner at least meant well, and as a former drama critic he realised the deep reportorial truth that administrators can be as amateurish as they like, provided that their amateurism keeps the Fourth Estate contented:

> Convinced that a new age of open diplomacy and exposed government had dawned, he conducted Bavaria's affairs in public. [...] Visitors found Eisner's desk strewn with proclamations, telegrams and memoranda. He made no particular effort to hide even the most confidential documents. Would the visitor care to see a copy of a telegram only just sent off to Ebert in Berlin? Here it was. Would the journalist like to read the minutes of the cabinet meetings of the Bavarian Socialist Republic? They were available in full for the journalist's immediate inspection.[21]

Eisner's open-handedness did him no good whatsoever when he fell out with the local Communists, having already antagonised the local Ebert-style Social Democrats and the local Catholic conservatives. On 21 February of the new year, Eisner left his office for the state parliament (Landtag), planning to tender his resignation. Lying in wait for him was a young aristocrat, Count Anton von Arco-Valley. Denied membership of the Thule Society – a local group of Judeophobic occultists who refused him entry to the group because of his mother's Jewish blood – Arco-Valley decided to prove his credentials for homicide on a freelance basis. He fired two bullets into Eisner, who survived only seconds. When the news of Eisner's murder spread, one of his supporters – Alois Lindner, an apprentice butcher – entered the Landtag, drew a pistol, and shot the anti-Eisner Socialist politician Eduard Auer, having inaccurately concluded that Auer had conspired with Arco-Valley.[22] Auer survived, but the soldier who tried to subdue Lindner had less luck: with a solitary bullet, Lindner slew him. Banners borne aloft at the ex-Premier's funeral bore the slogan 'Vengeance for Eisner!'[23] Had Arco-Valley not been under arrest, he would have been lynched.

Soon Bavaria fell into the hands of rulers so out of touch with the reality-based community as to make Eisner look statesmanlike. Not the Social Democrats, who under their down-to-earth leader Johannes Hoffmann prudently moved their new government to Bamberg, where at least a detachment from the central government's Freikorps could protect it in that city. Meanwhile Munich's new rulers (fired by the nearby example of Béla Kun's Hungarian Soviet, and ranging across the entire political spectrum from Marxists to Anarchists) achieved novel and prophetic levels of mental disturbance.

One newly appointed commissar of the Bavarian Soviet Republic, playwright Ernst Toller, had no sooner accepted his role than he publicly pleaded for what he imagined to be the cowering ratepayers' most urgent needs: 'new art forms in sculpture, drama, painting and architecture which would permit the liberation of the spirit of mankind'.[24] Gustav Landauer, Toller's comrade at the Education Department, foreshadowed China's Cultural Revolution and America's religion of political correctness, by insisting that henceforth the entire population of Bavaria could attend the University of Munich without paying fees, and that no history courses would be required of any student there because the Soviet Republic had just banned 'the instruction of history, that enemy of civilisation'.[25]

To outdo this commissar in terms of derangement presupposed exceptional gifts, but these gifts the new Foreign Affairs Commissar Franz Lipp possessed in abundance. Within a week, Lipp – overcoming the difficulties in communication caused by 'a beard so immense that it seemed to cover his whole face'[26] – had declared war on Württemberg and Switzerland; had sought for this declaration the blessing of Pope Benedict XV, 'with whom I am well acquainted'; and had frantically cabled the USSR's leaders, to express his wrath at Hoffmann having taken with him 'the keys to my ministry toilet'.[27]

This approach to geopolitics having convinced the hitherto insouciant Toller that enough was enough, Lipp lost his job. So, within days, did Toller. Now it was the turn of the real, as opposed to the Groucho-type, Marxists: chief among them Max Levien, the confusingly named Eugen Leviné, and Tobias Axelrod, known collectively as 'the Russians.' Even when not born on Russian soil, the three men had lived on it for years. Gone now were the encomia to avant-garde daubs. In their place came decisions that bore immediate results. The new Bavarian Red Army, better paid than any other German military force, now enjoyed a constant supply of food, booze and prostitutes for free. Lest the troops' trigger-happiness be curtailed by insufficient weapons, the word went around: 'Citizens must deliver all firearms to the City Commandant within twelve hours. Anyone failing to do so will be shot.'[28] Membership of the middle classes or of the aristocracy was now punishable by incarceration. The Soviet Republic's currency having lost all value, Finance Commissar Emil Männer simply churned out more of the stuff, 'running the banknote printing presses night and day to pay the army'.[29]

Powerless, Hoffmann and his fellow Social Democrats seethed in Bamberg. Bavarian separatist instincts made them view with alarm the notion of requesting Ebert's cabinet to send the national army in. But someone's army had to be sent in, or else there appeared no prospect of Munich's primal-scream therapy session concluding any time before the Parousia. Reluctantly, Hoffmann and his colleagues went to Weimar in person and asked Defence Minister Gustav Noske for help. Noske, in a manner which he had already made his own, helped them good and hard.

Within three days, the already dreaded Freikorps units were on the march. From the Red Army came a trickle of desertions. The trickle became a river. Sensing that all would soon be lost, the Soviets' prison governor, Fritz Seidel (acting on orders from head office), had twenty of his right-wing inmates – including the monarchist Prince of Thurn und Taxis – killed, two by two, usually by being bludgeoned with rifle-butts until movement ceased. Not till 3 May did the Freikorps overcome the last Red leaders still in Munich. So thankful were most Müncheners for the Freikorps' arrival that 'a Te Deum was sung, and there was an open-air Mass for the troops'.[30]

Levien and Axelrod escaped to Austria; the latter eventually returned to the USSR, where he fell victim to Stalin's purges. Toller was more fortunate in the immediate term: he went to prison for five years, notwithstanding the efforts of Max Weber, a character witness at Toller's trial.[31] Of Leviné and Landauer, the Freikorps made short work. Landauer's captors first beat him over the head and then kicked him to death. Leviné shouted to the firing squad which executed him: 'Long live the world revolution!'[32]

At this stage the very word 'Freikorps' prompted panic in the hearts of left-wingers. The sanguinary Berlin events of January and March 1919 had given this panic every justification. Germany's Communist Party (KPD) had come into being during the last days of December; already two other groups, the Independent Socialists and the Revolutionary Shop Stewards, were among those seeking to force Ebert either to make concessions to them or to leave office. In 1914 Liebknecht and Rosa Luxemburg had formed a Marxist, anti-war subdivision of the Social Democrats, and accordingly were expelled for their refusal to back the German armed services. They and their allies called themselves 'Spartacists'. In January 1919 the Spartacist rank-and-file thought the moment propitious to launch a real proletarian revolution, as opposed to the restrained, legalistic, bourgeois processes by which Ebert had already become Chancellor (and would later become President). Liebknecht thoroughly supported the extremists; Luxemburg, and even KPD official Karol Sobelsohn – the birth-name of Lenin's Lviv-born confidant, who adopted the harsher-sounding alias Karl Radek – entreated the extremists to hold off. 'It would be a criminal error,' Luxemburg maintained, 'to seize power now. The German working class is not ready for such an act.'[33] But then she and Radek reluctantly concluded that they owed it to the activists to join them. Of the Spartacists' defeat later that month at the hands of the Freikorps, Noske, who had authorised the suppression, remarked: 'I was obliged [...] to fall back on the officers. It is quite true that many of them are monarchists, but when you want to reconstruct you must fall back on the men whose profession it is. An undisciplined army is a hollow mockery.'[34]

No officer expressed his fealty to the Hohenzollerns with greater passion than General Ludwig Rudolf Maercker. He told his Freikorps men:

I am an old soldier. I have fought and bled [...] in five wars and on three continents. Sentiments which one has cherished for thirty-four years cannot be thrown away and discarded like an old dirty shirt. One would act like a miserable, despicable scoundrel [*elender, verächtlicher Lump*] doing such a thing. I love and revere Wilhelm II just as much today as I did thirty-four years ago, when I swore my oath of allegiance to him. Noske knew very well that he could not expect us old soldiers to change our sentiments. Later he told me once he had special confidence in me because I had openly declared that I have been, and would always remain, a monarchist, and that I offered myself to the Republic only for the Fatherland's sake.[35]

Crushed in street-by-street fighting, the Spartacist militants could not save their leaders or, often, themselves. Radek escaped Berlin with his life, but Liebknecht and 'Red Rosa' were captured by the Freikorps, physically assaulted, and separately murdered. Though a fellow Spartacist, Leo Jogiches, had been Luxemburg's lover, he allowed no maudlin personal sentiment into the telegram which he sent to Lenin: 'Rosa Luxemburg and Karl Liebknecht have carried out their ultimate revolutionary duty.'[36]

During March, a further attempt by the surviving extremists at renewed violence – in the course of which they briefly captured no fewer than thirty-two police depots as well as the police headquarters in Berlin's Alexanderplatz[37] – moved the KPD to especially fierce invective. The KPD leadership referred to the rebels as 'hyenas of the revolution',[38] and warned (with good reason) that Noske would take ruthless advantage of their folly. This time the Freikorps, again enjoying Noske's full approval, reacted with such aggression as to make the force's behaviour in January look like a nuns' picnic. Under General Walther von Lüttwitz, Freikorps troops eliminated 'between fifteen hundred and two thousand revolutionaries'.[39] By this stage (ominously, in view of subsequent Teutonic events), an ethnic fault-line had emerged. In both Prussia and Bavaria, the revolutionary leaders (Liebknecht excepted) were disproportionately Jewish, the government leaders, overwhelmingly Gentile.

At the beginning of December 1918 German republicanism still had the charms of an untested, effervescent utopia. Six months later, approximately 2,400 German republicans had been killed by other German republicans; of these killings, Bavaria accounted for more than 600.[40] It could hardly escape retrospective notice that the Hohenzollern monarchy had shown far greater tolerance of domestic antagonists, however voluble. Germans could have been forgiven for concluding that there was a Hohenzollern-shaped hole where legitimate authority should have been. At the national election of June 1920, monarchist parties attracted four million more votes than they had obtained the previous year, and won 141 seats in the newly expanded 459–member Reichstag (as opposed to the sixty-five seats in the 423–member Reichstag which they had possessed before).[41] Here is British historian Sir John Wheeler-Bennett on early Weimar republicanism:

> The possibility of a restoration of the monarchy was ever present in the back of the minds of the founding fathers, to some a hope, to some a consolation, to some a source of fear, and this was nowhere more apparent than in the Weimar Constitution itself which was designed to facilitate the transition from republican to monarchical government should this prove feasible.[42]

An incident, trivial in itself, from August 1919 lastingly blackened the reputations of Ebert and Noske. On the 9th of that month, a conservative newspaper, the *Deutsche Tageszeitung*, published a photograph of the President and Defence Minister bathing in the Baltic Sea. The two men, vacationing along with other allies, had attracted the notice of a nearby photographer, Wilhelm Steffen. Steffen asked if he might be permitted to take a picture of the aquatic male-bonding session. By all means he might, but Ebert urged him to refrain from giving the picture any publicity. The utterly predictable outcome to this unenforceable caveat was that Steffen, having cropped his photo so as to omit Ebert's and Noske's fellow swimmers, gave the cropped image every publicity. He made it available (whether through selling it outright or, more probably, leasing it) to the *Deutsche Tageszeitung*, and secured for himself an enduring place in the annals of tabloid iconoclasm – particularly when the *Berliner Illustrirte Zeitung*, another prominent journal, plastered the photo all over its front page later in August. Daylight had blatantly been let in on what passed, Weimar style, for governmental magic. Whatever Kaiser Wilhelm's numerous deficiencies, at least when in the public eye he had always proven capable of staying fully clothed.

Monarchists' initial failure to make the most of Ebert's unpopularity had much to do with the shortcomings of the ex-Kaiser's eldest son, Crown Prince Wilhelm. The loathing and contempt which followed the Crown Prince (Allied propaganda of 1914–18 called him 'Little Willie', condemning him as 'a warmonger and murderer of children')[43] are not immediately explicable. True, he drank far too much, womanised far too much, and during the early 1930s would show undue indulgence towards Nazism; but others, including several of his own closest relatives, shared these faults without engendering comparable revulsion. He had charm, friendliness and courage – moral as well as physical – when he chose to reveal them. As an adolescent, upholding his homeland's glorious musical traditions, he learned to play the violin competently enough to perform in public. When in London in 1911 to watch George V being crowned at Westminster Abbey, he became (an otherwise bitterly hostile witness conceded) 'the most popular of foreign figures in the pageant'.[44] Allowances should therefore be made for him, and for the adverse effects on his temperament of his strict upbringing. (Even the most draconian among present-day parents will rarely sympathise overmuch with the Crown Prince's mother, the Kaiserin Augusta Victoria ['Dona'], who deplored her son's undue enthusiasm towards the female sex when the lothario concerned was only 8 years of age.)[45]

That said, Prince Wilhelm's personality gave the widespread impression of being forever unmoored. Had he been born in 1982 instead of in 1882, he would doubtless have incurred a diagnosis of being 'on the spectrum'. During the Great War, Admiral Tirpitz, having often seen him at close quarters, griped: 'He just doesn't know how to work.'[46] Well before 1914 he had many times infuriated his father and the political elite through the verbal incontinence which made him expound his relentlessly Pan-German political views in public, almost always to the incumbent Chancellor's detriment, often by means of loquacious telegrams despatched *en clair,* and at least once by absenting himself from regimental duties to visit the Reichstag, where from the gallery he greeted with enthusiastic clapping an attack on the government. (George V, having learnt of this behaviour, marvelled to a German consul: 'If I had acted thus as Prince of Wales they would have had me out of the House of Commons in less than two minutes.')[47] During a pre-war Hohenzollern hunting expedition, Alfred von Kiderlen-Wächter, long-time under-secretary of the German Foreign Office, told participants: 'Now pay close attention and don't shoot and kill the Kaiser, for the young one is much, much worse!'[48] When 34 years old 'the young one' inspired in Britain an anonymous, book-length, denunciation which mixed *ad hominem* abuse – 'The Crown Prince's face is almost that of a moral degenerate'[49] – with the occasional palpable hit: 'We see in fact a progressive worsening of the Crown Prince's character, reflecting as in a mirror the corresponding deterioration in the character of his fellow-countrymen. The end is not yet, but who would be so bold now as to call them his future subjects?'[50]

Max von Baden, once he had concluded that the Kaiser's rule had become unsalvageable but before he had reconciled himself to republicanism, hoped that the empire could skip a generation and that the Crown Prince's own eldest son (another Wilhelm) could reign, with Max as regent. 'If the dynasty had made the right decision,' reflected historian Friedrich Meinecke, 'the monarchy could have been saved. Kaiser and Crown Prince would have had to resign, but a regency would have found the recognition of the whole nation.'[51] Exacerbating the Crown Prince's reputational problems was his impetuous decision to move to the Netherlands independently of, and two days after, his father's journey there. General Friedrich von der Schulenberg, who in wartime had been military governor of Liège, passed after the war this grim verdict: 'The Crown Prince is finished in Germany, by his own fault [...] Today the Crown Prince is out of the running for the throne. Even the parties of the right discard him as unsuitable.'[52]

Clearly, 'Little Willie' had become lead in the monarchists' saddle-bags. The question arose as to whether he would remain so.

Even without the Freikorps, early Weimar governments had at their disposal the official peacetime army, the Reichswehr. By the pact made between Ebert and Groener shortly before Armistice Day, the Reichswehr would stay loyal to the Republic, while in return the Republic's politicians would hold the line against leftist rebellion. The politicians carried out their side of the deal. Would the Reichswehr commanding officers, and in particular the Reichswehr Chief of Staff Hans von Seeckt, carry out theirs? The coup attempt of March 1920 provided the first test in the matter. This time, the insurgency came not from left-wingers, but from right-wingers.

With the extreme Left temporarily in abeyance after mid-1919, the argument increasingly emerged that the Freikorps' *raison d'être* had ceased and that – however much resentment endured among Germans at the Treaty of Versailles's ban on their country's rearmament – the force should be scrapped. Even Noske, who owed more than any other German alive to Freikorps strength, had concluded that jettisoning the Freikorps would be desirable. But two big problems hampered him.

The first big problem was that mere governmental defunding of the Freikorps did not necessarily mean the same as doing away with it. Individual Freikorps divisions had an ingenious habit of renaming themselves as civilian operations, designed to engage in planting trees or building levees or plugging dams or some other such impeccably pacific, community-minded pursuit. Second of the big problems was that abolishing the Freikorps made the assumption that the Freikorps was willing to be abolished; this assumption carried inherent perils. While theoretically the Freikorps and the Reichswehr were separate entities, in practice cooperation between the two frequently prevailed, with elements of what later ages would call 'plausible deniability' if the cooperation got either group into trouble.

Noske's demand that one particular brigade dissolve itself, and that loyal Reichswehr soldiers enforce this dissolution if need be, generated indignant protests from brigade commander Hermann Ehrhardt and from the aforementioned General von Lüttwitz. Refusing to disband, the brigade (now augmented by survivors of Germany's ill-fated effort at preserving its hegemony in Latvia) declared war, negotiations between Lüttwitz and the cabinet having broken down. Noske appealed to Seeckt for help. Not for nothing had Seeckt acquired the nickname 'The Sphinx'. He expressed shock that Noske would recommend calling in patriotic German troops to attack other patriotic German troops, as opposed to calling them in to attack Bolsheviks. Whether or not Seeckt explicitly told Noske that 'Reichswehr does not fire on Reichswehr'[53] – and experts in German political history continue to debate the precise words used by Seeckt – he left Noske in no doubt as to his reluctance to quash Ehrhardt's brigade. By this time the insurgents had acquired a civilian figurehead in Wolfgang Kapp, a New-York-born but recently elected Reichstag member, belonging to the monarchist DNVP (*Deutschnationale Volkspartei*), of which political party much more anon. Him they declared Chancellor, while Lüttwitz continued as the military brains of the operation.

The putsch attempt nearly worked. Unfortunately for the putschists, they mistook Seeckt's fine words for active endorsement. Seeckt, cleverly described by one recent chronicler as 'a man who would advance to the Rubicon to fish in rather than cross,'[54] hedged his bets. That he retained his fundamental monarchist sympathies meant little to the outcome: almost every Reichswehr general in 1920 retained monarchist sympathies at the very least. More significant in his eyes was the widespread bureaucratic determination not to acknowledge Ehrhardt, Kapp and Lüttwitz as the legitimate new rulers. Of still greater importance was Ebert's desperate resort to a weapon which had actually been used against him by the revolutionaries of 1919: the general strike. Concerning the result of Ebert's demand for strike action, a historian of the Krupp firm commented: 'When Germans obey, they really obey; next day not a single water tap, gas range, electric light, train or streetcar would function. Within a week the putsch collapsed and Kapp fled to Sweden.'[55]

While some monarchists sided with Kapp (who two years later re-entered Germany of his own free will, dying a prisoner in Leipzig soon afterwards) and with Lüttwitz (who betook himself to Hungary after the putsch's failure), the Crown Prince in his Dutch exile held conspicuously aloof from the entire affair. Often overlooked amid the hurly-burly of those days was a distinctive feature of the Ehrhardt Brigade's uniform. Premonitorily the brigadiers wore, on their helmets, swastikas.

The government's two most conspicuous casualties were Chancellor Gustav Bauer – forced to resign for having failed to forestall the conspirators – and none other than Noske. Those union leaders who rescued Ebert by directing the industrial action to starve the putschists out of Berlin did so for a price: they wanted Noske gone from the Defence Ministry, and believed that he had been far too lenient towards Lüttwitz and the others. Had the putschists belonged to the political Left, as the unionists complained, Noske would never have let them come so close to triumph. Once Kapp had quit Germany, Noske lost his place in the cabinet. He lived another twenty-six years, and continued to be politically active in Hannover, but he never again played a major role at the national level.

Kapp's defeat had made German monarchists lose face; it had not made German republicanism any better loved. The very servants of Weimar's republican administration frequently despaired of it. In a wistful moment, industrialist turned Foreign Minister Walther Rathenau – who during the Great War had practically run the entire German home front, mitigating the severest impacts of the British blockade upon the citizenry – soliloquised:

> If I went down to the middle avenue of the Linden and shouted – 'Cheers for the good old days! Cheers for Bismarck! Cheers for Kaiser and Fatherland! Cheers for our old and glorious Prussian army!' – I should probably be arrested at once. But the men, apart from a few down-and-outs, would be deeply moved … and the women would all blow me kisses. Suppose I were to shout: 'Long live the Republic!' Everyone would begin to laugh.[56]

Bavaria's monarchist activism after 1918 took markedly, and necessarily, different forms from Prussia's. It had two advantages which Hohenzollern revivalism lacked. For one thing, Bavaria's Wittelsbach clan had enjoyed power in Continental Europe ever since the late twelfth century – even longer than the 'seven hundred years' to which Eisner's brag referred – and had produced two Holy Roman Emperors, as well as a king of Greece, a king of Hungary, and a king of (then-united) Norway and Denmark. By contrast, the Hohenzollerns were little more than parvenus, the German empire having been formally established only in 1871 (in the very Hall of Mirrors at Versailles where, on 7 May 1919, the famous Treaty was signed). For another thing, Ludwig III's son, Crown Prince Rupprecht of Bavaria (49 years of age when the war ended), suffered from none of Crown Prince Wilhelm's – to say nothing of the ex-Kaiser's – character flaws. During the Great War he had criticised much of the German High Command's policy, complaining: 'It seems to me as if I were in a rudderless boat which a raging storm is driving through the rocks.'[57] He also had the benefit, as the Hohenzollern father and son had not, of being permitted to remain on his native soil. The 1919 Soviets had confiscated Wittelsbach property, yet once the state's Supreme Court ruled in 1921 that the confiscation had no legal basis, the family reacquired its palaces and lived in them.

(As a matter of little-known but notable fact, according to the Jacobite line of succession, Rupprecht – being the eldest direct descendant of King Charles I – was from 1921 the rightful *British* sovereign. This claim, though, he never pressed: partly through fear that it would inspire further Teutonophobic feeling in Britain, and partly through all the other demands on his time, there being only twenty-four hours in each day.)

Along with possessing these strengths, Rupprecht faced difficulties similar to those which confronted the Hohenzollerns. Bavaria's so-called 'Bamberg Constitution' mandated, no less than did Article 17 of the Weimar Constitution, republican government.[58] Monarchist politicians themselves, several of them powerful – none more powerful than Gustav von Kahr, who from 1920 to 1924 dominated the state's administration even when not holding the premiership – quite often regarded bringing back the royals as something which, though innately desirable, needed to wait till more propitious times. In January 1922 Count Kuno von Westarp – among the most prominent of DNVP members in the Reichstag – specifically, if somewhat cryptically, informed Rupprecht (who claimed the title of king upon his father's death the preceding October) that 'at that time an attempt at restoration had to fail, due to the position of the working class in the industrial centres'.[59] Sometimes monarchists deplored in print the procrastination dominant in the DNVP and Kahr's own BVP (short for *Bayerische Volkspartei*):

> There was some truth to the common charge [...] that the BVP leaders trotted out royalist clichés only at election time to win more votes: 'For them there will always be "if" and "but" ... These people have no interest at all in Bavaria and the royal question, for they have long since inwardly reconciled themselves with the republic in which things go so well for them.'[60]

Westarp, Kahr and their fellow monarchists had, of course, an impeccable patristic precedent for their delaying tactics. Saint Augustine, after all, pleaded for the acquisition of chastity: but not yet.

One factor worked in Rupprecht's favour and, by definition, could not work in Crown Prince Wilhelm's favour: Bavarian particularist feeling. Only with reluctance had Bavaria agreed to incorporation in the German empire during 1871; and Bavarian resentment at Prussian overlordship continued after that date, save when wider national dangers in 1914–18 temporarily surmounted it. As has been wisely said, the average

Bavarian's attitude towards the rest of Germany resembled the average American Southerner's attitude – abiding for generations after Appomattox – towards states north of the Mason-Dixon Line.[61] Furthermore, Bavarians who sought either extensive autonomy or absolute independence from Berlin could play the Catholic card against Prussia's Lutheran ruling caste. (This final tendency endured despite Kahr himself, unusually among Bavarian right-wingers, being a Protestant.)

Causes for Bavarian monarchist optimism persisted. Newspaper editor Erwein von Aretin, an especially ebullient champion of the Wittelsbachs, condemned Prussianism as being 'to the core dishonest and untruthful'.[62] Constitutional minutiae about the juridical status of reborn Bavarian kingship within a republic run on federalist lines failed to dishearten him, or even to contain him. 'Fourteen days after the establishment of this kingdom,' he insisted, legalistic worries 'will seem just as odd as the former doubt of medical scholars about the speed of the railroads.'[63]

In the meantime, and for all Erwein von Aretin's euphoria, a circuit-breaker was needed. With the Teutonic traumas of 1923, a circuit-breaker came.

Continental strife, civil strife, hyperinflation; for Germans, 1923 had never a dull moment. In January, the official German decision to delay reparations payments moved France (and – with far less public coverage – Belgium) to send troops to occupy the Ruhr. Prime Minister Poincaré, initially inclined to restraint, changed his mind when he realised how much French steel production depended upon German coal supplies. The Germans responded to French occupancy as they had responded to Kapp's and Lüttwitz's takeover attempt: with comprehensive strike action.

Somehow the strikers needed to be fed. If the causal relationship between subsidising passive resistance (not least via depleting gold reserves) and wrecking the economy is less clear than commentators once assumed, the passive resistance was undoubtedly followed by outrageous increases in the cost of living. Hungary and Austria, at a slightly earlier date, had suffered from spectacular price rises. But nothing in those lands' experience prepared the world for Germany's fiscal debauch. Inflation had already been a severe problem for German administrations in 1921 and 1922. From 1923 it became a national nightmare and an international joke. For a kilogram's worth of rye bread in January of that year, a German *Hausfrau* muttered in annoyance at being compelled to spend 163 Marks. That same amount of rye bread the following October cost her 1,389,000,000 Marks.[64] Human brains were not geared for processing the resultant denominations of paper currency: five million Marks, five billion Marks, five trillion Marks. Carrying banknotes around in a suitcase made it hard to keep the suitcase safe; keeping the worthless currency safe was far less problematic. Any city-dweller who ordered coffee in a coffee-house needed to eschew lingering over the drink, because its price would go up from five thousand Marks at the time of the order to eight thousand Marks once an hour had elapsed.[65] At least the banknotes, as numerous German home-owners discovered, made for inexpensive and very colourful wallpaper.

Not before time, the worst of the madness concluded. Chancellor Gustav Stresemann, as well as calling off the passive-resistance campaign, put former Dresdner Bank official Hjalmar Schacht in charge of the national currency. In November, on Schacht's orders, a new Rentenmark appeared which superseded the existing Mark. By the year's end, prices for goods and services had returned to something like normal. The German middle classes took to purchasing proper wallpaper again. But in November, Bavarians had few reasons to smile.

On the whole, Gustav von Kahr continues to be mysterious. As recently as 2015, Nebraska historian Roy G. Koepp noted: 'There exists no scholarly biography of him in either German or English.'[66] A strange lacuna, considering how many other aspects of Hitler's rise to absolute power have been studied almost to death. The lacuna can be partially explained by the initial shortage of features distinguishing Hitler's band from other groups of local toughs. Kahr, as Premier, never predicted that the Austrian corporal would leave 'a name at which the world grew pale'. Nor, had he predicted it, would he have been rendered squeamish by it. He had no love for Jews, although unlike Hitler he avoided punitive action against Judaism per se, preferring to threaten individual left-wing Jews with increased civil disabilities and possible expulsion.

Kahr's experience as a civil servant, of fleeing to Bamberg in 1919 along with the Hoffmann cabinet, made him determined to obtain and preserve access to paramilitary personnel. From this determination sprang the Bavarian Civil Guards, whom Kahr wanted to keep loyal to the state government, without the default mode of freebooting independence that the Freikorps had exhibited. There were 288,000 Civil Guards by early 1920.[67] Wishing to stake his entire career on maintaining law and order in Bavaria more efficiently and more economically than Ebert could, Kahr furiously denounced the disbanding (at the national government's insistence) of the Civil Guards in May 1921; and the following September, having failed to obstruct the disbanding, he resigned from the premiership. His successor as Premier – the gloriously named Count Hugo Maximilian Philippus Ludwig Franziskus von und zu Lerchenfeld auf Köfering und Schönberg – considerately arranged that Kahr be given the ill-defined post of *Generalstaatskommissar*, with the right to rule by decree if such rule became needful. In the very month that the Civil Guards were abolished, Kahr invited Hitler and some of the latter's followers to meet him, although he 'thought Hitler was a propagandist and nothing more'.[68]

Thus, in essentials, the situation remained in September 1923, when Ebert and Seeckt wanted a ban placed on the Hitlerite newspaper *Völkischer Beobachter* (by this stage already three years old), while Kahr – along with the Reichswehr's Bavarian commander-in-chief, General Otto von Lossow – desired no such prohibition. Seeckt informed Kahr, in language of almost Delphic impartiality:

> The Reichswehr must not be brought into a position in which it has to fight, for a government which is alien to it, against people who have the same convictions as the army. On the other hand it cannot permit irresponsible and unauthorised circles to try and bring about a change by force.[69]

Rumours abounded (and a speech given by Kahr on 6 November, though cautiously worded, did nothing to dispel them)[70] that Kahr planned to move on Berlin and do what

Kapp and Lüttwitz had done in 1920, but with more skill. Were this move to succeed, there would be nothing to stop him from making Rupprecht the sovereign, not solely of Bavaria, but of Germany as a whole. For Berlin's sway had grown considerably weaker *vis-à-vis* Munich's in 1923 than it had been in 1921. Hyperinflation, foreign troops overseeing the Ruhr, and October's KPD-directed uprisings in Saxony and Thuringia had all seen to that. (Amid these uprisings, 'Vicious mobs extracted food from recalcitrant farmers, or assaulted employers and draped red flags and placards around their necks in public degradation sessions reminiscent of what Nazis would later do to Jewish people, although this similarity is seldom remarked on.')[71] One non-Communist obstacle remained to any national ambitions on Kahr's part: the *Nationalsozialistische Deutsche Arbeiterpartei*, or NSDAP.

Innumerable volumes and television documentaries on the Third Reich's origins have made widely familiar the basics of the November 1923 Beer Hall Putsch and of its repercussions. The way in which Hitler burst, with his followers, into Munich's *Bürgerbräukeller*, interrupting a speech by Kahr, ordering a shot fired to frighten the 3,000 assembled auditors, and announcing that he and Ludendorff now ruled Bavaria; the deaths in the subsequent confrontation of four Bavarian state policemen and sixteen NSDAP followers, these latter constituting 'the Party's earliest, and hence most holy, martyrs';[72] the presence in Hitler's entourage of stalwarts – notably Hermann Goering, Rudolf Hess, Heinrich Himmler, Alfred Rosenberg and Julius Streicher – who subsequently held several of the most influential NSDAP positions; the pretext that the 1924 court case gave for Hitler to explain his credo to the world; the eventual imprisonment of Hitler, along with the acquittal of Ludendorff; the authorship of *Mein Kampf* during Hitler's captivity. All this is famous. Much less famous is why the putsch happened when it happened. Hitler demanded that the date be brought forward by two days from the original timetable, according to which the putsch would not be launched until the night of 10-11 November.[73]

In part, the answer lies with Hitler's inability to trust Kahr as far as he could throw him. Kahr had become more outspokenly pro-Wittelsbach since ceasing to be premier. Addressing the BVP's student subdivision in May 1922, he had recommended for his hearers the motto '*Vivat Ruppertus Rex!*'[74] In his *Bürgerbräukeller* speech which Hitler disrupted, Kahr described himself and his hearers as 'loyal monarchists', interpreting his own political function as 'lieutenant of the kingdom [*als Statthalter der Monarchie*]'.[75] Two months before, Kahr had refused to grant permission for the NSDAP to hold public rallies in Bavaria. Contributors to the *Völkischer Beobachter*'s pages snickered at Kahr's monarchism and advocated armed struggle against the state government; Kahr retaliated by forbidding the newspaper's publication for two weeks.[76] At no point had Kahr's distaste for Jews been sufficiently vindictive, obsessive, or biologically-based to meet NSDAP standards (he employed a Jewish press secretary, Adolf Schiedt).[77] Already putschists had arrested the Premier, who by this time was no longer Lerchenfeld but Eugen von Knilling.[78] Kahr, Lossow and Bavarian police commissioner Hans von Seisser were ushered into a nearby room and ordered to support the coup if they cared for their own lives.

Late that same night, almost unbelievably, Ludendorff decided on his own initiative to let all three men go. He had accepted their mere spoken assurances of willingness to back Hitler. Among the first things which Kahr did on gaining his freedom was meet Cardinal Michael von Faulhaber, Munich's archbishop; Rupprecht; and Franz Matt, Bavaria's Deputy Premier, who had spent the evening dining with Faulhaber and with nuncio Eugenio Pacelli (the future Pius XII). Rupprecht had, from the start, opposed the insurgency, though when Hitler first discerned that the putsch looked like failing, he frantically considered trying to recruit Rupprecht to the putschists' ranks.[79] At the meeting with Kahr, prelate, prince and politician all urged him to stand firm against the Nazis. Kahr did so, and thereby earned their undying detestation, which ensured payback during the June 1934 Night of the Long Knives. On that occasion, SS guards kidnapped Kahr, took him to Dachau, tortured him, killed him, and mutilated his corpse.[80]

In 1923 Kahr had turned 61. For Hitler and his clique, Kahr's chief sin – worse than his loyalty to the Wittelsbachs and his Bavarian separatism, worse even than his volte-face during the putsch itself – was probably his year of birth. It needs to be stressed how much National Socialism, above all in its formative years, stipulated not mere revolution but consciously demographic revolution: the young and virile versus the old and hidebound. Various salient statistics: 'In 1931 in Berlin seventy per cent of the SA [*Sturmabteilung*, storm-troopers, literally 'Storm Detachment'] were men under thirty, and in the Reichstag in 1930, sixty per cent of the National Socialist deputies were under forty, while only ten per cent of the Social Democrats were.'[81]

For the leading NSDAP figures, Kahr (to cite Koepp's words afresh) 'was not the man of the moment, he was the man of the past'.[82] They consigned Kahr to the same fusty, irrelevant museum inhabited by Wilhelm II: the museum of former Teutonic leaders who had outlived their usefulness. Hitler could well have sincerely believed that he needed to act on 8 November specifically to stop Kahr from enthroning Rupprecht.[83] If he did sincerely believe this, then the extent to which aversion to monarchism actuated him in 1923 – *Mein Kampf* bristles with censure of the Habsburgs – throws a new light on his policies a decade later.

As if 1923 had not been dramatic enough for Germany in other respects, it also witnessed the Crown Prince's reappearance. He returned during November with not merely the permission, but the full approval, of Stresemann. Like many others in the governing class at the time, Stresemann acquired the appellation *Vernunftrepublikaner*. This almost untranslatable noun (literally meaning 'sanity republicans') described those German politicians who, in their heads, had accepted republicanism for the time being, yet who in their hearts remained monarchist. To mark the ex-Kaiser's sixtieth birthday in January 1919, Stresemann had sent his former sovereign a congratulatory telegram.[84]

Within days of becoming Chancellor, Stresemann had initiated the process by which the Crown Prince could come back; an intermediary had personally given Stresemann Prince Wilhelm's application for a passport.[85] The heir had long chafed over his enforced political inactivity on the island of Wieringen, in the Netherlands' north. H.L. Mencken, an intense admirer of the Hohenzollerns, visited the Crown Prince and, in October 1922, recounted the meeting in a report which the *Baltimore Sun* assigned to its front page:

> [...] this deadly isolation has failed to make any noticeable impression on the spirit or frame of the Prince. There are touches of grey in his sandy hair, but he still is as erect as a drill sergeant, and as quick in speech and movement. Very tall, slim and lithe, and now smooth-shaven, he looks much like a big boy.

But certainly there is nothing immature about his ideas. Among all the Germans I have talked to during the past six weeks, ranging from high officials to newspaper editors and from university professors to businessmen, I can recall none whose views of past and present contain less of illusion. [...] 'I sincerely wish I could be more actively employed, but certainly have no desire to complicate the present situation by raising factional questions. It would be absurd, of course, to say dynastic questions do not interest me, but they assuredly take second place in my thoughts. In such days as these I am, first of all, a German citizen and soldier.'[86]

Stresemann, a year later (24 October 1923), wrote to the Crown Prince, alluding to the latter's Great War service, and warning him not to expect too much:

I should like to express my personal pleasure that this decision by the cabinet was made on my recommendation, and as I may add, unanimously without objection of criticism. At an earlier time, when I myself was not a member of a German Reich's cabinet, I repeatedly tried to work towards this end. Again and again political events opposed your wish. And even now, when your return is near at hand, the conditions in Germany are unfortunately just as gloomy as ever. [...]

Your Imperial Highness will find the German homeland, that you knew in splendour and greatness as a member of the German ruling house, in a state of great confusion, in poverty, and in misery. But it remains nevertheless the German land and the home of the Germans, and millions of Germans will rejoice with you at the thought that after nine years' absence from this German soil you can celebrate this most German holiday [Christmas] in the circle of your family. I have had the opportunity to exchange thoughts with you many times in the years since the war, and the days which I spent with you in Wieringen have remained in my memory.[87]

The severity of Poincaré's demands concerning German reparations' payments had the useful and unintended effect (from Germany's standpoint) of setting the Entente Powers against one another. Lord Curzon, then British Foreign Secretary, boasted to his wife in November 1923: 'I have just gained a considerable diplomatic victory over Poincaré, who wanted to play the fool and seize more German territory.'[88] The French leader could no longer prevent the Crown Prince's return, however much he wanted to. He might not even have wanted to: anything liable to cause civil unrest among Germans had, by definition, the virtue of making Germany less capable of threatening France. (Already the French army had backed the establishment of a separatist 'Rhenish Republic.')

Once returned to the Fatherland, the Crown Prince kept usually and uncharacteristically quiet. In general, a comparative tranquillity marked German politics between 1924 and 1929. Quite apart from the explosions of *furor teutonicus* in 1919 and 1923, the years 1921–22 had been disfigured by numerous politically motivated murders and attempted murders. To name only the most publicised instances: Catholic Centre Party cabinet minister Matthias Erzberger had been shot dead in August 1921, Rathenau in June 1922; in each case the ex-Freikorps gunmen imagined that they were ridding the country of subversives, as did those who, in the very month of Rathenau's assassination, sprayed ex-Chancellor Philipp Scheidemann's face with prussic acid. In response to Rathenau's killing, the suitably alarmed government led by Joseph Wirth passed a Law for the Protection of the Republic. This statute criminalised groups which openly demanded violence against their antagonists. While the law did not prevent the NSDAP and KPD outrages of the following year, it had its effect afterwards. From 1924 a certain sanity broke in. Paradoxically, monarchists' hopes for restoration were impeded by the acts of a man who himself permanently regretted the Hohenzollerns' fall.

After prolonged ill health President Ebert succumbed to peritonitis and septic shock on 28 February 1925. He had found his office to be less a badge of honour than a crown of thorns, so spiteful and so persistent had been the execration against him by newspaper proprietors, Reichstag members and other foes. At one point near the end of his life, he had concurrent defamation proceedings against almost 150 persons.[89]

From the day of Ebert's death until the day of his successor's swearing-in (12 May), Germany remained without an official head of state, though the Chancellor at the time (Hans Luther) carried out several of the presidency's functions on a caretaker basis. Unlike almost all other twentieth-century republican constitutions, Weimar's provided for no vice-president. In fact, the constitution is retrospectively distinguished by its failure to anticipate much of what actually occurred after 1919. Those who drafted the document, for all their pious intentions ('the power of the State,' Article 1 soothingly proclaimed, 'emanates from the people'), never supposed that the Constitution's famous and controversial Article 48 – permitting the president to rule by decree – would be invoked more than 250 times.[90]

Surely the vacuum of a presidential interregnum furnished the ideal opening for the Crown Prince and his supporters to act on their own behalf. An explicit imperial restoration need not, at first, have been involved. Napoleon I and Napoleon III supplied precedents for a candidate acquiring a republic's leadership prior to revealing his true monarchical colours; later in the 1920s Albania's Ahmed Zogu would make himself king after a three-year presidency. But in early 1925 the Weimar Republic stayed intact, and the best possible opportunity for the Crown Prince to show his mettle went begging.

Part of the difficulty for monarchists concerned what to do with the ex-Kaiser, by this stage ensconced comfortably in the eighteenth-century, fifteen-room villa which he had bought near the Dutch village of Doorn.[91] Many monarchists willing to champion Wilhelm Senior wanted no truck with championing Wilhelm Junior; among other monarchists the contrary was the case. Two singularly tasteless stanzas of a marching song from the early 1920s – vowing to dispose of Chancellor Wirth, and popular with certain of the father's more thuggish adherents – indicate the passions aroused:

Lasst uns froh und munter sein
Schlagt dem Wirth dem Schandel ein,
Lustig, lustig, trallalla
Bald ist Wilhelm wieder da.

Wenn einst der Kaiser kommen wird
Schlagen wir zum Krueppel den Wirth
Knallen die Gewehre, tack tack tack,
Aufs schwarze und das rote Pack.

('Let us be cheerful and lively / Crack the skull of Wirth / Gaily, gaily, trallalla / Soon Wilhelm will be here again. / When the Emperor returns, / We shall mutilate Wirth, / Sound the rifles, tack, tack, tack, / Against the black and red mob.')[92]

Yet on the surviving evidence it is legitimate to hypothesise that with the Crown Prince himself, a personal tragedy from almost five years beforehand, seldom made much of – and quite often going altogether unmentioned – by historians, demoralised him for good. The tragedy involved Prince Joachim, his youngest brother.

Joachim's eventful life included being seriously considered, when 26 years old, as a possible Irish king by Padraic Pearse and other Easter Rising leaders of 1916. (That Prince Joachim spoke no English redounded, in the Irish insurrectionists' eyes, to his credit. It would make all the easier the establishing of Gaelic as the official language of independent Ireland.)[93] The young man exercised little or no restraint concerning alcohol and skirt-chasing. 'In all his behaviour and mannerisms,' the older sibling's biographer records, 'especially in his amorous adventures, he copied his model and his ideal, the Crown Prince.'[94] Unlike his brother, Joachim had enthusiastically backed the Kapp-Lüttwitz uprising. When that failed, 'he was disappointed in his last hope'.[95] Gambling had impoverished him, and his marriage to the Duke of Anhalt's daughter, Marie-Auguste, had already ended in particularly humiliating circumstances. Gossip spoke of Marie-Auguste cuckolding and deserting her husband. On 18 July 1920, mere weeks after the decree *nisi* – while in a hunting lodge owned by his cousin – Joachim shot himself.[96] From this loss, his mother never recovered. The Kaiserin (who in any event suffered from cardiac trouble and had adapted to enforced residence in the Netherlands much less well than her husband) died nine months after Joachim's suicide.

During the Great War the German government had sought to raise public morale with a gigantic statue of Hindenburg. The statue was scarcely more impassive and awe-inspiring than Hindenburg himself. Yet beneath the gruff, stoic exterior of that 'wooden titan' – Sir John Wheeler-Bennett's unforgettable epithet – writhed a guilty conscience. He remained:

> stunned by the role he had played in the flight and the subsequent abdication of the Kaiser, whom he persisted in referring to as 'His Majesty, the King and my master.' The event had been, as Hindenburg conceived it, an indelible stain on his honour, even though the actual advice to the Kaiser had been left for Groener to give. The Field-Marshal ruminated constantly about his 'faithlessness' to his monarch.[97]

Ponderous and incorruptible, he had no desire to enter civilian politics. When people urged him to run for office, he always declined. He produced his autobiography (which became a best-seller) while, as far as possible, ignoring the post-war world. But his devotees would not leave him in peace. He had only to give a humdrum lecture to a veterans' club, and ecstatic crowds would form. Then Ebert died. The next presidential election would be via direct popular vote (unlike the majority-Reichstag vote which had given Ebert the presidency). No one could accuse Hindenburg of being unpopular. Suddenly, at 77 years of age, he looked electable.

Hindenburg held out against his devotees' supplications for as long as he could. Former Interior Minister Karl Jarres, a Stresemann ally, offered himself as a presidential candidate. The Social Democrats had their own nominee: Otto Braun, a tactful, coalition-building Premier of Prussia. Yet neither Jarres nor Braun made it past the first round. (Nor did the irrepressible Ludendorff, who won less than 2 per cent of the vote.) For the second round, the non-Hindenburg candidate with the best chances was Wilhelm Marx, who had been Chancellor once before and would hold the office again. Generally regarded 'as an umpire rather than as a dynamic and resourceful leader', Marx belonged to the Catholic Centre Party and therefore, unlike Hindenburg the Lutheran, 'was bound to alienate some of the Protestant voters'.[98] The KPD's Ernst Thälmann, having temporarily decided that armed proletarian struggle should be deferred in favour of the ballot-box, also survived to the second round.

Typically, Hindenburg had refused even to contest the election without requesting, and obtaining, permission from the ex-Kaiser to do so. The result scarcely amounted to a ringing endorsement either of Hindenburg himself or of the Weimar polity as a whole. Turnout was less than 69 per cent; Hindenburg won a little over 48 per cent of the popular vote, Marx a little over 45 per cent; Thälmann's spoiler campaign had cut into Marx's vote much more than into Hindenburg's. But at least the streets' gutters were not actually running with blood.

Monarchists gave the victor their full support. (In Berlin itself, and despite the red-black-gold republican flags being flown from government buildings, 'crowds welcoming Hindenburg from the sidewalks also waved little flags with the old Imperial colours' of white, black and red.)[99] Now that the Field-Marshal had become president, monarchists – so they reckoned – could not lose. Either he would pave the way for the returning Hohenzollerns, in which case monarchism's victory would be unassailable. Or else, were he to fail in effecting this restoration, he would still frustrate left-wingers and rule by decree when the circumstances required it. Since he had all the advantages of Hohenzollern governance with none of its handicaps, the actual Hohenzollerns looked like back-numbers. Two incidents over the coming years would impair their cause further.

In 1926 Seeckt received a request from an army captain representing the Crown Prince. The latter hoped that his eldest son, Prince Wilhelm, now 20 years old, could be given some military experience befitting his age and position. 'I gladly granted this wish,' Seeckt wrote, 'and decided that the prince could take part in the exercises of the Ninth Infantry Regiment in Münsingen.'[100] Whether Prince Wilhelm was allowed to be present in the regiment's training area as an active participant, or as a mere observer, became the subject of dispute. The whole business soon grew muddled. It suggested that Seeckt, the exemplary political survivor, had lost his touch. A left-wing provincial newspaper learned of Prince Wilhelm's army doings and reported on them during early October. More significantly, Berlin's *Montagmorgen* reprinted the report on the 4th of that month, thereby forcing it upon the unwilling attention of Otto Gessler, Noske's successor at the Defence Ministry. Gessler gave Seeckt twenty-four hours to prepare his resignation, and upbraided him:

> The parliamentary inquiry will create a situation which is impossible for you as for the government, not to mention the heavy attacks against the Crown Prince, who with his wish disturbs the peace of the German people and violates his solemnly made promises. In passing I should only like to mention that I myself have been made a laughing stock.[101]

Seeckt, by his preparedness to take full responsibility for what had happened and to step down, emerged from the contretemps reasonably well. Nobody else did. The Crown Prince was widely blamed by his own supporters for not coming to Seeckt's aid. He looked shifty and unreliable. His private life remained conspicuously public. A document from early 1929 in the files of Kurt von Schleicher, the future Chancellor who counted himself as a friend of the Crown Prince, includes the following account of monarchist meetings in Berlin and Munich:

> People complained about the conduct of the former Imperial Prince ['Probably the Crown Prince,' reads Schleicher's handwritten note at this point] whose relations with the artiste Ossi Oswalda are making his already damaged reputation completely ridiculous. One of the participants in the conference emphasised this point vigorously and recalled the example of King George V of England, who constitutes one of the strongest supports of the monarchy in England. One pointed out the necessity of advising His Highness to be cautious. Since the prince is in an unpleasant mood whenever he is supposed to get good advice, it will probably be difficult to find a go-between who can be trusted with this delicate task. [...][102]

Other monarchists increasingly despaired of the Crown Prince's prospects. An essay by Prussian DNVP official Walther Lambach, entitled 'Monarchismus', appeared in the 14 June 1928 issue of the magazine *Politische Wochenschrift*. The essay insisted that Lambach's party, which had lately seen its Reichstag representation fall markedly at the national election (from 103 seats to 73), had done itself great harm by clinging to monarchism at all costs. Lambach viewed that attitude as disastrously obsolete. Had not Germany's president won since 1925 the national affection hitherto lavished on Kaiser Wilhelm? Indubitably Lambach thought so and said so:

> The shadow of the king and emperor, which would have over-towered [*überragt*] anyone else, could not over-tower Hindenburg. On the contrary, Wilhelm II disappeared behind the great and pious old gentleman who now represents the Reich. [...] In the light of his greatness, the nimbus of the living Hohenzollerns collapsed.[103]

Lambach 'called for a full transformation of the DNVP; he rejected the idea of a party geared toward the restoration of the monarchy, and championed instead a kind of conservative people's party with a new program and leadership'.[104] He urged the party to stop assuring voters that any day now the Hohenzollerns would be in charge afresh, and to start attracting constituencies indifferent or hostile to the monarchist cause.

(Indifference already prevailed with much of the big public. A 1926 Reichstag campaign led by the KPD, and supported by the Social Democrats, to ensure the expropriation of monarchical properties had failed at a referendum. In 1926 approximately 39.5 per cent of Germans had the right to vote, women having gained this right seven years earlier, via the Weimar Constitution's Article 109. But only if at least 50 per cent of the electorate took part in the referendum would its outcome be legally binding. While those who cared enough about the matter to cast their ballots approved expropriation by a vast majority – the 'yes' vote was 96.1 per cent – this result had no statutory weight, because a mere 15,551,218 voters had bothered to visit the polling booths in the first place.[105] Hindenburg told a friend and fellow monarchist how much he resented the referendum having been conceived: 'That I, who have spent my life in the service of the Prussian kings and the German emperors, feel this referendum to be primarily a great injustice, and also as an exhibition of a regrettable lack of traditional sentiment and of great ingratitude, I need not explain to you.')[106]

No hint of apathy on monarchist questions characterised the DNVP, though. If Lambach had become a rabbi, he could hardly have caused greater scandal within the DNVP membership than he did with his article (which earned him expulsion from the party during July).[107] In particular, Lambach scandalised the baleful billionaire Alfred Hugenberg, the DNVP's most aggressive figure even when not running the party *de jure* (Westarp continued to lead its Reichstag contingent). Hugenberg enjoyed in his sixties 'a power greater than Rothermere's or Beaverbrook's in England, greater than Scripps-Howard's or Hearst's in the United States'.[108] No earlier German news publishers attained, and few approached, Hugenberg's level of influence, not only over the press but over film production. While in the 1920s his stable of newspapers was not large, he had already perceived the fact that if you owned the dominant news *agency* – his bore the name Telegraphen-Union – it hardly mattered who owned the actual mastheads. When only 44 he had become chairman of the board of directors of Krupp, and in everything but name the Krupp CEO. Other Teutonic managers sincerely adopted paternalism; Hugenberg preferred Social Darwinism, except when he felt threatened, whereupon his Social Darwinism abruptly switched to blatant Uriah Heepism. He represented an early example of that syndrome which again and again has appeared in Western political life down to our own epoch: the fantasy that each government should be run like a business, with the still odder fantasy that it requires a tycoon to run government at all.

Aggravating such myths in Hugenberg's case was his lack of personal magnetism. Photographs of him evoke the top-hatted, handlebar-moustached plutocrat now familiar to the world's children from Monopoly sets (his plump, diminutive frame prompted Berlin wits to call him 'The Hamster'[109]), and by all accounts his oratory could have rendered whirling dervishes narcoleptic. But in 1928, with NSDAP demagogues in eclipse, Hugenberg's lack of public speaking talent did not impede him as it would do after Hitler had returned to national prominence. Hugenberg wanted Westarp out of the DNVP leadership for good. Out Westarp went, not merely from the leadership but, in due course, from the party (he would form his own short-lived movement, the KVP [*Konservative Volkspartei*], on lines resembling Lambach's recommendations). Hugenberg described the DNVP republicans' outlook in an expressive monosyllable: *Brei,* meaning 'mush'.[110]

On the monarchist issue Hugenberg showed no greater political responsibility than on any other issue. Supposing that – particularly before the 1926 Seeckt controversy – he had bent his business empire's entire will to ensuring a Hohenzollern comeback; had played on Hindenburg's enduring sense of guilt over the monarchy's collapse; and had won over the leadership of the Reichswehr (a leadership which, theoretically, could have been penalised for violating the Allies' prohibitions on Teutonic rearmament). With all those missions accomplished, it is hard to see what could have prevented such a comeback. Yet Hugenberg never managed this. His visceral antipathies kept getting in the way. He hated Catholics like Erzberger as much as he hated Jews like Rathenau, which was a lot. In the Reichstag he had accused Erzberger, who had only months to live, of being a 'traitor' promoting 'international economic slavery'.[111] (For all his much-vaunted opposition to Communism, the DNVP repeatedly voted in the Reichstag alongside the KPD against the centrist parties.) Enjoying the support of Tirpitz, by this time a fellow DNVP legislator, Hugenberg sought the Chancellorship in 1923; but Stresemann blocked his path, no other past or future Chancellor encouraged him, and his future dreams of leading a government remained just that – dreams.

In practice, Hugenberg's public philosophy comprised little more than the Marx Brothers' dogma 'Whatever it is, I'm against it.' From his brand of monarchism, most sensible monarchs would pray for deliverance. Hugenberg, like most German nationalists after 1918, was 'more influenced by feelings of disloyalty to the Republic than of loyalty to the Kaiser.'[112] His modus operandi remains common enough in the twenty-first-century Anglosphere, from those self-styled conservatives who (whether through short-sightedness or deliberate malevolence) conserve zero. He possessed, in short, every trait of populism except popularity.

From 1915 until very late in the war, it had been an article of faith in the Allied countries that Wilhelm II was 'dying of cancer'. In 1918 Rudyard Kipling, who himself lived in terror of such a fate – and whose own son had been killed on the Western Front – devoted to the allegation one of his most horrific poems, 'A Death-Bed'. Various lines in the poem are put in the mouths of the Kaiser's surgeons; other lines purport to be uttered by the Kaiser at his most unbridled and Nietzschean:

> 'This is the State above the Law.
> The State exists for the State alone.'
> (This is a gland at the back of the jaw,
> And an answering lump by the collarbone.)

> Some die shouting in gas or fire;
> Some die silent, by shell and shot.
> Some die desperate, caught on the wire;
> Some die suddenly. This will not.

> '*Regis suprema voluntas Lex!*'
> (It will follow the regular course of – throats.)
> Some die pinned by the broken decks,
> Some die sobbing between the boats.

Some die eloquent, pressed to death
By the sliding trench as their friends can hear.
Some die wholly in half a breath.
Some – give trouble for half a year.

'There is neither Evil nor Good in life,
Except as the needs of the State ordain.'
(Since it is rather too late for the knife,
All we can do is mask the pain.) [...]

'The war was forced on me by my foes.
All that I sought was the right to live.'
(Don't be afraid of a triple dose;
The pain will neutralise half we give.

Here are the needles. See that he dies
While the effects of the drug endure.
What is the question he asks with his eyes? –
Yes, All-Highest, to God, be sure.)

To the surprise of adherents and adversaries alike, the former monarch found within a few years of moving to Doorn that he had never felt better. Fresh air, strenuous physical exercise (particularly sawing and chopping wood), the absence of political cares: these all improved his health. As one unfriendly historian declared in 1933:

> It is astonishing how this man, whose chief fault all his life was lack of concentration and perseverance, has for more than thirteen years, with the patience of a monk, with the uniformity of a machine, and with the industry of a Chinese coolie, been performing this, for him, useless and futile work during three solid hours day after day. [...] the man who can destroy nothing more in world politics wreaks his destructive fury – *faute de mieux* – upon innocent and defenceless trees.[113]

The bouts of nervous prostration which had overcome him at times of crisis before 1918, disappeared from his medical record thereafter. Convinced that history would vindicate him, he gave several interviews, including one in 1924 to his long-time American apologist G.S. Viereck. There he reverted to the theme of what would have happened six years earlier, had he taken his own life: 'Suicide on my part would have been accepted by my foes as a confession of guilt. I and my people are innocent of this war. I regard it as the most solemn obligation imposed upon me by fate to clear the name of my country.'[114]

He did not always talk like this. More frequently he read aloud to his household, especial favourites of his including the novels of P.G. Wodehouse. Part of him had always longed to be an English country gentleman, like Lord Emsworth pottering around Blandings Castle.[115] At Doorn he had come as near as he ever would, and much nearer than most people do, to that state of grace. He even contracted, in 1922, a second marriage, his new bride being a widow, Hermine, whose brother (Henrich XXIV from the principality of Reuss-Greiz) had been among the monarchical casualties of 1918. The Crown Prince and his siblings cared little for their new stepmother, who in later years would embarrass even the least fastidious Hohenzollerns by the ardour with which she sang the Third Reich's praises. But that her presence gave joy to the Kaiser's late middle age and old age could not be gainsaid. After turning 70, he made a point of napping during afternoons, and to recommending that his courtiers, however young, adopt the same practice. 'That way, he said, they would not snore through his readings from books and papers in the evening.'[116]

He appears to have been so convinced of the inevitability of a Hohenzollern reinstallation, that he devoted much less time to seeking this result than might be assumed. (A 1922 *New York Times* report quoted him as specifically disavowing the restored imperial crown for himself.)[117] The Allies' striving to extradite him from the Netherlands, as part of their 'hang the Kaiser' campaign, had failed dismally, irked Queen Wilhelmina – and, if anything, increased the goodwill towards him of his former subjects. Monarchist German politicians' appeal 'to save the Emperor from the revenge of his enemies was answered at the [1920] polls by many non-monarchists, who, in expressing their protest against the extradition demand, boosted the political strength of the monarchist factions'.[118]

Attempts – advocated by Britain's ambassador to The Hague, Sir Ronald William Graham – to have the Kaiser shipped off to Java (then still Dutch-ruled territory, but gratifyingly distant from Europe) came to nothing. Herman Adriaan Van Karnebeek, the Netherlands' Foreign Minister, rejected Graham's Javanese plans from the beginning. He 'explained, as he did repeatedly in the future, that Holland had enough trouble with the Islamic nationalist movement there without adding Wilhelm to it'.[119]

Outlawed after the Beer Hall Putsch, the NSDAP initially circumvented this ban by contesting elections via a front organisation, known as the *Nationalsozialistische Freiheitsbewegung* (NSFB for short), which consisted not only of NSDAP members but members of other blood-and-soil groups. Ludendorff attached himself to the organisation, and at the June 1924 Reichstag election it won a respectable total of thirty-two seats, before being reduced to only fourteen seats at the year's second election the following December. From 1928, the ban on National Socialism having been lifted, the NSDAP ran under its own name with poor results that May, when its Reichstag representation fell to twelve seats. Germany's comparative quietude and affluence worked electorally against extremists who required discontent and economic chaos to thrive.

But buried amid the foregoing well-known, much discussed indicators of limited voter enthusiasm for the NSDAP during the later 1920s dwells a surprising truth. Rather than losing active members (as would be expected with any radical party which had had diminishing legislative representation over four years), the NSDAP was gaining them. In 1928, when still less than a decade old, the NSDAP could call on at least 100,000 members and possibly 108,000: having had 55,000 members in 1923.[120] The party benefited from lacking what sociologists call 'the free-rider effect', this effect being the bane of most political movements. Individuals who joined demonstrated their devotion, their willingness to sacrifice themselves – financially or otherwise – and their enthusiasm for being at the ready whenever the Führer needed them. Furthermore, the NSDAP had started luring supporters away from the monarchist movements. An early convert to the party was erstwhile Freikorps leader Franz von Epp, previously of the BVP.

The BVP itself had conspicuously downplayed its monarchist principles since 1924, the year that former newspaper editor Henrich Held took over from Knilling as Bavaria's Premier. A *Manchester Guardian* report from November 1925 indicated the state government's displeasure with talk of formally installing Rupprecht as sovereign:

> According to precise and detailed information received by the *Frankfurter Zeitung* the two chief advisers of Prince Rupprecht – Count [Alfred von] Soden Frauenhofen and General [von] Möhl – approached the Bavarian authorities a fortnight ago, pointing out to them that the time for action had come, that the military organisation *Die Bayerntreue* had been formed for the purpose by General von Möhl himself, and that everything was ready for Prince Rupprecht to ascend the throne.
>
> But the Bavarian authorities who were thus approached did not for a moment hesitate to reply that these plans were futile and dangerous, and might, if they were to be attempted, mean the end of German unity. They, for their part, although convinced Royalists, would do all in their power to oppose them.
>
> Thus the Monarchist *coup d'état* which was being prepared has received its first setback.[121]

BVP leaders' description of themselves as 'convinced Royalists' seems hypocritical but might not have been. When Rupprecht turned 60 in 1929, birthday greetings arrived from Premier Held and the aforementioned nuncio to Bavaria, Eugenio Pacelli, while Crown Prince Wilhelm's brother August Wilhelm (known to his kin as 'Auwi') marked the milestone by a fervent speech in Rupprecht's honour to a Nuremberg gathering. 'I am proud to stand here as a speaker for his Bavaria and to ask all of you to join in the cry: "God bless your king, His Majesty King Rupprecht, hurrah!"'[122]

Hitler, who had announced when on trial after the Beer Hall Putsch: 'I am no monarchist, rather in the final analysis a republican',[123] had decided by 1928 – the year of Epp's defection to the NSDAP – that protestations on his part of monarchical sentiment suited his purposes. He went so far as to assert: 'My aim is the restoration of the Empire under a Hohenzollern.'[124] His remorseless pursuit of strategic ends cohabited with outstanding flexibility as to tactical means. On any showing, his recent urban campaign, by which his party had sought to win over Social Democrat and Communist voters in the working-class areas of Berlin and other major cities, had failed. This setback, combined with the awareness that long before Stalin's dictatorship Communist regimes had exterminated well over two million 'enemies of the people' – not counting the death toll from the USSR's man-made 1921–22 famine, cautiously estimated at one million – made Hitler conclude that if his movement were to become the only serious long-term anti-Communist game in town, acquiring some kingly and aristocratic supporters (who, besides, might well share his objections to finance capitalism) would be advisable. Fine words to the upper classes were cheap.

His initial evangelising method in monarchist circles needed, to say the least, work under warranty. Munich Police Chief Ernst Pöhner brought about a meeting between

Hitler and that Count von Soden Frauenhofen whom the *Manchester Guardian* article had cited. The Count had been briefly taken captive by the NSDAP during the crisis of November 1923. He reminisced:

> Hitler greeted me most politely, and excused himself for my confinement, which one of his subordinates, whom he did not wish to name, rather than he himself had ordered. Then he began to lecture, at first in a calm voice, which became increasingly louder and more agitated, until finally the great man, screaming and wildly gesticulating, ran up and down the room and delivered such an oration that I hardly got in a word. This lasted almost three hours! His exposition was so chaotic that, although it was my duty to make a written report of the discussion, I was unable to arrange a memorandum of Hitler's remarks. I laid the overall impression which I had received before HRH the Crown Prince [Rupprecht] when, immediately after the so-called 'interview', I gave my report in the following words: 'The fellow is out of his mind [*Der Kerl ist volkommen verrücht*].'[125]

Hitler and his party left an equally unfavourable initial impression upon another prominent monarchist, this time a Prussian: Rear-Admiral Magnus von Levetzow, who maintained frequent epistolary contact with the ex-Kaiser. In a missive to another naval officer, Admiral Erhardt Schmidt, Levetzow condemned the NSDAP's behaviour as 'too rough and revolting to lead to success. For Hitler lacks a *master*. He himself is simply not qualified to be a leader.'[126]

But at least one true believer in monarchism could be found among Hitler's closest associates: Ernst Röhm. Before Röhm and Hitler had become friends, he informed the future Führer that 'You will never make a Fascist out of me. I remain what I have always been, a Bavarian monarchist.'[127] Even after Röhm had become (so he heedlessly believed) indispensable to the NSDAP, he tried his utmost to combine his new devotion with his old, going down on bended knees to Rupprecht in the hope – a vain one – of persuading the Wittelsbach head to join the National Socialists.[128] An April 1930 letter from Röhm to Rupprecht includes the following:

> A healthy Germany must again have a monarchist head. My ideal, for which I am ready to fight, is a free Germany under the strong and responsible leadership of her hereditary rulers. What Your Majesty can do for us royalist soldiers today is for Your Majesty to hold yourself in close and confidential contact with the loyal fighters for freedom.[129]

Nothing like these effusions marks Goering's recorded observations amid the two visits which he made to Doorn, the first in January 1931 with his already sick wife Karin, the second in May 1932 after Karin's death. Levetzow had actively wanted, and might have helped to organise, the first visit.[130] Goering assured his hosts of Hitler's esteem for the Hohenzollerns, though he remained discreetly silent about his master's desire to keep both the ex-Kaiser and Crown Prince Wilhelm out of the running. Hitler regarded the least objectionable Hohenzollern as being the young Prince Wilhelm, whose desire to marry a fellow undergraduate, Dorothea von Salviati, appalled his grandfather.

('Remember,' the septuagenarian told the student prince with inspired gaucherie, 'there is every possible form of horse. We are thoroughbreds, however, and when we conclude a marriage such as with Fräulein von Salviati, it produces mongrels, and that cannot be allowed to happen.')[131] The Prince's and Dorothea's nuptials went ahead in any event.

Hermine found Goering to be most congenial – her husband felt less enthusiasm – and was still more taken with Hitler when she met him. Prince August Wilhelm, whose earlier tribute to Rupprecht has been quoted, fell in love with Nazism and joined the party. (A British visitor to Germany passed upon the prince this cantankerous verdict: 'He has been described as a bright young thing of forty-five, has aesthetic fads, paints fair amateur pictures, if not his face, and patronises the ballet.')[132] The head of the family took in his stride the newest enthusiasm of 'Auwi'. But he thundered against Crown Prince Wilhelm's expressed wish to become a presidential candidate for 1932, and to seek Hitler's assistance (he had Hugenberg's assistance from the outset). The ex-Kaiser 'could not stomach the thought that his son was prepared to take the presidential oath to support the republic'[133] – nor could Hermine abide the idea – and he ordered the Crown Prince to abandon his scheme at once, calling it 'absolute idiocy'.[134] Hindenburg shared this opposition to the concept of the Crown Prince running for elective office: if the Hohenzollerns were to return, Hindenburg wanted the sovereign to be Wilhelm II again and no one else.[135]

The collapse of the Crown Prince's presidential ambitions confirmed what had already become visible: Hugenberg's political decline. As the Great Depression struck and electoral support for the NSDAP surged, electoral support for Hugenberg's party crashed. In April 1932, six months after the Harzburg Front meeting of prominent right-wingers had shown Hugenberg's inability to overrule Hitler, he bewailed the NSDAP's muscling in on the DNVP vote: 'We owe it to youth and to our children, to stress loudly and clearly in this campaign that we are not National Socialists and that the National Socialists on their own and without us are unable to solve the problems of our time.'[136]

Perfectly accurate and perfectly immaterial. At Prussia's state election that month, the DNVP lost half its Landtag seats, but the NSDAP, having previously had only eight representatives there, now had 162. It made significant, though less dramatic, gains (at the expense of the conservative parties, as well as the Social Democrats) in other state legislatures during April: Bavaria, Württemberg, Baden and Anhalt. DNVP losses were relatively mild at June's national election, which left it with thirty-seven Reichstag seats instead of forty-one. Yet that same Reichstag now had 230 NSDAP members, an increase of 123 on its previous total. When Germans returned to the polls in November, Hitler's drive for power went briefly into reverse, and the NSDAP's tally of Reichstag members shrank from 230 to 196. The votes which the Nazis had lost went to the DNVP (fourteen extra seats) and to the KPD, still run by Thälmann (eleven extra seats, bringing it to 100). But before Hugenberg could capitalise on this trend, Hitler had become Chancellor in January 1933, outwitting Kurt von Schleicher – just as Schleicher, the preceding December, had outwitted his predecessor Franz von Papen – and reducing Hugenberg, as well as Papen, to lackey status. The Führer gave Hugenberg the titles of Economics Minister and Agriculture Minister, while ignoring most of his demands. Within six months Hugenberg had resigned in a sulk from the cabinet, to which he never returned.

None of the DNVP's decay was ineluctable. All of it could have been reduced, if not wholly averted, by Hugenberg with firm self-discipline and a little imagination.

Being devoid of both, he was seldom trusted, and in the end, seldom feared. With Hindenburg, what voters saw was what voters got: a deficient and uninteresting article in several respects, but one that hardly bespoke premeditated rancour. Whereas with Hugenberg (as with many another media mogul since his day) posterity is forced back on the conclusion that for all his 'survival of the fittest' bluster, he viewed politics fundamentally as performance art: an attitude which he shared with Bavaria's Marxist-Anarchist zanies of 1919. Promising monarchists almost everything, Hugenberg delivered them absolutely nothing.

As late as March 1933 Hitler (a German citizen since February of the preceding year) allowed the monarchists to feed on the assurances with which he had crammed them. A solemn ceremony at Berlin's Garrison Church that month not only had Hohenzollerns galore on its guest-list – Crown Prince Wilhelm, his wife Crown Princess Cecilie, and their sons were all present – but, in the foreground, a chair kept deliberately unoccupied, to stand for the ex-Kaiser. Hindenburg wore a uniform from imperial days:

> a spiked helmet on his massive head and the broad, orange cordon of the Order of the Black Eagle on his chest, quite overshadowing the smaller, cutaway-clad figure of Hitler at his side. Coming abreast the empty chair in the nave he turned and raised his baton in silent salute to his absent lord. Afterwards the British ambassador [Sir Eric Phipps] reported that the old man's role no longer appeared to be that of Reich President, but of Reich Regent.[137]

Over the preceding two years, monarchism had become as hard to exorcise altogether as Banquo's ghost. Heinrich Brüning, who in March 1930 had not only become Chancellor, but had won Hindenburg's warm if transitory approbation ('You shall be my last Chancellor and I will never give you up',)[138] planned to hinder both National Socialists and Communists through a returned Hohenzollern dynasty incarnating 'a constitutional monarchy on the British model, with Hindenburg as *Reichsverweser* [imperial regent] until his death and then the accession of the eldest son of the German Crown Prince'.[139] As late as 1949, Brüning mourned the opportunity forfeited during the early 1930s:

> When I think over these years, I come more firmly than I did at the time to the conclusion that only the restoration of the monarchy in some form by a plebiscite could have prevented Hitler from coming to power. [...] It was my last weapon and to keep it sharp I had to be very cautious, and somewhat vague in talking about it.[140]

Alas, the mixture of economic disaster, Brüning's undue belief in Schleicher's dependability, and Hindenburg's obstinate opposition sabotaged the plan. By the end of 1931 Brüning, now reviled as the 'Hunger Chancellor' [*Hungerkanzler*] because of his powerlessness to stave off the Great Depression's miseries,[141] had to take one day at a time and considered himself fortunate if his government survived till the following sunset. In May 1932 his chancellorship ended. He found Hindenburg's intransigence particularly galling, and afterwards wrote: 'Though I spoke with the tongues of man and angels, I could have made no impression on him.'[142]

Even then all was not lost for Germanic monarchism. The extraordinary – not to say unprecedented – Bavarian gambit initiated late in 1932 revealed two qualities: in some politicians, the courage born of desperation; in others, the cowardice born of inertia.

Germany's March 1932 presidential election (with two voting rounds, like the 1925 contest) had made the dire political situation still worse. Hindenburg won, but by nothing like a majority decisive enough to see off Hitler's ambitions. Hitler lost, but still obtained almost 37 per cent of the total vote (Hindenburg obtained 53.05 per cent), acquiring an extra two million electoral supporters between the first round and the second.

Thälmann in 1932, as in 1925, made it to the second round. This time his share of the total vote amounted to a little over ten per cent: a much better result for him – almost four percentage points better – than that of 1925. From this electoral improvement's premise follows the melancholy conclusion: that Thälmann's villainous and reckless policy, on Stalin's orders, of acting as if the main threats to Germany were the Social Democrats (or, as Politburo cant had begun describing them, 'social fascists') struck a sympathetic chord with the voting public's stupider members. For Thälmann's KPD at this point, Hitlerism constituted, at worst, a mere short-term interruption to the guaranteed triumph of the workers' paradise. Either it genuinely presented no wider peril, or else what wider peril it did present would ultimately work to communism's advantage by spurring the proletarian vanguard to new feats of revolutionary valour. (In a January 1931 Berlin debate Willi Münzenberg, Thälmann's equally misguided fellow KPD apparatchik, had treated his audience to one of the modern world's least correct predictions: 'Hitler we can ignore.'[143] This just four months after an election which had seen the NSDAP's representation jump from twelve Reichstag seats to 107.)

The higher the temperature of national politics' ideological fevers, the more alarmed Bavaria's rulers became. On 20 July 1932, Chancellor Papen had unleashed the so-called *Preussenschlag* ('strike against Prussia'), deposing that state's government (still led by Otto Braun). To quote the recent essay by a professor himself Bavarian, Winfried Becker:

> Bavaria joined the legal action that Prussia brought against the central government in the Reich Court in Leipzig, but the court paid little more than lip service to the principle of states' rights [...] It was against the background of these developments that the leaders of the Bavarian government and BVP began to consider whether the appointment of Crown Prince Rupprecht as general state commissar or king could prevent the establishment of National Socialist rule in Bavaria.[144]

Such considerations possessed merit ('general state commissar' had been, it will be recalled, Kahr's post after he ceased to be premier). On any criterion, Rupprecht's own aversion to the NSDAP had been straightforward and well publicised for almost a decade. Nobody could accuse him of the smallest tenderness towards Communism. He lived there, in Bavaria, thus obviating the complications which would inevitably be involved with bringing the ex-Kaiser back from abroad, always assuming that the ex-Kaiser refrained from an impulsive last-minute decision to stay at Doorn.

Even Bavaria's Social Democrats, heirs to the prudent Johannes Hoffmann, thought that government by Rupprecht warranted a try.[145] The Munich funeral (on 13 January 1933) of a prominent Wittelsbach, Rupprecht's cousin Prince Alfons, attracted so large and so vocal a monarchist crowd as to indicate copious popular goodwill towards the notion of Rupprecht being given real authority.[146] Rupprecht himself abjured attacks on Berlin, whether during Schleicher's Chancellorship or after Hitler had ousted Schleicher.

At the same time, Rupprecht made himself readily accessible to the Bavarian masses as an embodiment of local patriotism. When he attended (18 February 1933) a Munich National Theatre revival of *Der Vogelhändler* – a much-loved operetta by late-nineteenth-century Austrian composer and civil servant Carl Zeller – the crowd erupted in cheering and sang the Bavarian royal anthem.[147] The operetta's storyline, which involved an alliance between peasants and aristocrats against a military impostor, imparted an additional pertinence to the occasion. A Regensburg newspaper editorialised the next day: 'In the monarchic idea and its realisation we see the last and greatest power reserve of Bavaria. A Bavarian king will be the best guarantee for the preservation of our state.'[148] So forthright a comment, from a journal marked by long-standing support for Heinrich Held, could never have appeared without the Premier's approval.

While Hindenburg promised BVP delegate Albrecht Schaeffer that the Reich would let Bavaria look after its own affairs, the President's mind had started to wander; old age had augmented his innate tendency to tell people what they wanted to be told; and his promises counted for nothing against the threats of NSDAP hierarchs like Interior Minister Wilhelm Frick. 'Certain states,' Frick unctuously proclaimed, 'obviously have not understood the meaning of the new era.'[149] Still the Bavarian monarchists held their nerve. They intended to place Rupprecht in charge of their state on 11 March, however bitterly Hitler opposed the idea.

Then suddenly, and too late, they discovered that a Trojan horse had arrived in their midst. On 9 March this horse exuded its unlovely contents in the shape of apostate monarchist Franz von Epp, whom the Führer had empowered to act as *Reichskommissar*. After persistent Berlin pressure, Held's own monarchist enthusiasm had considerably cooled. The day of Epp's takeover, storm-troopers informed Held that he had now joined the ranks of Germany's jobless and that Bavaria no longer had such a thing as a state government for him to lead; he soon escaped to Switzerland. Other storm-troopers captured Schaeffer and thrashed him so severely that Epp himself needed to intervene before the victim expired under the goons' attentions.[150] Already Hitler had called a fresh election (5 March) for the Reichstag. At this poll, for the first time, the NSDAP not only defeated the BVP in Bavarian electorates – where before 1933 it had always fared badly – but did so by a sixteen-point margin.[151] Rupprecht, refusing to pay back evil for evil, despaired and fled temporarily to Greece. When back in Bavaria, he continued to despise the Nazi state, and sent his youngest son to Britain rather than expose him to Hitler Youth membership. To Britain, also, went Rupprecht's youngest daughters, otherwise liable for enforced induction into the League of German Girls. But never again did Rupprecht seem (as he had seemed for a few tantalising months before Hitlerism's full oppressiveness had revealed itself) the most inspirational figure in the whole land. Of the 'lost leader', twentieth-century Europe affords few more poignant examples.

Where Rupprecht had failed, it strained credulity to imagine that Crown Prince Wilhelm – whose benefactor Stresemann was long gone, having prematurely died in October 1929 – would succeed. A harangue by the Führer on 23 March (the very day when the Enabling Act became law) left no monarchists in any doubt as to what he thought of them:

> In view of the distress now prevailing among the people, the government considers at this time the question of a monarchist restoration as one not to be discussed. It would regard any attempt at an independent solution of this problem in the individual states as an attack on the unity of the Reich.[152]

Certain regal dynasts, notably the Princes of Hesse, had gone so far as to join the NSDAP, hoping by this means to buy an insurance policy for their own future after 1933. Disappointment awaited them. Previously the National Socialist press had avoided sustained vituperation against royal families; now it felt free to jeer at them. On 27 January 1934, Berlin monarchists wanting to honour Wilhelm II celebrated in public their hero's 75th birthday; their revelry ended when Goering sent the police in to disperse the revellers. The same month, the capital's deputy NSDAP chief Artur Görlitzer, addressing a group of bureaucrats, instructed monarchists to 'stop playing the fool!' Showing (on even the most uncharitable estimate) an impressive knack for ideological originality, Görlitzer went on: 'Men who work for a restoration of the Monarchy we will treat as we do those who think they must conduct propaganda for Moscow. Indeed we now regard the Monarchists as more dangerous than the Communists!'[153]

Hitler, on 30 January, railed in the Reichstag against 'the recently resumed thesis that Germany would be happier under her hereditary princes'.[154] Three days later all monarchist associations became illegal. 'There is no intention of returning to the German monarchy', intoned Alfred Rosenberg, in his role as the pre-eminent NSDAP ideologist.[155] That Crown Prince Wilhelm survived unscathed the Night of the Long Knives, which numbered among its victims his friend Schleicher and the latter's wife Elisabeth, suggested a miracle operating. It did nothing, at least for the time being, to embolden the heir. When (on 2 August, little more than a month afterwards) the 86-year-old Hindenburg breathed his last and Hitler smoothly united in himself the offices of President and Chancellor, not a single monarchist dog dared bark.

By now the ex-Kaiser's hopes of a restorationist deal with the NSDAP were as dead as the Schleichers themselves. Though also periodically inclined to Jew-baiting of a type unconnected with Hitler's (and finding expression before Hitler had even been born), he voiced disgust at the June 1934 purge. 'We have ceased to live under the rule of law and everyone must be prepared for the possibility that the Nazis will push their way in and put them up against the wall!'[156] Four-and-a-half years later came *Kristallnacht,* which 'Auwi' welcomed and which Auwi's father deprecated:

> I have just made my views clear to Auwi in the presence of his brothers. He had the nerve to say that he agreed with the Jewish pogroms and understood why they had come about. When I told him that any decent man would describe these actions as gangsterism, he appeared totally indifferent. He is completely lost to our family.[157]

Kristallnacht's bacchanalia of sadism moved the last Hohenzollern ruler to what could well have been his most innocently human utterance. 'For the first time,' he declared, 'I am ashamed to be a German.'[158] He abstained from reciprocating Hitler's public insults against him and the other former sovereigns; but his congratulatory telegram to the Führer, when France fell in June 1940, was bound to displease the telegram's recipient by its eulogy to the sender's nonagenarian grandfather, Kaiser Wilhelm I, the warlord of 1870.

Twelve months later, at Doorn on 4 June 1941, the erstwhile All-Highest died unobtrusively, of an arterial blockage in his chest, and with none of the pain that Kipling had longed for him to suffer. He had asked that his funeral be free from the display of Nazi regalia; the Netherlands' wartime *Reichskommissar* Arthur Seyss-Inquart overruled this request. Goebbels, eager to ensure that the former sovereign's passing would generate as little nostalgia as possible within Germany itself, had instructed newspapers' bosses as early as March 1933:

> When the news about the Kaiser's death is released, it is to be published with a single-column head on the lower half of the first page. Short commentary may follow but isn't necessary. The less, the better. Care must be taken on the one hand not to hurt the feelings of the old monarchists over sixty, nor on the other hand to offend younger Germany, which regards the Wilhelmine era as something that has long ago been relegated to the dustbin. [Wilhelm] is the representative of a system that failed. One may concede to him that he desired the best. But in this world it isn't a question of intention, but of success.[159]

It is seldom recollected that many of those who, from the late 1930s, planned to rid the world of Hitler favoured monarchism. Especially ardent in his monarchist convictions was Carl Goerdeler, erstwhile DNVP member, who at first (as mayor of Leipzig) had hoped to ameliorate the NSDAP by appeals to reason, but who always refused to join the party. By 1938 Goerdeler could no longer convince himself that Hitler's rule would lead to anything except catastrophe for Germany and for European civilisation. Hjalmar Schacht also supported a reinstated monarchy. So did Colonel Claus von Stauffenberg; so did the academic Johannes Popitz; so did clandestine Social Democratic and labour-union activists like Julius Leber and Wilhelm Leuschner. But the plotters never resolved, for good and all, the quandary of which monarchical candidate they should back. Goerdeler considered the Crown Prince's youngest surviving brother, Prince Oskar – who had a good anti-Nazi record – to be the best candidate. Schacht put his hopes on Prince Wilhelm, hopes dashed when the Prince died of wounds incurred during the Battle for France. Three candidates the plotters agreed to exclude: Auwi (hopelessly compromised by his unabashed allegiance to the NSDAP); before June 1941, the ex-Kaiser himself; and at nearly all stages, Crown Prince Wilhelm, who had briefly won Popitz's support, but who for the others (except perhaps for Goerdeler, as will soon emerge) had too dubious a political past to be acceptable.[160]

By the time the Second World War ended, most of the conspirators had paid with their lives – often by the most hideously degrading methods of capital punishment conceivable – for their resistance to the 'Thousand-Year Reich'. Nonetheless the Crown Prince, who did not thus pay, had one more surprise to spring upon future chroniclers. The papers which Goerdeler (hanged in February 1945) left behind him included a document which the Crown Prince himself authorised, and which came to the attention of the historian Gerhard Ritter, though Ritter insisted that 'Who drew it up is not known; it certainly was not Goerdeler.'[161] As the document indicates, the Crown Prince expected to benefit directly from a monarchical restitution, and envisioned this speech from the throne.

> When I relinquished the crown of Prussia and the rank of German Emperor, it was not done to clear the way for a development which has led to the destruction of the blameless reputation of the German people and the besmirching of its spotless shield of honour.
>
> A state of lawlessness, of unbridled despotism, and of moral degeneration has set in, which has never before been a part of our people's history. This condition now threatens to degenerate into complete defencelessness, to destroy the home front and with that to paralyse the striking power of the Wehrmacht. [The original document has here a partial list of the army's wartime atrocities.]
>
> [...] Not for such foul acts have your and my ancestors created the German Reich in centuries of work with many sacrifices, but in honour and fear of the Lord. The blood of German soldiers may not be shed, the happiness of all German families may not be destroyed, to enable inhuman criminals to commit such cowardly crimes. German youths must no longer be forced to carry out the bloodthirsty commands of unscrupulous leaders and thereby ruin themselves mentally and spiritually.
>
> When my ancestors took over the Mark of Brandenburg they established the law and order of the state against the self-willed nobility. Justice and honest have become the pride of the German people.
>
> I have not given up the throne in order to deliver the Reich to madmen and criminals. By secret murders the Führer has broken the oath he gave the German people.
>
> I stand before the throne of my ancestors where they did not tolerate injustice; I place myself before the work of our ancestors to save it and to prevent you from being cheated of the fruits of your hard work by knaves, who hypocritically but shamelessly have enriched themselves behind our soldiers' backs.
>
> I have taken over the leadership of the Reich and the supreme command over the Wehrmacht. Soldiers and officials will take an oath which they can keep with sincere hearts, as I also swear to God that I will lead the Reich in justice and decency, in loyalty and honesty. I shall therefore command that the responsible criminals be apprehended and placed before the court. The German people will have the opportunity to form for itself a judgement about the immensity of the crimes and the extent of the danger.

The war is still on. But we wish to strive for a peace in common work, a peace that fulfils our national needs for living, which secures the freedom of the whole people, and every German in an honest state established on justice and decency, without destroying the freedom and happiness of other peoples. Only the close cooperation of all peoples will bring prosperity and happiness to us and to the world. As soon as this goal has been made secure, my son Prince Louis Ferdinand will take over my position, since my eldest son Prince Wilhelm, destined for this place, died on the field of honour.

The work which we all have to do is difficult. To punish crime, to relieve injustice, is the concern of the state alone. Let us set to work, while once more each one looks the other fearlessly in the eye and confidently helps to secure these decent goals.

Then God will also help us to secure the honour and future of the Fatherland.[162]

Superfluous though any comment upon this astounding expostulation (assuming it to be genuine, and Ritter never questioned its authenticity) could well be, several reflections are forgivable. Each incendiary sentence of the above *cri de cœur* was enough – in the more than ever nightmarish atmosphere of NSDAP rule after Stauffenberg's execution, which supplied every possible motive for turncoats – to ensure for its author, first, a grotesque show-trial within the 'People's Court' system, and second, the most agonising death by strangulation on the gallows at Berlin's Plötzensee jail or at Bavaria's Flossenbürg concentration camp. Yet the Nazis left the Crown Prince unscathed. Why?

Did the Gestapo simply overlook the incriminating document's existence? That implies an ineptitude rarely associated with key Gestapo performance indicators. Or, in spite of everything, did there lurk within the Nazi ruling elite some vague, atavistic conviction that while ordinary generals and politicians who opposed the Führer deserved nothing but the most ignominious scaffold, a Hohenzollern (however severe his written indictment of the Hitler state) somehow remained, purely by virtue of being a Hohenzollern, hedged with a divinity?

In the tenebrous context of the NSDAP's *Götterdämmerung*, an epigram of Ludwig Wittgenstein, duly altered, becomes germane. Whereof the historian cannot speak, thereof he must be silent.

The Crown Prince died of natural causes at Hechingen, sixty kilometres south of Stuttgart, on 20 July 1951. He never truly emerged from his father's shadow in life, nor can he very well do so after his death. As for that father, Lloyd George eventually expressed a certain unease about the anti-Kaiser fury which his government had encouraged in the Great War's aftermath. To the young Prince Louis Ferdinand, upon meeting him in 1933, the former British Prime Minister remarked: 'We over here never expected nor intended the fall of your dynasty. [...] If your family had remained in power in Germany, I am certain that Mr Hitler would not be giving us any headaches right now.'[163]

But let Churchill (writing two years after Lloyd George's comment) have the last word on the boring, banal, rash, cosy, cranky paterfamilias of Doorn:

> But he [the ex-Kaiser] lived longer still; and Time has brought him a surprising and paradoxical revenge upon his conquerors. He has reached a phase when the greater part of Europe, particularly his most powerful enemies Great Britain and France, would regard the Hohenzollern restoration they formerly abhorred beyond expression, as a comparatively hopeful event and as a sign that dangers were abating. If it were accompanied by constitutional limitations, it would be taken throughout the world as an assurance of peace abroad and toleration at home. This is not because his own personal light burns the brighter or the more steadily, but because of the increasing darkness around. The victorious democracies in driving out hereditary sovereigns, supposed they were moving on the path of progress. They have in fact gone further and fared worse.[164]

Chapter III

The Double-Headed Eagle a Phoenix?
Austria and Hungary

Francis I [Emperor of Austria 1792–1835] [...] replied to the description
of somebody as an Austrian patriot, 'Yes, but is he a patriot for me?'
A.J.P. Taylor[1]

Still the old man, wrestling against bronchitis, coped as best he could with the incoming
official documents. For, like his distant ancestor Philip II of Spain, he was not only
the monarch but the chief clerk of his realm. During the previous sixty-eight years he
had disciplined himself to soldier on (an appropriate verb: seldom did he appear to the
public in any attire save his military uniform) despite often agonising circumstances.
He had lost his wife Elisabeth and nephew Franz Ferdinand to assassins; his hectic,
irresponsible son Rudolf had made a suicide-pact with a worshipful, dim-witted mistress;
his brother Maximilian had been judicially murdered by Mexican insurrectionists. These
disasters – each one accompanied by press coverage as sensationalist and indecorous
as the age could show – would have demoralised a man more creative, less implacably
diligent, than he. A veritable Marcus Aurelius with white side-whiskers, he tried as
far as possible to extinguish his own feelings through the governance of his polyglot,
ramshackle, improbable, seemingly indestructible empire. In 1904 he had announced:
'The Monarchy is not an artificial creation but an organic body. It is a place of refuge,
an asylum for all those fragmented nations scattered over central Europe who, if left to
their own resources, would lead a pitiful existence, becoming the playthings of more
powerful neighbours.'[2]

This empire he regarded, not as his own possession, but as a sacred trust, embodying
pride of ancestry and hope of posterity. In the very marrow of his bones he believed that
one day, he would be forced to give an account to a sovereign far mightier than himself,
concerning his stewardship of that trust.

Yet at 86 years old, even the indomitable Franz Josef had visibly and audibly
started to weaken. Emperor of Austria, he also bore the titles King of Hungary
and Bohemia, Dalmatia, Croatia, Slavonia, Galicia, Lodomeria and Illyria, Duke
of Lorraine, Salzburg, Styria, Carinthia, Carniola and Bukovina; and so on through
a roll-call of bombinating proper nouns that included an echo from mediaeval
conquests ('King of Jerusalem') and the retrospectively chilling appellation
'Duke of Auschwitz'. In early November 1916 *Der Alte Herr* – so the Viennese
frequently called him, since only one 'old gentleman' could possibly be meant by
the nickname[3] – surprised visitors by sometimes finding it hard to follow what was
said to him, and by becoming sleepy.[4]

64

He had grown so benumbed by age and ill fortune that when Austria's Prime Minister, Count Karl von Stürgkh, fell on 21 October to yet another murderer's bullets, his sovereign carried on almost as if nothing had happened, and promptly appointed a lawyer, Ernst von Koerber, as Stürgkh's successor. His promptitude sprang not in the slightest degree from innate callousness, but from hypertrophic conscientiousness. During 1914, Stürgkh had closed the increasingly chaotic Austrian parliament (though not the Hungarian parliament, over which, thanks to the constitutional arrangements of 1867's *Doppelreich* – 'Dual Monarchy' – he had no control); and his killer, a socialist malcontent called Friedrich Adler, took offence at the closure. Adler shared the touching belief, otherwise chiefly found among Anglo-Saxons, that when you have established a legislature you have automatically solved a problem. He saw nothing amiss in the propensity of this particular legislature's multicultural occupants for greeting any official acts they did not like with shrieks, filibusters, banging of desks, flinging of inkpots, and, when the spirit moved them, actual shooting. Amid one tempestuous parliamentary session of October 1911, Stürgkh (then Education Minister) narrowly escaped the marksman's gunfire.[5]

But that strife belonged to a distant yesteryear now. On 19 November 1916 the Emperor's bronchitic condition, combined with what his doctor identified as pneumonia, prompted him to ask that a priest administer to him the sacraments. This was done, yet later that day he insisted on resuming his desk work, and continuing it for most of the next forty-eight hours. Only on the afternoon of the 21st did he desist, not willingly, but because he had lost consciousness at his desk and his servants carried him to his room. Surrounded by family members (a telegram had summoned his great-nephew and heir apparent, Archduke Karl) and having received the viaticum from the court chaplain, *der Alte Herr* suffered one final coughing-fit, then peacefully expired.[6] 'The manner of his passing,' an early biographer wrote, 'was the symbol of his life. He died in harness.'[7]

One Viennese author of aristocratic background, Nora Wydenbruck – who turned 22 during the year Franz Josef passed away – remembered her girlhood:

> The Emperor had taken the place of God in my imagination, but unfortunately I already knew that he did not share one of the main prerogatives of the deity – eternity. Ever since I could remember, everybody had been saying: 'It will be the end of Austria when the Old Gentleman closes his eyes.'[8]

For 'the Old Gentleman' and for all his relatives, Habsburg funerary ritual had devised a unique *memento mori* which expressed the same sentiment that an eighteenth-century English poet had articulated: 'the paths of glory lead but to the grave'. Shortly before midnight on 30 November, when the Emperor's hearse, borne by four black horses, had reached Vienna's Church of the Capuchin Fathers (where most of his family had been interred), the court chamberlain, Alfred von Montenuovo, knocked on the church's front door with his staff of office. From inside could be heard the retort from the Capuchins' prior:

'Who is it?'

'His Most Serene Majesty, Franz Josef, Emperor of Austria, and Apostolic King of Hungary.'

'I know him not.'

Once more the chamberlain struck the door with his staff. Once more the prior asked: 'Who is it?'

'Emperor Franz Josef, King of Hungary.'

'I know him not.'

The chamberlain rapped the door a third time. Yet again the prior asked: 'Who is it?'

'A poor sinner, Franz Josef.'

Then, finally, the door opened and the cortège entered.[9]

In normal times the new Emperor Karl (who also bore the Hungarian royal title Károly IV) would probably have achieved great things. Young, personable, amiable, of unquestioned religious devotion, blessed with a wonderfully contented marriage to Archduchess Zita of Bourbon-Parma (which produced eight children), he combined these virtues with an imaginative insight alien to his predecessor. His insight took two principal forms: first, a horrified awareness (shared with Pope Benedict XV) that the Great War had gone on quite long enough, and that somehow it must be stopped before all of Europe's young men were in their coffins; second, that the Habsburg domains, having shown themselves flexible enough to accommodate a Dual Monarchy, could and should be turned into a Triune Monarchy with Slavs as active partners. Effect such a partnership, Karl maintained, and the menace of nationalistic grievances would be much diminished, if not altogether defanged.

These being sensible ideas, they inspired widespread shock among many other belligerents. They confirmed the belief of Kaiser Wilhelm (when he eventually learned about them) that the Austro-Hungarian empire could not be relied on as an ally. Also, they alarmed much of the Hungarian political class, which had rather enjoyed its half-century-old licence to blackmail Vienna into preserving its own special bureaucratic and linguistic privileges. Among the Slav émigrés pouring into Allied ears – most crucially, after April 1917, into American ears – their honeyed verbiage about the rights of 'oppressed peoples' within the Habsburg 'prison-house of nations', Karl's ideas gave outright scandal. 'Prison-house of nations' had been a slogan of genius coined in the late 1840s by the anti-Habsburg Hungarian separatist Lajos Kossuth.[10] It acquired a new popularity in the West after 1917, with Woodrow Wilson's increasing sway over public opinion, in Europe much more than at home. All the émigrés' rhetoric had derived from the automatic postulation that the Habsburg empire was dying and deserved to die. They dreaded Karl giving it a blood-transfusion and thus strengthening it.

Nevertheless, some heeded the 'still, small voice' of Karl the peacemaker. One of the leading French politicians, Aristide Briand (who in 1915 had become his nation's Prime Minister for the second time), took that voice seriously. Similarly, Lloyd George, whose own accession to power occurred only weeks after Karl's, paid the Habsburg monarch's overtures attention. He knew – as Briand knew, but as the newspaper-tranquillised general public had never suspected – something of the frightful casualty rates every day on the Western Front. For five months in 1916, the Battle of the Somme had inconclusively raged. On the battle's very first day, no fewer than 19,240 troops in Britain's army had perished: for that army, the figure remains an all-time record death-toll for British forces within a twenty-four-hour period.[11] Suddenly Karl's moves towards a negotiated peace, moves which a year earlier would have been laughed to jingoistic scorn, looked worth considering.

They promised well. Karl's trusted representative, Zita's brother Sixtus of Bourbon-Parma, approached France's President Poincaré and convinced him to write to both Lloyd George and King George V. This move Briand welcomed. Even when Briand was suddenly deposed from the prime ministry in favour of the more obviously bellicose Alexandre Ribot (March 1917), the communications continued. Ribot actually took, to his clandestine meeting at Folkestone with Lloyd George, a letter from Karl himself, stressing his desire for peace, whether or not he had German support for this desire. Lloyd George met Sixtus at 10 Downing Street the following May, and liked what he saw. He recommended to the emissary that the matter be dealt with by the leaders themselves, not by ambassadors – however well-meaning. In his words, 'Diplomats were invented to waste time.'[12] George V welcomed the idea of such a discussion, telling his diary: 'He [Sixtus] came to inform us that the Emperor of Austria had written to him to try and arrange for a separate peace with the Entente. The difficulty will be Italy. It is of course very secret: only M. Poincaré and M. Ribot know. It would be a great thing if it could be brought about.'[13]

In identifying Italy as the paramount obstacle, the King showed characteristic shrewdness. Now that the Great War is more than a hundred years in the past and no one lies awake at night worrying about Italian foreign policy, it is hard to explain – hard even to conceive of – how large, and almost always destructive, a function successive Italian governments had assumed in European affairs, both before and after 1914. A 1963 chronicler felt somewhat abashed about his limited coverage of Italy's opportunistic imperialist appetite ('a much more significant factor than it has been possible to indicate within the limited scope of the present work'), and blamed the appetite, which the 1911–12 Italo-Turkish conflict increased, on a national pride that 'reflected the tormented romanticism of delayed adolescence'.[14]

At first Italy had refused to enter the Great War at all. Then she did enter it, solely because Britain and France, by the April 1915 Treaty of London, had offered her swathes of mostly Austrian-ruled terrain, with some Greek-ruled islands for good measure. When Lloyd George and Ribot tried in April 1917 to persuade Italy's Foreign Minister, Baron Sidney Sonnino, to consider negotiating with Austria, they had no luck:

> Sonnino's position was that no peace on any basis short of complete fulfilment of the Treaty of London could even be discussed or the Italian public would withdraw from the war with a roar of outrage, releasing scores of enemy divisions for service on the Western front. Since the Treaty of London was secret, this was nothing but naked blackmail.[15]

All hopes of keeping the Treaty hidden from the rest of the world ended in December 1917, when the new Bolshevik regime revealed the Treaty's text, as evidence of the capitalist powers' perfidy. Ludendorff, by this stage Germany's de facto dictator, made it all too clear what destiny awaited an ally which made a separate peace behind German backs. Austria's own Germanophile Foreign Minister, Count Ottokar Czernin, had no intention of carrying out Karl's will, and faithfully primed the German embassy with reports on Karl's doings. When Clemenceau remade French politics on the principle of *revanche*, every prospect of national compromise ended. In a foolish panic, Karl denied – to Kaiser Wilhelm via a telegram – that he had ever sought to end hostilities on his own initiative. Clemenceau exultantly publicised the relevant correspondence, thus not only confirming Czernin's duplicity but completing Karl's public humiliation:

> The Emperor of Austria stood exposed to the world as a liar. In those days Europe, even in its death throes, was not hardened to such violations of the gentleman's code. [...] Monarchs themselves quibbled and cheated on occasion. But they did not put their signatures to a formal lie – least of all in writing to a brother monarch.[16]

Thus ended, with bangs as well as with whimpers, the Habsburg sovereign's efforts to conclude the war a year early. Thus vanished everything that this cessation entailed in terms of the European lives which it would have saved, and the European crowns which it would have preserved: not to mention the cutting-down to decent human proportions of Woodrow Wilson's messianic status. On 4 November 1918, Karl signed from a position of desperate weakness what he had wanted to sign the preceding year from a position of comparative strength: a separate peace treaty with Britain and France. It availed him and his empire nothing. The Slav republican separatists had tasted blood and wanted more. Within a week, chunk after chunk of Habsburg territory had fallen away. As early as July, a Czech deputy in the Austrian parliament (reopened at Karl's behest in the preceding year) bellowed the following imprecation to his hosts, and went unpunished: 'We regard Austria as a centuries-old crime against humanity [...] It is our highest national duty to betray Austria whenever and wherever we can. We shall hate Austria, we shall fight against her, and God willing, we shall in the end smash her to pieces.'[17]

Five days before Karl signed the treaty with the Allies, a Provisional National Assembly had set up a Republic of German-Austria, with the prominent socialist lawyer and academic Karl Renner in the Chancellor's role. Renner's talents for backing winners – talents which, another world war later, would enable him to appease Stalin and live to tell the tale – first manifested themselves in the Great War's final alarums and excursions. On 31 October (the day after Renner's elevation), István Tisza, who had been Hungary's Prime Minister for most of the preceding five years, shared Stürgkh's fate. Having survived three attempts on his life, Tisza fell victim to the fourth, when three soldiers burst into his Budapest villa and shot him. Refusing to flee when he had the chance, and ostentatiously casting aside his own revolver, he told his killers: 'As I have lived, so shall I die.'[18] Within seconds he breathed his last, in his distraught wife's embrace.

By 9 November, Karl could hardly count on the support of anyone outside the Schönbrunn Palace. Accordingly, on that day, he left Vienna, first staying with his family in Austria's north-east, at Schloss Eckartsau, which he himself (rather than the state) owned. The document which he signed before departing from the capital said nothing about formal abdication. To this legalistic nicety he and Zita would in after years cling, as to a lifeboat.

He won admirers in the most unexpected places. The doughty republican Anatole France, fully alive to the danger of Clemenceau imprisoning him for sedition, lamented Karl's failure.

> No one will ever persuade me that the War could not have ended long ago. The Emperor Charles offered peace. There is the only honest man to occupy an important position during the War, but he was not listened to. In my opinion, his offer ought to have been accepted. The Emperor Charles has a sincere desire for peace so everybody hates him [...] A king of France, yes, a king would have taken pity on our poor people, bled white, attenuated, at the end of their strength. But democracy is without heart, without guts. A slave to the power of money, it is pitiless and inhuman.[19]

Shortly before leaving Vienna, Karl appointed the 43-year-old Count Mihály Károlyi as Hungarian Prime Minister. Károlyi rewarded the sovereign's trust in him by proclaiming a Hungarian Republic within weeks. After Károlyi's childhood harelip had benefited from surgery, he made up for lost time by leather-lunged orations at every suitable juncture – and most unsuitable ones. If noisiness, juvenile optimism and garrulity in four languages (Hungarian, German, English and French) amounted to statesmanship, Károlyi would have been up there with the immortals. Sir Harold Nicolson, who saw much of him, commented after reading Károlyi's memoirs: 'He had many qualities, but unfortunately lacked those by which a man is taken seriously by serious people.'[20] Even Károlyi's fellow politicians, inured *ex officio* to waffle, thought his logorrhoea excessive. One office-holder in the new republic, the writer Lajos Hatvany, wrote: 'From the discussions no decisions arose, and from the decisions – no actions. A cabinet? No, it was a debating club.'[21]

Károlyi, one of Hungary's richest landowners, owed his socialist protestations more to his hatred of Tisza (who had wounded him in a duel) than to either reading of doctrine or acquaintanceship with poverty. The best that can be said for Károlyi's actions regarding his foe's murder is that he did not actually order it. His attitude towards Tisza – at whom he had screamed near the war's end 'Your time is over, and our time has come'[22] – can be summarised in the nineteenth-century couplet 'Thou shalt not kill, but needst not strive / Officiously to keep alive.' He never denied, and still less did he refute, the rumour that a guard who had been protecting Tisza's house was actually sent elsewhere before the killing. Within months all Europe had the chance to reflect on Károlyi's level of political aptitude, when his cabinet 'suffered the fate of all amateur left-wing radicals who play with real fire and had been duly smoked out of office.'[23]

Leading the expulsion of Károlyi and his ministers was Béla Kun, the Hungarian-born but Moscow-trained Marxist who, for 133 vertiginous days from March to August 1919, ran the Hungarian Soviet Republic, the first communist regime in the world outside the USSR (it came into being a fortnight before Bavaria's). Aware that the capitalist banking system had its merits, Kun had thoughtfully provided himself with a supply of Swedish kronor and Swiss francs – as well as fake documents allegedly from the Red Cross[24] – before arriving in Budapest from military service among the Russian Civil War's Bolsheviks. Once in Hungary's capital he incited a mob to ransack the head office of the Social Democrat newspaper *Népsava* ('Voice of the People'). Károlyi's government incarcerated Kun, but in such mild conditions that the captive enjoyed an unending stream of visits from comrades – sometimes several hundred visits within a day – and still ran the Hungarian Communist Party as he had done before. By March 1919 even these undemanding limits on Kun's freedom of movement no longer operated. Kun emerged from his cell with the glamour of martyrdom, took over the government (having cowed most of the leading Social Democrats into supporting the Communists), had Károlyi arrested, and then obliged the Count to escape, first to Prague, later to Paris. Seldom in modern times has a professional revolutionist so swiftly vanquished a virtue-signalling dilettante, one whom Kun himself called the 'Hungarian Kerensky'.[25]

Officially Kun was nothing more than the Soviet Republic's Foreign Affairs Commissar, the role of national president having been assigned to one Sándor Garbai. In practice, Kun was the unchallenged despot, whose aides included two fellow Marxist apparatchiks, both still in their twenties: Tibor Szamuely – leader of the regime's paramilitaries, who bore the comforting name 'Lenin Boys' (in the original Hungarian, *Lenin-fiúk*) – and Mátyás Rákosi, Commissar for Trade. Of the regime's forty-nine highest officials, thirty-one (Kun, Szamuely, and Rákosi included) were Jewish; and Rákosi – capable of genuine if macabre humour – defended entrusting the Gentile Garbai with the presidential office, on the memorable grounds that this guaranteed 'someone who could sign the death sentences on Saturday'.[26]

Within a month, the Hungarian Soviet Republic had managed the near-impossible feat of starving the nation known as 'the breadbasket of Europe'.[27] All those concomitants of Bolshevik rule which subsequent epochs made only too familiar were here already manifest. Revolutionary tribunals subverted the standard court system and decreed impromptu lynchings (not least at the hands of the Lenin Boys) of 'class enemies', whether genuine or, frequently, imagined. Urban managers of proven competence found themselves dismissed to make room for the most inept Party drudges, so that 'production almost ceased in the factories'.[28] Hungary's peasants, anticipating Ukrainian kulaks, refused to supply food to the cities until compelled to do so at gunpoint. Kun's Finance Commissar Eugen Varga hailed runaway inflation as the best method 'to liquidate bourgeois possessions',[29] with the result that no one left with any choice in the matter wanted to use the official currency. 'You were lucky if a cabman consented to take his fare in Comrade Varga's banknotes, instead of some more valuable object in your pocket.'[30]

Meanwhile Education Commissar György Lukács (whose father had been elevated to the Hungarian peerage) always had funds for his pet projects of musical and dramaturgical didacticism. Not content with defending his Marxist cultural rationalisations through prose of a viscosity that even 1960s French philosophers struggled to match,[31] he 'emptied the Budapest theatres by imposing on them his own taste [...] few people could bear [Henrik] Ibsen, [August] Strindberg, Gerhart Hauptmann and [Arnold] Schoenberg as their exclusive daily entertainment'.[32] Such proselytism – enforced over the protests of actors often too hungry to memorise their new roles[33] – inspired an underground joke at communism's expense:

Organiser	Come the Revolution, we will all eat caviar.
Recruit	But I don't like caviar.
Organiser	Come the Revolution, you will like caviar.[34]

Unlike Bavaria's Marxist carnival, Hungary's required foreign intervention to end it. During June, under French military protection, an anti-Communist government-in-waiting took shape at the southern city of Szeged. It appointed as its War Minister the most famous of Hungarian admirals, Miklós Horthy. Czech and Romanian armies had by this stage invaded. Even granting unlimited public access to stagings of Strindberg could no longer ensure the Hungarian commissars' political survival. Clemenceau made further military support for Hungary dependent upon the Soviet Republic being terminated. By 1 August Kun could hold out no more. Late that day, profusely weeping,[35] he resigned and absconded by train to Vienna, taking with him two dozen of his henchmen, among them Varga and Rákosi. (Accounts differ as to whether Szamuely, at the Austrian frontier, was gunned down by a border guard or killed himself.) Karl Renner's cabinet first kept the Hungarian arrivals under arrest, then ordered their deportation to the Soviet Union. Out of the blue, Lenin purported to discover a grand historical necessity in the embarrassing downfall of Kun, whom he had so long backed. At a 1924 executive meeting of the Socialist International, Lenin (as reported by Marxist intellectual Victor Serge, there present) upbraided his former protégé in the most derisive terms:

> Kun kept his big, round, puffy face well lowered; his sickly smile gradually faded away. Lenin spoke in French, briskly and harshly. Ten or more times, he used the phrase *'les bêtises de Béla Kun'*: little words that turned his listeners to stone. My wife took down the speech in shorthand, and afterwards we had to edit it somewhat: after all it was out of the question for the symbolic figure of the Hungarian Revolution to be called an imbecile ten times over in a written record![36]

❀ ❀ ❀

It appeared to Karl and Zita all too likely that Vienna would soon emulate Budapest in terms of berserker Marxism. Already in March 1919 Karl had penned, and sent by special courier, a missive to Alfonso XIII, explaining to him the Bolshevik danger not to Hungary and Austria alone, but to all the former empire's component states. Alfonso forwarded the message to George V, who felt ashamed about his failure in 1917 to compel Lloyd George's cabinet to offer asylum to the Romanovs. (Upon the news that the Tsar and his immediate family had been slaughtered in Ekaterinburg, King George seethed at the British political class's failure to rescue them in time: 'If it had been one of their kind,' he complained, 'they would have acted fast enough. But just because the poor man was an Emperor – !'[37]) The preceding February, Prince Sixtus, on Poincaré's recommendation, met both the King and Queen Mary at Buckingham Palace, wishing to impress upon them the urgency of Karl's concerns and the danger to the Habsburg family if Bolshevik influence spread to Vienna.

Queen Mary, 'very moved, turned to the King and said: "What Sixtus has told us is very serious"'.[38] In general George V had, like his spouse, sagacious political instincts.

Well before the Great War had finished but with an Allied victory on the horizon, he recommended that in a post-Hohenzollern Teutonic environment, 'the kings, princes, grand dukes and dukes [be] restored to the positions of prestigious independence which they had enjoyed before Bismarck's wars had united Germany under Prussia half a century earlier'.[39] While this plan had none of the vote-catching appeal which 'Hang the Kaiser' sloganeering enjoyed, it possessed over such sloganeering the advantages of prudence and foresight. (Nor was King George alone in advocating it. French historian Jacques Bainville – in his book *Les Conséquences Politiques de la Paix*, the very title of which alludes to John Maynard Keynes – independently counselled the same policy after the Treaty of Versailles had been signed.)[40]

But George too seldom acted on his instinctive horse-sense. He feared exceeding his constitutional limits – unlike his father, who had initiated in person what became the Entente Cordiale without asking permission from (or even consulting) his Foreign Secretary. Nothing alarmed George V more than the peril of Lloyd George doing to him what Groener and Hindenburg had done to Kaiser Wilhelm, or what Renner and Károlyi had done to Emperor Karl. The 'Welsh Wizard' harboured passionate republican sentiments, which he voiced years later, when he defied a royal request to abstain from publishing his embittered wartime memoirs. 'He [the King] can go to hell. I owe him nothing. He owes his throne to me.'[41]

At any rate, a certain Lieutenant-Colonel John Summerhayes, from the Royal Army Medical Corps, went to Vienna with King George's full approval. Karl wrote on 21 February – in French, then still the customary diplomatic tongue – to thank the British monarch, who had shown himself to be (as Karl's 1968 biographer neatly put it) 'a friendly head of state if not the head of a friendly state'.[42] But Summerhayes, whom the Emperor called '*un homme charmant* [...] *avec beaucoup de tact et d'amabilité*',[43] soon had his commission withdrawn: Britain's War Office regarded his presence as an excessive risk to future dealings with the Austrian republic. In his place went (at the King's own behest) another lieutenant-colonel, Edward Lisle Strutt, a Catholic and fluent in German, who – as emerges from the diary which he kept of his time with the Habsburgs – became genuinely fond of his imperial charges.

Mere goodwill, though, could not counteract Renner, whose hostility to the Habsburgs' continued Austrian presence grew more and more pugnacious. Renner (under pressure from radical leftists in his own ranks) demanded that both Karl and Zita give up all claims to the throne, and content themselves with being mere private citizens, if they wished to remain in Austria at all. Were they to keep making their claims, Renner would ensure their banishment; if they tried to resist banishment, they would be locked up. Strutt realised that meeting Renner face-to-face would be necessary, although it might not be sufficient, for helping the Habsburgs. Once in the Chancellor's office, Strutt showed Renner a telegram which he had prepared and, he said, was entirely willing to send to London's Director of Military Intelligence: 'Austrian Government refuses permission for departure of Emperor unless he abdicates. Consequently give order to re-establish blockade and stop all food trains entering Austria.'[44]

Strutt knew how Renner, or any Austrian in 1919, would react to the terrible word 'blockade'. Renner, after exclaiming '*Grosser Gott!*', paused and then added, 'All right, he [Karl] can go.' 'Without any conditions?', asked Strutt. 'Yes,' responded Renner.[45] The telegram was, of course, a total fake. Strutt had banked on Renner failing to comprehend how little power a mere 'Director of Military Intelligence' had to initiate

British policy, let alone to initiate policy that ran counter to everything which the anti-Habsburg Clemenceau wanted. But this 'wildest and most improbable of bluffs'[46] achieved its object. Renner caved in to Strutt's demand that Karl and his family be permitted to leave Austria for Switzerland, without any preparatory talk of abdication.

Before departing, the Emperor issued a document known as the Feldkirch Manifesto, in which he explicitly stated that he abandoned none of his monarchical rights, and that he considered Austria's republican administration to be 'null and void'.[47] Thus openly flouted, Renner pushed through the legislature a statute not only forbidding the Habsburgs to set foot in Austria again unless they specifically swore allegiance to the republic (which some of the dynasty's members did), but confiscating all Habsburg property in Austria. This vengeful law, unlike Kun's millenarian fantasies in Budapest, remained on the books for decades.

Meanwhile those Hungarians who had championed Kun's utopia were increasingly wishing that they had never been born. Admiral Horthy, no great thinker or great orator – he had spent so long outside Hungary that he 'spoke Magyar with a pronounced German accent'[48] – nevertheless knew the political chance of a lifetime when he saw one. Plausibly enough to attract the Hungarian masses, Horthy talked and acted as if Judaism and Marxism were one and the same. He knew that they were not; Hungarian Jews knew that they were not; and numerous extremely rich Hungarian Jews would afterwards give Horthy their full backing. But the state of absolute fright which Kun's antics had instilled in Hungary's non-Communists made most of them extend to Horthy tolerance, if not active approval. As a recent Hungarian historian commented:

> In vain did the representatives of the Jewish community and moderate conservative politicians, as well as independent writers, try to prove that most Jews not only did not ally themselves with Bolshevism but that, on the contrary, many industrialists, landowners and merchants [under Kun] were stripped of their assets, arrested or held as hostages.[49]

Likewise in vain did Horthy attempt to curb the lethal anti-Jewish excesses of his notional subordinates, among whom paramilitary leader Pál Prónay became particularly prominent. The chances are that Horthy (who did not achieve his subsequent career pinnacle through any excessive penchant for asking awkward questions) seldom wanted to know of pogroms carried out during the resultant White Terror, and that if he ever had wanted to know, Prónay would simply have continued ignoring any official calls for comparative restraint.

Briefly, in August 1919, Archduke Josef August, a distant relative of Karl's and one who had survived the Soviet Republic unscathed, served as Hungary's head of state. In this role, which he regarded as mere deputising for a restored Karl (the precise term used to convey the Archduke's function was the German *Reichsverweser*, roughly translatable as 'Regent'), he appointed a Prime Minister: not Horthy, but István Friedrich, who, before entering Károlyi's cabinet, had been – of all unexpected occupations – a soccer player at national level. The Archduke did not enjoy his new dignity for long. Duly overawed by the British and French governments' censure of him for his dynastic links (Clemenceau wrote a typically sharp note on the subject),[50] he resigned from his job within three weeks of accepting it, although Friedrich continued as Prime Minister until the following November. Never again did the Archduke attract international notice; he preferred quiet and useful labours at the Hungarian Academy of Sciences.

Eventually Horthy emerged as the most conspicuous candidate for the nation's leadership. The Hungarian parliament voted on 1 March 1920 in favour of Horthy (131 deputies supported him, whereas only seven deputies supported his sole rival, the septuagenarian Count Albert Apponyi). Yet, cannily, the Admiral refused to call himself president, nor did he wish the assembly to address him by that title. Instead, he became – like Archduke Josef August, but with much more durability – 'Regent'; and his homeland again bore the name 'Kingdom of Hungary', thereby prompting the famous witticism about Hungary being 'a kingdom without a king, ruled by an admiral without a fleet'.

That Horthy lacked a fleet was the Treaty of Trianon's doing. This treaty, in all respects a great deal more punitive than that Versailles arrangement which moved Western liberals to Keynesian dirges, 'sums up for all Hungarians to this day the most devastating tragedy in their history':

> In the Trianon Palace, in the park of Versailles, the Allies presented the death certificate of the 1,000-year realm of St Stephen, and two representatives of Hungary, whose names have long been forgotten, had to sign the dictated settlement on behalf of the government and parliament. On that fateful day, 4 June 1920, church bells rang all over the country, black flags flew over buildings, traffic came to a standstill, newspapers appeared with black borders, and funeral services were held in churches.[51]

Little wonder. Before the war, Hungary had covered 282,000 square kilometres. After Trianon, a mere 93,000 square kilometres were left to it. The Allies rewarded Romania, Czechoslovakia and Yugoslavia with copious spoils. Romania obtained 102,000 square kilometres of territory in which 5.4 million Hungarians lived; Czechoslovakia, 63,000 square kilometres of territory in which 3.5 million Hungarians lived; Yugoslavia, 21,000 square kilometres of territory in which 1.5 million inhabitants lived.[52] The Yugoslav acquisitions included the port of Rijeka, better known to the world as Fiume, which had previously been Hungary's main outlet to the sea. Whatever Woodrow Wilson had meant (on the optimistic assumption that he meant anything) by the 'right to self-determination', the exercising of this right by Hungarians cannot have been a part of it.

Even this crushing humiliation did not destroy Horthy's own fundamental Anglophilia. But it accentuated his eagerness to use that Anglophilia for his own benefit. If he could defend his enthusiasm for retaining office by invoking British desire for him to continue, so much the better. Outwardly he seemed like the sailor he had always been, rich in that dogged, unintellectual straightforwardness associated with the nautical life. 'He probably could not,' his biographer from 1994 concedes, 'have defined or explained such terms as the "Szeged idea", liberalism, or fascism.'[53] Nevertheless, in private he had few superiors when it came to self-interested guile. Lack of interest in, or talent concerning, abstract ideas can perfectly well coexist with impressive self-preservation. So it did with Horthy, who profited further from (to quote his biographer again):

> his tendency to blame others for his own failures or mistakes. […] Horthy truly believed that his own motives were always pure and honourable, and that he never told a lie or betrayed a friend. Yet the disinterested historian can identify numerous occasions on which Horthy told untruths. Already in the 1920s, in the face of much contrary evidence, he was explaining to visitors that he had never aspired to be Regent and had hoped that Count Apponyi would be elected.[54]

For Horthy, as for certain blithe heads of government after him, any foreign or domestic unpleasantness had to be someone else's fault. This instilled in him a confidence valuable for his own interests, not least against antagonists like Karl and Zita, hamstrung as they were by moral scruples about bloodshed.

Scarcely had Horthy been declared Regent than disquieting reports about his behaviour reached the imperial family in Switzerland's Wartegg Castle (itself belonging to Zita's father). At a time when Europe's upper classes regarded oath-keeping as sacrosanct, Horthy had sworn twice to obey his sovereign: first in floods of tears at a meeting with Karl himself during the Great War's very last weeks, and again when accepting the regency. To the Hungarian army officer Count Antal (or Anton) Sigray, Horthy proclaimed: 'You can spit in my face if I am anything but the most emphatic legitimist.'[55] Now he had not only ensconced himself in Budapest's royal palace, but begun to regard himself as his own king, and denied to British diplomats any enthusiasm for reinstating Karl on the throne:

> Initially he had sent his monarch loyal messages of support, requests for permission to act, and assurances that all government was being carried out in his name and in the prospect of his return, but gradually things changed. Horthy established a new oath of allegiance for officers in the armed forces, which bound men to the service not of their monarch but to Horthy personally.[56]

Such arrogance might have admitted of an innocent explanation. But the monarch concluded that there was only one way to find out.

Karl believed that his best course of action would be simply to turn up, unannounced, in Hungary and insist that Horthy make way for him. He chose the 1921 Easter weekend (26–27 March) for his journey, before which he shaved off his moustache and acquired a bogus Swiss passport.

After he arrived at Szombathely in Hungary's extreme west, he met several prominent supporters, including Colonel Antal Lehár (younger brother to Franz Lehár, composer of *The Merry Widow*) and József Vass, Education Minister in Horthy's cabinet. Szombathely's own bishop, János Mikes, also gave Karl his blessing. Hungary's Prime Minister – by this stage Pál Teleki – happened to be visiting Sigray's home for the

Easter break. At first Teleki expressed alarm over the arrival of Karl, whom he entreated to go back to Switzerland. But on realising that his pleas had no effect, he reluctantly joined the imperial party, hoping that the showdown with the Admiral would not be too painful. Whether accidentally or on the Prime Minister's instructions, Teleki's chauffeur took a wrong turn on the route to Budapest.

When Karl reached the capital's royal palace, Horthy had just sat down to lunch with his wife Magda. He initially appeared the model of friendliness, hugging Karl as if he were a beloved son. Then subject and monarch spent the next two hours in the palace's main office, which Horthy now occupied. 'The most difficult moments in my entire life', was how Horthy afterwards described those two hours, which he also called 'thoroughly odious'.[57]

Karl expressed gratitude for the Regent's service, but made it clear that he had no intention of letting the regency continue: he flatly told Horthy to 'hand over power to me'. Appalled, Horthy protested: 'This is a disaster. In the name of God, Your Majesty must leave at once and return to Switzerland, before it's too late and the [Entente] Powers learn of your presence in Budapest.'[58] Yet the more Horthy begged, the more imperturbable Karl became. Hoping to gain some ascendancy over the Admiral, Karl switched to speaking German, one of the seven languages in which he could fluently converse.[59] He reminded Horthy of the latter's pledges to serve the Habsburgs. Horthy tried to shirk this unpleasant topic by maintaining that his subsequent oath to serve the Hungarian nation (an oath which he had sworn to the parliament) outweighed any earlier vow. He also bemoaned the suddenness of Karl's arrival, and complained that he should have been given advance warning.

Obstinately Karl avoided rising to this bait, preferring to stress legal issues. Since he had never abdicated, all oaths made to him (whether by Horthy or by anyone else) continued to bind those who took them. He cited the names of Teleki, Vass and Sigray as being willing to hold office in an imperial cabinet, and threatened Horthy with 'simple revolution' if he refused to give the regency up. When the Admiral attempted to direct the conversation into side-issues about precisely where a restored monarch would live, and how the Admiral himself would fare in any new monarchical dispensation, Karl responded by emphasising that Horthy need not fear going unrewarded. Quite the opposite: he would be made Prince of Otranto and Szeged, as well as being admitted to the Orders of the Golden Fleece (membership of which he had long coveted) and of Maria Theresa. Yet not one of these prizes would he receive, unless and until he stepped down.

Horthy continued to reject resignation. Then the monarch put him unmistakably on the spot, asking him how he planned to circumvent the impasse. Did he envisage (Karl asked) the *arrest* of his sovereign? At the very idea of such impudence, Horthy 'turned red with shame and answered in the negative'.[60] Very well then, what choice (Karl wanted to know) did Horthy have, if he possessed no intention of putting his sovereign under guard, except to resign? 'I stick by my position,' the sovereign asserted. 'I'll give you five minutes to think it over.'[61]

Until this point, Karl held – the metaphor's regality is apposite – every court card in the pack. But he omitted to allow for Horthy's deviousness in playing for time. Horthy, simulating alarm at Karl's apparent fatigue, summoned a servant to bring dinner for himself and Karl: dinner which soon arrived, and which monarch and subject ate. The interval of this repast enabled Horthy to fortify himself with new objections to Karl's enterprise. He pleaded the precariousness of his regency's position against dangers, foreign as well as domestic; and (rather cheekily, in the circumstances) Karl's own less than stellar performance as monarch in 1918. 'Your Majesty,' he announced, 'I must choose between my loyalty to the dynasty and to my nation. I choose the nation, and will not hand over the government, because in twenty-four hours this unfortunate country would be occupied and partitioned.'[62]

Karl denied that this would occur, on the grounds that he had guarantees of support from a 'prominent statesman'. Quizzed as to who this 'prominent statesman' might be, Karl wrote on a slip of paper – after insisting that Horthy keep the matter confidential – one simple word: 'Briand'.

This revelation frightened Horthy a good deal. The preceding January Aristide Briand had become France's Prime Minister again. Horthy distrusted French politicians in general, not least thanks to their indispensable role in forcing the Treaty of Trianon upon him, and thanks to their having backed the so-called 'Little Entente' of Czechoslovakia, Romania and Yugoslavia against any Hungarian hopes of regaining lost lands. At first Horthy greeted Karl's mention of Briand by arguing that he had firm written evidence of French opposition to a Habsburg comeback. Karl continued to state the contrary. Fearing total defeat, Horthy sought a few weeks' grace in order to prepare for a transfer of power in Budapest. Karl pointed out that three weeks from 27 March would be 17 April. 'So, Horthy, if you are not in Szombathely on that day, I will be in Budapest on that date.'[63] To placate the Admiral – who, he honestly believed, would keep his word and spend the next three weeks making the capital Habsburg-ready – he gave him then and there the Order of Maria Theresa's Grand Cross.

Whereupon, anticlimactically, Karl departed (via one of the palace's back doors, at Horthy's insistence) and entered a chauffeur-driven car that took him to Szombathely. The car being without a roof, and therefore exposed to the elements, the exhausted and insomniac Karl, who had not brought or been offered an overcoat, was soon overcome by uncontrollable shivering. By the time he and the chauffeur reached Szombathely late that night, influenza had set in. Once again, as with Teleki's trip earlier, there occurred perhaps deliberate delays which made the drive much longer than it would normally have been, although this time the car's alleged mechanical faults, rather than any wrong turn on the driver's part, incurred the blame.

Having farewelled the monarch, Horthy greeted the group which now awaited him outside his office. The group included Teleki, two future Prime Ministers – one of them being Count István Bethlen, the other being Major-General Gyula Gömbös – and Prónay. Upon Horthy's announcement that Karl would soon be back in exile, Gömbös launched into a sycophantic encomium of the Admiral, maintaining that Hungary had been saved by Horthy's effort. Later Horthy revealed, not to Gömbös but to an aristocratic friend, how much that effort had cost him. He suddenly burst into tears and bewailed his action: 'I, the old soldier, have broken my oath!'[64]

Over the next week, a flurry of telegrams passed between Szombathely and Budapest. Teleki cabled Lehár, to state that henceforth any orders which Karl gave would be ignored. Horthy, meanwhile, asked Maurice Fouchet (the French ambassador to Hungary) whether Karl had told the truth in boasting of encouragement from Briand. Fouchet, with some of Horthy's own flair for postponing a tricky decision, asked if he might be granted leave to consult Paris. But unquestionably Briand had denied to Fouchet, the preceding month, that he had any desire to let a Habsburg be sovereign over Hungary again. Horthy, thus encouraged, sent to Szombathely Count Bethlen and another leading politician, Count Gyula Andrássy (whose father and namesake had been among Franz Josef's prime ministers). As backup, if these civilian figures proved insufficient to force Karl across the border, some of Prónay's troops accompanied them.

Despite all this, Karl continued to believe that he could trust Horthy, saying, 'I can't have been so dreadfully mistaken' about the Admiral's character.[65] On 5 April, a sadder but wiser Habsburg boarded, with his remaining retinue, the train from Szombathely to Switzerland. The Swiss government, having previously allowed Karl and his family to remain on Swiss territory as long as they refrained from political activism, made it clear to the refugees that it would now give 'political activism' a wider and wider definition. With the advantages which hindsight bestows, it is plain that Karl, amid his showdown with Horthy, made three fundamental mistakes.

In the first place, the monarch overestimated his bodily strength. Although during much of the Great War he had been robust enough to perform active military duty, from late 1918 onwards he seldom spent a month in good health. The influenza pandemic of 1918–19 nearly carried him off; he also suffered from heart disease; his post-1919 activities are an almost constant chronicle of great stoicism when faced with, at the very least, chills and bronchitis. Given the coincidence of his worst physical illnesses with his worst political hardships, pronounced psychosomatic elements cannot be excluded.

In the second place, Karl failed to press home his initial advantage over the Regent. Permitting Horthy to stall, by ordering dinner, meant that thereafter Horthy – however much the reference to Briand alarmed him in the short term – could set the tone of the discussion in the long term. The monarch's own personality rendered him liable to this misjudgement:

> Though no coward, he was also no *beau sabreur*, and that was what the emergency cried out for. A ruthless man of action would have driven straight from the palace to the headquarters of the Budapest garrison to summon the officers and men to fall in behind their crowned king, whose portrait was still looking down from the walls. [...] Returning as he did to Szombathely, his hands empty of anything but promises, left him with no chance at all.[66]

Throughout, Karl deluded himself into the supposition that Horthy meant the same things as he himself did when he spoke of loyalty and service. The Admiral, in truth, inclined to Humpty Dumpty's manipulative lexical fudging, as expounded by Lewis Carroll:

> 'When *I* use a word,' Humpty Dumpty said in rather a scornful tone, 'it means just what I choose it to mean — neither more nor less.'

> 'The question is,' said Alice, 'whether you can make words mean so many different things.'

> 'The question is,' said Humpty Dumpty, 'which is to be master — that's all.'

In the third place, Karl harmed his cause by not bringing Zita with him. Hungarians of Horthy's background prided themselves on their chivalric devotion to women, and especially to authoritative women. Zita demonstrated a ruggedness of temperament, and a sharpness of tongue, far surpassing her husband's. She had even dared to reprimand, at an official luncheon while the war raged, Germany's Admiral Adolf Karl Henning von Holtzendorff. When she deplored the suffering which the war had already brought about, Holtzendorff (campaigner for unrestricted use of submarines against Entente and neutral ships) snapped back: 'Suffering? What does that matter? I work best on an empty stomach. It's a case of tightening your belt and sticking it out.' Zita responded: 'I don't like to hear talk of sticking it out when people are sitting at a fully-laden table.'[67]

It is impossible to imagine Zita sharing her spouse's predisposition to allow Horthy's feints, attempts to divert the talk into trivia, and sheer greed for those trophies that lay within Karl's gift. Moreover, Zita, Karl and Horthy had known since childhood the role played by the chivalric impulses of Hungarian magnates during one of the empire's gravest crises: that moment in 1741 when the young Empress Maria Theresa – helpless against Frederick the Great's invading forces – pleaded for the magnates' military aid, and reinforced her plea by bringing to the assembly her infant son Josef. Overwhelmed by the spectacle of this beautiful blonde damsel in distress, the Hungarians shouted in Latin: '*Vitam et sanguinem pro rege nostro Maria Theresia*' [Our life and our blood for our king [*sic*], Maria Theresa!][68] All that Zita needed to do was combine outward vulnerability with inward determination, and Horthy would probably have done whatever she wanted. So would most ordinary Hungarians who saw her.

There remained, naturally, no chance of keeping the Karl-Horthy meeting secret. Horthy decided, after his Easter reprieve, to make an official tour of the nation. He met conspicuously less than wholehearted plaudits:

> Everywhere he was received either in silence or with cheers for the King, and he could not openly resent loyalty, for he still pretended to be loyal himself. The Hungarians, who have always prided themselves on their courage, were roused to enthusiasm by the action of a King who had ventured to come alone to claim his rights. They resented the airs and graces of the Regent, were shocked to see him take possession of the Castle of Gödöllö and shoot the Royal coverts. [...] In parliament, soon after the King's departure, a vote of thanks and confidence in Horthy was violently opposed, and Count Bethlen actually voted against it.[69]

Chastened but undaunted, Karl – in the spirit of 'If at first you don't succeed' – vowed to try again. He found the opportunity to do so in the following October, with a campaign that differed in many ways from the previous one. A particularly clear difference lay in the method of transportation:

> Although the Danube route seemed one obvious way of getting into Hungary, a far more efficient means of travel was now at hand and one which would minimise the need for elaborate subterfuge, forged passports, and the like. [Karl] could fly into his kingdom. His supporters went into action and through a discreet network of contacts a small

private light aeroplane was obtained, and plans laid for a great venture. The King would be flown into Hungary, muster support among loyalist troops and seize power at the palace in Budapest, putting Horthy's supporters under arrest.[70]

Air travel offered for the couple 'the triple advantage [...] of maximum speed, maximum security, and maximum surprise'.[71] Assurances of physical safety, not so much. We of the 2020s have become so blasé about aeronautics that without substantial imaginative feats, we cannot grasp the level of valour necessary for making any plane trip during the 1920s. (And for a long while afterwards. In 1936 and 1937, leading confederates of General Franco perished in two separate air crashes, their deaths helping to prolong Spain's civil war.) Neither Karl nor Zita had ever flown previously, and Zita was pregnant with her eighth child in October 1921. She later recounted, to Karl's biographer, the experience of being airborne in a Junkers *Monoplan* (which had a single 180-hp engine):

> The Emperor and I were seated right at the back of the plane, behind the wings, and both of us felt somewhat giddy. But [...] I remember the Emperor saying thankfully once we left the Swiss mountain scenery behind us and were safely coming down over the plains of our homeland: 'I would never have thought that a great flat stretch of stubble fields could be so beautiful.'[72]

Horthy suspected that something was afoot, since he commanded that Major Gyula Ostenburg's battalion, noted for its legitimist sympathies, leave its position near the Austrian border and return to Budapest. Ostenburg had been in contact with Lehár's nearby forces, and Lehár continued unshaken in his Habsburg fidelity. Once the royal couple had arrived in Hungary it looked at first as if nothing could go wrong with the royals' campaign:

> As the train rolled inexorably forward, town after town declared allegiance to [the Habsburgs], and soldiers, instead of stopping him, joined his forces. It seemed as though the tragic muddles and problems that had beset the Easter bid were not to be repeated and that finally all was going to be well and the great opportunity seized.[73]

The Regent had every reason to be afraid. As one commentator acridly observed, Horthy 'was at a loss to find enough regular troops who might be relied upon to fire at the King'.[74]

Alas, not being a Mafioso, Karl did not appreciate the deep wisdom behind the gospel 'Keep your friends close and your enemies closer.' Bethlen, who had taken over as Prime Minister from Teleki the preceding April – and who anticipated the British politician said to have 'sat on the fence so long that the iron entered his soul' – announced: 'We wish to solve the dynastic question with patience and honourable goodwill [...] therefore we will accept neither those who think they can restore the King by force nor those who are only concerned with taking his crown from him.'[75] The last thing which the Habsburg troops wished or needed to hear was Bethlen's declaration of 'A plague on both your houses.' József Vass now equivocated. General Pál Hegedüs, who had hitherto been fond of proclaiming his Habsburg loyalty, did more than equivocate. He so worried about a showdown with the Regent that (notwithstanding the little matter of having sworn not once but twice, like Horthy, to defend his monarch) he ostentatiously relayed details of the royal progress to three Entente officials based at Sopron – seventy-three kilometres to Szombathely's north – 'as it would make a better impression not to deceive them'.[76] Karl, having suspected Hegedüs from an early stage, nonetheless promoted him to the role of commander-in-chief solely because the all too self-effacing Lehár, who would have been much better in the post, had vouched for him.

In the long run (indeed in the short run also), where Horthy was, there would Gömbös be; and that fact, more than any other, decided the outcome. Unlike Hegedüs who had turned his coat, Gömbös disdained any concealing of his Habsburgophobia. Manpower he lacked, since so many professional servicemen had defected to the royals. His best hope lay in attracting male undergraduates to the colours. Fortunately for him, his political armamentarium still contained one weapon not yet used – a veritable Big Bertha among weapons – to be aimed at the royal troops with terrifying outcomes, and Gömbös now resorted to it, evincing an ingenuity which commands reluctant respect.

The weapon was simple and bold. Gömbös accused his monarch of being ... a Bolshevik puppet.

Discharged as it was when memories of the Hungarian Soviet Republic's miseries remained open wounds on the body politic, Gömbös's armament did the intended damage. Karl's 1932 biographer takes up the story:

> Technical students [of Budapest's university] had proved very useful patriots, resisting Communist attacks after the withdrawal of the Romanians. They might serve again. Gömbös had the town plastered with posters during the night, announcing that hordes of Czechs and Communists were at the gates, that it was the duty of every able-bodied man to shoulder a musket and save the population from pillage, ravage and destruction such as had been known in the days of Béla Kun. He called the students together and addressed them as follows: 'Our poor, well-beloved King has been led astray by Czechs and bands of Communists and is now advancing at their head against the capital. It is our duty to deliver the King out of their hands and save our country from a foreign occupation.'[77]

Falstaff asked, rhetorically:

> What is honour? A word. What is in that word 'honour'? What is that 'honour'? Air. A trim reckoning! Who hath it? He that died o' Wednesday. Doth he feel it? No. Doth he hear it? No. [...] Therefore I'll none of it. Honour is a mere scutcheon. And so ends my catechism.[78]

So, in 1921, ended Hegedüs's catechism too. Gömbös, by contrast, at least joined battle – the battle being the events of 23–24 October at Budaörs, a suburb of Budapest.

Karl, from a wholly divergent standpoint to Hegedüs's, loathed the thought of warfare as much as Hegedüs did. No one needed fewer reminders than Karl of how the cataclysm of 1914–18 had turned much of Europe into a necropolis. But also, no one needed fewer reminders than Karl of what it means to be a monarch. Forces on the royal train were fired on by approximately eighty of Gömbös's student irregulars. Karl's loyalists soon deterred these students; but the loyalists, shocked to discover that they were driving off mere uniformed boys, waited for their sovereign to give further commands. The commands never came. Characteristically but ill-advisedly, Karl, instead of taking the lead, insisted on going to Mass. The delay did his campaign great hurt.

Horthy, having found professional troops still loyal to him, led them into action. For the royalists, confronting lads from technical college was one thing; confronting an established army was something else. No soldiers can ever predict how they will cope at the very first time in their lives when they hear shots fired in anger. Some of Karl's rawest recruits decided that they could endure no more, and deserted. A ceasefire came into effect before nightfall; under cover of the ceasefire, desertions from the royal ranks continued, while Horthy's ranks mostly stayed intact. The following morning, Ostenburg and Lehár rushed from the train, 'prepared to lay down their lives in his [Karl's] defence'.[79] Their sovereign wanted none of it. From the train he yelled at his champions: 'Lehár! Ostenburg! Stop and come back here! I forbid any more fighting. It's all quite senseless now.'[80] The two men returned to the carriage, and the train left. Never more would Karl set eyes on the land over which he had once reigned.

On Horthy's side, nineteen soldiers had been killed, and sixty-two wounded. The precise body-count on the other side is mere guesswork: there were, at any rate, enough dead royalists to require the hasty digging of mass graves, with no markers. For Horthy, the proverbial 'fog of war' had its benefits. When issuing commands to his forces, he gave as little publicity as possible to his foes' exact leadership. Many of those under his command – in the artless words of one royalist participant, Aladar von Boroviczényi – 'did not know that they were fighting the King, still less that they were firing upon the Queen'.[81]

After 1921, with a repetitiveness comparable to a broken gramophone record, Horthy and his apologists (whether at home or elsewhere) insisted that letting Karl regain his Hungarian crown would have so angered the Entente powers as to guarantee another war in Eastern Europe, and probably another war in the rest of Europe. How much validity did this contention have in practice?

There cannot be a scintilla of doubt that insofar as the definition of Entente anger included mere words, Horthy was right. In London and Paris especially, cabinet ministers and newspaper editorialists greeted the vanquishing of Karl with unconcealed relief. Similar official sentiments came from their counterparts in Prague, Bucharest, and Belgrade. But Horthy did not confine his predictions to the issuing of such official communiqués. It behoves us to examine the surviving evidence for his strenuous allegations that mere words would have been followed up by actual blows.

If any Western country in late 1921 was likely to have sent in troops to thwart Karl's comeback, France was that Western country. Within two years, it will be recollected, the French (who kept conscription after the Great War, as the British did not) occupied Rhineland territory. But however habitual such defiance in foreign affairs became under Clemenceau and Poincaré, it operated nowhere when more emollient leaders occupied the nation's two highest offices, as in 1921. Between 1914 and 1918 almost two million Frenchmen, from a population of thirty-nine million, had lost their lives: with all the demographic implications of such a casualty rate. What likelihood existed that any of the most prominent French politicians in 1921 – Briand himself as Prime Minister; President Alexandre Millerand; cabinet ministers André Maginot (of subsequent Maginot Line celebrity) and Jean-Louis Barthou – would have aggravated France's demographic disaster by waging additional warfare to bail Horthy out? None of these men can, by any accurate use of language, be called a warmonger. Briand's aversion to warmongering was exactly what made Karl's trust in his help a substantial risk for royalist ambitions.

That which can be said of French politics in 1921 goes double for British politics. By 1921, the calls for Kaiser Wilhelm's hanging had faded to complete silence. More and more, Britain's leaders put their faith in the League of Nations, wanted to help Germany back on her feet, and had reverted to the centuries-old pre-1914 national resentment of anything Gallic. Profound war-weariness dominated all political parties: a war-weariness so great that Ireland's declaration of independence – the very suggestion of which independence had destroyed Gladstonian liberalism decades earlier – became a mere *fait accompli*. Lloyd George, failing to register this spectacular change in the public mood, rattled the British sabre in 1922's Chanak Crisis, wrongly convinced that he could repeat his former magic spells, this time against Mustapha Kemal's leadership of Turkey. He soon discovered that those spells had lost their efficacy. Most of his own followers opposed him, most Conservatives opposed him, and (perhaps most humiliating of all) Canada and Australia – dominions which for four years had given abundantly of their blood and treasure to assist Britain – refused all military aid to Lloyd George. Soon afterwards he had to leave 10 Downing Street, never to re-enter. As Stanley Baldwin would find to his great electoral advantage, most Britons in the 1920s longed, above everything, for European peace (they continued longing for it until well after Hitler emerged). If peace entailed acquiescing in Karl's enthronement at Budapest rather than squandering British lives upon essaying his expulsion, then that seemed a bearable penalty.

As for the USA, its leaders in 1921 craved, if anything, even more obliviousness to continental European squabbles than Britain's did. Woodrow Wilson, whose aims of a third term in the White House were doomed by a massive stroke, completed his transition from world messiah to national pariah. His preferred presidential candidate James Cox had lost the 1920 election in a landslide to the placatory Warren G. Harding, who said what isolationists wanted to hear. Any American chief executive who in 1921 had recommended despatching doughboys across the Atlantic anew, this time to prevent Karl from wearing the Magyar crown, would have been viewed as a certifiable lunatic. Wilsonian tropes about the evils of Old World monarchical corruption still played, now and then, in Peoria; but they were oratorical boilerplate rather than signals of actual Washington policy. At elections and elsewhere, most American citizens showed that while they bore the League of Nations' members no ill-will, they wanted their country to mind its own business.

So much for the (Big) Entente, in connection with the Habsburgs. What of the Little Entente?

Granted, Romania's government wanted to make Hungary's admission to the League of Nations conditional upon its repudiation of Karl. But Count Apponyi, on Hungary's behalf, pointed out that the League had no authority to dictate the constitution of any country within the League or outside it; that the Treaty of Trianon had been silent about prohibiting a monarchist restoration; that requiring Hungary to throw away its rights as a sovereign state before it could enter the League was unacceptable and would antagonise other sovereign states; and that if the League's vows to protect states against foreign aggression applied anywhere, they must apply to protecting Hungary against the Little Entente. The League allowed Hungary to join in September 1922;[82] Romania preferred not to press the issue overmuch, being forced to concentrate upon the more immediate problem of Soviet ambitions in Bessarabia.

Czechoslovakia, unlike Romania, possessed a government anti-Habsburg in its very essence. The government's two principal figures, President Tomáš Masaryk and Prime Minister Eduard Beneš, yielded to none in their determination to make Hungarian monarchism unviable. But they overplayed their hand. Britain and France grew so vexed by obstreperous Czech talk of invading Hungary during November that they sent Beneš an official warning to end such talk.[83] The Czechs, in any case, 'could not depend on the Slovaks'.[84] That scission between the two peoples which in 1993 would become complete, had its origins in Slovaks' umbrage, between the two world wars, at rule from Prague.

Yugoslavia's King Alexander I proved equally reluctant to turn anti-Habsburg pronouncements into renewed anti-Habsburg martial action. Though the King had long fought against everything that Karl embodied (Serbia had been among the most severely affected of all Great War belligerents, in terms of casualty rates relative to the national population), during the 1920s he had his hands full trying to stop his Serbian, Croatian, Bosnian and Slovene subjects from wiping each other out. Amid an otherwise unmemorable June 1928 session in Belgrade's parliament, a Serbian deputy suddenly produced a pistol and slew three Croatian deputies in cold blood. Eventuall,y Alexander himself would meet a violent end; in 1934 at Marseille, he was murdered by a terrorist doing the Croatian Ustaše's ugly work. (The aforementioned French politician Jean-Louis Barthou, sitting beside Alexander, died from police crossfire.) This was the first political assassination captured live, in part, by movie cameras.

Nor did bigger powers have any greater taste for intervening against the Hungarians. Italy's administration in 1921 had grown so pusillanimous, and its established legislative groups so incapable of overcoming Communist-derived unrest, that it was no longer a question of *whether* the Fascisti would constitute the leading movement in national politics, it was a matter of *when*. (The March on Rome occurred the following year.) In short, the menace – however obsessively Horthy spoke about it – of foreign armed wrath against a Hungary incautious enough to revert to Habsburg kingship was among the feeblest, and the most cynically deployed, of all possible paper tigers.

There is little to tell about the remaining six months of Karl's brief, poignant, humbled terrestrial existence. The Swiss authorities had by this stage decided enough was enough, punctilious though Karl had been in notifying them of his voyages. Monarchists who stayed on Hungarian soil, Andrássy and Sigray included, developed a disturbing tendency to find themselves inside Budapest's Pestvidék prison. Ödön Beniczky, one of the persecuted monarchists, dared to ridicule his interrogator, who had asked: 'Which office did the Right Hon. Gentleman contemplate in case of success?' Benicky answered: 'My hobby, photography. I have an amateur ciné-camera. It would have given me great pleasure to snap you all, Gentlemen, in case of success, while you were doing homage to His Majesty.'[85]

Briand, washing his hands of their incriminating Habsburg residue, 'invited' – Briand's own word – Horthy's cabinet 'to hand over the King's person to the British naval Danube flotilla presently in Budapest'.[86] At first Lloyd George and his cabinet colleagues contemplated bringing Karl and his family (now, on Horthy's orders, confined to Tihany Abbey, more than 100 kilometres southwest of the capital) to Malta, but before long they discarded this plan, since 'the majority of those present were opposed to Great Britain being his gaoler'.[87]

One other destination remained; Portugal continued to be Britain's oldest ally. Which is how, on 19 November, the Habsburg exiles – Horthy being only too glad to see the last of them – came to be deposited at Funchal, on the Portuguese island of Madeira.

Penury now loomed. The governments of Britain and France decided that the Little Entente's rulers, plus Poland's, should pay for the upkeep of the imperial family. No such payments arrived: 'not a farthing was either offered by or extracted from Warsaw, Prague, Belgrade and Bucharest'.[88] Archduke Robert, one of the Habsburg children, needed to undergo an operation by a Zürich specialist early in the New Year. With great reluctance, Switzerland's government allowed Robert and his mother to visit the city, but the local law enforcers kept vigilant eyes on them. 'Each sister leaving the Zürich nuns' hospital […] had her veil lifted by the police to make sure it was not the royal visitor slipping away in disguise.'[89]

To raise funds both for the Funchal tenancy and for young Robert's surgical procedure, Karl and Zita decided to part with some extremely valuable heirlooms, consigned to a Zürich bank vault. Bruno Steiner, an Austrian lawyer, had the responsibility of looking after them. When Zita's brother Prince Javier made inquiries, fearing the worst, he discovered that Steiner had vanished from the city. He managed to locate Steiner not in Zürich but in Frankfurt, at a hotel into which the lawyer had far-sightedly checked under a pseudonym. Once tracked down, Steiner hastily assured Javier that the jewels continued to be safe, and that he himself would give them to the prince next morning at eight o'clock. With laudable scepticism concerning Steiner's honesty, the Prince returned to the hotel an hour earlier than the planned rendezvous. Even that proved too late, because by seven o'clock Steiner had already fled. The jewels which the Habsburgs had intended to sell were nowhere to be found. Nor was Steiner.[90] Once again, Karl had let his gullibility be exploited by a confidence trick.

By March 1922 the last Emperor's wife and older children realised that he had not long to live. Apart from anything else, the shortage of affordable fuel at the family home meant that he was freezing to death. Even in our own age, when central heating and electric radiators are common, Portuguese residences – predominantly built for comfort in summer – often manage to be shatteringly cold in winter. A hundred years ago they were much more disagreeable. At least one servant felt indignant on the refugees' behalf. An Austrian chambermaid who waited upon the Habsburgs at Funchal wrote the following to her parents:

> Down in the town it was very pleasant, but their poor Majesties have no
> money and were no longer able to pay the expensive hotel and therefore
> a banker who was a joint owner of all the hotels on the island of Madeira

offered this villa to their Majesties free of charge, and because of their money embarrassment, they accepted this gratefully. Up here on the Monte [Quinta do Monte], the weather is only bearable in May and June. Down below, the sun shines every day and when it rains, it is not for long, but up here we have had only three warm days. [...] I am terribly upset about this. I am writing without their Majesties' knowledge. I just cannot bear that these two innocent people should be left for so long in this completely inadequate house. Someone ought to lodge a protest![91]

Any ordinary man too ill to leave his bed (as by March 1922 Karl usually was) would have consented to the calling of a doctor. Karl, no ordinary man, held out for a week against this. He believed that summoning medical help would be irresponsibly extravagant. By the time he relented and allowed two physicians to examine him, he could not stop coughing, while his temperature had shot up to 104°F. The doctors tried their best, but in that pre-antibiotic epoch, their best wrought no improvement. His lungs ravaged, he soon could no longer breathe without extra oxygen supplies, and those supplies on Madeira were few enough. No self-pity passed his lips. He regarded his afflictions as a sacrifice, saying at one point: 'I must suffer like this, so that my peoples can come together again.'[92]

On 27 March he summoned his eldest son, Archduke Otto, to the sick-room. He told Zita on the morrow: 'I would have liked to have spared him [Otto] all that yesterday. But I had to call him to show him the example. He has to know how one conducts oneself at times like this – as a Catholic and as an Emperor.'[93] Thereafter Karl kept praying to Christ and to the Virgin Mary. As he clutched a crucifix, his mouth formed one last word: 'Jesus'.

From early in the afternoon of 1 April, after life's fitful fever, Karl slept well. He had not yet turned 35. Zita, for the rest of her days, wore black.

Few in Britain, other than King George and Queen Mary, grieved over Karl's demise. (One Briton who did was Hilaire Belloc, a repeated eulogist of the last Habsburg ruler in the pages of *G.K.'s Weekly*.)[94] Much grief manifested itself elsewhere. When the news of Karl's death reached Austria, his 1932 biographer happened to be in that country. 'I found mourning almost universal,' the biographer reminisced:

> especially among the poorest classes. Subjects, who had listlessly accepted a sort of anarchy, seemed to forget their share in the catastrophe, recalled only the virtues and the misfortunes of their lost Lord. Flags were flying at half-mast, shops closed, dour Tyrolese peasants in tears. [...]
>
> A solemn Requiem was held in the Coronation church at Budapest. A vast concourse thronged round a lofty catafalque, filled every crevice, overflowed into the square, where, five years previously, the Monarch had received the frenzied acclamations of his people. Now a motor-car suddenly thrust through the kneeling worshippers. Police outriders loudly demanded passage. 'Make way for his Highness the Regent!' and a figure in full uniform, bedizened with medals of valour and crosses of chivalry, stepped out clutching a garish wreath in his arms, stride briskly

into the church, deposited his tribute, turned and departed whence he came. Five short months ago he had ordered out machine-guns; now he had the insolence to offer flowers.[95]

Not all Hungarian politicians appeased Horthy. The national parliament's sole female member, Margit Schlachta (who later founded the Sisters of Social Service), vigorously dissented from the November 1921 law by which the Regent stripped the Habsburgs of all their rights. With boldness rare among Hungary's male legislators, she announced: 'I vote against this law which exiles an exemplary Christian family, I vote for a noble Queen and mother and her children, I vote against this bill and I pray for a great Christian woman, benefactress of the poor people of my apostolic Hungarian country!'[96]

❀ ❀ ❀

Otto was still a mere 10 years old in 1922. Those willing to fight on an adult claimant's behalf understandably jibbed at doing so for the sake of a claimant far too young to shave. Zita conceded the justice of this attitude, and contented herself with overseeing her eldest son's education until he reached man's estate.

While Hungary's politics groaned and travailed, Austria's had settled down to a certain trucial shabbiness. Karl Renner, who knew whereof he spoke, called Austria 'a republic without republicans'.[97] At the Requiem Mass in Vienna's *Stephansdom* for the repose of Karl's soul, shouts of 'Down with the Republic!' emerged from the crowd.[98] In Budapest, or in Hitler's Berlin, these shouts would have provoked whiffs of grapeshot (and probably much more). Not in Vienna, where, for well over a year after the war, simple shortage of food mattered much more to the masses than squabbles over different forms of administration. Foreign correspondents, though in many instances battle-hardened, expressed shock at the scene: 'Death itself is not so tragic as the lives of the Viennese children, who are now a race of pygmies. Children ten years old look as if they were seven. In the public kitchens there were children of three or four years who were unable to walk.'[99]

Herbert Hoover, already one of the best known and most esteemed living Americans because of his food aid programs, helped to quieten Vienna down (and would play a similar role in assisting the end of Kun's regime) by making charitable assistance to the capital conditional upon political peace. A 1974 survey informs us that Hoover:

> To counter a reported uprising in Vienna scheduled for 1 May, authorised the city government to post the following proclamation on the city walls:

> Any disturbance of public order will render food shipments impossible and bring Vienna face to face with absolute famine.
> HERBERT HOOVER.

In his description of the incident, Hoover states tersely: 'May 1 came and went quietly.'[100]

Every description of Austria, however terse, is apt to include the untranslatable German-language noun *Schlamperei*, perhaps best rendered as 'bet-hedging slovenliness', the opposite of that steel-helmeted militarism traditionally associated with Prussia. *Schlamperei*, more than any other motivic force, kept the First Austrian Republic alive. Few hated it enough to slay it. Brief right-wing coalition cabinet succeeded brief right-wing coalition cabinet. That Austro-German union which Renner had sought, the Treaty of Saint-German (which the Entente imposed on Austria in September 1919) now prohibited. The Socialists, with the hard-nosed Renner in temporary eclipse after the Treaty came into force, merrily set to work making themselves unelectable by campaigns vociferous enough in their Marxism to scare the electorate, but seldom merciless enough to threaten regime change. Except in July 1927, when a Socialist mob took to Vienna's streets and set on fire the Justice Ministry; in response, government troops had no compunction about shooting into the crowd, killing almost ninety of the insurgents. By the gory criteria of Budapest and Berlin in 1919–20, this pacification counted as almost benevolent. Dominating the political landscape, whether Chancellor or no, was Ignaz Seipel: more exactly, *Monsignor* Ignaz Seipel, he being one of two twentieth-century priests who headed Central European governments. (The other was Slovakia's wartime leader Jozef Tiso.) Seipel, when discussing monarchism in a 1925 periodical article, dismissed monarchist dreams in one devastating sentence: 'I believe in the resurrection of the dead, but only on Judgement Day.'[101]

Once Seipel relinquished the chancellorship (1929), his dauphin Engelbert Dollfuss came increasingly to the fore, despite not heading the government till 1932. To quote the blunt description of Dollfuss's 1961 biographer: 'he was born a bastard and only grew to be five feet high'.[102] One atrabilious English observer complained of Dollfuss that 'the expression of his face is feeble, he walks like a well trained marionette'.[103] This was not the general view of the Chancellor's compatriots. Origins out of wedlock caused nothing like the scandal in the Catholic Austria of 1892 that they did in, for instance, Presbyterian Scotland and Unitarian Massachusetts at the time. As for Dollfuss's small size, he took most jokes about it in good part, though not the widespread description of him as 'Milli-Metternich', a taunt devised by National Socialists.[104] Both in boyhood and in adulthood Dollfuss inspired adulation as well as aversion. (In surviving newsreels he bears a curious resemblance to his almost exact coeval and fellow vertically challenged authoritarian: Louisiana Governor Huey Long, similarly cut down by gunfire at his political zenith.)

During the year in which Dollfuss became Chancellor, Otto celebrated his twentieth birthday. (He undertook some of his university tuition in Belgium: specifically, at Louvain, where his French counterpart, the Comte de Paris, also studied.)[105] Upon the death in 1930 of another Habsburg scion, Archduke Rainier, Zita had given orders for the Viennese obsequies to be a grand production number as of old: complete with the call-and-response ceremony outside the Capuchin crypt. A report by the unidentified Austrian correspondent for *Time* magazine burdened the ailing Seipel with the full weight of those Homeric compound-adjectives which the weekly's house style then decreed:

> In the opinion of Zita it is about time that her Otto received proper publicity in Vienna, for he reaches his majority next November. She therefore staged the first full-dress Habsburg funeral in Vienna since the War. Pope Pius XI is supposed to favour the candidacies of Otto, which would account for the presence of beak-nosed, bald-headed former Prime Minister Seipel, a Monsignor. Quite unimportant was

the presence of the dead man's father, Archduke Leopold Salvator von Habsburg who recently published his piquant autobiography: *From Archduke to Grocer*.[106]

Zita's approach had reason behind it. Her biographer explained why:

> Horthy now seemed immovable as regent in Budapest and the monarchist movement which swirled around him was divided into several opposing currents. But in Republican Austria, which the Habsburg exiles had for so long written off as a hopeless cause, their prospects were growing steadily brighter. Sympathy had begun to flow both from the bottom and the top of the political scale […] It seemed to be lapping too around the Chancellery in Vienna.[107]

Dollfuss's ferocity in hounding the organised Left during February 1934 disturbed both Zita and Otto, who both believed that a monarch should transcend the strife which sundered parties and social classes. But at least Dollfuss had metamorphosed into what can best be called an anti-anti-monarchist. He knew that, were Austria to keep any prospect of resisting both Berlin's and Moscow's lures, hard martial power would not suffice. What we nowadays call 'soft power' had become equally vital. An Austrian newspaper report from 28 September 1933 included the following explicit condemnation by Otto of the National Socialist pressure that threatened Dollfuss:

> Through Duke Max [von Hohenberg], son of the Crown Prince Franz Ferdinand who was assassinated at Sarajevo in 1914, the Archduke Otto has accepted honorary citizenship in the towns of Hain, Mamau and Ragelsdorf and [these] have pledged allegiance to the Pretender, hoping that he will soon be sovereign. … Duke von Hohenberg presented the Mayors of the three towns with letters signed, 'Otto in Exile' stating that the exile was doubly hard when the fatherland was heroically fighting for existence against malicious and unscrupulous attacks. Archduke Otto condemned the Nazi movement and added that he trusted the present regime would remove the remaining unjust laws of the revolutionary period against the Habsburgs. He trusted the day was not far distant when relying on God's help, and with a strong hand, he would lead the Homeland to a happy, certain, and great future.[108]

Sir Charles Petrie – British historian, Conservative Party activist, unsinkable monarchist – knew Vienna at first hand, met Dollfuss, and summarised the Chancellor's strategy:

> The textbooks used in the schools were revised, and all uncomplimentary references to Austria's previous rulers were excised; the old pre-war uniforms were restored for ceremonial purposes; and the regimental bands toured the rural districts playing such national airs as the 'Radetzky March.' […] In the past it had been the dynasty, rather than any national feeling, which held the country together, and the ordinary Austrian thought of the state in terms of the reigning monarch.

Such being the case, it was hardly surprising that the first result of this traditionalist campaign should have been a widespread revival of Royalist feeling. For more than a decade the Habsburgs had seemed forgotten in the land which they had ruled for centuries, but when Austrians were officially requested to direct their gaze upon the past, they naturally began to remember their old dynasty. Photos of the Archduke Otto were seen in the shop windows, and township after township made him an honorary citizen. How far Dr Dollfuss was prepared to go in the direction of a restoration of the monarchy it is impossible to say, and in an interview which the present writer had with him a few months before his death he was manifestly unwilling to discuss the subject. Nevertheless, he was too intelligent a man not to see whither this movement must tend, and that the exaltation of dead Habsburgs must inevitably stimulate interest in their living representative. At this time, too, not a few Socialists were quite willing to see the Archduke on the throne, for they felt that under his rule they would have far greater freedom [...][109]

Sadly, Dollfuss reckoned without the sheer scale of Hitlerite infiltration. On 25 July 1934 Austrian Nazis stormed the Chancellor's headquarters. Though they failed in their aim of seizing power for themselves, they shot Dollfuss and deliberately let him bleed to death, scorning to summon for their victim either medical or sacerdotal assistance. Sir Austen Chamberlain, who had been Baldwin's Foreign Secretary, voiced his disgust in a letter to his sister Ida:

> I feel almost physically sick when I think of the murder of Dollfuss & I cannot get it out of my thoughts. Cold-blooded murder of a defenceless man is always revolting, but to leave him to linger on in agony, refusing to allow him either a doctor or a priest, seems to me to reach the limit of callous brutality. I have never met a man who captured my sympathy more quickly; he was so transparently honest, so simple & so brave & withal had a personal charm which is so rare.[110]

Dollfuss's burial interred the Habsburgs' best Viennese hope. The Chancellor's successor, Kurt von Schuschnigg, talked a great game about his fundamental pro-Habsburg beliefs; but Zita and Otto found to their exasperation that the more he talked, the less he acted. He refrained even from repealing the law which blocked Otto and his mother from visiting Austria. Conscious Horthy-type deceit towards royalists played no discernible part in his outlook. Rather, as his résumé showed on numerous occasions between his accession to the chancellorship and the 1938 *Anschluss* which hurriedly ended his career, he never missed an opportunity to miss an opportunity.

Long before Dollfuss became Vienna's most powerful man, but long after Horthy became Budapest's, occurred a bizarre postlude to the saga of Hungarian monarchism. It had as its protagonist Harold Sydney Harmsworth, first Viscount Rothermere, owner of the *Daily Mirror* and *Daily Mail*. (Baldwin, not in most circumstances a vituperative man, famously denounced at a public meeting Rothermere and his fellow newspaper tycoon Lord Beaverbrook for having sought 'power without responsibility – the prerogative of the harlot through the ages'. Upon which outburst a habitually tactless member of the House of Lords is said to have spluttered: 'Good God, that's done it. He's lost us the tarts' vote.')[111]

Rothermere – like the other press baron in his family, his elder brother Lord Northcliffe – possessed in good measure that attribute which mass media titans so often find beneficial: a sublime imperviousness to reality's constraints. In this attribute, as in the ease with which he could be hoodwinked, he resembled his most renowned fictional analogue: Lord Copper, from Evelyn Waugh's *Scoop*. ('Mr Salter's side of the conversation was limited to expressions of assent. When Lord Copper was right, he said, "Definitely, Lord Copper"; when he was wrong, "Up to a point".')

Those who found it essential to hoodwink Rothermere included his mistress, Stephanie Hohenlohe, who first met him by design at Monte Carlo's roulette tables in early 1927. Beautiful and crafty, Stephanie paid dutiful attention to Rothermere's grumbles about how boring the *Daily Mail* had become, after which recital of woe she took the opportunity to explain to him Hungary's fate. The country's post-Trianon plight moved her to great eloquence, but given her pulchritude, she could have discoursed about trigonometry or Hegelian metaphysics and she would still have held the infatuated Rothermere spellbound.

Over lunch at the Rothermere home, Stephanie showed her new admirer a map of Hungary that she found in a volume of *Britannica*, Rothermere having hitherto been ignorant of where Hungary was. At no point had geographical details figured in what Rothermere's well-wishers charitably called his education. He assured Stephanie: 'My dear, until today I had no idea that Budapest and Bucharest are two different cities.'[112] Clearly this man deserved to be entrusted as soon as possible with the destinies of several million benighted foreigners.

Under Stephanie's guidance, Rothermere wrote and published articles fervidly denouncing the Treaty of Trianon. To say that the articles inspired pleasure among Hungarians is to understate the case. Hungarians adored the articles, vying with each other to contrive the most insanely inflated estimates of Rothermere's cosmic significance. 'Rothermere,' proclaimed Budapest newspaper editor János Rákosi (unrelated to the Communist Mátyás), 'will have a full chapter in Hungarian history to himself.'[113] According to Ferencz Herczeg, novelist and anti-Trianon activist, Rothermere's articles had left the greatest impact on humanity 'since Gutenberg invented printing'.[114] Two hundred thousand telegrams, letters, and postcards reached Rothermere from Hungary, compelling him to hire two Magyarophone assistants to deal with the epistolary inundation. So many Hungarians (more than a million of them) wrote and signed expressions of gratitude to Rothermere that before these thank-you notes could be presented to him in person, they needed to be leather-bound in twenty-five volumes. 'Had there not been a deadline for the presentation,' Horthy asserted, 'the entire nation would probably have added their signatures.'[115]

The hysteria must have amazed even Stephanie. It indubitably delighted her. And it delighted the German Nazis to whom she clandestinely answered. She corresponded with Hitler himself, who either did not know about or did not object to her Semitic blood. He supplied her with a photograph of himself, on which he had written: 'To my dear Princess Hohenlohe – Adolf Hitler.' (Czech Foreign Minister Jan Masaryk, speaking of this photograph, loftily referred to Stephanie as 'this world-famous secret agent, spy and swindler, who is a full Jewess.')[116] Though armed with a Hungarian passport, Stephanie spoke none of the Hungarian language: her English was near-perfect. When she sneezed, her besotted lover caught cold.

Not that Rothermere needed much inducement from her to praise the NSDAP's boss. Once Germany's 1930 Reichstag election produced a spectacular upsurge in the National Socialist vote, it made Hitler a front-page news story again, as he had ceased to be after the Beer Hall Putsch's failure. Once Hitler had gained the chancellorship in January 1933, Rothermere sent to him a letter of congratulations. He would send another letter of congratulations each January until 1939; and panegyrics to the Third Reich characterised his newspapers. Like every other right-wing *nouveau-riche* fool at the time, Rothermere imagined that Hitlerism amounted to nothing more than an unusually argumentative form of conservatism. That Hitlerism involved actual revolution, he never comprehended this side of the grave.[117]

Yet Hungary, not Germany, remained Rothermere's principal preoccupation. The more paeans from the Hungarians came his way, the more enamoured he grew, from 1927, of what he hoped would be his future. A member of the Harmsworth clan had already been acclaimed as Hungary's saviour. Why (he thus wondered) should not another member of the Harmsworth clan be acclaimed as Hungary's *king*?

Happily for the Magyar race, Rothermere had for the monarchical role the perfect candidate: his own son, Esmond Cecil Harmsworth, 29 years of age, wartime officer in the Royal Marine Artillery, and House of Commons backbencher since 1919. Esmond could no more speak Hungarian than Rothermere could, though military service had at least acquainted Esmond with aspects of continental life closed to his father. His existence lacked all Hungarian connections. No matter: Rothermere determined that his son, while not born to the purple or desirous of achieving the purple, would have the purple thrust upon him.

Paternal pride is explicable; but it speaks volumes for the surreal atmosphere of Budapest politics in 1927–28 that those influential Hungarians championing King Esmond the First were taken very seriously, rather than being ushered into the nearest detoxification unit. Rákosi, for one, recommended that a Harmsworth mount the throne. A letter from Rothermere to Stephanie includes the following delirious opinion: 'If they want to save the monarchy in Hungary, then there is only one man who is able to do so – Esmond Harmsworth. No Habsburg or royal prince from somewhere else can accomplish it.'[118]

When Esmond visited Hungary, to collect the honorary doctorate from the University of Szeged which had been awarded to his father, the mayor of Budapest greeted him, along with 'several former prime ministers [...] and a crowd of about 100,000 appeared in front of his hotel'.[119] In the capital, Boy Scouts marched in his honour, as did employees from the post office and the railway network. He met Horthy, Bethlen (still Prime Minister), and Cardinal-Archbishop Jusztinián György Serédi. Lest the foregoing welcome should bespeak undue moderation, the government arranged still more rejoicings:

> Organisations ranging from the right-wing 'Awakening Hungarians' to
> the Jewish Ladies' Auxiliaries were represented at the various festivities.
> A firework display from the citadel of Buda and a grand map of the old

and the amputated Hungary, symbolically depicted in a football stadium by girls wearing national costume, completed the program of events in Budapest. Harmsworth next travelled with his escort by special train to Debrecen and to Szeged, where a street was renamed 'Rothermere.' An array of other streets, parks, gardens and settlements throughout the country and even a tennis trophy were named in his honour, and articles, songs and odes were dedicated to him.[120]

Then Harmsworthomania dissipated as abruptly as it had started. Rákosi found that his own enthusiasm for a kingly Harmsworth irritated Mussolini, whose favour the Regent courted. The Duce, with considerable asperity, informed his Hungarian guest that just as he opposed the idea of a Habsburg restoration, he also opposed the idea of a foreign journalist's offspring making Hungary into a global laughing-stock by wearing the crown.

Horthy and Bethlen, though willing to entertain Harmsworth at a banquet, drew the line at enthroning him. They had not banished Karl in order to undergo the dubious privilege of submitting to an English commoner. Gömbös, as might be predicted, rejected Rothermere-style monarchism with contempt; and his contempt counted for a large amount in national life, especially from 1932, when Horthy appointed him prime minister. He remained in this position until his death in October 1936. Obituarists quoted Horthy's words on Gömbös's passing: 'I've lost my right hand.'[121]

By that stage Stephanie and her paramour had fallen out. From 1932 to 1939 Rothermere gave Stephanie regular monetary gifts, and when these stopped, she took legal action against him. The outbreak of war meant that more pressing suits than hers occupied the British courts, and Rothermere's book on the subject of Hungary – not to mention the subject of Hitler's political genius – appeared shortly before Wehrmacht tanks barrelled into Poland. Its embarrassed author, who in the book had concealed Stephanie's pivotal importance in the whole business, died in November 1940 while on a Bermuda vacation.

Rothermere's majestic pipedreams had their farcical elements; but such farce never ventured long from tragedy, as is the case with the single most popular novel that the Habsburg imperium ever inspired.[122] Historian Edward Crankshaw referred to this novel's military anti-hero, when pondering the former Habsburg lands' inter-war calamities:

> In the end the whole terrible story was reduced to the horizon of 'the good soldier Schweik'. That, perhaps, could have been endured if only the good soldier Schweik had been determined to defend his birthright, instead of surrendering it to the first plausible rabble-rouser.[123]

Chapter IV

The Shadow of the Bourbons
France

Even paranoids have real enemies.
Anonymous 1960s American
bumper sticker[1]

No mere Eurostar train can hope to bridge the gap between England's political ethos and that of France. For proof, we need only consult the history of French monarchism, not least during its inter-war zenith.

Let us imagine a milieu where a lad of powerful but unfocused literary gifts, brought up in a respectable Catholic middle-class household, has his religious belief destroyed in adolescence by the combined effect of deafness and positivist metaphysics. Primarily an autodidact – his loss of hearing having cut him off from most possibilities of interaction with equals – he reveals in adulthood an awe-inspiring gift for attracting followers, and a flair for journalism at its most ruthless. This flair he devotes to a program that in 1890s Paris seemed only marginally more promising than flat-earthism: re-establishing monarchy, not as mere constitutional ornamentation, but as the founding principle of all government, allied to a church in which he himself has ceased to believe. His brilliance wins grudging respect even from those with most cause to resent him, and when he joins forces with a colleague as Rabelaisian and epicurean as he himself is austere and eremitic, cabinet ministers tremble. Half a dozen world-famous authors have him and his colleague to thank for publicising their output. Cherished by several-hundred-thousand fellow Catholics but eventually excommunicated by the Vatican, he wins over new admirers (and repels many old ones) by his anti-German invective, only to go on trial for his life a generation afterwards on charges of collaboration with the Wehrmacht. He avoids the death penalty but spends six out of his last seven years in prison. While incarcerated, he maintains a protracted and mutually polite correspondence with Portugal's prime minister.

In England, and probably in Scotland and Wales also, at any period over the last century-and-a-half, this odyssey would have been so unthinkable as to seem insane. Political life in those countries does not work that way; neither does scholastic life. But in France, the odyssey did happen. The biography of Charles Maurras, who along with his ally Léon Daudet, made the Action Française movement into a political powerhouse, shows both the virtues and the dangers of a culture in love (sometimes to the point of disaster) with ideas as ideas: a culture where English-style slothful anti-intellectualism remains to this hour inconceivable.

France's Third Republic had stumbled into existence not because of any importunate demand for it, but because, after the collapse of Napoleon III's empire with defeat in the 1870–71 Franco-Prussian War and after the suppression of Paris's brief Commune, the two most obvious alternatives to middle-of-the-road republicanism were unworkable. The loss to Germany of Alsace and Lorraine continued to be the great national humiliation ('Think of it always,' Prime Minister Léon Gambetta counselled, 'speak of it never':[2] his countrymen obeyed the first injunction but ignored the second). Successive French republican cabinets became international by-words for corruption. A seemingly unstoppable 1889 coup attempt by the populist General Georges Boulanger, presenting himself as a new broom sweeping clean the executive and legislature, failed at the last moment when the great man suddenly backed down and remembered a previous engagement with his mistress. (He nevertheless had so terribly panicked the incumbent administration that to this day, French officials have never dared to name a street after him.)[3]

Above all, from 1894 to 1906 the Dreyfus Case – many Frenchmen referred to it simply as *l'Affaire*, not needing to specify it further – turned into a low-level civil war. It pitted parents against children, brothers against sisters, and tore apart innumerable decades-old friendships, in the same way that the Vietnam War did well within the memories of millions now alive. A much-anthologised two-panelled cartoon from around 1900 has, in its first panel, a host at a French family dinner instructing everyone: 'Above all, let's not speak of the Dreyfus case!' In the second panel the dinner has turned into chaos, the chairs have been overturned, and the caption says: 'They spoke of it.'

With no true leader visible on the horizon after Boulanger's disgrace, the long-standing French itch for personal despotism had no outstanding candidate to scratch it. There remained, though, recollections (fading recollections, since fewer and fewer people in the late nineteenth century could personally recall France before Napoleon III's tenure) of conventional, non-Bonapartist monarchy: first the Bourbon restoration of 1814–1830 presided over by Louis XVIII and Charles X (both brothers of the martyred Louis XVI), then the Orléanist constitutional monarchy of 1830–1848 embodied in the humdrum King Louis-Philippe, arguably the biggest bore France's ruling class has ever produced. There is something to be said for boredom; how much, was detectable from the ordeals and feuds of French politics between 1870 and 1914, when political boredom had grown rarer than four-leaf clovers.

Earlier in the nineteenth century, the Bourbons and the Orléanists hated each other – the Bourbons found unforgivable the vital role of Louis-Philippe's treacherous father, Philippe Égalité, in the 1793 regicide – yet the passing of time had softened this mutual aversion, and by the 1890s the two parties had arrived at a truce. The direct male line of the Bourbons had ceased in 1883, with the death in Austrian exile of Charles X's grandson Henri, the Comte de Chambord ('Henri V' to his adherents). Shortly after the Commune's suppression, the Comte looked to have a good chance of becoming the next French crowned head. This chance he botched, through his insistence that his future subjects forsake the tricolour flag of republicanism and revert to the flag which had characterised earlier Bourbon rule. His demand so outraged republican feelings that his monarchical candidacy died then and there. Pope Pius IX, though himself monarchist to the core, deprecated the Comte's self-defeating vexillological stubbornness: 'Who ever heard,' the pontiff allegedly asked, 'of a man giving up a throne for a napkin?'[4]

But the monarchist dream did not disappear with Chambord. Nor could it disappear, the French being almost as habitually inflamed by their history as the Irish are by theirs. (Marshal Pétain was never more wrong than when he protested in a 1941 broadcast: 'French people, you have a short memory [*Français, vous avez la mémoire courte*].⁵' French people's memories tend to strike most politicians as uncomfortably protracted.) While Chambord's heir dwelt perforce in Belgium, forbidden under pain of imprisonment to put one foot on French soil, this émigré status did not doom his hopes and in some respects it improved them. The whole Jacobite saga confirms that a 'king over the water' can, and sometimes does, possess a power of enchanting the public mind that no mere king in our midst can do. (It is the gallant fugitive Bonnie Prince Charlie who flourishes in the collective imagination: not Prince Charlie the self-pitying, prematurely aged Roman tosspot whom the reality-based community needed to deal with until he drank himself to death in 1788.)

For certain monarchs, a still better reputational move than being exiled involves being dead. (Witness King Arthur: *Rex quondam, rexque futurus,* 'the once and future king'.) Centuries-old Teutonic popular tradition speaks of Frederick Barbarossa not having perished at all, but having immured himself in a cave at Kyffhäuser in Thuringia, whence he will emerge in all his imperial glory, to save the German nation in its hour of direst need. (Neither in 1918 nor in 1945 did the memo reach him.) Or take Portugal's young King Sebastião: had he really died in 1578, as most historians assure us, on the North African battlefield of El-Ksar el-Kebir? Not according to vast numbers of Portuguese, who reckoned that he would one day return, like Barbarossa, with immediate salvific effect. Believers in 'Sebastianism' existed well into the nineteenth century and even, it is said, into the early 1950s.⁶ As these words are being printed, there could well arise a Sebastianist Facebook page.

France itself, in some ways, only became 'France' after 1880, when the program – by Prime Minister Jules Ferry – of free, compulsory, secular school education broke down linguistic barriers, obliged all French citizens to speak French (which beforehand surprisingly large numbers of them did not, or did so with reluctance), and purged differences of dialect in the melting-pot of conscription. Regional sensitivities took a long time to fade. Before they faded, Brittany kept its own counterpart to the Barbarossa-Sebastian legendary archetype: because memories of Nevenoe, the first Breton monarch, endured in local bards' utterances. This one is called *Kan Bale Nevenoe* ('Nevenoe's Marching Song'):

> *Ma'z eo du an noz*
> *Dindan wask pounner ar Gall*
> *Disonjet-krenn eo ho anv [...]*
> *Piv a sammo bir ha kleze*
> *Nevenoe, Nevenoe, Nevenoe!*⁷

(How black is the night / Under the heavy oppression of the Frank / Your name has been lost completely [...] Who will brandish the sword? Nevenoe, Nevenoe, Nevenoe!)

All this nostalgic mythopoeia might seem far removed from late nineteenth-century France. It was not. At that very period, the unclassifiable French political philosopher Georges Sorel explored the power of myth, not in a Grimms' Fairy Tales sense, but in a specifically political sense. Sorel's world-view resists summary. The syndicalist doctrine of triumph through general strike action had a role in it. So did a heterodox Marxism largely stripped of determinism. So did the *élan vital,* that mysterious 'life force' about which Sorel had learnt from Henri Bergson's lectures. So did the conception of discrete historical cycles, one that he derived from reading Giambattista Vico. So did the theory of 'circulating elites' which a much later Italian theorist, Vilfredo Pareto, expounded. And so did meditations on the nature of violence that could well have had their origin in watching many a Parisian gendarme on the job. Nevertheless, Sorel, in his unsystematic, way arrived at a conclusion pertinent to monarchism not in France alone, but also elsewhere.

The conclusion (simplifying it outrageously, with the purpose of keeping this section within manageable length) can be epitomised as follows: we are foolish if we regard politics as purely a matter of what Max Weber called slow boring through hard boards. Nor are we ourselves the more or less insensate playthings of vast impersonal powers, as conventional Marxism would preach. People's shared beliefs as to what is politically true can matter quite as much as, or more than, what actually is politically true. The Hollywood scriptwriter who coined the line 'When the legend becomes fact, print the legend' encapsulated part of Sorel's credo in one immortal sentence.

Besides, although people can adopt their political allegiances through logic, or heredity, or self-interest, or racial background, or class background, these methods of transmission (as Sorel appreciated) are by no means failsafe. Often, people adopt their allegiances through a kind of intuitive, oceanic consensus instead. Contemporaneously with – but independently from – Sorel, Italian Prime Minister Giovanni Giolitti 'spoke revealingly of "beautiful national legends" which sustain a country (and which he didn't want undermined by allowing inquisitive scholars into the archives)'.[8]

'Sustain a country': those, surely, are the operative words. General de Gaulle's entire political survival (and at first his physical survival) would depend upon his ability to construct a 'beautiful national legend' in which forty million Frenchmen somehow heard his defiant radio transmissions; forty million Frenchmen somehow gallantly resisted Pétain and the Wehrmacht for four solid years; Stalingrad, Kursk and D-Day had not the faintest bearing on the outcome; and Vichy was always the fault of the other fellow. Were these lies? They were certainly fantasies; and if they deceived others, they probably deceived de Gaulle too after a while. ('Apart from a handful of wretches,' he surrealistically announced as early as October 1944, 'the vast majority of us were and are Frenchmen of good faith.')[9] But what was his alternative to peddling such arrant nonsense? Civil conflict all over again, this time with Communists calling most of the shots. More sensible, in de Gaulle's view, to impose on the French populace a collective oblivion – a kind of ideological deep-sleep therapy – until everyone with adult experience of the Occupation was safely entombed, and the uncomfortable archival discoveries occurred on some other French ruler's watch.

The oblivion served de Gaulle's interests in another, more personal, sense. It enabled widespread amnesia regarding an exceedingly embarrassing and inconvenient truth: before the Occupation, he had revered none other than Sorel's sometime-ally Maurras, and had esteemed Action Française in general.

From which connections, it will be clear that French inter-war monarchism differed from other countries' inter-war monarchism as plainly as French cuisine differs from Portuguese, German, Austrian and Hungarian cuisines (not to mention Spanish, Greek and Albanian cuisines). Accordingly, this chapter bears little structural resemblance to other chapters. In France, far more than anywhere else, inter-war monarchism was a project of philosophers. It died amid the gory recriminations of 1944–45; it had been born in what we would nowadays call a think-tank. Far from depending on the whims of a particular would-be monarch, it often enough viewed particular would-be monarchs as obstructive nuisances.

An ancient joke defines the typical French intellectual as one who asks: 'Yes, it would work in practice, but does it work in theory?' Action Française lived and breathed theory. To quote the verdict of American historian Eugen Weber, a verdict authentically Gallic in its mixture of neatness with cheerlessness: 'by neglecting the politics of power, the Action Française lost out on the power of politics'.[10] Was it obliged to lose out? Solely by examining Maurras, its *maître à penser* – an untranslatable description which the English language can hope to convey through no more adequate or comely term than 'guru' – will anyone reach an answer to that question.

'My life,' Maurras once avowed, 'is my ideas and my books.'[11] Indeed it was. His birthplace, the Provençal town of Martigues, still seems as if it inhabited a different planet from Paris; how much more different it must have seemed in 1868, the year Maurras was born to a tax-collector father and an exceptionally pious mother. The intellectual and spiritual climacteric in his life came early, at the age of 14; he had to abandon his dreams of joining the navy, because he went almost stone-deaf. From such blows of fate, others have had their religious fervour increased (as did Beethoven); Maurras, by contrast, lost his own Catholic faith, which exposure to Comtean positivist dogmas had already much weakened. Absurdly reductionist though it would be to explain all his subsequent thinking by invocations of his hearing deficit, we may conjecture that a Maurras able to conduct normal conversations with ease – more especially, to conduct with ease normal conversions involving persons less intelligent, less well-read, than himself – would have been likelier to retain, if not faith and hope, then at least a prudential modicum of charity.

But if Maurras had been of the sunniest disposition imaginable, he would still have been faced with the threat to him and to his loved ones from successive French governments determined to retaliate against Dreyfus's enemies, and in particular on the anti-Dreyfusard Catholics. Revenge took such forms as the 1905 Law of Separation (eliminating government funds for religious groups, often driving abroad the members of religious orders), and the previous year's *Affaire des Fiches*, 'Affair of the Cards'. In that imbroglio, officials belonging to Masonic lodges were shown to have kept elaborate card-filing systems for ensuring as few Catholics in the army as possible. (Again, the contrast with Britain is telling. Granted that many British, Canadian and Australian politicians have wished to keep Catholic employees out, they have usually avoided being so stupid as to maintain documented proof of their wish. They have preferred a nod and a wink and the Old School Tie.)

Contrary to what has too often been assumed, Maurras conceded that Alfred Dreyfus might have been guiltless of the charges against him, although on the subject he managed to be thoroughly original and thoroughly offensive. Years after officialdom pardoned Dreyfus, Maurras wrote:

Je ne veux pas rentrer dans le vieux débat, innocent ou coupable. Mon premier avis là-dessus avait été que, si par hasard Dreyfus était innocent, il fallait le nommer maréchal de France, mais fusiller une douzaine de ses principaux défenseurs pour le triple tort qu'ils faisaient à la France, à la Paix et à la Raison.[12]

(I do not want to enter into the old debate [as to whether Dreyfus was] innocent or guilty. My view at first and all along was that, if perchance Dreyfus was innocent, he should have been appointed a marshal of France, but that they should have shot a dozen of his chief defenders for the triple wrong that they did to France, to Peace, and to Reason.)

This is to anticipate. In 1896 Maurras, representing the newspaper *Gazette de France*, had visited Athens (which hosted the first modern Olympics that year) and had undergone some kind of indescribable life-changing epiphany during his visit. 'The glory that was Greece and the grandeur that was Rome' had long been deeply familiar to him, but exclusively when mediated through innumerable poetical and prose texts in Greek and Latin. Now, by contrast, he experienced the classical world for himself. It overwhelmed him cognitively and viscerally. The late Hungarian-American political scientist Thomas Molnar described Maurras's experience thus:

His Greek-Latin *forma mentis* translated for him the image of classical columns to the political architecture of sharp contours and hierarchies within which the citizen occupies his place. Expressed otherwise, there are the multiplicities of civil society, but institutions and finally the hereditary king are at the top. [...] This is not fascism, nor even Nazism, both being too turbulent for Maurras's classical preferences, both alien on account of their socialistic ingredient and enthusiastic but temporary unity, not fixed in institutional form. The Maurrassian edifice is also different from that of Carl Schmitt, the German critic of the modern state, who faulted the Weimar constitution for its failure to make room for a supreme arbiter in case of turmoil and danger. Precisely, the Maurrassian State needed no appointed arbiter, it possessed such a function in the monarch, surrounded by the loyal civil servants of the common good. Thomas More would be a good illustration.[13]

Nine out of ten intellectuals before 1914 would have reacted to the ancient world in the spirit of the most bacchic romanticism. Maurras, ever the maverick, found that the ancient world reinforced his classicism. He prefigured T.S. Eliot and the much lesser known T.E. Hulme – both admirers of his, Eliot's admiration having bordered on idolatry – through the scorching emotion with which he fulminated against the whole concept of scorching emotion. Maybe a self-conscious classicist is by definition a romanticist turned inside-out; undeniably Maurras was, as Eliot and Hulme were. (Maurras owed a much greater literary debt to nineteenth-century French romanticism than he ever wanted to acknowledge.)[14] An American scholar of Third Republic France remarked in 1959: 'Spinoza once urged that the task of the political thinker was to show how men, even when full of passion, could still have fixed and stable laws. Maurras's solution was not to permit the passion.'[15]

Another American expert on the subject, writing in 1962, is similarly emphatic:

> Maurras detested anything that he considered feminine or effeminate, whether it was Romantic literature or what he called 'sentimental' socialism – Maurras once accused Jean Jaurès [the Socialist and pacifist assassinated shortly before the Great War] of having a feminine spirit that sought only to stir up the emotions of his working-class audiences.[16]

There might have been a homoerotic element at work with Maurras, judging by his apostrophe to a young man depicted in a statue at Athens's National Museum.[17] Various friends and foes of his believed that while in Paris he occasionally consorted with female prostitutes, but 'he seems never to have had a steady mistress'.[18] Perhaps he was simply asexual, as his younger contemporary and fellow anti-Romantic Maurice Ravel appears to have been.

Whatever the truth of Maurras's private life, he had systematised by 1900 his principles in what remains his best-known book, *L'Enquête sur la monarchie*, which emerged that year. The anecdote appears too good to be true but is well authenticated: when a Paris journalist, Henri Vaugeois, had finished reading the *Enquête*, he informed Maurras: 'You are the only royalist in France.' Maurras – who, however deaf, could presumably lip-read and could incontestably manage an apt retort – answered: 'Join me and there will be two of us!'[19]

Vaugeois did join Maurras, as, soon, did thousands more. No French readers, however erudite, had previously encountered anything quite like Maurras's style. Against the hieratic *fin de siècle* languor of Arthur Rimbaud, Paul Verlaine and Stéphane Mallarmé, Maurras offered parade-ground commands. Almost every sentence he penned was like a slap to the reader's face. His two most famous epigrams illustrate his method.

The first much-quoted Maurras epigram is straightforwardness itself: *Politique d'abord*: 'politics before all' (a better rendition than the usual 'Politics first'). Maurras was fond of saying that action without politics is as useless as a plough without an ox to pull it. The second, and specifically monarchist, epigram is more elaborate but equally memorable: 'For monarchy to work, one man must be wise. For democracy to work, most people must be wise. Which is more likely?'[20]

Action Française, the movement which – though already existing before Maurras – became the outward and visible sign of Maurras's inward and spiritual creed, impressed large numbers of French people who had never before given sustained thought to the matters that Maurras raised. Never again, while Maurras at the height of his powers held court ('court' being the appropriate term), would monarchism seem musty, quaint, defensive, redolent of the faded photographs in Grand-Tante Marie-Thérèse's album. Edmund Burke and his younger contemporary Joseph de Maistre had made monarchism widely convincing; it took Maurras and AF to make it widely chic. (In this chapter, to minimise confusion, 'AF' will be used to mean the organisation itself, whereas the name of its chief newspaper will be given as *L'Action Française*.) The movement's increasing vogue – which included a large and pugnacious youth wing, the Camelots du Roi – elicited from André Gide one of his few recorded jokes: 'I do not read the *Action Française*, for fear of becoming a Republican.'[21]

During the decades before television, the Internet, and mass higher education had done their frequently destructive work, all Western European lands had periodical markets which flourished to an extent that became unimaginable later. But the flourishing of France's periodical market when Maurras first found a large audience was freakish even then. Six factors, above all, contributed to its strength.

First, the uncompromising and often murderous seriousness of French politics as such, a seriousness which discouraged dilettantism. *Second*, the astoundingly high standards of French school education, which guaranteed that even people who in adult life abhorred each other could communicate via a shared comprehension of Descartes, Racine, Balzac, Stendhal, Baudelaire, Victor Hugo and the rest of the national literary canon. *Third*, the decentralisation (remarkable by Anglo-Saxon or even German criteria) of media ownership: France never possessed a William Randolph Hearst, a Lord Northcliffe, a Lord Beaverbrook, a Rupert Murdoch, or for that matter an Alfred Hugenberg, so that in the early twentieth century almost any Frenchman with something to say could afford to set up – and to disseminate – a magazine of his own. *Fourth*, the tendency of French publishers (both books and periodicals) to release print runs remarkably small by Anglo-Saxon standards; these publishers were less likely than their British or American counterparts to do themselves lasting economic damage by issuing titles in quantities too big to sell. *Fifth*, the absence of an Anglo-Saxon-style lending-library system: those who wanted to read a book or a periodical needed to buy it. *Sixth* (and connected with the first factor), the Gallic distaste for journalism as a mere undergraduate lark: France had – it still has – no equivalent to the Cambridge Footlights, Oxford's *Isis Magazine*, the *Harvard Crimson*, or any such vehicle for generalised yet chiefly apolitical mischief.

The multiplicity of outlets available astonished the young Orwell, when in Paris during 1928. One of his earliest printed essays, 'A Farthing Newspaper' (which appeared under his real name, Eric Arthur Blair), marvelled at the embarrassment of journalistic riches:

> At present France is the home of free speech, in the press if not elsewhere. Paris alone has daily papers by the dozen, nationalist, Socialist and Communist, clerical and anti-clerical, militarist and anti-militarist, pro-semitic and anti-semitic. It has the *Action Française*, a Royalist paper and still one of the leading dailies, and it has *l'Humanité*, the reddest daily paper outside Soviet Russia. It has *La Libertà*, which is written in Italian and yet may not even be sold in [Mussolini's] Italy, much less published there. Papers are printed in Paris in French, English, Italian, Yiddish, German, Russian, Polish, and languages whose very alphabets are unrecognisable by a western European. The kiosks are stuffed with papers, all different. The press combine, about which French journalists are already grumbling, does not really exist in France.[22]

When Orwell wrote, both *L'Action Française* and its parent organisation had just passed their peak of popularity. In the immediate aftermath of the Great War, both had enjoyed exceptional influence. The 1919 general election had seen Maurras' comrade-in-arms Léon Daudet win a Paris seat in the National Assembly, having adopted an openly monarchist campaign platform.

A year older than Maurras, Daudet could not have formed a greater outward contrast with his associate. Expansive in build, a lover of the good life (so determined a diner-out that one wonders how he found time to write his two-dozen odd novels and his six-volume autobiography, not to mention stupendous quantities of journalism), Daudet was the son of Alphonse Daudet, then renowned throughout Europe for his fiction – *Lettres de mon moulin, Tartarin de Tarascon* – and for his play *L'Arlésienne*, which the young Georges Bizet adorned with glorious music. What most of Alphonse's readers never suspected during his lifetime was the nightmare of his final decade, riddled with tertiary syphilis. The available mercury-based remedies for this disease, in that pre-penicillin environment, approached in gruesomeness the disease itself: *Une heure de Vénus, trois ans de Mercure*, ran the astringent French proverb. All these horrors Alphonse faithfully chronicled in a diary called *La Doulou* (preferring the Provençal word over the French *douleur*), so harrowing in its detail that his family dared not release it until 1930, when Alphonse had been thirty-three years in the grave. Life knows few greater torments than watching impotently while a loved parent dies centimetre by excruciating centimetre; and this torment Léon, for all his belligerent audacity, could not avoid. Like Maurras, he needed no private distress to make him a truculent writer. Yet, again like Maurras, he came to regard the outside world as having it in for him personally: a view which a second, much more public, family tragedy in 1923 (the year he left the legislature) would confirm.

For AF and its eponymous newspaper, the French Revolution represented a septic wound so painful that it might as well have happened yesterday. It was to Maurras, Daudet and their adherents what the Great Famine was (and, to a lesser extent, still is) to the Irish: not just an atrocity but *the* atrocity, from which all later evils derived. 'Political realism,' Maurras stated, 'sets against this revolutionary liberty, which destroys the state and the citizen, the concept of the land's traditional liberties [*Le réalisme politique oppose à cette Liberté revolutionnaire, qui détruit l'État et le citoyen, la conception des libertés traditionelles du pays*].'[23] Among those evils AF included Freemasonry, Protestantism, centralism (Maurras's heroes included the Provençal separatist poet Frédéric Mistral, winner of the 1904 Nobel Prize), German militarism and – often Jewish-administered – finance capitalism.

These antipathies did not make AF unique. They were shared by many at the time, in France and elsewhere, who found AF repellent. Surveys like *The Lost Literature of Socialism* (1998), by the late Anglo-Australian political scientist George Watson, demonstrate the fervour with which countless left-wingers raged against their foes in openly racial language. Treated with embarrassed silence ever since, this language was par for the course before 1914. Marx himself, as is (or should be) well known, expressed himself in the grossest terms when discussing both Jewish and Gentile rivals, notably the Jewish socialist Ferdinand Lassalle: 'The Jewish nigger Lassalle,' Saint Karl breezily announced in 1862 to Friedrich Engels, 'is descended from the negroes who accompanied Moses's flight from Egypt (unless his mother or paternal grandmother interbred with a nigger).'[24] One will pore over *L'Action Française* in vain to find in any save its most vitriolic articles Marx's brand of demonisation. But such vulgar abuse as Marx's indicates that blunt ethnic talk was almost as ubiquitous in the nineteenth century as was inadequate plumbing.

AF differed from other French movements not in its concentration of vitriol, but in its conviction that France needed to return to hereditary Catholic kingship in order to be saved. (And not any hereditary Catholic kingship, but hereditary Catholic kingship with some muscle.) By expounding this hereditarian conviction, Maurras in particular hit on an important point which eluded his opponents. To cite Eugen Weber once more:

> The crux of Maurrassian doctrine is not legitimate authority alone but its continuity: the problem of regulating the succession and thus ensuring order untroubled by the seismic effects of political change is solved by the hereditary system, hence by monarchy. [...] Maurras's solution may have been an impossible one, and its form was certainly unpopular; but he came face to face with a question that others continue to ignore.[25]

Hilaire Belloc, himself of half-French parentage, knew Maurras's output as well as anyone in Britain. His 1920 book *The House of Commons and Monarchy*, the product of his own disillusion with the Westminster party system (he himself served in his own nation's legislature for four years, just as Daudet did in his), is imbued with Maurrassianism on each page. A typical excerpt from *The House of Commons and Monarchy* echoes Maurras's championship of regal strength:

> The definition of Monarchy is that there is one real and attainable human head ultimately responsible in any moment for the fate of society. Who prevents an Englishman today from getting a glass of beer when he wants it? Fifty years ago the answer would have been clear – 'The Governing Class' (only no governing class would have been so tyrannical). Who *today*? You cannot answer. It is anonymous. A lot of (unknown) rich men got richer through it. That is all you can say, and that sort of thing cannot last. Well, under *monarchy* the answer would be clear. 'Who stopped your beer?' 'King John.'
>
> 'Why can this man perjure himself unpunished in an attempt to rifle the public treasure? Why is he not punished? Who will punish him?' Today there is no answer. But there should be an answer. 'King Edward.'[26]

Belloc remained a Catholic all his life; Maurras, as we have seen, no longer practised the Catholicism in which he had been nurtured. It may legitimately be wondered what Maurras saw in the Catholic Church that led him to fight for its French subdivision in season and out of season, when he himself had scarcely darkened an ecclesiastical door since his teens.

To this question, Maurras gave two answers which may be summarised thus: Catholicism as national culture; and Catholicism as crowd-control. The former was by no means as eccentric in France as it would have been in, say, Austria or pre-unification Italy. Louis XIV, with his Gallican brand of Catholicism, had been almost as contemptuous of supranational Vatican jurisdiction as Henry VIII had been a century-and-a-half earlier; but unlike Henry, *Le Roi Soleil* remained technically within the Catholic fold. That suited Maurras: a country administered by the Sun King could match almost anything in Protestantism, dictate for dictate, while avoiding the Protestant dangers of atomised individualism. Besides, in Maurras's eyes the Catholic Church at least had the advantage of preserving the best in Greco-Latin civilisation. Through this advantage, it could minimise the harm which, he believed – as the second-century heretic Marcion had believed before him – the Hebraic mindset had done to the world. Marcion condemned the entire Old Testament; Maurras went further, expressing (in a sentence which he afterwards, on reflection, bowdlerised) his doubts about the Gospels: 'I shall not leave the learned retinue of Fathers, of Councils, and of Popes, and all the great men of the modern elite, to put my trust in the scriptures of four obscure Jews [*Je ne quitterai pas ce cortège savant des Conciles des Papes, et de tous les grands hommes de l'élite moderne pour me fier aux Évangiles de quatre juifs obscurs*].'[27]

Regarding Catholicism's crowd-control aspect, Maurras had the acuity to realise that someone or something has to control crowds; and if not Catholicism, what? Mainstream Marxism he wholly rejected, because he rejected all warfare of class against class. Capitalism in its boorish pre-1914 form he equally rejected, as Pope Leo XIII had formally done with his encyclical *Rerum Novarum*.

Socialism, when in a non-Marxist form, did pique Maurras's interest. In 1900 he had declared that 'a socialism freed from the democratic and cosmopolitan element can go with nationalism as a well-made glove goes with a beautiful hand [*un socialisme libéré de l'élément démocratique et cosmopolite peut aller au nationalisme comme un gant bien fait à une belle main*].'[28] The simile was less apposite than Maurras intended, since as Marxist historian Robert Stuart sourly observed, 'Hands manipulate gloves, not vice versa.'[29] Yet that AF actively sought to increase its blue-collar following, and took leading socialists' arguments seriously, is beyond dispute. *L'Enquête sur la monarchie* – in which Maurras quoted both admirers and antagonists at length – cited with approval various prominent socialists from Central Europe.

> When the Austrian socialist [Karl] Kautsky remarked, in 1905, that in no country had there been shed more working-class blood than in the French Republic during the last twelve years, our most progressive journals strangely applauded him. The following year, at the Amsterdam Congress [of socialists], M. Jaurès, who offered the defence of the Republic, had to suffer a cruel martyrdom. 'In a certain sense,' [August] Bebel told him, 'I must be the defender of monarchy against you ... Monarchy does not fundamentally engage in class struggle. It must take the people into account. In all the republics, we witness the intervention of the army to quash strikes. The French government is thus a class government' [*Quand le socialiste autrichien Kautsky remarqua, en 1905, que dans aucun pays il n'a été répandu plus de sang ouvrier que dans la République française pendant les douzes dernières annees, nos journaux les plus avancés l'applaudirent étrangement. L'année suivante, au Congrès d'Amsterdam, M. Jaurès qui présentait la défense de la République eut à souffrir un martyre cruel. « Dans une certaine mesure, » lui disait Bebel, « je dois être l'avocat de la monarchie contre vous ... La monarchie ne peut s'engager à fond dans les luttes de classe. Elle doit compter avec le peuple. Dans tous les républiques, on constate l'intervention des troupes pendant les grèves. Le gouvernement français est lui aussi un government de classe »*].[30]

Furthermore, Maurras's book had discussed Sorel with respect, and when its author sent to Sorel a copy of its second (1910) edition, the recipient 'expressed his admiration in a four-page letter'.[31] Maurras's cordiality towards Sorel had an acrimonious conclusion. Sorel grumbled to a friend in 1914 that 'Maurras never had any serious idea of what social forces were necessary under a monarchy.'[32] The royalist scribe had better luck in his interactions with the working-class publisher and syndicalist Alfred-Georges Gressent (himself profoundly affected by Sorel's teachings), better known under his pseudonym 'Georges Valois'. That Maurras eventually took the trouble to expel Valois from AF circles indicated something of the closeness with which both men long worked.

Others found AF attractive thanks to the willingness through which, confronted by the German military threat, it had put its monarchism into cold storage throughout the Great War. Before 1914 it had decried Clemenceau; from 1917 it could not praise 'the Tiger' highly enough, since Clemenceau himself behaved like an absolute monarch, imprisoning real or putative traitors to the war effort whenever they showed themselves.

It needs to be stressed that Maurras, in his preoccupation to the point of obsession with national culture, never thought in primarily racial classifications. He, along with all his contemporaries across the political spectrum (Jewish and Gentile alike), believed that races existed. But labours by the Comte de Gobineau and other late-nineteenth-century authors to tabulate racial hierarchies moved him to contempt, not least because of those labours' origins in Teutonic scientism. He dismissed Gobineau as 'inept, false, lying'.[33]

This constituted one of AF's tamer reprimands. Daudet's literary aggression matched, when it did not outdo, that of Maurras. Still, neither man's idiom could be mistaken for the other's. Maurras's prose contains numerous brisk declarative sentences and is for the most part not too difficult to render into English; Daudet's prose, abounding in baroque decoration and subordinate clauses, resists translation almost totally. Yet translation must be attempted. Here is Daudet going to work on the scientist and left-wing politician Alfred Naquet:

> Alfred Naquet, hunchbacked as in the *Arabian Nights*, with the shining eyes of a sadistic almea [an Oriental female singer-dancer], and who resembles a spider and a crab. You see him, in a nightmare, coming down askew from the ceiling, bypassing the bed-curtains, to go and drink from the toilet bucket. Destiny forced me during my youth, with constant horror, to rub shoulders with, if not hobnob with, this deformed and hirsute being, whose physique is certainly nothing more than the projection of his inner nature. From what hereditary conjunctions of the Sabbath did Alfred Naquet descend? What witch's cauldron cooked and recooked the elements of which he was formed?[34]

Elsewhere Daudet aimed much higher than the likes of Naquet. He faithfully attended every session of the legislature during his term as representative, hoping not merely to spread the monarchist gospel but to obtain memorable copy for his ferocious memoirs. Of course no one in government had the slightest intention of allowing him anywhere near ministerial office, but it hardly mattered, because he soon became by a considerable margin the most daunting member of the legislature. Aristide Briand, whose insufficient Teutonophobia made him particularly objectionable to Daudet, inspired this diatribe (the 'tribune' was the platform where each deputy stood while giving a formal speech):

> I was watching from where I stood on the tribune a number of individuals of varying merit, among them Briand, Aristide Briand, down below me, with his little hump on the left shoulder blade looking like a piccaninny perched on its mother's back! A lustreless golliwog mop, eyes which looked almost white because of their admixture of green and blue, a miserably twisted mouth, a body warped by the massive invasion of those rheumatic twinges which afflict men in their sixties – such was Briand. [...] when I saluted him as the bright star of this democratic comedy which is based on the exploitation of the unfortunate workers, he began to squirm and crawl, sending out impalpable tentacles and pseudopods like a shellfish sprinkled with lemon juice.[35]

Often Daudet the monarchist deputy scared his fellow legislators even more when he was not talking than when he was. Worse, we are told, than his explicit insults 'were his great resonant bursts of laughter which could and did make his opponents' carefully prepared oratorical effects instantaneously ridiculous'.[36]

Maurras and Daudet had – if the anachronism of *Spinal Tap* imagery may be pardoned – dials always turned up to eleven. Amid all their sulphurous invective and derisive bellows, we must not overlook that *déformation professionnelle* of political militants, a *déformation* confirmed in our own age by a thousand blogs and ten thousand Twitter wars: the desire to shock for shock's sake, beyond what one firmly believes. Now and then, for want of more distant targets, Maurras and Daudet delivered backhanders to each other. Maurras once complained: 'I doubt if Daudet has ever deeply understood anything. He is drunk on words and also on certain images [*Je doute que Daudet ait jamais rien compris profondément. Il est ivre de mots et aussi de quelques images*].'[37] Daudet could give as good as he got:

> He was even prepared to defy the xenophobic Maurras who took exception to Daudet's too frequent eulogies of the Englishman, Shakespeare. 'Yes, Maurras,' Daudet exclaimed genially when someone mentioned this little difference between the two men, 'what a great political brain! But as for his literary views – *ah, ça, non!*'[38]

That said, Daudet had a far greater general capacity for pleasure than Maurras ever possessed. Repeatedly he gave his support to writers whom he found politically or personally revolting, simply because he admired their output:

> Daudet was a prolific literary critic (the articles he chose to preserve fill eight volumes) and perhaps the only critic at that time who could, as they say, make or break a book. He preferred to make them. That niggling inability to enjoy anything whatsoever, which is the distinguishing characteristic of most modern critics, was not part of Daudet's temperament. And he was concerned with books, not with their

authors. For much of his life he was strongly antisemitic, yet he did as much as anyone to promote Proust's career; [Louis-Ferdinand] Céline's anarchic masterpiece, *Voyage au bout de la nuit,* was a compound of everything he most loathed, and yet, according to Céline himself, 'it was Daudet who launched me.' He had no great liking for Protestants or homosexuals, yet these mild antipathies did not prevent him from coming to the defence of André Gide.[39]

On occasion, a victim whom Daudet targeted would take the onslaughts in good part. We are informed:

> Then there was the deputy whom Daudet had sliced, opened up, resected, boned, and eviscerated on the front page of *L'Action Française* and who greeted his executioner later in the day with, 'My dear M. Daudet, I must tell you that I thought what you wrote about me was extraordinarily brilliant and extremely funny.' Daudet contemplated him for a moment. 'Too bad, too bad,' he said glumly. 'After that, I'll never be able to attack you again!'[40]

It will have been noted that the foregoing coverage of Maurras-style and Daudet-style monarchism has contained remarkably few mentions of French royalty itself. For this there is good reason. The more elaborate the ideological superstructure of AF, and the greater the impact which its example left on French intellectuals (whether or not they took monarchism seriously otherwise), the less appealing AF seemed for actual French royals, usually based in Belgium, since they were still forbidden to live in France. Philippe, Duke of Orléans, claimed the French crown from 1894 until his death in 1926, whereupon the claim devolved to his own son Jean, better known throughout his life as the Duc de Guise. Jean, as early as 1912, had admonished AF: 'Maurras and Daudet are not true Royalists [...] They do not serve monarchy; they use it for the satisfaction of their ambitions or their literary grudges.'[41]

This censorious note the dynasty's leaders would strike time after time. Willing enough to let AF champion their cause, they resented Maurras, Daudet and the movement's other leaders telling them what to do. Most direct in his criticisms of AF was Jean's son Henri, the young Comte de Paris, who maintained more frequent personal associations with the movement than his father and grandfather had done, but who refused to be AF's sycophant. During his undergraduate years at the University of Louvain, Henri routinely attended lectures by the visiting Maurras. (A photograph of the two men in conversation dates from 1934 and has been often reproduced.) Nonetheless, he completely rejected – in bolder language than his father had used – Maurras's urgings that the dynasty back AF to the exclusion of every other political group.

For Maurras, Henri's attitude constituted the second great betrayal of his organisation. The first, still more devastating for him both personally and politically, had taken place in 1926.

'I bless his work.' Thus Pius X, Pope from 1903 to 1914, had told Maurras's mother at a Vatican audience.[42] The pontiff, in his 1910 encyclical *Notre Charge Apostolique,* sided with Maurras and AF in their opposition to *Le Sillon* ('the Furrow'): a movement, led by politician Marc Sangnier, that tried to square the circle through seeking to reconcile Catholicism with anticlerical leftist agitation. But Vatican doubts about the liceity of AF and Maurras's own writings, doubts which Pius X privately voiced seven months before his death in August 1914, came to the surface twelve years and a world war later. By this stage those actively involved with AF included the historian Jacques Bainville (whose commentary on the Versailles peace settlement has been noted in an earlier chapter) as well as two Catholic intellectuals who would afterwards break with it: the novelist Georges Bernanos (who had been a member of the Camelots du Roi) and the theologian Jacques Maritain. In 1922 Maritain wrote to Maurras with affection – the Jewish origins of Maritain's Russian-born wife, Raïssa, cannot have been an issue between the two men – and also with a touch of raillery:

> I think that one day, you and I will need to produce a manifesto explaining that we don't reject *en bloc* everything that has happened since 1270, and that we regard as imbeciles, beneath all discussion, those who can only cite that belief for opposing our reasons [*Je pense qu'un jour, il faudra que, vous et moi, nous fassions un manifeste expliquant que nous ne rejetons pas en bloc tout ce qui s'est passé depuis 1270, et que nous tenons pour des imbéciles, inférieurs à toute discussion, ceux qui ne trouvent que cela à opposer à nos raisons*]!*[43]

A decree of Pius XI (born Achille Ratti, and Pope since 1922), promulgated in 1926, astounded the faithful by asserting not only that various books by Maurras were dangerous to Catholic morals, but that *L'Action Française* now came under the same ban. The Pope followed this decree the following year by announcing that all active supporters of AF would henceforth be automatically excommunicated. Why AF should have been considered beyond the pale in 1926–27, when both Pius X and the French episcopate had lauded it earlier, was never explained. In 1926 the features of AF's pronouncements most likely to irk twenty-first-century readers – the chauvinist devotion to France and the bouts of Jew-baiting – went unrebuked. (So, more surprisingly, did certain risqué passages in Daudet's fiction which had worried French censors.) Those Maurras volumes to which the Vatican now took such strenuous exception had been tolerated by earlier popes, and few Catholics had so much as heard of them, let alone read them. In each case, the objectionable passages could have been easily cut, as Maurras himself sometimes did with the books' later editions. Moreover, complaints about Maurras's own acknowledgement of pagan forebears came oddly from a church whose leading systematic theologian, St Thomas Aquinas, had famously 'baptised Aristotle'. (Further, Dante had spoken of 'Sovereign Jove who was on earth crucified for us'[44] without officially jeopardising his Catholic credentials.) Meanwhile there remained the uncomfortable facts that Maurras's influence was bringing vast numbers of hitherto lukewarm French Catholics back to the pews, and that since 1905 this influence defied successive anti-Catholic French cabinets more effectively than any Catholic prelates did. AF leaders put into practice Pius X's own call – in his allocution *Gravissimo Officii* – for civil disobedience against France's new anti-Catholic statutes.[45] Jesuit historian Peter J. Bernardi conceded as much in a recent (2021) article: 'Maurras's political program offered a concrete and practical outlet for those who despaired of reversing the inimical, anticlerical policies of the Third Republic by constitutional means. 'Order, discipline, and hierarchy' were AF's watchwords.'[46]

Instead of admitting these truths, the Vatican performed the doctrinal equivalent of cutting off its nose to spite its face. One has only to read eyewitness accounts of Pius XI's behaviour to detect how this occurred. A pontiff who, like Pius XI, insisted on his own sister and brother addressing him as 'Your Holiness', and who so lost his temper at a mistake committed by nuncio Angelo Roncalli (the future John XXIII) as to make him kneel before the Pope for three-quarters of an hour, may be described in all justice as a narcissistic bully: and a bully by his own epoch's criteria, not only by ours. The chastisement of Roncalli showed him at his worst: it later came to his notice that Roncalli had a reasonable pretext for making his error, but Pius insisted on apologising to him purely as 'Achille Ratti', because if he had apologised to him as Pope, he would have looked foolish. He demanded that the Superior-General of the Holy Ghost Fathers dismiss the French seminary's rector, who had expressed sympathy with AF; when the Superior-General answered 'Yes, Holy Father, I'll see what I can do', the pontiff 'grabbed his beard and shouted, "I didn't say, see what you can do, I said fire him."'[47]

By this stage the AF-allied weekly *Candide* had become well established. (Contributors to *Candide* included several important figures well outside Maurras's inner circle: the playwright-actor Sacha Guitry; the playwright-poet-novelist Jules Romains; and the Jewish conservative deputy Georges Mandel, future Interior Minister, who would be murdered in 1944.)[48] A *Candide* editorial of 16 September 1926 made, with deadly blandness, a point which defenders of Pius XI ignored at their peril: 'It is not likely, in any case, that the Church would prefer to have unbelievers as enemies rather than as friends, as if she had too many friends and not enough opponents [*Il n'est d'ailleurs pas vraisemblable que l'Église aime mieux avoir les incroyants pour adversaires que pour amis, comme si elle avait trop d'amis et pas assez d'adversaires*].'[49] The same point can be phrased more bluntly: how many dutiful and articulate Catholics, not in France alone, could Pius afford to alienate? French Catholics had mostly kept the faith against government persecution from 1905: this, apparently, was to be their reward.

From 1927, not only were regular readers of *L'Action Française* to be refused communion; not only were they to be prohibited from marrying in Catholic nuptial Masses, prohibited even from acting as godparents; but those who died while still adhering to AF were to be denied Catholic funerals. The punishments were so disproportionate to the crime that it is hard to interpret them as anything other than ebullitions of the Pope's individual rancour. Their long-term consequence (like the consequences of certain even more misguided outbursts from later pontiffs in our own time) was to demoralise ordinary devout Catholics without making Catholicism one skerrick more attractive to its self-identified foes. During 1937, events obliged Pius XI to issue, within the space of a week, two ringing encyclicals in fierce reproach of anti-Catholic regimes: *Mit brennender Sorge*, denouncing the Third Reich; then *Divini Redemptoris*, which condemned the official godless terrorism in the USSR, Mexico and Red Spain. Alas for his own credibility on these issues, the French political movement most consistent in reprehending both Nazi and Communist regimes had been precisely that AF which he had anathematised. As the French themselves say, quoting Molière's 'be careful what you pray for' maxim: '*Tu l'as voulu, Georges Dandin.*'

Sir Shane Leslie, Irish Catholic diplomat, editor and biographer, gently hinted at the importance of offended papal *amour-propre* in the determination to destroy Maurras and all his works. With a fleeting reference to Belgium's recently deceased Cardinal Désiré-Joseph Mercier, Leslie wrote:

> As a theorist, Rome could have passed him [Maurras] over, but as he has succeeded in captivating Catholic youth to such an extent that Belgian students voted him the palm in a competition which left Cardinal Mercier with a derisive six votes, Rome has felt hurt in a very tender spot. [...] *Paradise Lost* and Gibbon's *Rome* [*Decline and Fall of the Roman Empire*] have been condemned by Rome, but both works have been cited by converts as reasons for their conversion. Maurras caused converts by the score, and his atheist or agnostic friends often trembled to find themselves on the point of being somersaulted into the Roman camp.[50]

Back in 1924 another Irish Catholic, the journalist Denis Gwynn, though recklessly hostile to Daudet (whom he called 'at best a master of objectionable vituperation, and at worst the extremely popular author of pornographic novels'),[51] spoke in much more measured and sensible tones about Maurras. He called the latter:

> one of the most effective critics in all the French press of the disastrous policy pursued by Émile Combes and the anticlericals in proscribing the religious orders and in so dividing Frenchmen from one another with the bitterest resentments. Considering all the assistance that M. Maurras has given to the Church in this way by his unfailing support and his deadly attacks upon the old Radical policies, it is not surprising that most French Catholics regard him as an ally whose aid is to be accepted with gratitude and enthusiasm. Even the Jesuits have pronounced in favour of cooperation with him on all matters of Catholic policy when he is willing to lend his aid, and this whole question was discussed in all its bearings with remarkable lucidity in a large book about M. Maurras and his policies, which the Père [Pedro] Descogs, SJ, published before the war.[52]

Cardinal Louis Billot, rather than enforce the papal condemnations, resigned: the only man in the twentieth century to have given up his red hat by choice. Jacques Maritain decided that he could no longer support Maurras, and ceased to do so; Bernanos stayed with Maurras till 1932, then separated himself from AF amid much mutual blame.[53]

Between 1910 and 1926, according to the aforementioned 1962 scholar who examined the organisation's records, AF had between 30,000 and 40,000 members.[54] Around 15 per cent of the membership during this period consisted of minor nobility; 10 per cent consisted of monks or priests; almost 50 per cent consisted of lawyers, doctors, army officers and writers; and a smaller but still substantial proportion of the membership (25 per cent) consisted of white-collar workers, often civil service clerks. Remarkably few farmers, small shopkeepers, or proletarians joined AF, despite persistent outreach by the leaders towards all of those groups. After 1926–27, most clergy stayed away from AF, and although to a certain extent increased support form colonial administrators in North Africa compensated for the post-1927 ecclesiastical shortfall, the pontifical campaign against AF did hit Maurras and Daudet in their hip-pocket nerves.[55] It reinforced the two men's belief that ultimately they could rely on no one except their own followers.

Certainly not the Third Republic's police forces, as a crime three years before the condemnation had shown. A 22-year-old Anarchist and trade unionist, Germaine Berton, had already come to official attention when she demanded in print that French soldiers desert en masse. She had, furthermore, been convinced (or had convinced herself) of the falsehood that AF and the Camelots du Roi had arranged for the slaying of Jean Jaurès. At first she wished to avenge Jaurès by killing either Maurras or Daudet; ultimately, in January 1923, she entered the AF headquarters and fired five shots into Marius Plateau, secretary-general of the Camelots. After a nationally publicised murder trial, during which Anarchists and Communists loudly defended her, the jury acquitted her the following December.

A month beforehand, Daudet had suffered a terrible loss in his own family. His son Philippe, something of a Dostoyevskyan ne'er-do-well, had himself toyed with Anarchism and had purloined a thousand francs from his parents to go on a trip to Alaska which never eventuated.[56] Several times earlier, the boy (a mere 14 years old) had run away from home, though never on those earlier occasions had he stolen parental funds. After days in which neither the Daudets nor anyone close to them knew of Philippe's whereabouts, the dreaded news came. The authorities announced that the youngster had shot himself while occupying the back seat of a Paris taxi, and hours later had breathed his last in hospital without regaining consciousness. Charles Bajot, the cabdriver, insisted that at first he had mistaken the sound of the shooting for a tyre exploding.[57] At first the distraught father had been prepared to accept the official verdict that his son's death had been a suicide (Philippe had already been allowed Catholic interment, a compassionate doctor having declared that even if the youth had taken his own life, he had done so while the balance of his mind was disturbed). Yet soon Léon Daudet concluded that Moscow-trained, pro-German Anarchists had killed Philippe with the connivance of Bajot and of the police. *L'Action Française* ran on the front page of its 2 December 1923 edition the upper-case headline 'L'ASSASSINAT DE PHILIPPE DAUDET', and then as a sentence-case subhead 'Innocent blood [*le sang innocent*]'.[58]

Till his dying day, Léon believed that Philippe had been murdered. He was by no means unique in this assumption: left-wing politician Édouard Herriot, who served three short prime ministerial terms between 1924 and 1932, thought it likely (though by no means proven) that Philippe had met with foul play.[59] Bajot, enraged by the persistence with which Léon, in the pages of *L'Action Française*, had accused him of helping to kill Philippe, sued Léon for libel. Few libel suits in France have ever succeeded, but this one – which dragged on until 1927 – finally did. The court found Léon guilty, ordered him to pay a fine of 1,500 francs, and condemned him to five months in gaol; despite a petition to the government, signed by the poet Paul Valéry among others, which urged that Léon be spared incarceration. The trial's outcome moved *The New York Times* to elegant sarcasm: 'M. Léon Daudet, long famous for his sobriety of language'.[60]

In fact Léon spent only a month deprived of his freedom: because enterprising friends of his, pretending to speak on behalf of Interior Minister Albert Sarraut, telephoned the governor at La Santé prison and ordered him to release Léon on the government's behalf. By the time the call's bogus nature had been officially realised, Léon had taken refuge in England. He 'told me,' Sir Charles Petrie afterwards remembered, 'the story of his escape while we were waiting for a bus in Trafalgar Square.'[61] Rather than return immediately to France once the fuss had died down, Léon lived in Belgium until 1930, when he received a governmental pardon, and deemed it safe to re-enter his homeland.

Concerning AF and its leaders, Petrie had mixed views. He found interacting with Maurras predictably effortful, the latter being 'as deaf as a post, making conversation impossible; his writing, too, was almost illegible.'[62] The newspaper's production processes could never be called streamlined, though they delivered the goods:

> I was present in the offices of the *Action Française* one night when, in the absence of Maurice Pujo, the editor, he [Maurras] was putting the paper to bed. It was a memorable experience: confusion reigned everywhere, everybody was talking at once as Maurras went to work with a will armed with a large pair of scissors and an enormous blue pencil, but the number came out on time with its accustomed brilliance.[63]

Nor could Petrie reconcile himself to 'a narrow nationalism and a violent anti-Semitism in the movement which not only alienated many moderate people but was diametrically opposed to the true principles of kingship'.[64] He concluded that while Maurras and Daudet ranked with:

> the glories of French literature ... they were not intended to lead political parties. So in spite of the brilliance of its leaders and the activity of its propaganda the Action Française achieved precisely nothing in the political field. [...] It always remained a gathering of intellectuals, and though hundreds of thousands of people read their articles and books with relish they never translated what they read into political action.[65]

Petrie, when discussing AF, concluded that the articles which the newspaper published over the initials 'C. de G.' were in fact Charles de Gaulle's work.[66] De Gaulle, in a manner that his subsequent reputation would render most awkward, had assiduously courted Maurras's goodwill before 1940. When he released in 1934 his book *Vers l'Armée de Métier* (*Towards A Professional Army*), he sent a complimentary copy of it to Maurras, and wrote separately to *L'Action Française*'s military correspondent about the book, voicing in his letter the hope that – as he put it – 'M. Maurras will bring his powerful support to the professional army. In truth he has been doing so for a long time already, through his body of doctrines.'[67] Maurras, in short, remained hard to ignore, despite the decline in his influence from its pre-1926 levels.

PORTUGAL

Assassination of Carlos I.
The 1908 Lisbon murders of King Carlos 1 and his elder son fatally weakened Portugal's monarchy. This illustration's circular side-panels depict the killers. (Wikipedia's Creative Commons)

Plaque commemorating the murders.
The Portuguese text reads: 'On this spot, 1 February 1908, His Majesty King Carlos I and the Royal Prince Dom Luís Filipe died for their country.' Photo © Robert James Stove, 2023. (Image Author's Own)

Manuel II.
Carlos's successor Manuel II would lose his throne in 1910, when scarcely out of his teens. (Wikipedia's Creative Commons)

Gaby Deslys.

Gaby Deslys, Manuel's mistress during his exile. Anglican episcopal censure of her revealing stage attire moved her to retort: 'Tell your bishops, I love them – but they show too much leg!' (Wikipedia's Creative Commons)

Henrique Mitchell Paiva Couceiro.
The most intrepid and assiduous of Portugal's monarchist campaigners, Henrique Mitchell Paiva Couceiro. (Wikipedia's Creative Commons)

GERMANY

Above: **Wilhelm II, Crown Prince Wilhelm, and Prince Wilhelm of Prussia.**
Three generations of Hohenzollerns, 1927: the erstwhile Kaiser Wilhelm II (centre); his eldest son, Crown Prince Wilhelm (left); and the Crown Prince's own eldest son, yet another Wilhelm, killed in 1940. (Wikipedia's Creative Commons)

Right: **Gustav von Kahr.**
Gustav von Kahr, Bavaria's pro-monarchist Premier 1920–1921. He tolerated Hitler, then helped doom the Beer Hall Putsch, and for this apostasy paid with his life eleven years afterwards. (Wikipedia's Creative Commons)

Prince Rupprecht of Bavaria.
Bavarian monarchism's great white hope after 1918: Prince Rupprecht, from the House of Wittelsbach. (Wikipedia's Creative Commons)

AUSTRIA AND HUNGARY

Above: **Emperor Karl, Empress Zita, and Archduke Otto at the Budapest coronation, 1916.**
The Budapest coronation (1916) of Habsburg Emperor Karl and Empress Zita of Bourbon-Parma as, respectively, Hungary's King and Queen. Between the crowned couple stands their four-year-old son, Archduke Otto. (Wikipedia's Creative Commons)

Right: **Admiral Horthy.**
A much-repeated 1920s-1930s joke called Miklós Horthy 'an admiral without a fleet' ruling a 'kingdom without a king'. In theory he was a mere regent for the absent Karl. In practice, his 'temporary' regency lasted twenty-four years, and endured despite both of Karl's attempts to re-occupy the Hungarian throne. (Wikipedia's Creative Commons)

Lord Rothermere.
Lord Rothermere, newspaper tycoon and possible model for Evelyn Waugh's Lord ('Up to a point') Copper. He required a geography lesson from his mistress to teach him 'that Bucharest and Budapest are two different cities'. This cognitive breakthrough sharpened his desire to make his son Hungary's king. (Wikipedia's Creative Commons)

FRANCE

Above left: **The Duc de Guise.**
Prince Jean d'Orléans, claimant to France's throne from 1926 until his death in 1940. To his followers he was 'Jean III'. Successive French republican governments kept him and his family in exile. (Wikipedia's Creative Commons)

Above right: **Charles Maurras and Léon Daudet.**
At a 1926 Paris ceremony honouring Saint Joan of Arc, the two guiding spirits of Action Française: Charles Maurras (left, with beard) and Léon Daudet (right, with smile and holding hat in left hand). Their vehement monarchism coexisted with fierce scorn for individual monarchs. (Wikipedia's Creative Commons)

SPAIN

Above: **Alfonso XIII and Queen Victoria Eugenia ('Ena').**
A 1906 wedding photograph of Spain's Alfonso XIII and his English-born bride, Victoria Eugenia ('Ena'). The nuptial day was marred by a hideous terrorist attack in Madrid, and the union went downhill from there. (Wikipedia's Creative Commons)

Left: *Alfonso XIII and General Primo de Rivera From 1923 to 1930 General Miguel Primo de Rivera (right) was Spain's de facto ruler, reducing his sovereign (left) to a mere figurehead. 'Had I known in my youth that I would one day have to govern this country,' the General endearingly mused, 'I would have spent more time studying, and less fornicating.' (Wikipedia's Creative Commons)*

Don Jaime, the Carlist claimant.
*Don Jaime, the Carlist claimant to Spain's throne from 1909 till his death in 1931.
No firebrand, he once allowed himself the wistful observation: 'I would have liked
to be a dealer in emeralds in Colombia.' (Wikipedia's Creative Commons)*

The Duke of Alba.
Jacobo Fitz-James Stuart y Falcó, the seventeenth Duke of Alba. Friend of Alfonso XIII, who nevertheless failed to give him political power commensurate with his gifts, despite or because of the striking facial resemblance between monarch and subject. Alba's descent from the Duke of Marlborough's sister gave him the right – enthusiastically exercised – to address Churchill as 'cousin'. (Wikipedia's Creative Commons)

GREECE

King Constantine I, King George II, Queen Sophie, Princess Irene, King Paul, King Alexander.

The Greek royal family, circa 1910. From left to right: Queen Sophia; Princess Irene; the Princess's father King Constantine I; Irene's elder sister, Princess Helen, who married Romania's Carol II; and two of Constantine's sons, the future King Alexander and the future King Paul. (Wikipedia's Creative Commons)

Eleftherios Venizelos.
The kingmaker of Greek politics before, during, and after World War I: Eleftherios Venizelos, who served no fewer than eight terms as Prime Minister between 1910 and 1933. His British admirers included John Buchan – who based on him the character of Karolidis in The Thirty-Nine Steps *– and Lloyd George. (Wikipedia's Creative Commons)*

Ioannis Metaxas.
Venizelos's antipode and bitter antagonist: Ioannis Metaxas, devoted royalist who from 1936 to his demise in 1941 enjoyed supreme power over Greece. Though a general, Metaxas preferred to wear (as here) civilian clothes. Mussolini underestimated him, with disastrous consequences for Italy. (Wikipedia's Creative Commons)

ALBANIA

King Zog.
In 1928 Ahmed Zogu, having served three years as Albania's President (notwithstanding numerous attempts to kill him), upgraded himself to the status of King Zog I. His moustache inspired Salvador Dali's. (Wikipedia's Creative Commons)

Queen Geraldine.
Small wonder that Albanians called her 'the White Rose of Hungary': Geraldine Apponyi, the Catholic who married the Muslim King Zog in an ecumenical 1938 outdoor rite. Proficient in many languages, Geraldine also knew how to use a typewriter. (Wikipedia's Creative Commons)

An extremely popular French novel from 1931, still quite well remembered nine decades later, throws a memorable sidelight on French monarchism generally. It is one of the earliest volumes in the Maigret series by Georges Simenon (who derived some of the volume's local colour from his own brief experience of employment, as a young man, in an eccentric monarchist's office). Originally entitled *M. Gallet Décédé,* the book has been published in two separate English translations: *Maigret Stonewalled* (1963) and *The Late Monsieur Gallet* (2013).

As always with Simenon's novels, the plot is secondary to the elegiac atmosphere of Paris and the provinces, and to the depictions of the protagonists' mental anguish: above all the frustration of being socially and geographically deracinated, as the Belgian-born ex-Catholic Simenon himself was. But this time the plot could probably never have worked except in the context of the years between the wars. (Internal evidence indicates the plot's date: the story cannot take place after April 1931, since in the first chapter Alfonso XIII continues to occupy Spain's throne.) *Spoiler alert*: those who have not read the book, but wish to do so and to retain the element of surprise, need to skip the next nine paragraphs.

Jules Maigret must investigate the death of one Émile Gallet, found shot and stabbed in a Sancerre hotel room. At first there appears no problem in identifying the dead man. Gallet, thin, shabby, in his early fifties, and afflicted with liver trouble, was a commercial traveller specialising in the sales of jewellery; he left behind him a widow, Aurore (née Préjean), and a son, Henry. Nevertheless, the more Maigret examines the dead man's background, the odder it seems. The firm for which Gallet purportedly worked as sales representative (and whose letterhead he used) had not, in fact, employed him for the previous eighteen years. What grounds, moreover, would Gallet have had for his quarrel with Tiburce de Saint-Hilaire, the local aristocrat?

Especially important clues come from an effusive tax inspector, who assures Maigret of having known Gallet from a shared Indo-China youth. The Gallet who emerges from the tax inspector's account is exuberant, cynical, and lecherous, willing to engage in a sham marriage with a local girl: the very opposite of the liverish, put-upon Gallet whose character Maigret had thought he knew.

In actuality Gallet had been living for eighteen years a lie, or rather, two lies. The commercial travelling had been a cover for an elaborate swindle, with prominent royalists as its victims, and he had kept for his own use the sums which the royalists gave him in their belief that he would further the royal cause. Aurore Préjean's father (dead long before the story begins) had been a passionate monarchist, in charge of a magazine called *Le Soleil* devoted to reinstating kingship. *Le Soleil* had expired, but Aurore's husband retained access to the subscribers' list, from which he chose his most promising targets. He needed the money for two reasons above all. In the first place, his liver condition had made it extremely difficult for him to qualify for life insurance – the only hope left for his wife to inherit any money from him – and the premiums from the sole coverage which he could obtain were extortionate. Second, his son and the latter's mistress, Éléonore Boustang, had been blackmailing him over his illegal bilking of the royalists, while pretending that the actual blackmailer was a certain 'Monsieur Jacob'. Henry, who had inherited his father's liver ailment and thus needed funds for medical care as much as his father did, benefited from a quirk in French law which ensures that 'there has been no crime or offence when a son lays hands on his father's property by fraudulent means'.[68]

Little by little, with that almost infinite patience and unflappability which characterise the Police Judicaire's most famous inspector, the bleak truth comes to light. Various passing oddities (the hand which Tiburce de Saint-Hilaire uses to pick up a stone, for instance) point in one direction. What had happened could be called a case of – as we would now say – 'identity theft', except that in this instance both parties were privy to the faking involved. The desperately impoverished man whom Maigret had assumed to be Gallet (and who could never extract more than a few hundred francs at a time from the royalists) was none other than the real Tiburce de Saint-Hilaire; and the exuberant, cynical lecher whom the world took for Tiburce de Saint-Hilaire was none other than the real Gallet. Both men had known each other at school. Maigret explains:

> I felt for too long anyway that there was something creaky about this story. You needn't try to understand, but when all the material clues manage to confuse matters rather than clarify them, it means they've been faked … and everything, without exception, is fake in this case. It all creaked. [...] But most of all Gallet. He sounded as wrong dead as he did living.[69]

The real Tiburce, who had sold his identity to his Indo-Chinese sometime-companion, longed to commit suicide, but knew that suicide would invalidate his life insurance policy. To circumvent that problem, he tried to make his death look like murder. The fake Tiburce tells his interrogator of the troubles which his Indo-Chinese debaucheries had brought upon him:

> 'I had to go back to France anyway. It was about women … I went too far when I was out there. There were husbands and brothers and fathers who bore me a grudge. So I had the idea of looking for a Saint-Hilaire, and I can tell you it wasn't easy. I picked up the trail of Tiburce at the school in Bourges. They told me they had no idea what had become of him. I knew he was a gloomy young man, reserved, who never had a friend at school [...]

> 'It took me three months to lay hands on him, in Le Havre, where he was trying to get taken on as a steward or interpreter on a liner. He had ten or twelve francs left. I bought him a drink and then I had to get the information out of him word by word – he never replied except in monosyllables. He'd been a tutor at a chateau, a proof-reader, an assistant in a bookshop [...] So I staked everything on getting it all. I told him I wanted to go to America and make my fortune and I said that out there nothing helps a man more, particularly with women, than an aristocratic name, and I wanted to buy his. [...]

> 'I paid 30,000 francs for the right to call myself Tiburce de Saint-Hilaire. As for the real Saint-Hilaire, we were almost the same age. All we'd had to do was exchange our papers.'[70]

From the late 1920s AF grew much weaker. The Great Depression did not help the viability of regional branches. Although overall France suffered less in an economic sense during the 1930s than most other Western countries did, AF supporters were likelier than the national average to depend on fixed incomes, and therefore to feel the pinch financially in a way that farmers, for instance, did not. Post-1926 subscriptions to *L'Action Française* greatly and consistently fell, so that the newspaper's 'income in 1928, itself less than half what it had been in the same period in 1925, was almost double that of 1930'.[71] (A report in *The Atlantic* that as late as 1936 AF retained 60,000 members[72] is almost certainly an exaggeration: as stated above, it lacked that membership base even in its pre-1926 glory days.) For six months, from February to July 1933, *L'Action Française* made particularly fervid attempts at fund-raising.[73] Most significant of all, the movement had forfeited much of its previous hold over youth. Increasingly those Frenchmen in their twenties who had once done so much to keep the Camelots alive were looking elsewhere, to more militant leagues. Some joined the *Cagoule* (literally 'cowl'), which waged campaigns of sabotage against left-wing cabinets, particularly against the Popular Front of 1936–37 led by Socialist Léon Blum. Others joined the *Parti Populaire Français* (PPF), founded in 1936 by ex-Communist Jacques Doriot. Still others joined the *Croix de Feu* – originally a pressure group for war veterans – which had attracted many Catholics frightened away from AF by Pius XI's denunciation. (The *Croix de Feu* had a youth wing for those too young to have served in 1914–18; it included the teenage François Mitterrand.)[74]

AF appeared ever more old-school, particularly after its failure to profit from Paris's 6 February 1934 riots, inspired by the Stavisky crisis: the probable murder (some insisted suicide) of Kiev-born confidence trickster Serge Alexandre Stavisky, who for years had notoriously done as he wished with such politicians as Camille Chautemps and Édouard Daladier. The riots, during which the police slew fifteen protesters, so unnerved Daladier (who had taken over the prime ministry from Chautemps a week beforehand) that the AF of old would have had no difficulty in seizing the initiative from him and dictating conditions. On 1 February, two days after Chautemps had been driven from office, London's *Evening Standard* ran a long and detailed article by Daudet that included these observations:

> May I add that I was elected Deputy for Paris in 1919 on the cry of '*Vive le Roi!*' and that I have never ceased to proclaim my hatred of democracy – democracy killed my son when he was 14½ years old – before the largest possible public, and to audiences numbering between 10,000 and 30,000?
>
> I have done this without being heckled or contradicted. [...]
>
> During the Paris floods of 1910 the lids were forced off the manholes in the sewers. The forcing of the lid off the Stavisky sewer is the beginning of the general collapse of the band of brigands to whom democracy and parliament have given the chief political, judicial, and police offices of the nation. [...]
>
> One need hardly add that no attempt at a dictatorship is possible at the moment in Paris. The very idea is laughable. I ask you, who would be the dictator? The Neo-Socialist [Adrien] Marquet has been credited with such intentions. Nobody in the great city knows Marquet. Besides,

to put it briefly, we of the Action Française would break in half an hour any demagogue who tried to play the role of Sylla [Sulla] or Caesar. We have no time to waste on puppets. That explains the futile rage against us with which these puppets are animated.

Only one solution, then, is possible: the king, that is to say, Monseigneur the Duc de Guise, now in exile at Brussels, whose recent proclamation has made all French patriots thrill with hope. Behind him is his son, Monseigneur the Comte de Paris, himself the father of a little Dauphin.

When the Comte de Paris married Princess Isabel of Orléans-Braganza 1200 Royalists and Camelots du Roi, among them Maurras and myself, went there to celebrate the happy event. It was there that Madame, who tomorrow will be queen of France, said in her beautiful and melodious voice to our chief, 'This rebirth of the Royalist ideal shown here is due to you, Charles Maurras.'

The 1200 guests wept with joy.[75]

But while AF's bosses wrote such declarations as this, those Camelots on 6 February who took to the streets were left to their own devices. Maurras, Daudet, and Pujo – who at the time were respectively in their sixty-sixth, sixty-seventh and sixty-second years – no longer had enough activist fire in their bellies to satisfy dissidents like the young novelist and film critic Robert Brasillach, employed by the new periodical *Je Suis Partout*. Brasillach and his fellow apostates regarded monarchism as irrelevant to their concerns, and they were pro-Hitler enough to scandalise Maurras and Daudet. An unidentified figure whose disenchantment with AF prompted him to leave the Camelots lamented to PPF official Paul Marion (who during September 1935 described the encounter in the short-lived newspaper *La République*) that 'Charles Maurras is the Léon Blum of royalism'.[76] Erstwhile AF member Louis Darquier de Pellepoix, unblushing in his zeal for punitive physical measures against Jews *en bloc*, went so far as to accuse Maurras and Daudet of being themselves Jewish.[77] Decorated Great War veteran Joseph Darnand, who late in the Vichy era would establish the much-feared *Milice*, abandoned AF with the typically callous announcement that he viewed the organisation as no longer anything more than 'a gang of c**ts [*Une bande de cons*]!'[78] 'The trouble was,' a 1970 chronicler of French royalist sentiment decided, partly on the testimony of an ex-Camelot:

> that he [Maurras] never really quite meant what he said, while his disciples mistook his message for the real thing. For many of them, who had long followed him blindly in the delusion that they were working toward the immediate redemption of France, February 6 came as a rude awakening. They now came to the conclusion that nothing was ever to be expected of the Action Française.[79]

It could have been inevitable that Maurras would be misrepresented and eventually laughed to scorn by those who owed almost everything to having been his disciples. Maybe this problem is inherent in discipleship, as Kipling clearly assumed that it was:

He that hath a Gospel
  To loose upon mankind,
Though he serve it utterly –
  Body, soul and mind –
Though he go to Calvary
  Daily for its gain –
It is his Disciple
  Shall make his labour vain. [...]

It is his Disciple
  Who shall tell us how
Much the Master would have scrapped
  Had he lived till now –
What he would have modified
  Of what he said before.
It is his Disciple
  Shall do this and more.

He that hath a Gospel
  Whereby heaven is won
(Carpenter, or cameleer,
  Or Maya's dreaming son),
Many swords shall pierce him,
  Mingling blood with gall;
But his own Disciple
  Shall wound him worst of all![80]

Partly through a genuine trepidation regarding the peril to France which the Popular Front (and in particular those Communists ordering around Blum's cabinet), represented in his eyes, but partly in the hope of competing with Brasillach and the rest in terms of polemical outrageousness, Maurras devoted editorial after editorial of *L'Action Française* to attacks on Blum that went beyond all bounds of taste and of sanity. Not content with calling Blum 'that old Semitic camel [*ce vieux chameau sémitique*],'[81] he went so far as to call for Blum's elimination ('There's a man worth shooting, but in the back [*C'est un homme à fusiller, mais dans le dos*]'),[82] and went to prison for inciting violence. He would probably have avoided captivity had he not affixed to the incitement his own name, but subterfuge never had a prominent – or any – place in Maurras's skill-set. The same 1970 chronicler quoted previously also called Maurras, 'the very antithesis of a man of action. [...] was he the type of man to practise what he preached? One tends to doubt it. One of the agents detailed to watch him by the Sûreté once reported that "Maurras is incapable wilfully to harm a fly."'[83]

Now it is perfectly true that France's Communists often used similar homicidal language about their own targets. Yet from Communists, and from Communists immediately answerable to Stalin at that, it was futile to expect any better, whereas Maurras had serious powers of intellectual application. These powers gained formal acknowledgement when, in 1938, he improbably won election to an Académie Française which contained numerous political opponents of his. (His verses, for the most part severely traditional in temperament and form, helped gain him votes.) The preceding year a nobleman, the Marquis Xavier de Magellan, nominated Maurras for – of all unlikely awards – the Nobel Peace Prize.[84]

Shortly after the Anschluss, Maurras condemned, in much of *L'Action Française*'s front-page editorial, what his headline called 'A stupidity: Hitlerism.' The following extract retains the original's staccato paragraphing: proof that the man himself, amid all his empyrean flights into classical and neo-Gothic reverie, had never stopped being a journalist.

> *Certains conservateurs français nous dégoutent.*
>
> *Pourquoi? Par leur sottise. Laquelle? L'hitlérisme.*
>
> *Les grands succès du dictateur allemand ont consisté à oser quand il n'avait rien devant lui. J'avoue qu'à son point et à celui de son pays, il a bien fait. Mais était-ce donc si malin!*
>
> *Ces conservateurs se prosternent.*
>
> *Ces ex-nationaux s'agenouillement.*
>
> *Et les plus coruscant d'entre eux se vautrent dans la boue, dans leur boue avec des* heil*! à non plus finir.*
>
> *Des idiots pommés se sont mêmes trouvés pour établir une sorte de système de comparaison entre le Communisme et l'hitlérisme sur le territoire français.*
>
> *Plus ils sont riches, plus ils possèdent, et plus il importe de leur montrer qu'un hitlérisme établi chez nous les tondrait de plus près encore que Blum, que Thorez, et que Staline coalisés!*

(Certain French conservatives disgust us.

Why? By their stupidity. What sort? Hitlerism.

The great successes of the German dictator have consisted of being daring when he had nothing facing him. I acknowledge that from his viewpoint and that of his country, he has done well. But was it so clever after all?

These conservatives prostrate themselves.

These ex-nationalists kneel.

And the loudest among them wallow in the gutter, in their own gutter, with unceasing *Heils*.

Facile idiots can even be found who wish to establish a kind of system of comparison between Communism and Hitlerism *on French territory*.

The richer they are, the more they possess, the more important it becomes to show them that Hitlerism, if established here, would flay them much more thoroughly than Blum, Thorez [French Communist leader Maurice Thorez], and Stalin combined!)[85]

As if the loss of AF's right wing to pro-Hitler organisations did not weaken Maurras's position enough, the years before 1939 also saw the open estrangement between AF and the French royals whom it was meant to be backing. In 1937 the Comte de Paris voiced his irritation at AF's political narrowness, founded a magazine of his own called

Courrier Royal (far less controversial than anything in the AF publishing stable), and used the *Courrier Royal* to siphon off much of the journalistic talent on which Maurras and Daudet had relied. When Maurras and other AF officials met the Comte in Brussels to complain about this policy, the Comte reminded Maurras of the latter's own youthful jibes against the prevailing political establishment, and told him: 'You were young then; I am young now. The future is with me.'[86]

Partial consolation for these disappointments came AF's way in April 1939, two months after Pius XII had become pope. The new pontiff revoked the bans on AF and its literature. For all his frequently noted gentleness of spirit, he realised – unlike his predecessor – that according to Catholic teaching the Church Militant is an army like any other, and that no army can hope to defeat its enemies' forces if it has systematically disheartened its own. Against the clear and present dangers of Hitler and Stalin in 1939, Catholicism could no longer afford the luxury of vendettas against French individuals whom a particular pope might not like. Mainstream left-wingers throughout Western Europe, locked inside their unquestioned delusion that Berlin must at every possible juncture oppose Moscow, failed to prophesy the Molotov-Ribbentrop Pact. Daudet, with much greater prescience than they, had foretold this very outcome, predicting 'the Germans and the Russians overrunning Poland, after which the former, reassured as to their eastern front, will turn on France'.[87] When the panzers barrelled west, as noted by Pennsylvania political scientist and historian Paul E. Gottfried (several of whose relatives were killed by the Nazis):

> It was not Maurras and his followers in Action Française, many of whom fell in the Battle of France, but rather Communists who refused to take up arms against the invader as long as Nazi Germany remained allied to the Soviet motherland. A lifelong adversary of the 'German Menace,' Maurras had already called for a French preventive war against Hitler in 1936, when the German government remilitarized the Rhineland.[88]

The Vichy *État Français* from July 1940 – voted into power by deputies across the political spectrum, including such left-wing stalwarts as Senate President Jules Jeanneney and the above-cited former Prime Minister Herriot[89] – won Maurras's and Daudet's emphatic approval. Maurras referred to Pétain's ascension, in his April 1941 book *La Seule France*, as 'a divine surprise'.[90] For him, in a recent British historian's words, 'this meant unconditional loyalty to Pétain without needing to take up a position on collaboration: he wanted to pretend that Germany was not there'.[91]

Pétain, for his part, described Maurras as 'the most French of all Frenchmen', despite never actually seeking out Maurras's advice.[92] Obeisance to the *Maréchal* did nothing to make AF more attractive for the hard-core collaborationists in occupied Paris: Brasillach, Doriot, ex-Socialist deputy Marcel Déat, ex-AF member Marcel Bucard and the like. Both Maurras and Daudet remained in what was, until November 1942, France's unoccupied zone; and there, early in July of that year, Daudet succumbed to a massive brain haemorrhage. Maurras's funeral oration ascribed Daudet's death, more poetically, to 'the sufferings of France'.[93] *L'Action Française* kept going, after a fashion, in Lyon until August 1944, Maurras having insisted on preserving it, though the historian Pierre Gaxotte had unsuccessfully recommended to Maurras that he close it.[94] On the rare occasions that French monarchism made international news during the war, it did so for reasons entirely unwelcome to Maurras. The Comte de Paris had thrown in his lot with the Free French – de Gaulle made to the Comte various promises of post-war support for a monarchical restoration, promises predictably honoured more in the breach than in the observance – while a self-confessed royalist youth, Fernand Bonnier de La Chapelle, shot dead Admiral François Darlan on Christmas Eve 1942.

With the collapse of both the Third Reich and Vichy, Maurras had every reason to fear for his life. Authorial renown proved insufficient to protect Brasillach from a firing squad, while Darnand and Bucard likewise paid the supreme penalty for siding with Nazism. Maurras (whose Académie Française seat, along with Pétain's, had formally been declared vacant) underwent at Lyon a show trial conspicuous for the profusion of doctored evidence offered against him.[95] When given leave to speak, he 'held the floor for six tedious hours, reading an interminable memorandum which no one, he least of all, could hear'.[96] Very easy to hear, on the other hand, was his response to the verdict passed against him: life imprisonment. He shouted: 'It's Dreyfus's revenge [*C'est la revanche de Dreyfus*]!'[97]

Such limited contact did Maurras have by this time with the outer world that he probably enjoyed as much or as little contentment in his prison cells as he did in the year before his trial and conviction. First the authorities kept him in the town gaol of Riom in the Auvergne. Then they transferred him to similar quarters in Clairvaux, where earlier inmates had included the anarchist Prince Pyotr Kropotkin and the teenage Communist Guy Môquet. Neither prison resembled a gulag: Maurras kept up a substantial correspondence, including letters exchanged with Salazar. Portugal's ruler had publicly expressed disagreement with AF's *Politique d'abord* slogan,[98] but never in such a way as to imply denigration of Maurras himself, to whom he sent a case of port wine.[99] When Salazar havered in 1951 over whether he should seek to become Portugal's president – the incumbent, Óscar Carmona, having recently died – Maurras wrote to advise him firmly against such a move: '*Restez! Tenez!*'[100] 'Stay where you are! Hold on!' This Salazar did, happy to have had his own inclination applauded by the captive Frenchman.

In early 1952 on the government's orders, Maurras was moved to the more comfortable environs of a private clinic not far from Tours. His letter to France's President Vincent Auriol combined, characteristically, expressions of gratitude with demands that the left-wing Justice Minister, François de Menthon, be put to death.[101] The following November he himself died, having been reconciled in his last months to Catholicism and been given extreme unction.

By this point, French invocations of monarchism had grown increasingly ritualistic. From the year before Maurras's demise came Nancy Mitford's best-seller *The Blessing*, which near its end includes a scene where the aged aristocrat Madame Rocher – of Paris's Faubourg Saint-Germain – expounds to the visiting British parliamentarian Mr Clarkely (in the presence of the book's English-born heroine, Grace de Valhubert) her monarchist sentiments. These, nevertheless, are becoming more a formula than a call for action:

'Give us back our King, my dear sir, and then speak to me of politics,' she said, rather as if her King were kept a prisoner in the Tower of London. […]

'Is she really so royalist?' he [Clarkely] turned to Grace. Madame Rocher was telling Sir Conrad her summer plans and begging him to go with her to Deauville, Venice, and Monte Carlo.

'Like all the Faubourg,' said Grace, 'she has a photograph of the King on her piano, but I don't think she'd raise a finger to get him back.'

Thomas Molnar observed in 1999 that 'Maurras and his oeuvre are practically unknown in the United States, where occasionally college students will sidle up to you showing some Maurrassian texts as if they were dirty pictures.'[102] Of such texts there would never be a shortage: Maurras, as his follower Lucien Rebatet coarsely put it, 'could no more cease writing than he could cease his physical functions'.[103] There were a million things which Maurras knew that a semi-literate municipal functionary never knows; but there are also certain things which the semi-literate municipal functionary knows that Maurras, by his deafness-aggravated isolation from the ruck of common humankind, never began to grasp.

De Gaulle himself is said to have devoted to Maurras what Alistair Cooke engagingly called 'one of those blasting sentences with which Frenchmen love to seal off whole tunnels of enquiry'.[104] (And what tunnel of enquiry stood in greater need of sealing off than the 1930s' Gaullist-Maurrassian connection?) 'Maurras,' this sentence runs, 'was so right that it would drive him mad.'[105] A haunting extract from G.K. Chesterton – whose work Maurras knew and, in translation, occasionally published – possesses a certain applicability to the French sage, especially in its concluding parallelism:

If you argue with a madman, it is extremely probable that you will get the worst of it; for in many ways his mind moves all the quicker for not being delayed by the things that go with good judgement. He is not hampered by a sense of humour or by charity, or by the dumb certainties of experience. He is the more logical for losing certain sane affections. Indeed, the common phrase for insanity is in this respect a misleading one. The madman is not the man who has lost his reason. The madman is the man who has lost everything except his reason.[106]

Chapter V

Death in the Afternoon
Spain

If you can keep your head while all around you are losing theirs, it's just possible that you haven't grasped the situation.

Jean Kerr[1]

Shortly before noon on 12 November 1912, a 58-year-old, bespectacled, moustachioed man of solid build stood outside a bookstore in Madrid's Puerta del Sol, examining the display in the shop-window, when his reverie was abruptly terminated by two bullets fired straight into the back of his head. José Canalejas, the Prime Minister of Spain, died without regaining consciousness.

In Canalejas's person there expired one of the few twentieth-century Spanish politicians who could be credited with statesmanship without inspiring mirth. During his term of office (which began in February 1910) he had pacified once-roiling Barcelona, had done his considerable best to save Spanish Catholic officialdom's more obtuse leaders from their own folly, and had seen with Disraelian acumen – but without sharing any of Disraeli's fashionable advantages or novelistic flair – the potential for intelligent blue-collar conservatism. This he managed with prudence and, wherever possible, good humour. (When good humour would have availed him nothing and when the situation justified sarcasm, his skill as a mimic[2] counted for much in a political class sensitive to loss of face.) He avoided ham-fisted over-reaction to genuine threats, let alone fictive ones. 'All the newspapers which are hostile to monarchical government,' he pardonably complained to republican novelist Benito Pérez Galdós, 'enjoy not only liberty of thought which you advocate but a tolerance given in no other country.'[3] To sum up, he carried out (albeit with much less severe methods) the same moderately reformist function that his younger contemporary Pyotr Stolypin carried out in Russia. So both men had to be disposed of. It should be added that Canalejas had always refused to accept police protection,[4] although he spoke of having foreseen the manner in which he would die.[5]

Historian Salvador de Madariaga, no friend of crowned heads, found himself paying tribute to Canalejas' work:

> Though firm, he was not harsh. Far from it. No Spanish prime minister ever took more to heart the responsibilities of life and death which power implies. His advice was always for leniency [...] Had Canalejas lived, it is almost certain that the forces which were disrupting the system which had been slowly evolving from the Restoration [of the

Bourbon monarchy in 1875, eleven years before Alfonso XIII's birth]
would have been controlled by his masterly hand and keen intellect.
The petty party intrigues, above which he had not always been able to
remain, would have been met by frank exposure and attack, and the
help which they were apt to meet with in the royal palace, energetically
checked; the progressive forces of the nation would have been absorbed
into active partnership; the Army and Church reduced to obedience by
a moderate, yet firm, handling of their preposterous claims; and foreign
affairs conducted with tactful vigour. But Canalejas was killed by an
irresponsible fanatic and the Liberal Party found itself without a head.[6]

Manuel Pardiñas, his assassin, eventually evaded arrest by taking his own life. Yet not
before Canalejas's state funeral, where King Alfonso XIII – who had arrived on the
scene too late to see the Prime Minister before he died – insisted on serving as chief
mourner. His expressed intention to do so horrified his courtiers, all too conscious that
Pardiñas remained on the loose. Their attempts at dissuasion merely strengthened the
King's resolve. So did the Madrileño crowd which voiced its displeasure at him. 'More
than once that crowd broke past the police. But Don Alfonso never quailed. If he must
face the industrialisation of crime, he would face it.'[7]

Quailing did not, at least before 1931, form part of Alfonso's emotional repertoire.
Unlike poor Manuel II in Lisbon, Alfonso seemed to relish physical danger; and he
had plenty of it to cope with, including five nearly successful assassination attempts.
In June 1905, while making a state visit to Paris, he and French President Émile Loubet
narrowly escaped death in the Rue de Rivoli when an anarchist threw a bomb at their
carriage. Eight years later, in Madrid's Calle de Alcalá, he cheated a would-be killer
still more narrowly:

> I saw a man coming towards me armed with a revolver. He fired, and
> I rode at him. When he was quite close he tried to seize my bridle as he
> fired a second time, the flash singeing my glove, while the ball grazed
> my horse. I immediately wheeled *Atalun*, who knocked the man over
> with his shoulder; at that instant a policeman sprang on him; his third
> shot was fired from the ground and whistled overhead.[8]

As the King observed to an admiring Churchill: 'Polo comes in very handy, on these
occasions.'[9] But the single most impressive demonstration of Alfonso's steadfastness
had taken place on his own wedding day: 31 May 1906. As he and his bride, Victoria
Eugenia of Battenberg – 'Ena', to give the most common form of her Christian name –
were on their way to the reception after the Nuptial Mass at the monastery of San
Jerónimo el Real, there occurred the bloodiest terrorist attack that Western Europe had
then seen. (In a prefiguration of the aftermath to Canalejas's slaying, the perpetrator
died by his own hand before he could be imprisoned.) Eyewitnesses to the attack
included America's Ambassador to Spain, William Miller Collier, who wrote:

> Suddenly from out of an upper-storey window something was tossed.
> It looked like a bouquet of flowers, such as had been thrown to the
> King and Queen by many persons along the route, although police

regulations had forbidden such acts. There was a flash, a deafening noise, a rattling of broken glass, shrieks and cries. A blinding smoke concealed the royal carriage. When it cleared away one saw soldiers stretched out on the ground, horses kicking in agony, men dead, men dying. Panic seized the crowd, which fled precipitately, men, women and children falling over each other. The Captain-General, *aides-de-camp,* and equerries who were riding at the side or just behind the [royal] carriage rushed to the door of it. The King, whose first thought had been of his bride, and who had assured himself that she was uninjured, answered their inquiries with calmness, saying, 'We are not injured. We will go on.'[10]

A more prosaic eyewitness account came from the future George V. This provides a telling detail unknown to Collier, of how Alfonso could not indefinitely maintain his public stoicism, but subsequently wept in private:

Of course the bomb was thrown by an anarchist, supposedly a Spaniard and of course they let him escape. I believe the Spanish police and detectives are about the worst in the world. No precautions whatever had been taken, they are most happy go lucky here. Naturally, on their return, both Alfonso and Ena broke down, no wonder after such an awful experience.[11]

One might think that a marriage that had started in so sanguinary a fashion could not grow any unhappier; one would be wrong. It might have been better for Spain, and for Europe as a whole, if the union had never taken place. Alfonso had married Ena on the rebound, his original choice of an English bride having been Princess Patricia, daughter of Edward VII's brother Arthur, the Duke of Connaught. Princess Patricia, most unusually among womenfolk of the period, found Alfonso's charms eminently resistible; or perhaps she simply disliked the notion of any husband from the Iberian Peninsula, since matchmakers' hopes of affiancing her to Manuel II's unfortunate elder brother had come to nothing as well. Ena, unlike Patricia, expressed a willingness to become a Catholic, a procedure on which Alfonso insisted.

The trouble resided not in Ena's rational, sane, and conscientious character, but in her heredity: the haemophilia gene. She had a haemophiliac brother, Leopold of Battenberg; and there existed a 50 per cent possibility that she herself was a haemophilia carrier, as her mother, Queen Victoria's youngest daughter Princess Beatrice, had certainly been. Victoria herself had had a haemophiliac son – the short-lived Duke of Albany, also called Leopold – and another daughter of hers, Alice, had borne a haemophiliac son of her own: Prince Friedrich of Hesse, only three years old when he died after a fall in 1873.

That said, even if Alfonso had been more scientifically literate than he was, he would have slighted pessimistic auguries. His habitual love of adventure made him view matrimony in the same spirit with which he viewed his beloved baccarat: risks were there to be taken, not to be shied away from or whined about. He knew that Ena had a one-in-two chance of transmitting 'the royal disease' to any sons she had; and he accepted the hazard.[12]

It proved ruinous. Sympathy for Russia's imperial house, and for the agonies endured by the haemophiliac Tsarevich Alexis, needs to be balanced by the realisation that from 1907 onward the Spanish royal family had not one but *two* haemophiliac sons: Alfonso (alias 'Alfonsito'), the Prince of Asturias; and Gonzalo, seven years his junior. (A third son, Fernando, who lived for only hours after his birth in 1910, might also have been a haemophiliac.) 'Many Spaniards,' we are told, 'believed the gruesome story that a young soldier had to be sacrificed every day so that his fresh blood could keep the haemophiliac sons of the king alive.'[13] As if that were not domestic misery enough for Ena, yet another son, Jaime (born 1908), suffered a childhood bout of mastoiditis so malign that it rendered him deaf and mute. Only the fourth son, Juan (born 1913), enjoyed good health. When sectarians in England described the familial tragedies as heavenly punishment on Ena for abandoning her native Protestantism by converting to Rome, they little knew how Ena dreaded the hypothesis that they could be correct. Nor did this fear on her part mollify Alfonso. Were any husband, however saintly – and Alfonso was no saint – to have three profoundly disabled sons under his roof, he would be superhuman if the prospect of repeated straying from the marital bed did not tempt him.

With forlorn percipience, Ena observed of Alfonso: 'He tires of everything. Some day he will tire even of me.'[14] He eventually fathered at least six extramarital children by at least five mothers. Possibly the most succinct description of his world-view is the saying of Portugal's early nineteenth-century queen-consort Carlota Joaquina:

> I adore God and I fear the Devil; but if God or the Devil were to confront me while lovemaking preoccupied me, I would kick them both into the street [*Eu adoro Deus e tenho médo do Diabo; mas si Deus ou o Diabo si puserem na minha frente quando a amor me preoccupa, eu os porei na rua a pontapes*].[15]

Nonetheless, whatever Alfonso's numerous failings in the chastity department, he nowhere disputed – and openly admitted to believing in – divine interventions at certain crises of his life. On a shooting expedition in Nottinghamshire, organised by the king's politician friend the sixth Duke of Portland, someone (we are not told whom: perhaps the Duke himself) asked Alfonso whether he had been rendered lastingly nervous by the carnage of his wedding day. The monarch's gentle but firm retort: 'No. You see I do really believe in God.'[16]

Few were the European rulers in August 1914 whose reputations for statesmanship had been enhanced by November 1918. Alfonso belonged with those few. The Great War showed him at his best. It purged him, not forever but for years, of his proneness toward brilliantly clever dilettantism; it curbed, or at least rendered purposeful, his complex mind's natural tendencies to undue intrigue; it forced on him the habits of humdrum desk-work; it put to practical purpose his natural reserves of compassion.

As Alfonso's refusal either to help Manuel II openly or to oppose him openly had revealed, he had not shone in pre-1914 foreign policy. He shone in it now. For once he had a clear goal, or rather, two clear goals: to keep Spain neutral; and to do whatever a neutral power could do to shorten the conflagration, or at least to temper it. To achieve these aims, personal sympathy must not be allowed to dominate. Had it done so, Spaniards would have fought and perished alongside British Tommies and French *poilus* in the mud and barbed wire of Flanders. But as Churchill reported Alfonso saying: 'Only I and the mob are for the Allies.'[17]

María Cristina, Alfonso's own mother, was a Habsburg, with everything that this implied in 1914–18. Shortly after Italy had entered the war on the side of Britain and France, the Queen Dowager snapped at Sir Arthur Henry Hardinge, by this time British Ambassador to Madrid: 'Don't you find that these Italians are behaving like pigs [*Ne trouvez-vous pas que ces italiens agissent comme des cochons*]?' Hardinge recollected: 'I was a good deal embarrassed, but I replied as politely as I could: "*Madame, il m'est assez difficile d'appliquer le terme de «cochon» aux allies du Gouvernement du roi mon maître*" ["Madame, it is rather difficult for me to apply the term 'pig' to the allies of the Government of the King my master"].'[18] The response mollified her.

Meanwhile, Alfonso brought all his substantial energies to charitable work. One of his biographers informs us:

> a special Bureau was set up. In due course this came to employ forty people, and the whole cost was borne by the Sovereign personally. Its main activity was tracing the missing, and this work gradually spread all over Europe. The Bureau collected information regarding both civil and military prisoners; forwarded correspondence concerning health and cognate matters to and from prisoners and the occupied countries; gave material help to prisoners; arranged the repatriation of civilians; watched over the welfare of those who were interned; secured the mitigation of punishments; obtained special indulgences for prisoners-of-wars; and acted as the medium of communication between individuals and families in occupied countries and their friends and relations all over the world.[19]

Through his Brussels plenipotentiary, the amazing Villalobar, the King did his utmost to save Wilhelm II from a crime that was also a gaffe: the shooting of Edith Cavell. After she had been put to death, we are told, 'three people did not sleep the whole night through: they were the Empress Augusta in Berlin, the Emperor Francis Joseph in Austria and King Alfonso in Madrid.'[20] No mere Spanish legislator – least of all the Count of Romanones, Prime Minister from December 1915 until his desire to end all diplomatic relations with the Central Powers caused the King to force his resignation in April 1917[21] – could have carried out Alfonso's corporal works of mercy; and, as a matter of indisputable fact, no mere Spanish legislator tried to carry them out. Alfonso in 1914–18 justified, if ever he justified, Churchill's tribute to him: 'superior, not alone in rank, but in capacity and experience, to the ministers he employed'.[22]

More and more the King won admirers in unexpected circles. Republican philosopher Miguel de Unamuno was quoted as having observed of him: 'I have not spoken often with the King, but it has been sufficient to show me that one must look elsewhere for the obstacle to certain necessary reforms to establish the supremacy of justice and education. I hope more – much more – from the King than from the Parliament.'[23]

A year before the war, another veteran critic of royalism, the liberal Cortes member Melquíadez Álvarez, could say nothing worse than: '[L]isten to me attentively,

Republicans. I would do justice to the King; he has fulfilled his duty attending to the requirements of opinion and respecting constitutional principles. He has been a sovereign who knows how to inspire the confidence of his subjects.'[24]

That such eulogies would become unthinkable within Spain itself had little or nothing to do with direct action on Alfonso's part, and much to do with his acquiescence in the direct action of others. It was somehow typical of him that when, from September 1923, he found himself cast in what public opinion regarded as a subordinate role, the figure thus relegating him to subordination was no swaggering despot – nor a vociferating orator like Mussolini, who had then been Italy's strongman for only eleven months – but the impetuous, un-bookish General Miguel Primo de Rivera. So little inclination did the General possess for Man of Destiny rhetoric that he candidly admitted: 'Had I known in my youth that I would one day have to govern this country, I would have spent more time studying, and less fornicating.'[25]

The three years before Primo de Rivera's takeover indicated that all Spain's international prestige in the Great War had vanished, so completely did political life revert to pre-1914 'business as usual'. In foreign as in home affairs, disaster abounded. During July and August 1921, Spain's troops had suffered utter, shameful defeat at Annual, in north-eastern Morocco, at the hand of a Berber force led by local revolutionist Abd el-Krim. The Spaniards under General Manuel Silvestre lost 13,000 dead. Four thousand of those 13,000 perished within two days, not counting another 3,000 Spanish captives slaughtered by the Berbers in cold blood, with lofty disregard for international law regarding prisoners' rights.[26] Silvestre himself was never seen alive again. His corpse, when found, could be identified only by his general's insignia.[27]

Along with this humiliation, domestic mayhem – in abeyance to a certain extent during the war – exuberantly resumed. On 8 March 1921 Eduardo Dato, who had served thrice as Prime Minister, was being driven from the Cortes to his home. He never reached it. Three motorcycle-riding Catalan separatists (Ramón Casanellas, Pedro Mateu and Luis Nicolau) halted alongside the automobile and fired twenty-seven shots at their target, wounding him in seven places. Dato's killers had done their homework: their bullets, a contemporary newspaper report tersely announced, 'had been filed to make them explosive'.[28] Cardinal Juan Soldevilla y Romero, the 79-year-old Archbishop of Zaragoza, met a similar fate to Dato's on 4 June 1923. He was en route to the scheduled episcopal visitation of a convent, when members of an anarchist group called *Los Solidarios* blocked the path of his car and shot him dead.

None of the prelate's murderers suffered the inconvenience of arrest. A Spanish correspondent for a British newspaper, recollecting the nation's ethos prior to Primo de Rivera's ascension, lamented:

> Terrorism invaded new zones and adopted new forms – attacks on banks, on restaurants full of people who with inexplicable cowardice allowed themselves to be robbed, waylaying of passers-by in the open street. The aged and virtuous Cardinal-Archbishop of Zaragoza succumbed in his car, pierced by bullets, and the assassins were never found. In Madrid preparations were being made for the inquiry into the Morocco disasters. Passion, in this as in all else, clouded the clear vision of justice […] General Aguilera, President of the Supreme Court of the Army and the Navy, sent to Señor Sánchez de Toca, ex-Premier, an insulting letter,

which the offended party read aloud in the Senate, and in the Senate also another ex-Premier, Señor Sánchez Guerra, struck General Aguilera in the face.[29]

In such chaotic circumstances, it would have required a far more patient soul than Alfonso to avoid concluding that playtime had lasted quite long enough and that the kindergarten's wider viability remained questionable. At least Primo de Rivera looked, to the King, like one capable of cracking down on subversive elements.

The General's dictatorship (with characteristically maladroit public relations, he freely admitted that it *was* a dictatorship) began with a certain populist verve. Aware that the national bureaucracy needed trimming, he acted on this awareness during mid-1924:

> He ordered all the State officials to report for duty at one and the same time. It was a shocking scandal. There were not to be found in the government offices seats enough to accommodate all the muster of employees. On the payroll marquises figured as porters, lawyers as street-cleaners, girl clerks as messenger boys.
>
> General Primo de Rivera proceeded to cut the most inflated, costly, and corrupt army of officials in Europe down to reasonable dimensions. The Puerta del Sol was thronged with a twofold stream of *cesantes* [unemployed] suddenly expelled, like quicksilver, from both sides of the political barometer at once.[30]

Committed socialists found little enough to object to in the General's attitude, which favoured blustering over outright bullying. He himself espoused an unofficial rural socialism, raising some of the highest tariff walls in Spanish agriculture's history; anticipating FDR's New Deal by devising infrastructure projects to reduce unemployment levels; and making public transportation more efficient than it had previously been. In foreign policy he achieved one signal success: the 1926 conclusion of the Rif Wars, with smashing victories – more than ever welcome to Spaniards after the horrors of Annual – for combined Spanish and French forces. (The French leaders included two already famous names: Marshal Lyautey, then Resident-General, and Marshal Pétain. A leading figure in the Spanish contingent was one Francisco Franco, of whom the world would likewise come to hear far more.)

Yet with passing years, the central problem of Primo de Rivera's rule became ever more obvious: while it could harass and needle its domestic antagonists, it could never frighten them. Unacquainted with *The Prince* and suchlike textbooks of power, the General remained ignorant of Machiavelli's warning that rulers are better off being feared than loved. Sometimes his actions took such petty forms as banning long-practised public urination at railway termini.[31] When the capital's students noisily but peacefully protested against him, he ordered the University of Madrid to be temporarily shut down, thus inconveniencing numerous innocent people but not in the smallest degree harming the recalcitrant students themselves.

Worst of all, the General became a figure of fun; and among no European people is ridicule a more devastating weapon, than among Spaniards. A head of government in an English-speaking country has nothing to lose by joining in satirists' laughter against himself; a Spanish head of government has little enough such self-deprecating tolerance even in the 2020s, and had none whatsoever in the 1920s. One mischievous couplet which entered folklore derided Primo de Rivera's aristocratic title as well as his extracurricular pastimes: 'Playing cards, women, and the bottle are the Marqués de Estella's escutcheon [*Naipes, mujeres, y la botella / Son el blasón del Marqués de Estella*].'[32] Other jibes at his expense did his repute much more damage than this versified avowal of what Dickens would have called amiable weaknesses.

The General's aversion to academe coexisted with a fierce yearning (one surprisingly widespread among politicians with little formal education) to acquire honorary degrees. Two Madrid students – fervently begrudging the university's earlier closure – obtained a donkey, around the neck of which they 'placed a placard [...] on which was written in huge letters "Honoris Causa", and marched through the streets of Madrid. When the police stopped them, they said that it was only an advertisement.'[33]

Another, and still more galling, incident struck directly at the General's machismo. A bitter foe of the regime thought it amusing to pretend to be a 14-year-old girl, in which persona the foe mailed to Primo de Rivera a short poem, lauding him in the most extravagant terms. The subject of this encomium took such pleasure in it that he arranged for a newspaper to publish it. Thereupon the newspaper's readers gleefully noticed a fact which had eluded the General himself. 'When interpreted acrostic-wise, taking the first and last letters and reading downwards, the phrase was anything but laudatory.'[34]

Given that national governments much shrewder and more pitiless than the General's found themselves overwhelmed from 1930 onwards by the Great Depression, it is unsurprising that Spain should have been hard hit, although the country never suffered from Britain's, Germany's, and the United States' levels of joblessness. Illness had a more immediate effect on Primo de Rivera's fortunes than did wider economic trends. Diabetes clouded his judgement, and the idea of quitting office grew on him. He decreasingly bothered himself with gaining the needful royal assent to his policies. As a historian noted in 1983:

> The Dictator's sequence of transitional plans had become an unbearable nuisance to him [Alfonso]. Indeed, the way in which Primo de Rivera fixed for himself timetables was seen by the king as an affront to his sovereignty, a blow to his prerogative to designate and unseat prime ministers.[35] [...] The most striking thing about the last days of the régime was the almost total isolation of the Dictator.[36]

Óscar Carmona's recent behaviour in Lisbon offered the General, or so he wrongly assumed, a solution worth copying. Carmona had sent a round-robin to the leading generals in Portugal's army, asking them if he should continue as head of state, and concluding from their responses that he should. In January 1930, fortified by news of Carmona's success, Primo de Rivera wrote to his own generals, asking their opinions as to whether he should stay on. Many of the generals furnished non-committal answers. The remainder thought it desirable to stay silent. Moreover, he had dispatched the round-robin without notifying, never mind gaining permission from, the King beforehand.

Alfonso learned nothing of what had happened until he read about it in the newspapers. He summoned Primo de Rivera, chastised him in the strongest terms over his failure to appreciate the juridical difference between a republic such as Portugal versus a monarchy such as Spain, and ordered him to retire or else be dismissed. In a drastic *mea culpa,* the abashed Prime Minister not only resigned but crossed the border, spending in a Parisian hotel most of what little time remained to him. Possibly he had disseminated the round-robin with the deliberate aim of committing, as it were, political suicide. Anyhow, an attack of fever, worsening the impact of his existing diabetes, ended his life on 16 March. For all his unpopularity with the intellectual set, he had always retained a considerable popular following; and when his coffin was brought back home for a magnificent Madrid funeral, crowds mourned. Through their tears, nevertheless, they could descry the conspicuous absence from the funeral of Alfonso himself. From this 'blunder of the first magnitude',[37] the King's reign had not a hope of recovering.

At first Alfonso reverted to improvisation, such as had served him well before. He appointed to the Prime Minister's post another general, Dámaso Berenguer, hoping that the latter would be able to win over to the monarchy those whom Primo de Rivera had antagonised. (There are good grounds for supposing that Magnus, the frantically clever sovereign whom Bernard Shaw depicted in his 1928 play *The Apple Cart* as constantly seeking to outwit elected politicians, owed something to Alfonso's outlook.)[38]

In truth, Berenguer's government, unofficially known as the *Dictablanda* ('soft dictatorship'), satisfied almost no one. Within months, it had united against itself liberals, socialists, Marxists, moderate conservatives, and – a particularly worrying development for the King – champions of an autonomous Catalonia. During August 1930 representatives of these diverse movements signed the Pact of San Sebastián, which formally stated that whatever their disagreements with each other, they all sought a republic (such as Spain had been once before, in the 1870s). They included numerous figures who would make front-page news later in the decade: Niceto Alcalá Zamora (who became their formal leader), Manuel Azaña, Santiago Casares Quiroga, Alejandro Lerroux and Indalecio Prieto.

Several signatories kept in contact with republican elements of the army. Certain headstrong soldiers pre-empted the politicians' plans by declaring, on 12 December, a mutiny at the barracks in the north-eastern town of Jaca. This mutiny, though crushed within three days, so perturbed Berenguer that he had two of its leaders, Fermín Galán and Ángel García Hernández, put to death by firing-squad. He also consigned Alcalá Zamora to prison. A wave of strike action resulted (the Socialist Party's industrial-relations subdivision, the *Unión General de Trabajadores*, had backed the Jaca uprising). Already such hitherto cautious scholars as Ortega y Gasset had declared themselves republican. With atypical wrath, Ortega demanded as early as 15 November, on the front page of the liberal Madrid newspaper *El Sol*, a Carthaginian punishment for Alfonso and Berenguer alike. His essay ended with the menacing words *'Delenda est monarchia'.*[39]

Berenguer, thus identified by both allies and adversaries as a drag upon Alfonso, resigned on 18 February 1931. For a substitute, the King looked again to the armed forces, and in particular to Admiral Juan Bautista Aznar Cabañas. Scarcely had the Admiral become Prime Minister than he made it clear that he defended the Crown only with reluctance. Several members of his own cabinet had started explicitly negotiating with republican spokesmen. Paralytic strike action continued, and Aznar Cabañas himself began talking in republican accents. The King was not so much 'rearranging deckchairs on the *Titanic*', as making futile efforts at explaining deckchairs' innate usefulness to sailors determined upon throwing all furniture overboard.

Then, on 12 April, came nationwide municipal elections: the first major ballot-box initiative which Spain had witnessed since 1925. They represented the most frustrating possible outcome for the King. In absolute electoral terms, his adherents did very well, with 22,150 monarchist councillors given office, versus only 5,875 republicans.[40] The problem was that from a standpoint of political power, the monarchists notched up this huge overall majority in all the wrong places: specifically, in the countryside. All three of Spain's largest cities – Madrid, Barcelona and Valencia, whence the tallies came in first – went solidly republican. This protest vote discouraged the monarch as no mere would-be regicide could have discouraged him. He greeted it with the memorable lamentation: 'I feel as if I had gone to call upon an old friend and found that he was dead.'[41]

It had, nonetheless, become second nature for Alfonso to disguise his fears in public; and Ena herself paid her husband an unwilling compliment by saying that 'He was never more calm than in this gravest crisis.'[42] His aviator cousin, the Duke of Galliera, tried to dissuade him from departing, as an entry from the Duke's diary confirms. The Duke showed this entry to the British Catholic journalist Sir Arnold Lunn, who in an article of 1963 (printed when the diarist was still alive) quoted its admonition to the King. 'If you call on the army to suppress the riots,' the Duke warned, 'you may kill a hundred people in Madrid and as many in Barcelona. If you leave, a million will die before this mess is cleared up.' Lunn went on to remark: 'A million is the widely accepted estimate of those who died in the Civil War.'[43]

But nothing, least of all ducal caveats, could shake the King's resolve to go into exile rather than allow Spaniards to slay other Spaniards in his name. 'I do not wish one drop of blood,' he explained, 'to be shed for me.'[44] At this late stage the King might yet have gambled, as Alcalá Zamora (set at liberty just after the council elections) half-expected him to, on a reaction in his favour. He could have proclaimed martial law, with reasonable hopes that his proclamation would have been broadly obeyed and that the Admiral would have fallen into line. To the republicans' amazement, no such proclamation emerged. Berenguer – now Aznar Cabañas's War Minister – announced to the army's high command, whether through mere innumeracy or active mischief-making, that 'The elections have been lost.'[45]

José Sánchez Guerra, who had been Prime Minister for part of 1922, proposed to Ena that Alfonso abdicate and that Ena be a short-term regent until the Infante Juan came of age (Juan's eighteenth birthday would fall on 20 June). Alfonso toyed with this notion, but Ena herself wanted none of it.[46] Mere survival looked a more urgent concern than constitutional niceties. Spectres haunted the royal family: the spectres of Louis XVI, Marie Antoinette, and the Romanovs. 'All night the mob howled about the palace, filling the great rooms with the threatening sound of their voices. Sleep, even rest, was impossible. It was as though the nightmare would never end.'[47]

On 14 April the King's reign, for practical purposes, ended. He allowed his wife and children to stay in the palace for the night while he himself was driven to Cartagena, where he boarded a ship called the *Principe Alfonso,* bound for Marseille. Only after he arrived at Cartagena did anyone telephone the Queen to assure her that her spouse was still alive. His parting words, not published in Spain itself until after newspapers in other countries had printed them, were a weird mélange. They combined undue pessimism (beginning with the opening sentence's misinterpretation of the municipal polls) with defiant optimism:

> The elections held on Sunday have revealed to me that I no longer hold the love of my people, but my conscience tells me that this attitude will not be permanent, because I have always striven to serve Spain with utmost devotion to the public interest, even in the most critical moments. A King may make mistakes, and without doubt I have sometimes done so, but I know that our country has always shown itself generous towards the faults of others committed without malice.
>
> I am King of all the Spaniards and I am a Spaniard. I could find ample means to maintain my Royal Prerogatives in effective resistance to those who assail them: but I prefer to stand resolutely aside rather than provide a conflict which might array my fellow-countrymen against one another in civil and patricidal strife.
>
> I renounce no single one of my rights which, rather than being mine, are an accumulated legacy of history for the guardianship of which I shall one day have to render strict account.
>
> I shall await the true and full expression of the collective conscience and, until the nation speaks, I deliberately suspend my exercise of the Royal power and am leaving Spain, thus acknowledging that she is the sole mistress of her destinies. In doing so I believe that I am fulfilling the duty which the love of my country dictates. I pray God that all other Spaniards may feel and fulfil this duty as sincerely as I do mine.[48]

Sir Austen Chamberlain grieved at Alfonso's downfall:

> He was such a sympathetic figure, and, whatever his failings, Spain was making real progress under his rule. I entirely mistrust the competence of the new governors – not to mention their honesty [...] it is possible that the Republic may not be long-lived and that Alfonso may be recalled; but on the whole experience seems to show that it is easier to get out than to go back.[49]

Trotsky, from his Turkish bolt-hole, had predicted – via an exultant pamphlet written as early as January 1931 – his comrades' role in republicanism's triumph. 'Upon the Spanish Communists lie glorious historic tasks. The advanced workers of the world will follow with impassioned attention the course of the great revolutionary drama, which will, a day sooner or a day later, require not only their sympathy but also their cooperation. We will be ready!'[50] More surprisingly, Alfonso's downfall inspired satisfaction in certain monarchists: those who adhered to the Carlist movement.[51] For this satisfaction, ancient reasons existed.

Carlism's immediate origin lay in the quarrel that divided King Ferdinand VII (reigned 1813–33) from his younger brother, Don Carlos. Ferdinand's decision to leave the throne to his 3-year-old daughter Isabel – with his wife María Cristina in the position of regent – infuriated Don Carlos, who wanted the crown for himself and had the political advantage of being a male adult rather than a female toddler. Rather than quietly admit defeat, he declared open hostilities. Not just for dynastic reasons: he considered Ferdinand and (still more) Ferdinand's spouse to be intolerably left-wing, enslaved to the French Revolution's spirit. The Carlists, who derived their name from Don Carlos himself, 'were taking up arms against Liberalism, which in their eyes was but a second wave of the old Lutheran heresy'.[52] Fratricidal warfare ravaged Spain three times: 1833–39; 1846–49; and again (despite Don Carlos's own death in 1855) 1872–76. Much of the warfare took the form not of pitched battles, but of guerrilla raids. The struggles' eventual end occurred through general exhaustion rather than decisive governmental victory.

Alfonso XIII, true to his peace-loving nature, behaved with the utmost politeness towards the Carlist claimant, who by this time was Don Jaime (Don Carlos's great-grandson). In September 1931 he and Jaime met in Paris. It appears – details of the encounter are very sketchy and much disputed – that the childless Jaime accorded some kind of recognition, not to Alfonso, but to the Infante Juan, conditional upon the Infante embracing Carlist principles and eschewing Alfonso's own monarchical liberalism. Only a month afterwards, though, Jaime (aged 61) suddenly died, without having imposed the policy change on his fellow Carlists.[53] The great difficulty, if not the impossibility, of this imposition for anyone had already been made obvious by a setback which Jaime experienced during the Great War. Back then, he showed strict impartiality towards the Allies and the Central Powers; but the Cortes' Carlist leader, leather-lunged Anglophobe Juan Vásquez de Mella, refused to do likewise.[54] Condemning Jaime's leadership, Vásquez de Mella left the party with his own followers, known as 'Mellists,' by contrast with the 'Jaimists' faithful to Jaime. Within Carlism such splits, mergers and demergers were commonplace, prefiguring the mutual detestation between the 'Judean People's Front' and the 'People's Front of Judea', familiar to cineastes from *The Life of Brian*.

The Second Spanish Republic, with Alcalá Zamora as its first Prime Minister, had no outstanding successes in encouraging most sports. But it led the entire Western world in one form of organised al fresco entertainment: the burning down of churches. Unlike soccer or bullfighting, church-burning presupposed no individual ability. It signified an inherent egalitarianism, since it could be undertaken by anyone with adequate supplies of petroleum and matches. By the end of May 1931, 107 of Spain's churches had been incinerated, and local police often refused to intervene.[55] In June, a horrified Pope Pius XI issued an encyclical (*Dilectissima Nobis*) which avoided condemning republican rule *qua* republican rule, but which reprobated the 'serious offences committed against the Divine Majesty, with the numerous violations of His sacrosanct rights and with so many transgressions of His laws'.[56]

At this stage Alcalá Zamora was starting to look like a Spanish Kerensky. While remaining the titular head of government, he failed to halt the incendiarism.

In practice he ceded power to such hard men as Azaña and Largo Caballero, the latter a working-class socialist, the former a middle-class liberal. Alcalá Zamora, still a faithful Catholic when push came to shove, gave up the Prime Ministry in September. Azaña succeeded him, and the Cortes kicked Alcalá Zamora upstairs by electing him to the presidency.

Within weeks of the changeover, so much legislation plainly inimical to Catholicism had been rammed through the Cortes (despite the new President's misgivings) that Azaña could boast: 'And with these measures Spain ceases to be Catholic.'[57] It is not known for certain whether, as has been often alleged, Azaña – despite having a wife and mistress – was fundamentally homosexual. But it can be confidently asserted that had he been an Englishman or an American, he could have inhabited academe as a licensed atheist jester, in the fashion afterwards exemplified by Bertrand Russell and Richard Dawkins. In Spain, and for all his literary preoccupations (his complete published works run to seven volumes), he had few if any career outlets save day-to-day politics at something like its nastiest. Unamuno issued a warning: 'Beware of Azaña. He is an author without readers. He would be capable of starting a revolution in order to be read.'[58]

Foreigners fretted too. Reflecting in 1933 on the Primo de Rivera epoch,[59] Sir Charles Oman, by this time 73 years old, noted:

> I do not think that the recent dictatorship was nearly so autocratic as previous XIXth-century dictatorships had been: it certainly did not deal so drastically with all opponents as does the Fascist régime in Italy. But all the same it was, and could well be represented as being, a reactionary anomaly. And the plea that it was keeping down worse evils could not be proven to be true until it had been removed [...] The new Government has invariably had to employ armed force, within a few months of coming into power, against the left wing of the body of the revolutionary party. At the same time it has to beware of a recrudescence of monarchical feeling, and has always acted with more energy against 'reactionaries' than against 'extremists'.[60]

Also in 1933, a much younger Englishman than Oman – Richard Aldington, novelist, poet, and biographer of T.E. Lawrence – made his first Spanish visit. At the northern seaport of Castro Urdiales, Aldington disliked and feared what he saw:

> We sat at a café, and being new to Spain and fresh from France, were surprised to be openly jeered at as foreigners. The priests, I noted, were big burly men who might have been soldiers; and the soldiers undersized, underfed men who might have been priests. I said to my companion:

> 'These people seem to be doubly ignorant, ignorant of the outsider world in that they are astonished at the sight of foreigners and feel hostile to them, ignorant of the plenty they accidentally enjoy through having kept out of the war. What will you bet that they don't destroy themselves by some violent imbecility in the next ten years?'[61]

134

Surveying Spanish politics during October 1931, Alexander Leeper, a high-ranking civil servant in Britain's Foreign Office, had written in an internal memorandum: 'I think we should hear of a monarchist reaction in 1932.'[62] In August 1932, two prominent Carlists – Manuel Fal Conde, the Carlist party's secretary, and the Count of Rodezno, the party's Cortes leader – supported a coup attempt by General José Sanjurjo, who had previously gone along with the Republic, but who had lost patience with Azaña's leadership. Although *la sanjurjada* (for thus Sanjurjo's rising became known) briefly won over Seville, it totally failed in Madrid; and there clung to the whole affair, as to the Kapp Putsch attempt in Germany twelve years beforehand, a certain atmosphere of comic opera. The government cannot have viewed *la sanjurjada* as a great danger, because although Sanjurjo originally incurred a death sentence soon commuted to incarceration for life, he served in practice only two years' imprisonment.

No hint of comic opera marked the Asturias rebellion (October 1934) and its aftermath. This rebellion aimed at rendering unsustainable the conservative coalition which in November 1933 had become the Cortes's largest group, Azaña having been defeated at the polls. (At that election, the Carlists won twenty Cortes seats of their own, six more than the Alfonso-backed monarchist party, the Renovación Española, then led in the Cortes by the Catalan Antonio Goicoechea.)[63] The rebels' particular aversion: 35-year-old José María Gil Robles, the coalition's leader, who struck many – Vatican officials included – as the Spanish political scene's great white Catholic hope.[64] Alcalá Zamora refused to appoint Gil Robles as Prime Minister, fearing the consequences of enraging the left: fearing, also, that Gil Robles's avowals of monarchism were sincere (certainly Gil Robles's father had been an active Carlist).[65] Instead, he gave the role to a much longer established figure: Alejandro Lerroux, once a demagogic leftist, but by the 1930s decidedly centrist. Convinced that Lerroux would do Gil Robles's bidding, leftists seized power in the coal-mining city of Oviedo. There they set up soviets – their own term – and brought a new dimension to church-burning for fun and profit. This time, rather than confining their efforts to mere architectural revisionism (impressive though that was: fifty-eight local churches went up in flames), they also slew thirty-three local clergy, at least twelve local businessmen, and Carlist legislator Marcelino Oreja Elósegui.[66] It required 20,000 government troops – many of them led by Franco – to subdue the insurrection's chiefs, who refused to surrender until no fewer than a thousand of their comrades had been killed. In short, nobody who witnessed the events of October 1934 had any cause for surprise at the still gorier events of 1936–39.

With the Asturias thus made a desert and being called peaceful, a respite of sorts followed. One movement of radically right-wing orientation, the Falange Española (or FE for short), made copious headlines for a while under the leadership of José Antonio Primo de Rivera, the late General's son. José Antonio had much greater charisma and erudition than the General ever managed. (He alone, among FE candidates, won election to the Cortes in 1933.) But although the FE received subsidies from the Duce, it represented a poor return on Italian investment, and by early 1936 it was waning. Leaders of Carlism and the Renovación Española publicly distanced themselves from it.[67] Moreover, the frequency with which leftists assassinated Falange adherents – ten such adherents had been murdered in 1933 and 1934 – made Falange membership a dubiously attractive career option for the uncommitted. At the February 1936 Cortes election, José Antonio was defeated, and no other Falange candidate did any better. Nor was this the election's only portentous aspect.

Those who imagined that the result would be an unqualified triumph for Azaña, and for the left-wing Popular Front (*Frente Popular* in Spanish) which he led, were disappointed. True, the Popular Front gained seats; the Gil Robles coalition lost seats, as did both the main monarchist parties, Carlist and Alfonsist; while the Lerroux-style centre groups, plagued by financial scandals, declined greatly from their 1933 representation (Lerroux failed to carry his own electorate). In the 473–seat Cortes, the Popular Front won 263 seats and the Gil Robles alliance only 132 seats. But the popular vote told an almost unrecognisably different story. Altogether 9,864,763 Spaniards cast ballots; of these, almost as many went to the right-wingers (4,503,505 votes, or 45.7 per cent of the total) as went to the left-wingers (4,654,116 votes, or 47.2 per cent of the total). We now know from such historians as Stanley G. Payne, Jesús Palacios, Roberto Villa García and Manuel Álvarez Tardío the debt which even this wafer-thin left-wing majority owed to intimidation at voting booths by pro-Azaña activists, and the zeal with which Azaña insisted on Alcalá Zamora making him Prime Minister before all the returns were in.[68]

As for Gil Robles, well before the campaign (which left thirty-seven persons dead)[69] had finished, he announced his absolute confidence in a victory for his own forces. Prudence would have mandated that he postpone such rejoicing till ballots had actually been cast. His failure to demonstrate such prudence confirmed the suspicions of left-wingers and monarchists alike: that for all his tough talk, all his allusions to rulers like Mussolini, he would shrink from any tough action. 'If Gil Robles,' one British chronicler acerbically commented the following year, 'had known what he was about there would have been no need for Franco.'[70]

Azaña could scarcely believe his fortune. Convinced that the political Right was a busted flush, his government amnestied left-wing political prisoners, while also banning the Falange Española, imprisoning José Antonio (no longer protected by Cortes membership) on an accurate but trivial charge of unlicensed gun possession, and banished from the mainland those generals considered insufficiently loyal (these included Franco, sent to the Canary Islands). Alcalá Zamora, having served his purpose, dutifully resigned from the presidency on 10 May to make room for Azaña, who handed over the prime ministerial duties to his fellow Pact of San Sebastián signatory Santiago Casares Quiroga. The latter's term lasted for little more than two months.

By the time it ended, all pretence of neutrality had been perforce extinguished. On 13 July, the Cortes's most outspoken Renovación Española figure José Calvo Sotelo had been kidnapped and shot dead by members of the Popular Front's Shock Police (*Guardias de Asalto*), who painstakingly gouged out their captive's eyes;[71] these guards also tried and failed to capture Gil Robles, then outside the capital on holiday. On the 17th, the war officially began when the garrison at Melilla, in northern Africa, revolted against the government. On the 19th, the despairing Casares Quiroga stepped down. His successor, Diego Martínez Barrio, lasted less than a day in the job. During that day Martínez Barrio tried to win General Emilio Mola to the Popular Front's support. This effort having proven unavailing, Azaña dismissed the hapless Prime Minister in favour of a reliably ruthless figure, José Giral. About an infinitely more dignified and peaceable régime change than Spain's travails of

1936–39 would prove to be, Lord Macaulay had written: 'In revolutions men live fast: the experience of years is crowded into hours: old habits of thought and action are violently broken: novelties, which at first sight inspire dread and disgust, become in a few days familiar, endurable, attractive.'[72]

This is not the place (no mere book chapter is the place) to attempt a description of the Spanish Civil War. Antony Beevor's *The Battle for Spain* runs to 526 pages;[73] Burnett Bolloten's *The Spanish Civil War: Revolution and Counter-Revolution* contains 1,074 pages;[74] the third (1977) edition of Hugh Thomas's much older and more renowned volume on the subject occupies no fewer than 1,115 pages.[75] More than 10,000 tomes to do with the war have been published, with almost all the major European languages represented. All that can be essayed here is a concentration upon, and a summary of, the war's specifically monarchist aspects.

With the 1931 death of Don Jaime, the Carlist claim to the crown had passed to his uncle, Alfonso Carlos, a veteran of the 1870s' Carlist warfare. Much more vehement by nature than Jaime (who had once poignantly mused 'I would have liked to be a dealer in emeralds in Colombia'),[76] Alfonso Carlos greeted the insurgent generals' July 1936 campaign as a 'spectacular renaissance of Carlism'.[77] Five years earlier he had issued an equally robust manifesto: 'The banner which was raised by my glorious ancestors [...] and was unfurled with the same enthusiasm by my dear nephew Jaime, I shall keep intact as the intangible palladium of the Spanish Catholics and Monarchists.'[78]

This 'intangible palladium' was soon torn. On 28 September the 87-year-old Alfonso Carlos, while he crossed a busy Vienna street, abruptly ceased walking; a tramcar, its driver unable to brake in time, knocked him over. The stricken pedestrian died in hospital the following day. It seems a curiously banal fate for so obstinate and bellicose a figure; some insisted that his death had not been at all accidental.

At any rate, since Alfonso Carlos died childless, his demise left open the question of whom the next Carlist claimant should be. No other direct descendant of Don Carlos remained. It could therefore be argued, and by many Carlists it was indeed argued, that after September 1936 the rightful Carlist heir was (of all people) Alfonso XIII. This idea, with its implication that the previous hundred years' wars over the Spanish crown need not have occurred, Alfonso Carlos himself had rejected. He regarded his legitimate heir as his wife's nephew, Prince Javier of Bourbon-Parma. The old man, near the end of his life, had identified Prince Javier – brother, it will be recalled, of Empress Zita – as a regent. When such a regency would take place, and whether it was to operate while Alfonso Carlos was still alive but absent from Spanish soil, remained ambiguous. The dramas which such ambiguity intensified confirm the wisdom of the Duke of Wellington's words, spoken from bitter Iberian Peninsula experience: 'Spain is the only country where two and two do not make four.'[79]

Meanwhile the Carlists, as the political situation worsened and the Popular Front's homicidal tendencies increased, exemplified Trinculo's aphorism in *The Tempest*: 'Misery acquaints a man with strange bedfellows.' The Alfonsists, whom they once considered beyond the pale, soon looked like allies. As early as 1934, prominent Carlists Rafael de Olazábal and Antonio de Lizarza had attended a meeting in Rome with Mussolini and with Goicoechea. The three Spaniards sought Italian aid for their respective movements if Spain did descend into civil war.[80] When the war did break out, it broke out independently of Olazábal's, Lizarza's and Goicoechea's plans, but outsiders were not to know that.

Moreover, other exercises in political ecumenism occurred, through necessity, on the right-wing side before the 17 July eruption. Sanjurjo, who had cooled his heels in Portugal once his prison sentence had ended, concluded that he needed the Carlists still. Collective memory of their courage in the nineteenth century worked in their favour: they revived for themselves the name *Requetés*, coined in the 1830s, and the red beret from the same period likewise came back into use. General Mola also sought out Carlist cooperation, and Fal Conde, believing that his hour had arrived, spurned to mince words in his ambit claim:

> We Carlists, who stand for the old traditions, have made great but willing sacrifices. We have abandoned for the time being our idea of the restoration of an absolute Monarchy, but on the strict understanding that this movement is not to favour one or other of the different political parties, but is to establish authoritative government.[81]

Mola could not promise enough to keep the Carlists content. Sanjurjo could, but before July was out, he had lost his life in a crash near Lisbon, when his De Havilland plane's propeller hit a tree. *Faute de mieux*, it became clear that some sort of rapprochement with the Falange Española had to be undertaken, particularly since the FE's numbers had expanded still more rapidly during 1936 than Carlism's numbers had done.[82] And Carlist recruitment proceeded with impressive swiftness, above in the movement's ancient stronghold of Navarre. 'Between July and December 1936 some 40,000 Navarrese – a tenth of the population of the province – donned the red beret and took up arms against the republic.'[83]

The fact that Fal Conde and José Antonio had enjoyed a civil relationship with one another, despite their great political divergences, promised to facilitate a Carlist-Falange pooling of resources.[84] Yet of José Antonio's whereabouts, all the knowledge which outsiders at first had was that he mouldered in a Popular Front jail. His own movement's members, and other right-wingers, habitually spoke of him as *El Ausente:* 'the absent one'. In fact, during November 1936 he had been subjected to a kangaroo court set up at Alicante's main prison. Amid this mock-trial – where, to give the proceedings a patina of legality, three non-political judges were hired to supplement the 'people's tribunal' – he had defended himself with such embarrassing eloquence that the judges refused to impose a capital sentence on him. The government, not to be cheated of its prey, had him shot on 20 November.

With José Antonio and Sanjurjo both in the grave, nothing and no one could stop Franco from attaining supreme power on the Nationalist side. Particularly after 3 June 1937, the day on which Mola (whom Stanley G. Payne has called 'the only subordinate capable of talking back to Franco'[85]) perished when his plane hit a mountain. The 'last man standing' factor benefited the Caudillo immensely, however irksome his movement's external and internal opponents found it to be vanquished by one so obviously unintellectual. He did have his hard core of personal loyalists. Alfonso XIII's aunt, the Infanta Eulalia, somewhat bathetically reflected: 'We all believed in Franco. We gave money till it hurt, even selling our jewels.'[86]

Yet most Carlists and Alfonsists regarded the alliance with the future Caudillo in the spirit of a shotgun wedding, arranged in great reluctance. Already in April (that is, two months before bad weather and poor visibility caused Mola to lose control of his aircraft), a proclamation by Franco himself forced upon his philosophically diverse followers a unity ticket. From now on, Franco decreed, there would be no separate FE, no separate Renovación Española, and no separate Carlism. These groups henceforth would all be subsumed under the cumbersome title *Falange Española Tradicionalista y de la Juventud Ofensiva Nacional Sindicalista.* (The title's very acronym defied straightforward vocalisation: *FET y JONS.*) The name's full version being too elaborate for all but a handful of militants to utter in casual chitchat or indeed to remember, the collective soon became more generally known as simply the *Movimento Nacional.* A National Council (*Conseja Nacional*) of forty-eight persons included representatives from all the constituent blocs, but to make sure that the Council did not arrogate any authority to itself, Franco alone retained the right to nominate its members. María de las Nieves, Alfonso Carlos's widow, fumed at the way in which the decree forced Carlists to break bread with Falangist vulgarians – 'It is an infamy that has been done to us'[87] – but could do no more than fume. Prince Javier, bolder than María de las Nieves, told Franco to his face in December 1937: 'If it were not for the Requetés I very much doubt if you would be where you are. [...] Do not forget that I am the last link between you and the Requetés; or that I shall always work for Spain, but not for you personally.'[88]

The Prince's own younger brother, Cayetano, had joined the *Requetés* and had been severely wounded in action the preceding May.[89] But Javier might as well have saved his breath. Many Falangists, rather than wear the Carlist red beret with its ineluctable royal symbolism, preferred to stow the berets in their pockets and remain hatless.[90] One important Falangist, asked by visiting French journalist Georges Oudard how he would react if a monarchy really were established on Carlist criteria, retorted: 'There would simply be another revolution. And this time, I assure you, we would not be on the same side.'[91] Carlism had advocated, from the start, decentralised regional administration: the very antithesis of the FE's demand for a unitary state, a state which offered no special privileges for Navarrese, Catalans, or anyone else.

While Fal Conde had grown less and less enamoured of Franco, his views counted for little by this stage. He had fallen out with his colleague Rodezno, whom Franco found considerably more tractable. When Fal Conde established a Carlist military college without seeking prior approval from Franco, the latter decided on a judicious dialectic of carrots and sticks. Through a go-between (the Nationalist Defence Minister Fidel Dávila), Franco urgently besought Fal Conde to consider the advantages of banishment: or, should he find such consideration uncongenial, to let his mind be concentrated wonderfully by the prospect of a firing squad.[92] Fal Conde chose banishment. (Later, in November 1937, Franco appointed Fal Conde to the National Council, only to cancel this appointment the following March.)[93] Very likely the threat of a firing squad was hollow, Franco being – his subsequent career confirmed – much more inclined to neutralise right-wing antagonists through promotion than through violence; but hollow threats mistaken for deadly serious threats can serve useful purposes. They equally curbed the Falangist enthusiasms of Manuel Hedilla, one of José Antonio's closest friends, increasingly aggrieved by how limited his political power within the movement was, compared with what José Antonio had enjoyed. Hedilla tried to thwart the April 1937 amalgamation; failed; defied a demand from Franco that he accept a post on the National Council; and was himself sentenced to be shot. That shooting, similarly, never occurred – in part because of interventions by Ramón Serrano Suñer, Franco's pro-Falange brother-in-law (afterwards Spain's Foreign Minister), and in part because making a martyr out of Hedilla would create extra enemies whom Franco could ill afford. Better to keep Hedilla alive but politically and militarily impotent. Consequently, Hedilla spent the next four years in a prison cell, and gave the Caudillo no further trouble.[94] Nor did Goicoechea, placated with a well-paid but politically insignificant governorship at the Bank of Spain.

Nor, for the matter of that, did Alfonso XIII, now based in Rome, but eagerly following the war's progress. On 4 December 1937 Franco fired off to his quondam sovereign an insolent letter, which included the following reproach: 'The new Spain which we are forging has so little in common with the liberal and constitutional Spain over which you ruled that your training and old-fashioned political practices necessarily provoke the anxieties and resentments of Spaniards.'[95]

What was wartime life within Spain's monarchist forces like? Compared with the Republicans' International Brigades, which sometimes give posterity the impression of having inspired reminiscences from half the authors of Britain and America, few records of combat in Franco's army survive. The eminent South-African-born poet Roy Campbell had hoped to serve with the *Requetés*, but the Nationalist press officer Pablo Merry del Val – whose uncle Cardinal Merry del Val had been Vatican Secretary of State – rejected his application, telling him that he would be more useful to the Nationalists writing on their behalf than donning a uniform.[96] (Later in the war Campbell would publish his epic verse in heroic couplets, *Flowering Rifle,* that displayed Maurrasian ferocity.) One foreigner who did don a uniform, and wrote at length about the experience, was the English journalist Peter Kemp. He took his 1957 memoir's title, *Mine Were Of Trouble,* from lines by A.E. Housman ('The thoughts of others / Were light and fleeting, / Of lovers' meeting / Or luck or fame. / Mine were of trouble, / And mine were steady; / So I was ready / When trouble came.')

In his early twenties, Kemp had partied his way through Cambridge with so little academic benefit that his father, a retired judge, wrote him a letter which concluded with the minatory observation: 'Sometimes I think that God must have made you for a bet.'[97] Kemp, though active in the university's Conservative Party association, was not a Catholic and had no particular Spanish connections; but he felt genuine shock at the Popular Front's anti-religious campaigns, harboured a marked spirit of wanderlust, and had convinced himself that 'This war isn't likely to last more than six months […] the experience is bound to be useful, and anyway I've nothing to lose.'[98] Armed with a basic Spanish-language textbook,[99] with a letter of introduction from London's *Sunday Dispatch* newspaper (owned by Lord Rothermere),[100] and with certificates from Cambridge's Officer Training Corps which gave foreigners the impression of far more comprehensive military experience than Kemp could actually boast,[101] he quickly 'abandoned for ever my journalist's cover' and, 'the ideals of the *Requetés* [having] fired my imagination',[103] achieved admission to a Carlist regiment at Ávila. He met Fal Conde – 'Falconde', as he always spelled the latter's name – who warned: 'I do not know if we can take you as an officer when you speak no Spanish.' Kemp 'assured him that I was quite happy to enlist in the ranks'.[104]

To the ancient military proverb that soldiering consists of 90 per cent boredom and 10 per cent terror, the *Requetés* proved no exception. Nor did the terror invariably derive from Republican threats. Kemp recounts a searing instance of how Carlist Lieutenant Carlos Llancia, Marqués de Cocuhella, administered a discipline incomparably more cold-hearted than anything in the OTC:

> The day after my arrival two troopers reported for duty incapably drunk; apparently they were old offenders. The following evening Llancia formed the whole Squadron in a hollow square in the main barrack-room. Calling out the two defaulters in front of us he shouted, 'There has been enough drunkenness in this Squadron. I will have no more of it, as you are going to see.' Thereupon he drove his fist into the face of one of them, knocking out most of his front teeth and sending him spinning across the room to crash through two ranks of men and collapse on the floor. Turning on the other he beat him across the face with a riding crop until the man dropped half senseless to the ground. He returned to his first victim, yanked him to his feet and laid open his face with the crop, disregarding his screams, until he felt inert beside his companion. Then he turned to us: 'You have seen, I will not tolerate a single drunkard in this Squadron.' The two culprits were hauled, sobbing, to their feet to have a half-pint of castor oil forced down their throats.[105]

The punishment, however dreadful, did the job. Kemp reports: 'They were on duty next day, but I never saw either of them drunk again.'[106]

Elsewhere Kemp experienced a surprising amount of kindness from the locals, despite never speaking Spanish as well as he would have preferred. One awkward problem he (along with other non-Catholic volunteers for Franco) found hard to solve: as a Protestant, he had marked difficulty in persuading Nationalists, including a Catholic chaplain with whom he became friendly, that he had never joined the Masons.[107]

With moments of comparative freedom from danger came opportunities for Kemp to meditate upon the grandeurs and miseries of Carlist life. Although he had made his way up through the Carlist ranks, he grew to find that life wanting:

> I had learnt one thing about the *Requetés*; for all their courage and endurance, their patriotism and self-sacrificing idealism, they lacked the strict discipline and technical training that are so necessary in modern warfare. This war had altered radically since the early days, and the old qualities of willingness and valour were no longer enough. Only in the [Spanish] Foreign Legion, I was convinced, could I hope to learn first-class soldiering. They were the troops on whom General Franco depended for the most difficult operations. Somehow, I decided, I must join the Foreign Legion [...][108]

This Kemp did, after favourably impressing the Legion's one-armed, one-eyed, much-revered, much-reviled General José Millán Astray, who 'shot questions at me like a machine-gun, concentrating his one eye upon me in a fierce unblinking glare. Apparently my answers satisfied him.'[109] But if Carlist discipline could be alarming,

Legionary discipline constituted a whole new order of fear and misery for Kemp. About one incident, especially, he commented: 'The horror of it is still with me as I write; nor, I fear, will it ever leave me. I can scarcely bear to write of it now.'[110] An Irish deserter from the International Brigades had given himself up to a Nationalist patrol:

> He knew that if he tried to escape in Republican Spain he would certainly be retaken and shot; and so he had bided his time until he reached the front, when he had taken the first opportunity to desert. [...] Translating his account to [Legion Captain Eduardo] Cancela, I urged that this was indeed a special case; the man was a deserter, not a prisoner, and we should be unwise as well as unjust to shoot him. Moved either by my arguments, or by consideration for my feelings, Cancela agreed to spare him.[111]

Cancela's commanding officer, Major Alfonso de Mora, conceded the justice of Kemp's entreaties. Alas, de Mora's own superior, the sadistic Colonel José Peñarredonda, angered at Kemp's interruption of his meal, refused to be assuaged:

> 'I have the fellow here, sir,' I concluded, 'in case you wish to ask him any questions.' The Colonel did not look up from his plate: 'No, Peter,' he said casually, his mouth full of egg, 'I don't want to ask him anything. Just take him away and shoot him.'
>
> I was so astonished that my mouth dropped open; my heart seemed to stop beating. Peñaredonda [*sic*] looked up, his eyes full of hatred:
>
> 'Get out!' he snarled. 'You heard what I said.' As I withdrew he shouted after me: 'I warn you, I intend to see that this order is carried out.'[112]

Somehow Kemp nerved himself to obey, and to explain to the captive what he had been instructed to do:

> It was almost more than I could bear to face the prisoner, where he stood between my two runners [...] [who] nodded, and raised their rifles. I looked away. The two shots exploded simultaneously. 'On our honour, sir,' the senior of the two said to me, 'he could not have felt a thing.'
>
> I went to examine the body. There was no doubt that death had been instantaneous.[113]

Soon afterwards, Kemp learned from Cancela that Peñarredonda took no chances. He had (Cancela revealed) sent two Legionaries in pursuit of Kemp, 'to shoot you if you did not immediately carry out his order'.[114]

By the time the war ended, Kemp had had his jaw smashed during a mortar attack: 'my mouth and throat felt numb and soggy, I could not speak, and my jaw hung loose – I realised that it was shattered'.[115] Through discreet wire-pulling and, not least, the aid of Jacobo Fitz-James Stuart y Falcó, the seventeenth Duke of Alba (Franco's chief emissary in London), Kemp convalesced in Britain. 'I was far from well. Fortunately for me, the Duke of Alba [...] had observed this himself. He sent for me to say that he had caused my leave to be extended for another two months and forbade me to return earlier.'[116] Franco himself had known of, and had approved, Kemp's leave request. Before the intrepid young Englishman left Spain, he obtained a private interview at Burgos with the Caudillo himself, of whose utterances Kemp remembered:

> Throughout the interview his tone was informal and friendly, neither didactic nor condescending; sensitive, no doubt, to the embarrassment I should feel if I had to express my own views, he invited no comment. At the end he rose, shook hands gravely, thanked me for my services and wished me luck.
>> 'What will you do now?' he asked.
>> 'Join the British Army for the coming war, I suppose, Your Excellency.'
> He cocked his head, then gave a wintry smile:
>> 'I don't think there will be a war.'
> I wonder what he really thought.[117]

If the post-Civil-War Kemp had not existed, Graham Greene would have needed to invent him. During the 'coming war' of which he spoke to a sceptical Franco, Kemp enlisted in Britain's Special Operations Executive. He saw nerve-racking action in occupied France, Albania, and Poland; the NKVD captured him while he served in the Polish Home Army. Released by the Soviets after only a month – an improbable feat in itself – he went to the Far East and, in Bali and Lombok, threw himself into the struggle against the Japanese when not smuggling weapons to the French for use against the Vietminh. As if his résumé had not been already eventful enough, he covered the 1956 Hungarian uprising and its swift defeat for Britain's Catholic weekly *The Tablet*. The 1960s found him reporting from Africa, while the initial exhilaration of Congolese independence from Belgium gave way to the warfare which made Patrice Lumumba, Moïse Tshombe, Joseph Kasavubu and Mobutu Sese Seko household names in the Western world. When Ian Smith's rule over Rhodesia crumbled in 1978–79, Kemp was there, this time as *The Spectator*'s representative. The Nicaraguan Contras, profiting in the 1980s from the Reagan presidency's support, found in Kemp a useful military adviser. Back finally in Britain, he died of natural causes in 1993, aged 80.

At first Alfonso coped with expatriation tolerably well. Baccarat and bridge lost nothing of their appeal to him because of his enforced new environment. Neither did travel: he spent much time in Lausanne (with side-journeys to Northern Ireland, Austria, and Egypt) before settling in Rome, where a special dispensation from the Duce let him reside tax-free. The same liveliness of character that had charmed so many in the past prevented Alfonso from becoming too bored. Actually, boredom could have been a welcome change for him, given the tragedies which pursued his family. His younger haemophiliac son, Gonzalo, during an Austrian vacation in August 1934, succumbed to road accident injuries that a man of his age (20) in decent physical health would have survived. Within four years, Gonzalo's older sibling and fellow haemophiliac Alfonso Junior – 'Alfonsito' – met a similar doom.

Good-looking and charming, a rock-star before rock-stars were invented, Alfonsito had crossed the Atlantic (prefiguring the 1960s' Dionysian principle of 'I'm here for a good time, not a long time') and had developed the reckless habit of acquiring, both in Cuba and afterwards in Florida, wives who were not merely commoners but Protestants. (Before the Second Vatican Council, any Catholic who underwent marriage to a non-Catholic in a non-Catholic rite incurred, at least *de jure* and very often de facto as well, automatic excommunication.) His father, hardly in a position to censure womanisers as such, fretted over the lad's preoccupation with *marrying* his heretical mistresses. But soon Alfonsito made – as many other Old World immigrants have made – the delightful and astounding discovery that in the USA, unlike in Europe, getting divorced constitutes almost as much of a social obligation as getting a driver's licence. His marital commitments, then, could be as readily doffed as donned, leaving himself in a euphoric, impeccably democratic limbo of all bachelorhood's pleasures and none of its pains. 'Merry Mildred' Gaydon, a cigarette-seller, had the privilege of being Alfonsito's last attachment. One night in September 1938 found prince and cigarette-girl driving along Miami's Biscayne Boulevard, until Alfonsito lost control of the car and, desperately trying to evade an oncoming truck, careened into a telephone pole. Before medical help could reach the scene, the young man had died from sheer loss of blood. In spite or because of his canonically ambiguous status, he was interred (at Graceland Memorial Park) according to Catholic ceremonies. Miss Gaydon attended the funeral, along with 'a handful of friends'.[118]

Some marriages can withstand, can be strengthened by, disgrace and bereavement; not so for Alfonso and Ena. While husband and wife kept up the public forms of connubial duty for as long as possible, they increasingly led separate lives. Ena at least still had her health, which was more than Alfonso did. Heart disease sapped his strength and his bravado, so that on at least one nocturnal occasion he came 'weeping into her room'.[119] In his early fifties he seemed much older. And as sick men of a certain age will, he turned to religion anew, finding a particularly valued confidant in Cardinal Pedro Segura y Sáenz, Archbishop of Toledo, whom the Republic had deported for his impenitent royalism. Cardinal Segura 'wore a hair shirt next to his skin, and believed that a bath was a heathen invention'.[120] Nonetheless, clearly Alfonso considered the Cardinal's company congenial, as the company of a man clad in soft garments would not have been for him.

Ena continued to tough things out. Her recent biographer, Gerard Noel, rather cattily observed: 'She was not a crier over spilt milk. She would never have felt that the world was coming to an end unless she had suddenly had to do without meals or maids.'[121]

There survived some genuine affection between her and her spouse, after time and chance had done all their draining, empoisoning work. But by early February 1941 the end could not be long delayed. On 15 January, and not before, the 54-year-old Alfonso had formally announced his abdication from the throne, in favour of the Infante Juan. As Alfonso weakened, he initially resisted letting Ena visit him at all.[122] Once he relented, Ena found the last meeting painful:

> When she was shown into Alfonso's room at the Grand Hotel she was appalled at what she saw. 'Forgive me if I don't rise,' he said to Ena with the grave courtesy more appropriate to the receiving of a relative stranger. 'I'm suffering like mad.' Ena could not hide the shock she felt at his appearance.[123]

Never did Alfonso show himself a truer Spaniard than in the religious scruples which afflicted him as his strength ebbed. He felt so nauseated as to voice the fear that, if his chaplain Father Ulpiano López administered communion to him, he would inadvertently choke on the Host.[124]

On 28 February, the end came. His three doctors had pleaded with him to let them give him (an almost unimaginable luxury in a Rome already suffering wartime shortages) extra oxygen. This offer he chivalrously refused, insisting that 'There are so many of the poor who have more need of it than I.'[125] Perhaps nothing in Alfonso's life became him like the leaving it, but as an exemplar of *ars moriendi*, Alfonso's deathbed commands admiration.

An obituary for the ex-monarch in *The Tablet* commented:

> [...] history will increasingly question whether he did not make a tragic error in accepting as final the anti-monarchical feelings which dominated the municipal elections of 1931. Precisely because he knew so well how little the Republic was likely to succeed, he was tempted to let it disprove itself; but for the same reason he should have seen his office as a remaining bulwark against disintegration and collapse. The effect of his withdrawal was that everybody had to accept the Republic, and accepted it with very different ideas of what they intended it to become, and with increasing bitterness at other men who used the same vocabulary to cover opposite ideas. [...]
>
> The revolt from the anonymous and soulless capitalism of the last century is the main thing which the Carlist traditionalists and the new Phalangists [*sic*] have in common today. What they defeated in the civil war were movements bred in the corruption of the last century, the doctrines of Bakunin and Marx, which arose directly out of capitalist society and presuppose it, and all that exclusive and violent emphasis on man as a producer and consumer which the capitalist philosophy brought in and the Socialist philosophy had adopted.
>
> The traditionalists are very strong in Spain today. The Phalangists are so directly imitative of Italian and German models, that their credit must be impaired when the foreign precursors are proved either hollow or evil.[126]

Why, ultimately, did Spain's monarchist leaders, the Carlists in particular, not achieve more? Why did they form only a second-order threat to the republican establishment, not at all comparable to the difficulties which Portuguese republicanism experienced in suppressing Paiva Couceiro's campaigns? Several possible reasons can be listed.

Sir Samuel Hoare, former British Foreign Secretary and Home Secretary, who during most of the Second World War served as Ambassador to Spain (and who came to loathe Franco), regarded Spanish monarchism's essential problem as its lack of firm local leadership. Vásquez de Mella had died in 1928; Calvo Sotelo's assassination has already been discussed. Fal Conde remained little known outside Spanish political circles. Goicoechea strikes posterity as a natural second-in-command, inspiring no impassioned enthusiasm or impassioned distaste on his own account. The one right-wing leader of incontrovertible evangelistic gifts had been the republican José Antonio, who continued to resent the way in which his father had been cast aside by Alfonso XIII, and who saw no need to rescue monarchy from itself.

> Unlike the Republicans who had too many leaders, the Monarchists had no leader at all. [...] In the absence of such a leader they dissipated their very considerable strength in inconclusive discussions as to whether or not it was best to cooperate or break with Franco, as to when they should act, and as to how they should carry out the change of régime when the perfect moment arrived. More than once they were given the chance to succeed if they had been prepared to take resolute action. There were moments between 1940 and 1942 when Serrano Suñer's policy of fraternisation with the Germans seemed to point unmistakably to Spanish intervention in the war against the Allies. The country was overwhelmingly for peace and many Republicans were prepared to join the Monarchists in an effort to remove a government that seemed bent upon war. At that time the general talk in the back streets of the towns and in the country villages was that 'nothing had gone right since the King left Spain'.[127]

Hoare correctly observed that much of Franco's officer class maintained, at the very least, monarchist sympathies; but that these sympathies were seldom if ever capitalised on: 'The Generals, almost all of whom were monarchists in theory, remained inert.'[128] This despite the fact that the brief First Republic during the 1870s had been chaotic enough to leave bad national memories of republicanism *per se* – quite apart from the Second Republic's multitude of sins – and such memories should have worked in monarchism's favour.

A complicating (and, in practice, enervating) factor for Spanish monarchism lay in a problem which also damaged its French counterpart: over-supply of intellectuals. The Latin political classes' inherent propensity to imagine that to write a manifesto is to overcome all administrative difficulties much weakened the Spanish monarchists' collective hand and much strengthened the hand of Franco. (Paiva Couceiro in Portugal knew better than to let monarchist intellectuals, however laudable in themselves, dictate military policy.) If half of the dynamism which went on establishing Carlist magazines, arranging Carlist conferences, and issuing Carlist pamphlets had been devoted to the hard grind of encouraging Carlist administrators, the history of twentieth-century Spain would have been very different. As it was, the Caudillo always exhibited what Carlist policy-makers usually never showed and what Alfonsist policy-makers showed too seldom: unpitying single-mindedness of purpose, by which almost any tactical change could be accommodated, on condition that Franco's two fundamental strategies – keeping Spain Catholic, and preventing the USSR from controlling the Mediterranean – remained undamaged.

Alfonso XIII's closest friend the Duke of Alba, Kemp's benefactor, was a monarchist to the very marrow of his bones and, rarer still, a practical politician with abundant cabinet experience. He far surpassed General Primo de Rivera in aptitude, imagination, self-discipline, and ability to win over the intellectual classes. Clearly he captivated the British historian Sir Arthur Bryant, whose obituary notice for him in 1953 includes the following vivid pen-portrait:

> With his spare, eager face, long features and brilliant eyes, his quick, precise, clipped speech, his grave courtesy and uncompromising courage and integrity, he could never have been mistaken for anything but a Spaniard of Spaniards [...] Yet, with all this, he was the most internationally-minded man I have ever encountered: a European who, unlike the average Englishman of Spaniard, Frenchman or German or Italian, thought always of Europe as an indivisible and living unity – a unity which could never be broken without disastrous consequences to every nation in Europe.[129]

No illusions about the nature of Red rule afflicted Alba. Early in the Civil War he had been compelled to take sides when the Communists murdered his younger brother, the Duke of Peñaranda.

But neither Alfonso nor Franco made adequate use of Alba's talents. The King, though on occasion he gave Alba a fairly minor cabinet post, denied him what he accorded several much less versatile figures: the prime ministry. He preferred keeping the Duke in the role of mere boon companion, without even being able to dominate him as the newly crowned Henry V abruptly and unanswerably dominated Falstaff. (It might have spoken to something at a deep level of Alfonso's psychology that Alba *looked* like Alfonso's identical twin brother. Staring at caption-less photos of the two men, the beholder is hard pressed to differentiate monarch from subject, though the subject was the monarch's senior by eight years.) Franco, for his part, happily neutralised a probable rival by making the Duke Ambassador to Britain. There, he did good work in smoothing Anglo-Spanish relations.[130] (Alba's descent from the Duke of Marlborough's sister Arabella, mistress of James II, accorded him the right – which he exploited with relish – to address Churchill as 'Cousin'.)[131] Nevertheless he had little chance of influencing policy in Madrid, as others without his gifts could do purely by virtue of living in the capital. After the Second World War, the Duke deserted Franco's cause, on the incorrect but then understandable assumption that Franco never had the faintest desire to reinstate the Bourbon monarchy.

Not all of monarchism's failure in the early days of Franco's government can be ascribed to the monarchists' own faults. No one predicted the completeness of Franco's conquest except, possibly, Franco himself. And indubitably he at first assumed, as did his fellow generals, that July 1936 would be a matter of a short sharp coup, resembling many a nineteenth-century *pronunciamento*, instead of the almost three years' slogging combat that actually resulted. As of July 1936 the rational betting was on half-a-dozen other figures, all with more obvious and flamboyant abilities than Franco's, leading the Nationalist campaign. By January 1938 none of those figures remained a serious competitor and few of them remained alive.

Ultimately the chief blame for Spanish monarchism's inter-war frustrations lies with Alfonso XIII's own loss of nerve in April 1931. The fact that (like his Austrian counterpart thirteen years earlier) he fled his native country without ever having signed a formal deed of abdication counted, in reality, for naught. Probably no more than two or three Spaniards in ten thousand knew that in the narrow statutory sense Alfonso had never forfeited the crown. His subsequent rationalisation of his exile, as quoted by Churchill – 'I hope I shall not go back; for that will only mean that the Spanish people are not prosperous and happy'[132] – did much credit to his good-heartedness but little credit to his intelligence. It failed to suggest even the beginnings of a political creed, least of all a political creed for which brave men wanted to endure, and to inflict, the most atrocious hardships.

Churchill's son Randolph, evincing that oafishness which never deserted him, briskly pooh-poohed those existential clashes of doctrine that turned 1930s Spain into a slaughterhouse. When Randolph visited the Franco front (soon inspiring by this action the widespread hope that he would depart as quickly as possible for the Republican front), he treated the world to his considered opinion of the hostilities: 'A few excitable Catholics and ardent Socialists think that this war matters, but for the general public it is just a lot of bloody dagoes killing each other.'[133]

'This war' was in fact rather more than that.

Chapter VI

The Monkey That Changed the Balkans
Greece

> Love thy beloved little country with thy whole heart; be bold, but also patient: never be over-hasty; rather let the night pass before taking thy decision; be not angry, and let not the sun go down upon thy wrath; be calm in thought and mind, and never forget that thou art King of a southern people, whose wrath and excitability are kindled in a moment, and which at such a moment is capable of saying and doing many things which a moment later it will perhaps forget; and remember that it is often better for the King himself to suffer, even morally, rather than the people, whose interests should take precedence of all others.
>
> Political testament of Greece's King George I
(reigned 1863–1913),
to his son, the future Constantine I[1]

Fritz, a Newfoundland dog as boisterous, cuddly and friendly as most other Newfoundland dogs, inadvertently brought about his master's demise. He belonged to Alexander, who since 1917 had been King of the Hellenes.

On 2 October 1920, the sovereign visited the manager of the vineyard at the royal palace, Tatoi. The manager possessed two monkeys, a male and a female, who at the sight, sound and smell of Fritz's arrival in the manager's garden, set upon the hound with screeches. Alexander, who had been working on the engine of his car and whose hands were covered in grease, tried to separate the warring animals. The enraged male monkey administered to Alexander severe bites, on the leg and in the stomach. It required several assistants of the manager to remove the monkey's teeth from the King's person. No other bandage being available, they covered the leg wound with a bandage stained in oil: the first of several mistakes made by Alexander's carers.

The manager's wife, more sensible than most of the others present, insisted on giving the leg wound a thorough clean. Once the King had left Tatoi for Athens, doctors saw him and did some more cleaning, but neither they nor their patient took the whole incident seriously enough. Alexander himself, regarding it as a minor inconvenience, requested that his physicians keep it secret from the public.[2] Why they never cauterised the injuries remains mysterious.

Before nightfall the King was overcome by a high fever. The following day there could no longer be any hope of keeping the incident quiet: medical men needed to be summoned from other countries. Septicaemia had set in. Then the patient came down with jaundice, dysentery and pneumonia. No surgeon dared amputate the affected leg, though some briefly considered doing so. The unfortunate Alexander continued at first to joke about his illness, assuring the doctor who dressed his leg 'that he was using such a lot of bandage that he must have shares in the company'.[3] No intervention worked. Soon the King was yelling with pain, beseeching those attending him to summon his mother Sophie, then enduring banishment with her husband Constantine. He fell into a delirium in which:

> he called for his driver and asked if the brakes of one particular model had been repaired, as he wanted to go for a drive. His hands curled round an imaginary steering-wheel as, in his mind, he took himself on a final journey around the lanes of the estate.[4]

His mother implored the government to let her visit Athens. The government – then led by Greece's best-known and most controversial politician, Eleftherios Venizelos – rebuffed her entreaties. 'Petty political spite denied the exiled Queen Sophie the right to come to her dying son's bedside.'[5] Sophie's Lausanne-based mother-in-law, Dowager Queen Olga, made a similar request. This time the government yielded a little, and issued Olga with an entry permit. It arrived too late. So, thanks to a rough sea voyage, did she. Twelve hours before she reached (in the small hours of 26 October) the Greek capital, her grandson had given up the ghost. The preceding August he had turned 27.

Alexander's fatal accident was merely the most freakish of the many disasters to afflict Greece's royal house, the members of which (as has often been noted) had not a drop of Greek blood in their veins. The house originated in Denmark, its founder having been (in 1863) Prince Vilhelm, alias King George I, son of the Danish king Christian IX and brother of Britain's Queen Alexandra. Prince Vilhelm possessed no particular Hellenic connections or particular desire to rule over Hellenes; but the British, French and Russian governments – with rare unanimity – compelled him to take on the job, believing that he would be more malleable than their last candidate, King Otto, who belonged to the House of Wittelsbach and who during his 1832–62 tenure had shown alarming independent-mindedness. (No European power then wished Greece to go republican: it had been a republic once before, from 1827 to 1832, and its first president, Ioannis Kapodistrias, had been murdered by rivals on the steps of a church.)

The dutiful 18-year-old Vilhelm learned Greek, married in the Orthodox faith (to the Russian-born Olga, daughter of a Romanov Grand Duke), and reigned long enough – almost fifty years – to become something of a national institution. But the ill luck which afflicted so many of his successors eventually claimed King George. In March 1913, while strolling through Thessaloniki and having refused the protection of bodyguards, he was shot in the back by a vagrant named Alexandros Schinas, who might or might not have committed the crime for political reasons. A month and a half afterwards, Schinas fell, or jumped, or was pushed, out of a window at the city's main police depot.

At the time, many people assumed that Schinas had acted in the pay of Bulgaria. From October 1912 to May 1913 Greece – having appreciated the fact that it could not hope, as in the 1890s it had tried, to defeat Turkish encroachments by itself – joined forces with Serbia, Bulgaria and Montenegro in what became the First Balkan War. The league's spectacular success against the Ottoman Empire resulted in Greece (whose troops had been inspirationally led by Prince Constantine, George I's eldest son) doubling its population and its geographical area. It took over great tracts of land which had been ruled by Turks for much of the previous half-millennium, though it failed to take over the former Turkish territory which became independent Albania. An ancient folk tradition prophesied that Constantinople, which in 1453 had been lost to Christendom by one ruler named Constantine, would eventually be reclaimed for Christendom by another ruler named Constantine. When the eponymous Greek commander-in-chief succeeded to the Greek throne after his father's assassination, this chiliastic assumption seemed newly justified.

Bulgaria had other ideas. It had suffered a disproportionate number of the war's casualties while failing to acquire many of the war's spoils. Fearful of Greek resurgence in the disputed territory of southern Macedonia, and of Serbian resurgence in the equally disputed territory of northern Macedonia, Bulgaria attacked its erstwhile allies (plus Romania) in June 1913. The Second Balkan War thus broke out, ending in mid-August with a severe Bulgarian defeat. Greece, Romania and Serbia enriched themselves with slices of Bulgarian territory; the Ottoman Empire actually won back East Thrace. Nursing dreams of retribution, Sofia's rulers vowed to side, in any wider European conflict, with whoever became Greece's chief foe.

Not that the Bulgarian threat induced Greek caution in foreign affairs. When Greek politicians used the phrase *Megáli Idéa* (Big Idea), as they often did, they meant the irredentist dream of a Greece not just assured of all its existing regions but dominating the Mediterranean and, in extreme forms, emulating Byzantium's territorial zenith. Like most other Big Ideas in history, this one presupposed more-or-less unlimited supplies of other people prepared to do most of the fighting and dying on its champions' behalf; but invocations of the *Megáli Idéa* indubitably imparted to town-hall speeches and legislative sessions a liveliness that mere tedious references to housing projects or municipal drainage never achieved.

Venizelos, who had been Prime Minister since 1910, espoused the *Megáli Idéa* as passionately as anyone. Sir Charles Petrie, surveying Venizelos's career, concluded:

> He was a political gambler, and he gloried in the fact. [...] No impartial person can deny that [he] did much for Greece, and all over the country one comes across evidence of his foresight. On the other hand, he was an inveterate intriguer, and long before his death he had become a liability to his fellow-countrymen. As he grew older he was surrounded by an entourage who always represented a situation to him as he wanted it to be. One of the curses of modern Greece has been that so many of her leaders have passed their early days in opposition to an Oriental despotism, and the political habits and outlook thus acquired have remained unaltered for the rest of their lives. So it was with Venizelos, and in old age he reverted to the mentality of his youth.[6]

Born in 1864, Venizelos resembled Napoleon, Hitler and Éamon De Valera in one respect: he came from outside the land which he eventually ruled. He hailed from Crete, in 1864 still under Ottoman control, although thanks to British interventions during the 1870s the law required that the Ottoman empire always appoint a Christian to the post of Crete's governor. Not till an anti-Ottoman revolt in 1897–98 – in which Venizelos himself took a vital part – did Greece formally take possession of Crete. Even then the island possessed a quasi-colonial status, with a governor appointed by Athens rather than by Istanbul. Only in 1913 did Crete become a Greek province, with the same rights as any other.

Wilhelm II once disdainfully asked: 'Who is this man Venizelos?'[7] In fairness to the Kaiser, it is not at all easy to define Venizelism, whenever it amounted to more than a mere personality cult. While it opposed the undue exercising of royal power, this opposition did not always denote republican rule, though after the mid-1920s it generally did. (A 1931 chronicler highly sympathetic to Venizelos maintained that the Greek leader 'had always been in theory strongly in favour of a constitutional monarchy', and had as late as 1930 expressed 'his personal sentiments of respect for their former majesties, George I, Constantine, and George II').[8] Anglophilia, the doctrine of parliamentary supremacy, increased secular schooling, and elements of classical liberal thought: these things all made sizeable contributions to Venizelism – which latterly adopted the party name 'Liberal' – but they never dominated it. Nor did Venizelism's much-vaunted tributes to constitutional processes automatically mean accepting those processes which displeased it. Possibly its greatest feat lay in public relations, aimed above all at Britain's (and to a lesser extent at France's) governing class. Here Venizelos proved a virtuoso in the highest league, able to turn into political success what would have doomed almost anyone else to permanent political failure.

Part of this result sprang from Britain's almost century-old tradition of philhellenism. 'At least since the time of Byron,' a recent authority comments, 'there was a line in British public opinion that connected ancient with modern Hellenes.'[9] But too much must not be made of this, particularly given the bitter disillusionment which so many of Britain's philhellenes suffered upon actual contact with real live Greeks. As General Sir Charles James Napier (future Commander-in-Chief of British India) sardonically remarked, 'The bulk of the English came expecting to find the Peloponnesus filled with Plutarch's men, and returned thinking the inhabitants of Newgate more moral.'[10]

Central to Venizelos's own acclaim in Western Europe, and much more significant than any Byronic ancestral memories, was his combination – shared with his most powerful benefactor, Lloyd George – of charm (altogether compatible with ruthlessness), national pride and mental agility. John Buchan, in *The Thirty-Nine Steps,* firmly based the character of Constantine Karolidis on the real-life Greek leader, and expected all his original readers to recognise the portrayal, which most of them did. Between 1915 and 1921 four different biographies of Venizelos, all encomiastic in the extreme, emerged from London publishing houses.[11] His very countenance abetted (whether through conscious design or not) his flair for pleasing the British: with his white goatee and look of habitual mischief, unencumbered – if anything enhanced – by his spectacles, he resembled the pleasure-loving uncle whom almost every Edwardian Englishman wanted to have. (Contrariwise, one of George I's sons, Prince Christopher, loathed the Prime Minister and 'had to fight down my distaste [for] his fox-like smile'.)[12]

Through regrettable contrast with Venizelos, King Constantine I had no sense of public relations whatsoever. A soldier through and through, with a contempt (thoroughgoing even by military standards) for double-talk and for the imagination more generally, he said what he meant and meant what he said. The plan which he recommended to the Entente powers for assailing Gallipoli had been been drawn up not by him but by his ally, General Ioannis Metaxas. It was rejected without having been considered. According to one account, the British returned the envelope containing the plan to Metaxas unopened.[13] A suppler intelligence than Constantine's would have dictated a refusal to twist the knife in the wound of subsequent Allied military disaster, whereas Constantine did the exact opposite. He informed Britain's military attaché, Sir Thomas Montgomery-Cuninghame: 'I have never heard, and I never read, of a more amateurish method of approaching a serious military enterprise than your people employed at the Dardanelles.'[14]

A remark this abrasive could only give shocking offence to the British, whether it was accurate in strategic terms or not; and the greater its accuracy, the greater its offensiveness. Coming as it did from a man who had married Kaiser Wilhelm's sister – and who had accepted a field-marshal's baton from his brother-in-law – it left him with a lifelong repute for grovelling to the Germans. This repute Venizelos sedulously and cleverly fostered, the outcome being the National Schism (*Ethnikos Dichasmos*, to use the Greek-language words).

The truth of Constantine's, and his wife's, allegiance defied Venizelist over-simplifications. Both King and Queen spoke English at home for preference, sent several of their children to English schools, and holidayed in England whenever they could.[15] Constantine's favourite poems included Kipling's 'If', which he had a habit of quoting whenever adverse fate threatened to overcome his resolve. Sophie, for her part, bitterly resented the memory of her brother's complaints when she had entered the Orthodox Church, as that body's Greek bishops expected her to do upon her marriage to Constantine. Her husband, meanwhile, refused to permit either Venizelos or any foreign power to push him around. 'He was neither pro-German nor pro-Allied, he insisted to friends and detractors alike, merely pro-Greek.'[17] Conserving what remained of the nation's military strength, after not one but two wars since 1912, mattered far more to Constantine the fighting man than making pious noises about gallant little Belgium.

One prominent Englishman remained a steadfast friend of the Greek king: to wit, Lord Kitchener. The two men met in Athens during November 1915, and felt mutual approbation, as fellow military professionals compelled to endure civilian politicians' amateurism. 'I spoke to him as one soldier to another,' Kitchener subsequently reported; 'He is in the right. When we want the Greeks we can have them on our side.'[18] Alas for Constantine, his British admirer had only seven more months to live: a German mine sank the cruiser, *HMS Hampshire*, on which Kitchener travelled with a view to reaching Russia. Lloyd George despised Kitchener and had become so smitten with Venizelos's initiatives that he usually refused to hear a word against them.

So determined had Venizelos become to flout Constantine on the Allies' behalf that in September 1916 he left Athens, set up his headquarters at Thessaloniki (taking with him two cabinet ministers, both in the armed forces), and there proclaimed his own Provisional Government of National Defence. Unanswerable either to Athens or to Constantine, though careful to avoid explicit republican forms, this government declared war on Germany and Bulgaria during October. Two months afterwards began an

Anglo-French blockade, intended to starve the monarchy into submission. Constantine relented enough to permit his troops, at a parade the following January, to salute the flags of the Allied nations.[19] But for Britain and France, such gestures of goodwill no longer sufficed. The steady drip of anti-Constantine propaganda released by the novelist and editor Compton Mackenzie, performing with relish his role as British counter-espionage agent (though ostensibly nothing more than a 'supernumerary Greek'),[20] enraged the King and delighted Whitehall. When Russia overthrew Tsardom, and Nicholas II with it, in February–March 1917, Constantine lost a valued friend. By June 1917 the Entente, now benefiting from America's entry in the war, had decided that the sovereign needed to go. One concession, but an important one, Britain and France made to dynastic sentiment: they permitted the King's second son, Prince Alexander, to stay behind and to reign in his father's stead.

Through fear that Athens itself remained sufficiently monarchist and anti-Venizelist to frustrate the royals' departure, General Charles Jonnart (Allied plenipotentiary in the capital) demanded that this departure occur at a port obscure enough to discourage sympathisers with the kingly cause. But word of Constantine's imminent exile preceded him, and when the royal party took its leave at the bay of Oropos, 'fishermen knelt and wept'.[21] Jonnart afterwards admitted to his French political masters that he had overestimated his knowledge of Greek politics and underestimated the local devotion to Constantine, whose deposition he called 'a far from glorious page in the history of France'.[22]

From 1917 to 1920, Venizelos and his supporters treated Alexander with barely disguised impatience. Alexander played along with his enforced servitude. When someone pointed out to him that his signature adorned a state paper which in fact he had not examined, he justified his behaviour by the embittered remark: 'My father read papers before signing them, and is in exile. My grandfather signed papers before reading them, and died a King.'[23]

Official revenge against the departed sovereign included the purging from the army of no fewer than 3,000 officers for loyalty to Constantine.[24] Sometimes revenge took remarkably malicious forms against the most harmless creatures, as Prince Christopher (then still in Athens) reported. A song entitled *Son of the Eagle,* written in Constantine's honour after the First Balkan War, had become so popular among ordinary Greeks as to have attained the status of an unofficial national anthem. For which very reason, Venizelos banned the song – it was as if a British Prime Minister were to prohibit renditions of *Jerusalem* – and Prince Christopher discovered that the interdict covered not merely human but psittacine performances:

> Once a party of Venizelists on their rounds could hardly believe their own ears when they heard its familiar strains being sung lustily from one of the houses. Following the sound they rushed upstairs to a top room, flung open the door and found an old woman sitting alone in an armchair, beating time to the proud song of her parrot. Not troubling to waste time on explanations, they wrung the neck of the unfortunate bird and marched out of the room, slamming the door on the poor old lady's lamentations.[25]

Then Alexander's unexpected death threw Venizelos's plans awry. So accustomed had the Prime Minister become to viewing Alexander's political survival as dependent upon him, that he never entertained the hypothesis of his own political survival being dependent on Alexander. Yet, on this occasion, it was. Venizelos sounded out Alexander's youngest brother, Prince Paul, as a monarchical candidate. Paul, in accents of dignified principle which Venizelos had never expected and probably could not comprehend, retorted: 'The Throne does not belong to me; it belongs to my august father, King Constantine, and constitutionally my eldest brother [Prince George, then aged 30] is his successor. Neither of them has ever renounced his rights.'[26]

Genuine public grief at losing the amiable and youthful Alexander manifested itself in political terms. Dowager Queen Olga was allowed, in the immediate aftermath of Alexander's demise, to serve as regent until an election could be held. That election occurred on 14 November, and the Venizelists – who wanted to make the poll into a referendum upon Constantine, and who assumed that the voters would not dare to advocate the former King's return – won only 120 parliamentary seats. The openly royalist opposition, led by Venizelos's long-standing enemy Dimitrios Gounaris (who had been Prime Minister for part of 1915), had 246 seats, while four seats went to independent candidates.[27] Venizelos himself, having been clearly repudiated, exiled himself to France. On 5 December a plebiscite produced a still more lopsided outcome: only 10,883 voters declared themselves to be against Constantine's restoration, whereas 1,010,178 voters declared themselves to be in favour of it.[28] When the King's train from Corinth reached Athens, 'so excited was the crowd which awaited him at the Peloponnisou Station that people flocked down the railway track itself, preventing the train from pulling into the platform'.[29]

Could Constantine, after so many reversals, now lead a quiet and contented life? On the contrary. Few guessed it, but his worst troubles lay in the future.

Never had Venizelos abandoned his allegiance to the *Megáli Idéa*. In the Great War's aftermath, with the Ottoman Empire crushed, the Big Idea struck him (and many others) as, more than ever, an idea whose time had come. That Mustafa Kemal was no mere sybaritic Turkish Sultan, that he would show himself to be among his epoch's most brilliant military commanders, and that Turkey would recuperate with stunning speed from its 1918 defeats: these circumstances failed to enter the Venizelists' calculations. Those who, like Gounaris, proposed restraint and compromise regarding the Turks found themselves swept up in the prevailing exultant mood.

It is seldom a wise procedure to belittle the strength of the forces you are fighting against. But of this foolhardiness, the Greek high command was undeniably guilty (just as the Russian high command had been in 1904–05 when confronted with the Japanese, and just as the American high command would be in the 1960s when confronted with the Vietcong). When Nikolaos Kalogeropoulos – Greece's Prime Minister from January to March 1921 – sneeringly referred to Kemal's forces as 'a rabble worthy of little or no consideration', one bound to be 'annihilated within three months',[30] he spoke for Venizelos, for most of his compatriots, and for much of the West. The Greeks assumed that Britain would not dare let them down. Their supply chains and lines of communication soon stretched to (indeed beyond) the limit, they fatally overestimated

Lloyd George's capacity for survival, and fatally underestimated Kemal's. Constantine, against his better instincts, went along with Athens's hawks. To no avail did Italy's Foreign Minister, Count Sforza, urge prudence upon Greece and make the comparison with Napoleon in Russia.[31]

Smyrna, which Greek forces had captured in May 1919, became the war's flashpoint. Turkey's army conquered Smyrna on 9 September 1922, having been helped since the preceding year by military assistance from the Soviet Union (Lenin had no hope of turning the Kemalists into communists, but he wished to avenge himself on the British for their support of the anti-Bolshevik cause during Russia's civil war). Despite Kemal's threats of the death penalty for any soldier guilty of harming Smyrna's civilian population, he could not or would not enforce these threats. The city's Greek and Armenian quarters went up in flames (its Jewish and Muslim quarters remained intact), and at least 30,000 Greeks and Armenians were killed in the city within the next week.[32]

George Horton, the city's American consul, aghast at the horrors which he powerlessly beheld, wrote: 'one of the keenest impressions which I brought away with me from Smyrna was a feeling of shame that I belonged to the human race'.[33] The very name 'Smyrna' acquired for the Western public the same minatory power that the name Hiroshima would do a generation afterwards. A hundred years later, many Greeks still call Kemal's triumph and Smyrna's bloodbaths 'the Catastrophe', as if no other catastrophes had occurred in Greece's annals.

Supposing that it is ever valid for historians to call any nation united in its overwhelming thirst for vengeance, Greece in September 1922 was that nation. Already, on the eleventh of that month, a military coup led by Colonel Nikolaos Plastiras had driven from office the civilian cabinet. Two days later King Constantine fled to Italy, this time inspiring none of the public grief which his departure five years earlier had caused. Again, the forms of monarchy persisted: this time under Prince George, who in 1917 had been vetoed by the Entente powers for insufficient tractability.

Venizelos, true to form, had managed to remain absent from Greece for long enough to leave him undamaged by the clamour for sacrifices. Colonel C.M. Woodhouse, British expert in Greek political history, admitted:

> [T]he first steps towards disaster were taken by Venizelos before he fell. It was on his orders that the Greek army began to advance to the interior. [...] King Constantine was an obvious scapegoat: he was antipathetic to Greece's traditional allies, Britain and France, and he was nominally in command of the defeated armies. But it was not he who had launched Greece upon the fatal adventure in Anatolia. Venizelos had done so, yet his reputation was hardly tarnished and his voluntary exile could be ended wherever he chose.[34]

Prince George, now George II, wielded no more influence over the politicians than Alexander had done. If anything, he wielded less. Practical authority rested with Plastiras and with his fellow head of the Revolutionary Committee, Lieutenant-General Stylianos Gonatas. Both men selected for the office of prime minister a civilian, Sotirios Krokidas, who proved agreeably biddable.

With no challenge from that quarter, the Revolutionary Committee set up a military tribunal, before which it hauled six defendants: Gounaris, now suffering from typhoid;

Nikolaos Stratos, who had succeeded Gounaris as Prime Minister in May 1922; Petros Protopapadakis, who had taken over from Stratos and stayed in the post until September; Georgios Hatzianestis, former commander-in-chief in Asia Minor; Georgios Baltatzis, former Foreign Minister; and Nikolaos Theotokis, former Army Minister. The 'Trial of the Six' (in Greek, *Díki ton Éxi*) lasted fifteen days. For all the concern with judicial niceties which it displayed, it might as well have been finished in fifteen minutes. A kangaroo court pure and simple, it condemned all the six officials to death.

We must recall that in 1922 Europe's political leaders had not yet become hardened to the *vae victis* spirit of physical aggression against their counterparts in other lands. They lived in a continental culture where Hitler's Night of the Long Knives, Stalin's sequence of show-trials, and the Austrian National Socialists' decision to let Dollfuss die in slow agony remained inconceivable. British and French ambassadors lodged firm protests against the sentences, never fundamentally imagining that the Revolutionary Committee would presume to carry the sentences out. It did. The front page of *The Buffalo News*'s 29 November edition included the following eyewitness commentary on the executions:

> Finally the hour arrived. Priests went to the jail and the doomed men were offered communion. They partook, kneeling in the barred chamber, the men who once were all highest and all powerful in Greece, whose words moved armies – now unable to save their own lives. [...] Gounaris was lifted out of the ambulance and placed before the firing squad. He was too sick to pay attention to what was going on. Indifferent, huddled, with hands thrust deep in his pockets, he stood there with his head bowed until the volley crashed.[35]

This report bore the instructive headline 'Six Greek Firing Squad Victims Go to Death Like Gentlemen.' A century ago, the word 'gentlemen' could still be employed in a major city's newspaper without the faintest derisive intent.

Upon Constantine's and Christopher's brother Prince Andrew, who had been in the field at the time of the military disasters, the Revolutionary Committee demanded the same penalty. But the Prince's sheer lack of command experience weighed in his favour, as did his royal blood. His sentence commuted to lifelong banishment, Andrew left Greece for Italy with his family upon a British warship, *HMS Calypso*, in December 1922. This family included the 18-month-old Philip, who would spend most of his life in Britain and would become internationally famous long after most of his father's persecutors had been forgotten. In adulthood he was none other than Prince Philip, Duke of Edinburgh.

George II, having been browbeaten by the Revolutionary Committee into authorising the death sentences, considered permanently going abroad. The British government convinced him to stay in Athens, but he had never benefited in the past from anything like Alexander's personal following, and he did not do so now.

He had, it is true, followers in very high places. Some of his supporters attempted to intervene on his behalf in October 1923, under the direction of Lieutenants-General Georgios Leonardopoulos and Panagiotis Gargalidis. Neither man had a long royalist record. Both men had backed the September 1922 coup, and the Trial of the Six. Yet the sheer zeal with which Plastiras and his henchmen cast out from the army anyone whom they thought likely to harbour royalist convictions (whether or not evidence for such convictions existed) affronted Leonardopoulos and Gargalidis, who decided that they should endeavour to make George II the ruler in fact rather than in legal fiction. They won over to their plans General Metaxas, who had never weakened in his monarchical fervour, whoever controlled Athens. A diary entry of Metaxas's from back in 1898, his twenty-seventh year (and the thirty-fifth year of George I's reign), reads: 'Amidst the moral and national debris my soul has been filled with, only one institution remains standing: the King and his dynasty. And my devotion to them became even greater. There was a moment – only a moment – when I hated my country, but never the King.'[36]

Had the two Lieutenants-General taken Metaxas's advice, their plot could well have succeeded. Metaxas, from his base in Corinth, sensibly urged them to strike in the capital. They preferred the gradual route of conquering the provinces first, a decision which gave the authorities ample time to counterattack. In six days the whole insurgency had fizzled out. Leonardopoulos and Gargalidis unconditionally surrendered, faced a court-martial, and had death sentences passed on them. This time the Revolutionary Committee refrained from having the defendants shot – pleas from the Vatican helped in this regard – but for its atypical clemency, it wanted a quid pro quo. The quid pro quo concerned King George himself.

With what menacing terminology can be predicted, it was made very clear to the sovereign that he had hitherto tended to underprize the benefits of foreign residence. He took the hint and, on 19 December, went to Bucharest, the home of his wife Elisabeth, whom he had married in 1921. (In 1930, Elisabeth's brother Carol would become sovereign of Romania.) In 1923, unlike in 1920, Constantine no longer served as either a complicating factor or a monarchist rallying-point. On 11 January 1923, in his Palermo hotel room, the 54-year-old ex-king, long weakened by cardiac problems and influenza, suffered a cerebral haemorrhage. For much of his banishment he had carried with him a small packet containing a handful of Greek earth. The packet was still on his person when he died.[37]

Three days before George had left his realm (the preceding March, incidentally, Greece adopted the Gregorian calendar), another legislative election had occurred. In the past, Venizelists had boycotted such contests when boycotts suited them; now the royalists adopted the same method, and abstained from running candidates. Voters could choose between the hard republicanism of Gonatas, the Revolutionary Committee, and their Venizelist friends, versus the mild republicanism of the Democratic Liberal and Democratic Union parties, both newly established. Most of the electorate supported the former group. Out of 398 constituencies being contested, the Gonatas coalition won 250, giving it (unusually in Greek politics) a majority in its own right. In April 1924 another referendum indicated that popular enthusiasm for monarchy had plunged: this time the republicans won 758,472 votes, the monarchists no more than 325,322. The Second Hellenic Republic began.

Venizelos, back home from January 1924, 'was no longer the Venizelos of the great days; his health was impaired, he had lost touch with Greek affairs, and new men with new ambitions had arisen in his absence – for three years is a generation in recent Greek history.'[38] Nearly all 1920s cabinets were short-lived and ineffectual, with the same few ministers, some military, some civilian, leading them by turns. Outside a specialist textbook on twentieth-century Greece, these individuals resemble mere transient (to quote Disraeli's metaphor) and embarrassed phantoms. One alone among them, Venizelos excepted, demands lengthier coverage through his sheer flamboyance: General Theodoros Pangalos, whose inspired official eccentricity lasted from 1924 to 1926.

The reign of Pangalos, first as prime minister and then as president, included (October 1925) the so-called War of the Stray Dog, which acquired its name from a Greek soldier inadvertently crossing the frontier with Bulgaria in pursuit of his elusive quadruped, and being shot at by Bulgarian sentries. Greek troops managed to kill more than four dozen Bulgarians before a British-run sub-committee at the League of Nations instructed the combatants to stop, and mandated for Greece a reparations bill of £45,000, payable to Bulgaria before February 1926.[39] (The equivalent in today's currency is around £3,500,200.) Bulgaria's government, on the League's orders, paid compensation to the family of the frontier-crossing Greek soldier. The errant canine's fate went unrecorded.

On the domestic front Pangalos, well attuned to the needful overlap between political science and the entertainment industry, 'made the death penalty retrospective and publicly hanged two officials, guilty of malversation'.[40] But by general journalistic consent his finest hour occurred when, in November 1925, he forbade the hems of women's skirts to be more than thirty centimetres from the ground.[41] The prohibition, enforced by tape-measure-wielding inspectors in full view of news cameras, applied to every female over the age of 12. Infringements could be, and were, punished by imprisonment.

Five months after promulgating this sumptuary law, Pangalos made the error of judgement common among dictators who have let their guard down, and he ventured out of his capital. Therefore he gave an army detachment led by General Giorgios Condylis the chance to occupy the War Office and to announce his overthrow. (Condylis had been indispensable to the suppression of the October 1923 royalist campaign.) Pangalos, his flair for defiant theatricality undimmed, 'endeavoured to escape on board a torpedo-boat',[42] only to be arrested and incarcerated. (From the resultant obscurity he re-emerged during the Second World War, as a collaborator with the Nazi puppet regime.) Following three more brief administrations – including one led by Condylis himself, which lasted under four months – Venizelos regained the prime ministry in 1928 and held it for four years.

Economic crises vitiated many of Venizelos's latter-day objectives. While he coped no worse with Depression-induced miseries than most other Western heads of government did, he also coped no better. He belonged in essence to a pre-socialist, pre-Marxist world which the Wall Street crash had ended. Between May 1932 and March 1933 he left the prime ministry, then returned to it, then left it, then returned to it, then left it one final time after a mere two months. Despairing of further election victories, but with his personal fortune intact,[43] he let himself be conscripted into the role of front-man for a March 1935 military coup attempt, one that Condylis and Prime Minister Panagis Tsaldaris swiftly crushed. Two Venizelist generals who had organised the attempt suffered capital punishment, and Venizelos fled the country, spending the rest of his life in Paris.

Emboldened by the swiftness with which Venizelism collapsed, Tsaldaris called a fresh legislative election for June 1935. The outcome spectacularly reversed the December 1923 result. Whereas on that occasion the monarchists had held aloof, now the Venizelists held aloof. And while in December 1923 the voters could choose solely from different republican groups (plus a few independent candidates), in June 1935 they could choose (again, a few independent candidates excepted) solely from different monarchist groups. The Tsaldaris-led alliance, dominated by Tsaldaris's own Populist Party, wanted to bring the monarchy back at some stage; Metaxas's alliance wanted to bring the monarchy back with all speed. Of the 300 electorates being contested under Greece's first-past-the-post system, Metaxas's movement won only seven seats, but scored almost 15 per cent of the total vote; Tsaldaris's movement won a remarkable 287 seats, though it scored only 66 per cent of the total vote. (Independents won all the other seats.)

Most remarkable of all, the long-time republican Condylis, serving as Tsaldaris's War Minister, had by this time adopted monarchism with all the wild passion of a convert. Tsaldaris wanted to arrange a plebiscite on the monarchy issue before formally declaring George II the rightful king again. Condylis, whom his compatriots called 'The Thunderbolt', despised such scruples. After September came and went with no resolution of the issue, Condylis joined with the chiefs of the armed forces on 10 October and announced that his patience – a negligible quantity even at the best of times – was exhausted. In person, he and the chiefs commanded Tsaldaris either to abandon his plebiscite-before-restoration attitude, or to quit the prime ministry. Tsaldaris quit. Condylis took over as Prime Minister afresh. He then personally informed Alexandros Zaimis (who after serving more than four decades in the legislature had been an unobtrusive President since 1929) that the latter's term of office was at an end and that he himself would act as regent till George II returned from London. Zaimis, like Tsaldaris, obediently made way for 'the Thunderbolt'.

The plebiscite itself (to which George had consented while still in Britain) occurred on 3 November and was not, it may legitimately be hinted, a pageant designed for the squeamish. Voting had been made compulsory for Greek adults of both sexes in 1926. Literacy had not been. The proportion of Greek adults who could neither read nor write in 1935 was at least as high as the proportion of them after 1945, when a UNESCO survey found that one Greek adult in four remained illiterate.[44] A colour-coded scheme for ballot papers became, accordingly, imperative. Blue ballot papers signified a vote for restoring George; red ballot papers, a vote for keeping Greece republican. Pettifogging concepts of keeping the ballots secret meant little: at booths where the returning officers answered immediately to Condylis, 'one could cast a red ballot for the Republic and get roughed up'.[45]

Ninety-seven per cent of all ballots cast on this occasion were said to have supported monarchism. This implausible tally provoked much derision at the time in mellower, more sedate and less raucous political cultures than Greece's. (Whether it would attract equal derision in those cultures during the 2020s, after recent disclosures of internationally efficacious troll-farms and robot-propelled social-media campaigns, is open to argument.) But it needs to be read in the local context. By 1935 electoral fraud had become as quintessentially Hellenic a product as olives and ouzo. All political groups practised it: monarchists, republicans, republican Venizelists, republican anti-Venizelists, and any other movements craving more influence than they could win by meticulously fair methods. A prominent Greek-American columnist and publisher pointed out in 1976 that 'ballot-tampering has always been the rule, rather than the exception, in Greek elections'.[46] Political operatives who tampered with ballots incurred no disgrace, except when they tampered with ballots and somehow managed to lose. That jovial motto often ascribed to Stalin – 'Those who vote decide nothing; those who count the votes decide everything'[47] – simply crystallised what Greek politicians between the wars did to one another, Stalin or no Stalin, in any case.

George, on being told the plebiscite's outcome, telegraphed the Greek Foreign Ministry: 'This event by God's grace and the will of the Hellenic people will lead Greece to general prosperity and glory. The separation was hard for me and all of us have suffered deeply. But I harbour no resentment against anyone.'[48] So little resentment did he harbour that shortly after arriving in his homeland (which he did to scenes of ardent jubilation from crowds on 25 November), he proclaimed his intention to offer an amnesty for those leaders of the March insurrection who, like Venizelos, remained alive.

Flabbergasted and appalled by this announcement, Condylis watched with alarm as his vision for Greece's immediate political future melted away. He himself had planned to acquire Mussolini-like control over the nation, while reducing King George's role (as the Duce had already reduced King Vittorio Emanuele III's role) to that of a mere armigerous cipher. Sir Charles Petrie, writing in 1952, epitomised the battle of wills between the astute sovereign and the overweening subject:

> Condylis refused to give way, and so within a few days of his return the King was compelled to dismiss the man to whom he appeared to owe his crown. On this account he naturally acquired a good deal of odium in ultra-Royalist circles, but this was surely undeserved. Condylis only declared himself a monarchist when he saw that public opinion was coming to favour a restoration, and he was determined that the monarch should be a puppet, with himself as dictator. From the beginning he had played for his own hand, and King George in reality owed him nothing. It must be said in his favour that he took his dismissal with none too bad a grace, but as he died shortly afterwards it is impossible to say how long he would have continued to refrain from making trouble.
>
> This action threw a good deal of light upon the late King's character, and had Mussolini studied the Greek monarch a little more carefully he might have been spared a very unpleasant surprise five years later.[49]

Petrie knew whereof he spoke, because he had actively helped to bring about George's reinstatement. Surviving details of his efforts are meagre, but with George himself he remained on terms of lifelong friendship, and he had tried during 1935 to raise funds for the Greek royal cause. *The Times*'s December 1977 obituary of Petrie mentions his having been made a Commander of the Order of George I of Greece, 'this latter being a reward for his behind-the-scenes role he played in helping to secure the first restoration of King George II of the Hellenes in 1934 [*sic*]'.[50] Petrie's 1972 memoir sheds some, though not much, light upon his involvement; the 'he' at the start of the following passage refers to Dimitrios N. Levidis, master of the royal household:

> He and I, with a few others, worked closely together to bring about the first restoration, and it was a proud moment when, on 14 November 1935, the King, seen off by the members of the British Royal Family, left Victoria [*Station*] for Athens. Certainly no monarchy was ever restored

more cheaply. About twelve months before this event took place, and before Venizelos had played into royalist hands by his ill-considered rising, the maximum amount that the King and his friends could have raised was fifteen hundred pounds. At one moment there seemed a possibility that [*armaments tycoon Sir Basil*] Zaharoff might put up some money, but the King was rightly reluctant to accept anything from that source, and after some very complicated negotiations with a man who claimed to be acting for Zaharoff the project was abandoned.[51]

For years, the banished royal family had known what being cash-strapped felt like. Prince Christopher remembered that 'Our household servants had all followed us from Greece and served us out of pure devotion. Months went by without their being paid a cent in wages, but they never complained.'[52] King George had no intention of letting that financial embarrassment recur. While still staying at Brown's Hotel in London (and probably unsuspected by Petrie), he extracted from Condylis $US200,000 as an advance payment for the cost of the journey back home. Also, he kept secret from Condylis the cables which he had been exchanging with the anti-Condylis royalists in Athens under Tsaldaris's leadership.[53] Here was no latter-day King Alexander, but instead, a canny and calculating executive – refusing to accept a reiteration of his 1922–23 political impotence – who planned to rule as well as to reign.

Were today's Hollywood to depict the whole improbable saga of 1930s Greek politics, it would probably insist on calling the King's comeback *Son of George the Second* (notwithstanding the monarch's real-life childlessness) or *George the Second Reloaded*. What manner of man, then, was this potentate during his renewed occupancy of the job?

The *Time* magazine of 1935 seldom deigned to employ recognisable English, preferring its own madcap patois of inverted syntax, hyphenated descriptors ('moose-tall', 'blubber-lipped'), and gruesome neologisms ('cinemaddict', 'radiorator'). Averse to such boring nouns as 'monarchist', *Time* treated readers to its own coinage 'kingophile'. (In the following year Wolcott Gibbs, critic for *The New Yorker*, produced his justly admired parody of *Time*-speak, best known for including the words 'Backward ran sentences until reeled the mind. [...] Where it all will end, knows God!')[54] But every so often *Time*'s nameless scribes could supply, underneath the cornea-scalding hideousness of their prose, a closely observed portrait from life. So they did with George II, furnishing details seldom accessible elsewhere:

> With the dazzling candour of exalted birth he has said, 'I prefer brawn to brains'. He honestly thinks brainy people queer, commands ten languages, likes dancing, tennis, shooting, prizefights, the circus, slapstick at the Palladium and ginger ale with his meals. Untroubled by minor inconsistencies, he is a Mason, Greek Orthodox and divorced – all in good standing. [...] Seemingly the Greek Dictator [Condylis] did not realize how English George II has become in all these years, making himself at home to the point of picking his teeth while standing around with Queen Mary and Scottish aristocrats.[55]

Since the seventeenth century, if not earlier, exile has affected different monarchs in different fashions. With Charles II, banishment under the Cromwellian protectorate confirmed his natural good nature, his jaunty willingness to call black white and to call white black, provided that such disingenuous make-believe spared him the need to 'go on [his] travels again'. Kaiser Wilhelm felt in most respects happier at Doorn than he had ever done as a crowned head. For Emperor Karl, as has been shown, exile was a path hastening that sanctity which he might well have attained without such tribulations. But exile demoralised both Manuel II and Alfonso XIII, intensifying in the former a natural penchant for melancholy (as it had done in the 1620s and early 1630s for Frederick V, Bohemia's erstwhile 'Winter King'). George II resembled none of the above monarchical émigrés. In a thousand years he could not have managed jauntiness, his religious observances stopped well short of passionate devotion, and he never regarded banishment as anything other than demeaning; yet he avoided going to pieces. His general view concerning political setbacks – of which he experienced far more than most people – can be summarised by Alexander Pope's suggested addendum to Christ's Beatitudes: 'Blessed is he who expects nothing, for he shall never be disappointed.'

Taciturn and cool in a nation disposed to forgive almost anything from the voluble and warm, George II represented a throwback to his dour Scandinavian ancestors, and bore the marks of his protracted English residence. In few available photographs can he be seen to smile. Petrie reported of him:

> Unlike his father, King Constantine [...] he was reserved: to him the first approach of a stranger was generally difficult, which mattered a great deal more in Greece than it did in England; he was not one of those who found conversation easy when he did not have anything to say.[56]

When striving to sound jocular he frequently, and inadvertently, managed to sound sarcastic. To the British Ambassador, Sir Sydney Waterlow, he commented that given the Greek economy's Depression-exacerbated problems (and its dependence upon imported foods from Britain), the sole viable solution 'is that Greece should be taken over by your civil service and run as a British colony'.[57] Waterlow believed that the King 'faces his task in the spirit of one carrying the white man's burden among the tribes of the jungle'.[58] Nonetheless, Waterlow's American counterpart, Lincoln MacVeagh, who at first disliked the Greek monarch, found himself increasingly impressed by what he called George's 'attitude of Mr Facing-Both-Ways'.[59] As MacVeagh was reporting to Franklin Roosevelt, whose own 'attitude of Mr Facing-Both-Ways' amounted to genius, no more laudatory description could have been offered.

Furthermore, King George's position as still point in the turning – not to say frenziedly gyrating – world of Greek politics worked at last in his favour. The fact that he could never be accused of swindling or narcissism differentiated him from many of the prime ministers and presidents who had strutted and fretted their hours upon the stage from 1924 to 1935. Petrie quoted an unnamed Venizelist as saying, within seven months of George having reoccupied the throne, that 'Of course the plebiscite was faked, but today the King would get that majority on a free vote.'[60] This blunt and generous assessment exemplified a reluctant homage to the new system, from a vanquished spokesman for the old.

No longer did George find himself daily needing to fear Venizelist intrigues. The National Schism, still an open and painful wound in March 1935, had a year later been healed. From early 1936, George confronted a foe very different to his chief adversaries of earlier times: a foe much more disciplined than they were, much more violent – and above all, much more modern.

Greece's Communist Party, the KKE, had only limited impact for the first decade after its establishment in 1918. It eschewed the murderous inventiveness which enlivened its Bulgarian counterpart, and which guaranteed such terrorist coups as the April 1925 massacre at St Nedelya's Cathedral in Sofia. (Although this attack failed to kill its intended targets, King Boris and his cabinet, it left approximately 120 others dead.)[61] Elements of the Hellenic character impeded the KKE's initial plans:

> Greek individualism cannot easily adapt itself to the rigidity of Communism. Also, the fierce nationalism, not to say chauvinism, of the Greek does not readily take to communist internationalism. Finally, the Greek's belief in private property is almost sacrosanct, making him unlikely material for communist indoctrination.[62]

The Great Depression powerfully boosted the KKE's prospects, as it did the prospects of all communist movements in countries where such movements remained legal. (Venizelos's Interior Ministry had harassed individual KKE members – forbidding them to work as schoolteachers, for example – instead of criminalising the party outright.) In particular, Greece's post-1922 influx of refugees, part of the vast Greco-Turkish population exchange carried out after the 1923 Treaty of Lausanne, proved receptive to KKE campaigning. The KKE fared similarly well within the non-refugee population of 'New Greece', the areas that the First Balkan War had brought under Athens' rule. New Greece, in 1924, had 'voted overwhelmingly for a republic, with Old Greece remaining faithful to the monarchy'.[63]

King George appointed Dr Constantine Demertzis (a former legal scholar who had served in the first cabinet of Venizelos before falling out with him) to the prime ministry in Condylis's place. Two months afterwards, at the general election of January 1936, the KKE won fifteen seats in the legislature. The failure of either the right-wing coalition or the left-wing coalition to win a majority (the former obtained 132 seats, the latter 137 seats) gave the Communists great bargaining power. This power they proceeded to use, under the formidable leadership of a young immigrant born in north-western Turkey: Nikos Zachariadis, trained in the Soviet Union. Thanks to General Secretary Zachariadis's program, 'there were 344 strikes and disorders during the first six months of 1936 alone'.[64] To make matters worse, on 13 April Demertzis suffered a fatal heart attack. The King sent for Demertzis's Deputy Prime Minister and War Minister, who happened to be Metaxas.

In the drama of Greek politics, Metaxas had previously played a subordinate role, complete with occasional off-stage pronouncements ignored by other characters. From this point forward, he became the protagonist and the spotlight shone on him. This change of status wrought no apparent change in his personality. Other leading Greeks might assume and abandon monarchist doctrines almost as often as they changed shirts; not Metaxas. In 1919–22 he had criticised the strategy of letting the Greek troops be sucked eastwards into Anatolia, and while at the time his warnings had no effect, they helped to save him from the firing squad when the Revolutionary Committee took over. First he expatriated himself in Italy; then he compelled himself to return to Greece when he felt safe enough to do so, and reluctantly entered the republican legislature, always on the understanding that – whatever transactional lip-service he rendered to presidential privileges – monarchical restoration remained his aim. Towards Venizelos he felt visceral disgust, and he had never forgiven the mercurial Cretan's insolence towards King Constantine during the National Schism. In 1933 Venizelos was injured in an assassination attempt; though no evidence indicates that Metaxas ordered this assault, he openly rejoiced at the news of it.

He owed part of his survival to the astonishingly high mortality rate among other Greek politicians in 1936, a rate which eliminated rival contenders. Within weeks not only Demertzis but Venizelos and Condylis had died; former prime ministers Tsaldaris and Alexandros Papanastasiou followed them to the cemetery before the year ended, as did ex-president Zaimis. (To appreciate the impact of such consecutive disappearances, imagine if, in Britain five decades afterwards, Harold Macmillan, Sir Alec Douglas-Home, Harold Wilson, Edward Heath, James Callaghan, and Margaret Thatcher had all been taken from the scene inside twelve months.) Petrie, who along with Lady Petrie was invited that year to Greece by the King himself, noted:

> [T]he Attic wit enables the Athenian to mock his leaders as in the days of Aristophanes, for within a few hours of the death of Venizelos, immediately after that of his enemy Condylis, the newspaper boys were shouting through the streets, 'Meeting of Condylis and Venizelos.' The shade of Lucian must have smiled that day.[65]

In Britain's Foreign Office, Under-Secretary Sir Robert Vansittart sprinkled some characteristically sharp thorns on Venizelos's tomb. 'I always liked M[*onsieur*]. Venizelos personally,' Vansittart wrote, 'indeed I liked him immensely':

> But I could never understand the empire that he exerted over the minds of Mr Lloyd George and Lord Lothian [Lloyd George's private secretary] during the unhappy years when I had to act as liaison between the F.O. and the other F.O. at No. 10. I should have thought M. Venizelos one of the most amiable and overestimated men of his day – there were many less amiable – which has dragged on now like an indifferent summer afternoon. Whether dusk is finally at hand, and whether that in itself is a cause for rejoicing, I must leave to more expert local knowledge.[66]

Meanwhile Metaxas had two choices before him: he could either go along with the business-as-usual mindset which Demertzis, with whom he had amicably worked, sought to follow; or he could try something different. For him, the choices were not really choices at all. With mounting panic, he had watched the manner in which, since February 1936, communist bosses had been giving orders to successive cabinets in Madrid. He had no intention of letting Greece become as ungovernable as Spain.

Twelve people were killed at a Communist-organised demonstration of tobacco workers and other unionists during May in Thessaloniki. Whereupon a unit in the army itself changed sides, openly supporting Zachariadis and the KKE. Accordingly, Metaxas convinced the King that the parliament should be prorogued and that martial law should be declared. The KKE and its tame union leaders scheduled for 7 August a general strike. Metaxas got his retaliation in first: the previous day, King George granted his Prime Minister emergency powers.

One might have thought that Metaxas's high-handedness would have roused the febrile Hellenic citizenry to freedom-loving wrath. No such wrath occurred. A 1979 historian, scarcely an admirer of Metaxas, remarks: 'The reaction of the Greek people was one of resigned acquiescence. The general feeling was that the politicians, with their interminable feuds and intrigues, had not served the country well in recent years.'[67]

Abdyl Sino, an Albanian political activist, once quipped: 'Every second Greek is a prime minister.'[68] The country itself has an adage: 'Two Greeks, three political parties.'[69] Metaxas had seen for himself the obstructionism into which high-flown rhetoric over irrelevant philosophies had led national affairs. C.M. Woodhouse, looking back in 1948 upon the inter-war years, conceded the merits of Metaxas's outlook. 'A Greek politician,' Woodhouse explained:

> can talk as well as any western politician, if not better; and that is all he can do [...] He can understand, theoretically and academically, all the current political issues of the great world. He wishes to exercise his intellect upon them, and he does so; but he does nothing else, for there is still nothing else he can do. It is a scintillating exercise in a vacuum. Metaxas lost patience with politics so conducted: he sought realities.[70]

No 'Big Idea' for the pedestrian Metaxas, and no wishful assumption on his part that swords would miraculously turn into ploughshares by next week at the latest, purely because Geneva's delegates or America's League Against War and Fascism or Britain's Peace Pledge Union wanted them to do so. Instead, he promoted abundant defence spending and training, the better to discourage expansionism by Germany and by (a more immediate danger, in his opinion) Italy. More perspicacious than Albania's King Zog, Metaxas discerned from the beginning of his reign the perils of becoming an Italian satellite.

It should go without saying that Zachariadis and other KKE leaders wailed against Metaxas's dominance, as communists have habitually wailed when they find themselves receiving rather than imposing prison sentences. Equally, it should go without saying that the KKE condemned Metaxas as 'fascist' and 'Nazi'. Neither term fits. When an Associated Press interviewer (cited by *The New York Times*) asked Metaxas how he would describe his government, the new leader replied: 'Call it what you want. It is all the same to me.'[71] In fact Metaxas's rule, unlike that of Mussolini or Hitler, had no foundation in a mass movement: parades and salutes do not a mass movement make. It protected the safety of Greece's approximately 100,000 Jews (four-fifths of whom would perish at National Socialists' hands after Metaxas's death). It never joined the Rome-Berlin-Tokyo Anti-Comintern Pact. It refrained, unlike Plastiras's Revolutionary Committee of yore – or the Greek government of 1951–52, once again Plastiras-controlled – from slaying its opponents. In short, it resembled the paternalist conservatism of Salazar's *Estado Novo* rather than any dictatorship east of Portugal.

Unlike Salazar, Metaxas had never been an academic. But like Salazar (and regardless of his military experience), he preferred wearing civilian clothes to wearing any others. This taste, combined with his thick glasses, accentuated his outward resemblance to a dyspeptic solicitor. His world-view, shared with Salazar, can be encapsulated in words from Anthony Trollope's Barsetshire novels: 'It's dogged as does it.' He faced down the local Soviet-manipulated agitators with his characteristic single-mindedness: that trait which in 1935 had moved him to write no fewer than seventy newspaper articles explaining Venizelos's strategic blunders during the Great War.[72] At a press conference in September 1936 he revealed considerable insight into KKE bosses' motives:

> The communists trembled at the thought that my government would enact laws providing for compulsory arbitration and [a] minimum wage. The last thing they wanted was to have a non-communist government take action on behalf of the working class. It was a matter of clientele and the communists could never pardon having their clientele taken from them.[73]

Against the KKE, Metaxas devised a strategy that deserved to be implemented in other lands, and that speaks well for his sense of humour, not otherwise prominent. He established a sham Communist party under his own administration's auspices – complete with a bogus edition of the real party's official daily newspaper, *Rizospastis*, hard for the casual observer to distinguish from the genuine product – and enjoyed the confusion which the resultant doppelgänger caused in KKE ranks. Metaxas and his Interior Minister, Constantine Maniadakis, adopted another practice designed to embarrass the KKE leadership: 'releasing communists from detention provided that they would sign a humiliating declaration, not only renouncing their political past but also denouncing their erstwhile comrades [...] an aura of suspicion attached to those who, for whatever reason, did sign, and they were never subsequently able to shake it off.'[74]

Sometimes Metaxas's censorship seemed excessive to foreign observers, as when he banned books by Marx and Freud[75] (although non-government newspapers in Athens continued to be printed and to be quite outspoken).[76] George II had his private doubts about the Prime Minister – in public he remained methodically supportive – and sometimes expressed to diplomats, including Waterlow, the hope that Greece's state of emergency could be lifted sooner rather than later. 'The idea has always been,' the King said in Waterlow's hearing, 'that he [Metaxas] should retire when he has done his work.'[77] Metaxas begged to differ. Yet no outright showdown occurred between the two men, no lasting estrangement such as had terminated the duumvirate between Alfonso XIII and Primo de Rivera six years beforehand. Each man needed, and realised that he needed, the other. Scanning of the horizon yielded no candidate as an obvious prime ministerial alternative. The Liberals no longer had in their ranks any figure comparable to the dead Venizelos, nor the Populists any figure comparable to the dead Tsaldaris.

On 17 November 1936, both George and Metaxas officiated at a ceremony which underscored, and was fully meant to underscore, monarchism's resurgence. That day, the coffins of King Constantine, Dowager Queen Olga (who had died in 1926), and Queen Sophie (who had outlived Olga by six years) were borne on the cruiser *Averoff* from Brindisi to Piraeus:

> A solemn procession of eighty white-bearded church dignitaries intoned the prayers for the dead in the cathedral at Athens, and for six days the crowds filed past the catafalques before, on the following Wednesday, they were taken to the mausoleum among the tall pines on the slopes above Tatoi.[78]

Joachim von Ribbentrop hoped to be able to intimidate King George into giving up the crown, in favour of Prince Paul, who married Princess Frederica of Hanover in 1938, and whom the Hitler state therefore credited with pro-German promise.[79] Ribbentrop's hope came to nothing. With Metaxas's approval, Maniadakis and his security forces 'put under close surveillance' two Greek cabinet ministers whom he considered to be potentially pro-Hitler.[80] Metaxas himself, while recognising the uncomfortable truth that Germany accounted for 'almost a third of Greece's foreign trade',[81] described at a cabinet meeting his disillusionment concerning Teutonic ambitions:

> I studied in Germany, I believed in their military methods, and I liked the Germans as people. But since 1915 I have felt as a man feels about a friend who failed to keep his word and his promises, and deceived him. And since then I have hated them.[82]

British Foreign Office desires for an anti-Metaxas coup met no more success than did Ribbentrop's plans for tampering with the royal succession. An attempted July 1938 uprising in Crete – once Venizelos's stronghold – ended in a total fiasco. A 1998 biographer of Metaxas stated:

> The weakness of British intelligence about these events was that much of its information came from the so-called educated liberal classes. The poorer mass of the general public were indifferent [to] if not even perversely satisfied with the regime's populism, and more importantly the regime had the support of the Armed Forces.[83]

To Waterlow the King commented, in those disenchanted accents which his years in the political wilderness inclined him to employ: 'The Greeks are Orientals; they consider moderation in the exercise of power weakness. They are the most democratic people in the world, but once they take over power, they become automatically tyrannical. All know and accept this.'[84]

George had himself experienced a certain amount of tyranny at home. His marriage to Elisabeth had contented neither partner. On Elisabeth, her grandmother passed the scathing verdict: George 'ought to beat her, then she would like him'.[85] Quickly and blatantly, Elisabeth took a lover; and George sought consolation in the arms of a woman about whom he revealed so little that sources from the period usually call her simply 'Miss Brown' – MacVeagh's name for her – or 'Mrs Jones'. (In 1947, New York's *Daily News* identified her as Joyce Brittain-Jones, the former spouse of 'an officer in the Black Watch'.)[86] After the marriage of George and Elisabeth had been formally dissolved, George's relationship with 'Miss Brown' came up for discussion by Edward VIII and Wallis Simpson, amid their Mediterranean cruise on board the *Nahlin*. To Mrs Simpson's query as to why George did not marry his mistress, a fellow passenger answered 'with remarkable lack of tact under the circumstances'[87] that the mistress's status as a commoner, and possession of a husband still alive, made nuptials unthinkable. (Did 'remarkable lack of tact' truly inspire the answer? It reads in retrospect like a deliberate rebuke of Mrs Simpson, the twice-divorced American adventuress.) At any rate, George, though free to take a second wife according to Orthodox Church canons, never did so.

The ease with which Italy conquered Albania in April 1939, driving Zog from his throne, confirmed Metaxas's worst suspicions about Mussolini. Still, neither leader wished for all-out war yet. At first the Duce made soothing noises to Metaxas. These noises ceased the following year, when Italian ire at British naval intervention in the Aegean caused Rome to unleash an explicitly anti-Greek campaign in Italy's press. By this stage Italy had already declared war on France and on the United Kingdom. Mussolini wanted vengeance for the Corfu Incident of 1923, during which he had ordered the bombardment of Corfu itself (seeking revenge for the murder of an Italian general, allegedly by Greek bandits) but had been compelled by the League of Nations to retreat. On 15 August 1940 an Italian submarine sank the Greek light cruiser *Elli*; that the sinking occurred on one of the holiest days of the Greek Orthodox calendar – the Dormition of the Virgin Mary – added to Greek fury at the deed. Mussolini interpreted the Germans' October advance upon Romania as giving him carte blanche to treat Greece similarly. Convinced that the Greeks would put up little more resistance than the Albanians did, he ordered Italy's ambassador, Emanuele Grazzi, to issue on 28 October an ultimatum to Athens: allow free passage for Italian troops, or forget about maintaining neutrality.

A maxim from British historian H.A.L. Fisher (Lloyd George's Education Secretary and Ralph Vaughan Williams's brother-in-law) is relevant: 'No Greek loves an Italian, nor any Orthodox Greek a Roman Catholic.'[88] What Fisher said of the Mediterranean during the late seventeenth century held equally true for the mid-twentieth, and helped to ensure Metaxas's determination to punish the Duce's overconfidence. Concerning the events of 28 October, popular tradition credits Metaxas with having hurled at Grazzi one Greek word: *Oxi!* ['No!'] (To this day, Greeks around the world celebrate 28 October as *Oxi* Day.) Metaxas's actual response was less memorable, more formal, and conveyed in what then remained the chief language of diplomacy: '*Alors, c'est la guerre.*' ('Then it's war.')[89]

Italy's superiority in numbers proved no match for the determination of the Greeks to drive the invader back. Knowing extremely well the often inhospitable territory involved, and assisted by British air power, they fought to defend every square centimetre of it. They inflicted so much damage over the next fortnight alone that the Italian commander-in-chief, Sebastiano Visconti Prasca, had to be recalled home on 13 November.

Even Nikos Zachariadis, now imprisoned, urged the comrades (through an open letter to Maniadakis, which the Greek newspapers printed on 2 November) to rally behind the Prime Minister: 'In this war, directed by the Metaxas Government, we shall give every ounce of our strength without reserve.'[90] This was a remarkably heterodox proclamation during the Nazi-Soviet Pact, where the standard Communist line was to rage against the imperialist West. So heterodox, indeed, was the utterance that several KKE officials believed it to be either a counterfeit contrived by Metaxas and Maniadakis themselves, or else written by Zachariadis purely in the hope of effecting his release. From London exile, the Comintern bulletin *World News and Views* maintained that the utterance had been forged:

> The Greek Goebbels, [*Press and Tourism Minister Theologos*] Nicouloudes, went to characteristic lengths and released a story that the Greek Communists support Metaxas and the war. But it was done so blatantly and crudely that even an unpolitical person could see it was only a faked job. The Greek Communist Party never has and never will support Metaxas and the war which it understands as a feud between rival imperialists for markets and spheres of influence.[91]

Sure enough, less than a month afterwards (26 November), Zachariadis produced more conventionally Stalinist verbiage. On this occasion he furnished an open letter to Metaxas himself, wholly contrasting with the sentiments of his earlier proclamation, and wholly attuned to Moscow dogma as it existed before June 1941:

> Once we threw the Italians out of Greece, our basic effort should have been to conclude a separate peace, without concessions, which could have been accomplished only through the mediation of the Soviet Union; instead the Monarcho-Fascist dictatorship continued the war for the benefit not of the Greek people but of the plutocracy and English imperialism.[92]

Not that the workaholic Metaxas paid Zachariadis's volte-face conspicuous attention. Increasingly, as his seventieth birthday loomed, the Prime Minister devoted his diary entries to complaints about his health. As early as 1937 Waterlow, unable to conceal a certain reluctant respect for the Greek strongman's conscientiousness, had written to Anthony Eden: 'Metaxas has an almost superhuman disregard, not only of the ordinary pleasures of life, but of things, such as regular meals, which are necessities to most people; from sunrise until late at night he works without interruption, except occasionally to nibble some fruit.'[93]

Early on the morning of 29 January 1941, Metaxas died at his home. Though the death certificate speaks of 'septicaemia after a streptococcus infection',[94] and though he had suffered at least one massive internal haemorrhage (according to his daughter's subsequent account) 'in the spring of 1940',[95] a conspiracy theory soon arose, insisting that he had been murdered by British spies. A British soldier had brought the dying man an oxygen mask from a local army depot; from this slender basis, the theory took off. Since in January 1941 Greece was Britain's only European ally still in the war (and since two months earlier FDR had won an unprecedented third presidential term specifically through his promise to stay out of the war),[96] it is not obvious why Britain would have wanted to murder this ally's head of government, although modern history contains numerous instances of conspiracy theories gaining extra traction in direct ratio to their silliness.

❁ ❁ ❁

Most of Greece's sufferings over the next eight years belong in a separate book: the Wehrmacht's occupation from April 1941; the suicide in that month of Alexandros Koryzis, Metaxas's successor as Prime Minister; the famine which claimed more than 250,000 Greek lives; the onset of civil war, which (like its Spanish counterpart) left a legacy that poisoned political life for generations to come. Through it all, George II had at least the satisfaction of knowing that in the 1940s, by contrast with the 1920s, he had the backing of Britain – above all of Churchill personally – and of the USA. Once Crete had fallen, George and his entourage stayed first in Cairo, then in London. In December 1944, when the Third Reich looked as if it would soon end, the King acceded to the Allies' insistence upon a regency at home, one led by Damaskinos Papandreou, Archbishop of Athens.

On becoming regent, the Archbishop angered George by promptly appointing as Prime Minister none other than the veteran Plastiras, who presided over a largely republican cabinet. Nonetheless, with the Communists having been up in arms since 1944, the King could not protest overmuch. After 1944 Greek politics furnished the unexpected phenomenon of long-time royalists and long-time Venizelists fighting on the same side, against the KKE-run 'Provisional Democratic Government of Greece' and its army. A March 1946 general election gave a clear parliamentary majority to monarchists, now led by Constantine Tsaldaris, nephew of Panagis Tsaldaris. The following September, Britain gave King George permission to return to his homeland, and the prelate stepped down from his regency. Earlier in the month, the monarchist cause had prevailed at yet another plebiscite.

The King had little time to draw any satisfaction from his latest monarchical re-embodiment. Nor did he live for nearly long enough to witness the civil war's conclusion. The end came on 1 April 1947. An insomniac chain-smoker, he admitted to feeling sick after luncheon at Tatoi. Within an hour he had succumbed to arteriosclerosis. The cabinet – by this time the younger Tsaldaris had resigned the prime ministry in favour of former banker Dimitrios Maximos – 'was summoned to the palace and proclaimed 45-year-old Prince Paul his [George's] successor'.[97] (Had the Greek royal house permitted female succession, Paul would have needed to make way for King Alexander's daughter: Alexandria, the wife of Yugoslavia's unfortunate ex-monarch Peter II. But it permitted no such succession, and as the nearest living male relative of George, Paul became king automatically.) Fate had one last unkind trick to play on the deceased sovereign: the date of his death inspired a widespread rumour that reports of his passing were mere April Fool's Day jokes.[98]

By such nasty gossip, George II would have been saddened but scarcely surprised. Others greeted the news of his demise with suitable compassion, notably the Athens newspaper which announced: 'Last night was surely the first through which King George slept peacefully.'[99] About the Greek throne for which he had forgone so much, he once said: 'I loathe it, I hate it, I despise it, I would like to get rid of it, but what can I do about it?'[100] That cry of despair can stand as his epitaph.

Chapter VII

From President to Monosyllable
Albania

Land of Albania! where Iskander rose,
Theme of the young, and beacon of the wise,
And he his namesake, whose oft-baffled foes
Shrank from his deeds of chivalrous emprize;
Land of Albania! let me bend mine eyes
On thee, thou rugged nurse of savage men!
The cross descends, thy minarets arise,
And the pale crescent sparkles in the glen,
Through many a cypress grove within each city's ken. [...]
Yet in famed Attica such lovely dales
Are rarely seen; nor can fair Tempe boast
A charm they know not; loved Parnassus fails,
Though classic ground and consecrated most,
To match some spots that lurk within this lowering coast.

Lord Byron[1]

The political stability which Greece acquired in 1936, Albania had experienced for more than a decade. In November 1912 it had proclaimed its independence from centuries of Ottoman rule, and the rest of Europe recognised this independence in 1913, as a consequence of the First Balkan War. Who possessed the most suitable qualifications for governing Albania took longer to determine.

During (and apropos) the late twentieth century, Frank Zappa averred that 'You can't be a real country unless you have a beer and an airline.'[2] Before the Great War, much of public opinion considered it a *sine qua non* for a real country to have, not a beer or an airline, but a monarch. In 1905 this attitude had brought about the enthronement of a Danish prince as Haakon VII of Norway; it explained first Otto's, then George I's, Greek domicile; and it led to a profusion of candidates for Albania's throne.

Some urged Greece's Prince Christopher to become the Albanian king, but he refused, and turned out to be a master at deflecting unwelcome monarchist approaches. (In 1912 he also refused the crown of Portugal, partly out of esteem for Manuel II, partly out of aversion to Sir Basil Zaharoff, from whom the Portuguese offer came. A subsequent campaign to make Christopher king of Lithuania likewise went nowhere, the Prince disowning it on the somewhat specious pretext that 'my head was too bald to prevent the crown from slipping off'.)[3]

172

Between March and September 1914, Kaiser Wilhelm's second cousin, Wilhelm of Wied, presided as Albania's sovereign and lived in Durrës, then the nation's capital (the transfer of government functions to Tirana had to wait until the 1920s). The Albanian term for Wilhelm's position was *Mbret*, closer in meaning to 'king' than to 'prince', although his contemporaries in the West tended to refer to him by the lowlier title. Muslim rebels nostalgic for Turkish control made Wilhelm's life a misery; they benefited from the fact that their co-religionists constituted seven-tenths of Albania's population.[4] Many of Wilhelm's subjects concluded from his gentlemanly demeanour that he must be a weakling: 'when visiting Tirana he helped his wife from their carriage and allowed her to walk before him, an action which the people interpreted as a sign of feebleness!'[5]

Italian meddling in the country's politics took the form of giving bribes to Wilhelm's Prime Minister, Essad Pasha Toptani, provided that Essad organised the monarch's deposition. Greece, in the meantime, helped itself to Albanian land in North Epirus, justifying this action by the presence in the area of a large Greek-speaking minority. Essad's efforts to topple Wilhelm with Italian assistance came to naught, and once defeated he went into exile at Bari, thanks to Italy's intervention on his behalf.[6] Wilhelm, wanting (despite his Teutonic background and sympathies) to keep Albania neutral once the Great War had begun, found that neutralism rendered him deeply unpopular with the Central Powers. They cut off his money supply, and he fled Albania – for good, it turned out – while avoiding outright abdication.

From then until 1923, Albania's history proved to be an almost meaningless catalogue of invertebrate governments unable to prevent repeated military incursions by Austria-Hungary, Serbia, Venizelist Greece, and (most lastingly) Italy, which had been promised Albanian territory by the Treaty of London. In one year alone (1921) Albania had five prime ministers. Homicidal disputes among rival chieftains, rather than any police force or magistracy as Western Europeans understood such things, administered whatever justice most ordinary Albanians knew. In the wildest region of the country, called Toplana, blood feuds – according to one scarcely credible yet well authenticated statistic – accounted for *42 per cent* of all male deaths.[7] A local saying ran, 'In Toplana men are killed like pigs.'[8] (Such feuding left Albanian females secure, 'since female blood was not considered of any value'.)[9] The imbroglio inspired the following caustic paragraph from an English journalist, Joseph Swire:

> No Albanian had so risen above his compatriots that they would have accepted him as king, so the royalists looked abroad. Several European princes were approached, several men of title, and an English commoner whose tireless efforts for the Albanians' welfare had proved his love for them. Irresponsible individuals, caring more for dollars than decorum, went further, making overtures to millionaires and kings of industry; and some approached much humbler men who had happened to do minor services for Albania, among them a friend of mine. But in his case there was a condition – he must marry an American girl whose work had also gained Albanian appreciation, so that the sum of their joint benefactions might make up for their want of money and royal blood. But the condition evidently proved

beyond the bounds of their heroism. Our Popular Press broadcast these tales, so the Albanian authorities received letters from all kinds and conditions of people who thought they might shine as king – or queen – of Albania. Among them was an instructress of classical dancing who lived in Highgate – she claimed that she could soar like an eagle, a qualification she thought irresistible to the Albanians who call themselves 'Son of the Eagle'.[10]

Within the relevant period, 'there were about forty serious candidates for the throne, and at least twice as many replied to an advertisement placed in the "Situations Vacant" section of a London newspaper, which read "Wanted, a King; an English country gentleman preferred – Apply to the Government of Albania".'[11] Quite the unlikeliest of the 'forty serious candidates' was the all-round sportsman C.B. Fry.

An Oxford contemporary and friend of Max Beerbohm and Hilaire Belloc, in 1895 Fry had won (when 23 years old) *Wisden*'s award for Cricketer of the Year. He captained England's Test team, scored ninety-four centuries in first-class cricket – six of them, in 1901, consecutive – and somehow found time to equal the existing world long-jump record, as well as to play for Southampton's soccer team in the 1902 FA Cup Final. (His marginally less impressive record in rugby union still included being chosen for Oxford's team in that sport.) Until his seventies he also possessed the ability to jump backwards, from a standing position, onto a mantelpiece.[12]

After the Great War, Fry's old friend and former team-mate K.S. Ranjitsinhji – for whom, sometimes, he ghost-wrote – represented India at the League of Nations, and took Fry with him as a staffer. While at the League, Fry somehow came to the attention of Albania's representatives, recently disappointed in their hopes of offering the kingdom to British soldier Aubrey Herbert, whose daughter Laura Herbert became the second wife of Evelyn Waugh. At least Aubrey Herbert, thanks to his wartime service, knew Albania at first hand – in marked contrast to Fry.

An Albanian bishop, whom Fry's account does not name, made the initial approach. Since Ranjitsinhji had managed back in 1907 to obtain an Indian princedom (complete with 'his own crown jewels [...] and the title of "His Highness the Maharaja Jam Saheb of Nawanagar"),'[13] Fry understandably craved a comparable elevation. As he put it years later in his own sub-Wodehousian prose:

> It is quite easy to understand that as the personal friend and assistant of the only Sovereign Prince at Geneva, illumined by the reflected light of his magnificent hospitality, and being pretty busy all over the place without any careful solicitude to hide my own light under a bushel, I was spotted by the lambent eyes of the Bishop as an eligible Englishman. Nor would it be wholly improbable that somewhere or other an income of ten thousand a year was knocking about.[14]

Little did the Albanians suspect that 'an income of ten thousand a year' was precisely what Fry did not have. He spent money (much of it from his newspaper and magazine output) as soon as he earned it, depending for much of his upkeep on doles from his dragon of a wife. Belloc urged Fry: 'Do not accept the crown of Albania. Be content with a cellar of wine and the society of those who love you.'[15] Fry obeyed Belloc's advice. Afterwards he took politics seriously enough to contest, between 1922 and 1924, three elections in the Liberal interest. At the second of his attempts, in Banbury, he fell only 219 votes short of unseating the Conservative incumbent.[16] But he never again provoked wider European enthusiasm.

During 1922 there emerged in Albania's politics a remarkable, youngish (40 years of age) figure: Fan Noli – Theofan Stilian Noli, to give his full name – who promised dramatic change. At once a parliamentarian, historian, theologian, translator, composer, musicologist (his curriculum vitae includes a biography of Beethoven) and bishop of the Albanian Orthodox Church, Noli is a strong candidate for the most overqualified politician in modern world history. Much of his earlier career he had spent in America, where he graduated from Harvard, and where he ministered to the spiritual and economic needs of Massachusetts's Albanian community. First as Foreign Minister, then (June–December 1924) as Prime Minister, Noli embodied reformist and Anglo-Saxon attitudes. 'He was generally considered a man of principle and patriotism,' a historian wrote long after Noli's demise, 'but politically he was somewhat out of touch […] He had been removed from [Albania] for too long, and he no longer really understood it.'[17]

Noli's chief opponent, the Muslim Ahmed Zogu – born in 1895, and thus Noli's junior by thirteen years – understood the terrain all too well. Originally called Zogolli (a surname which he abandoned once its Turkish character became disadvantageous to him), Zogu had already become Prime Minister in December 1922. Any man who can head a national administration before the age of 28 possesses, by definition, an acute intelligence, whatever his pedagogic shortcomings. Zogu's father had been chief of the Mati tribe, supreme in much of central Albania, while Zogu's maternal uncle was none other than Essad Pasha Toptani. (In 1920, outside a Paris hotel, Essad had been cut down by an assassin's bullet; the assassin himself, parliamentarian Avni Rustemi, perished four years later in Tirana at a pro-Zogu killer's hands.)

To the limited extent that Albania had anything so tediously conventional as a ruling class, Zogu belonged from boyhood to this class. Far better travelled than most of his countrymen, he spent much of the Great War in Vienna, where he mastered German and appreciated the political benefits of observing his environs while keeping his own counsel. If his wife's testimony is to be believed, he met Emperor Franz Josef,[18] and a 1957 book on Albania maintains that the spectacle of Emperor Karl's coronation profoundly affected Zogu's eventual career dreams.[19]

Noli's brief term of office included moves to establish diplomatic relations with the USSR, and enough talk of comprehensive agricultural reform to scandalise the Islamic landowners who backed Zogu. After only six months as Prime Minister, Noli found himself confronted with troops (many of them supplied by Yugoslavia) under Zogu's command. It was no contest. Noli had the intellectual standing, but Zogu had the army, albeit a foreign-aided army.[20] 'Extensive precautions were taken to mask the complicity of Belgrade. Yugoslav soldiers were to wear native Albanian costumes.'[21] Other soldiers aiding Zogu were White Russians who had fought under General Pyotr Wrangel against Bolshevism.[22]

Zogu's government condemned Noli to death – the fallen Prime Minister escaped to Italy before the sentence could be carried out – and arranged the murders of two well-established politicians incautious enough to have involved themselves with Noli's movement. In January 1925, Zogu persuaded the intimidated legislature to elect him Albania's President. Hitherto Albania had continued to call itself a monarchy, and Wilhelm of Wied had remained its theoretical head of state, though Albanian monarchist ministers (like Admiral Horthy in Budapest) could never be accused of undue eagerness to extend the welcome-mat to their absent sovereign.

The Albania over which Zogu now ruled remained desperately poor and backward, not merely by Western criteria, but by Balkan criteria too. (Noli had tried to extract a loan from the League of Nations, which refused to supply any largesse.) Only a tenth of Albania's populace could read and write.[23] Two years prior to the Great War, the nation possessed a grand total of one water-closet.[24] In 1922 90 per cent of Albanians worked on farms, but a mere 9 per cent of the countryside permitted farming at all. Of the rest, 24 per cent was virgin forest, and 67 per cent was thankless scrub, plagued with erosion.[25] When Zogu took over, no trains existed, and the recorded automotive transportation in Albania consisted of three motor cars, all of them ancient Fords 'left behind by an American relief mission'.[26] As late as 1927, Albania's annual per capita national income amounted to US$40.07, whereas even cheerless Bulgaria managed in the same year $67.57, while the equivalent Yugoslav figure was $76.93.[27] Zogu's 1984 biographer commented:

> Clearly, some drastic measures were in order. Zogu had learned some lessons. He had learned that political stability was impossible without a measure of economic stability and fiscal sanity. More importantly, Zogu had learned that although it might be possible to eventually turn Albania into a Western state, the Western political model had been a miserable failure.[28]

Hidden from inquisitive posterity is the exact date on which Zogu conceived the idea of an upgrade from President Zogu to King Zog the First, thus making himself one of only three Albanians known by name to millions of non-Albanians, the other two being Enver Hoxha and Mother Teresa. (Were Albanian ethnicity to override the accident of non-Albanian birth, a fourth name would warrant inclusion: John Belushi of *Blues Brothers* fame, born in Chicago to Albanian parents, and according to his own testimony – albeit in a very different sense from Mother Teresa – 'on a mission from God'.)

Zogu himself could probably not have identified just when the upgrade concept dawned on him. At first, he remained content with mere presidential status, not least because after the recent national experiment of Noli-style liberalism, he 'did not want to give the Albanians the impression that he was an unregenerated conservative working in his own interests rather than in the interest of the country'.[29] Still, Zogu had long been fascinated by Napoleon's example, and by a more locally relevant avatar: Skanderbeg, the fifteenth-century Albanian general whom he falsely claimed as a blood-relative. (A certain piquancy attached itself on religious grounds to this championship, since although Skanderbeg had been raised as a Muslim, he apostasised from the Islamic faith – unlike Zogu – and acquired his greatest significance as a persistent military defender of Christendom against Turkish encroachment.) Zogu's impressionable years in late-Habsburg Vienna, and his earlier period of basic schooling in Constantinople under the sultanate, had exposed him to monarchical culture in its most elaborately ceremonious modern forms. More and more from 1925, the initials 'AZ' magically appeared on bureaucratic offices, on postage stamps, and on at least one mountain side.[30]

By the comparative efficiency and occasional ferocity of his government, the President did more for Albania in three years than his predecessors had done in thirteen. Though he had not altogether stamped out blood feuding, he had at any rate done much to nationalise it. His early tenure as Interior Minister served him well (Sir Harry Eyres, British Ambassador to Albania at the time of Zogu's rise, rated his performance more highly in that subordinate role than as absolute ruler).[31] This tenure gave him some gift for administrative mechanics, sharpening his talent in playing off Muslim, Orthodox and Catholic officials against each other. It also ensured that, for instance, his censorship policies inconvenienced his antagonists – at least, those among his antagonists who knew their way around the alphabet – without being so draconian as to bring endless Western obloquy down on his head:

> Fortunately for the small intelligentsia, the new regime lacked ideological commitment, was not the monopoly of one party, and did not use efficient means [...] many of the young men who served as censors were in secret sympathy with the ideas expressed by the university-trained writers. Consequently, there was some freedom of thought expressed in the press and books, except when Zogu himself was personally attacked. In such cases, and when communist oriented material was in question, Zogu never hesitated to ruthlessly crush his opponents.[32]

So obvious a supremacy over all rivals had Zogu established, that for many unlettered peasants (clueless about general republican or monarchist principles, but aware that schools and paved streets were now being constructed where no schools and paved streets had been constructed before), he already *was* king. He even brought to Albania its first telephone service.[33] Discovery in mid-1928 of a conspiracy against him increased his natural suspiciousness and his resolve to overawe his foes. (His dread of being poisoned meant that 'his mother, while she lived, supervised the preparation of his meals'.[34] In February 1924, during his first prime ministerial term, he had been shot and wounded at the legislature's entrance by a student radical, Beqir Walter, who then 'locked himself in the Parliament lavatory and sang patriotic songs to maintain his courage'.)[35]

A courtroom heard in June 1928 that three plotters, two of them Bulgarians and the third a native Albanian, had intended to blow up the President at his Durrës villa. In July, on a makeshift Tirana gallows, the defendants met their ends with a full complement of Grand Guignol horror:

> The hanging of one of the Bulgarians, a man named Georgieff, was a blundering atrocity. His giant frame brought the tripod down with a crash when the box was pulled out from under his feet and he was allowed to

drop. He had to be put back up and it was forty-five minutes from the time he was first hanged until he was pronounced dead [...] this did not prevent the usual mad scramble for slices of the rope, always in demand after a hanging as good luck charms.[36]

Regnal nomenclature posed an initial problem to Zogu. Should he style himself 'King of Albania', or should he style himself – after the fashion of nineteenth-century monarchs in Athens, Brussels, and Paris – 'King of the Albanians'? The latter choice prevailed, in part because Yugoslavia opposed it, fearing that the title would appeal to 'the half million or more Albanians living under Yugoslav sovereignty'.[37] By this stage, the Yugoslav leadership had grown so unpopular in Tirana that whatever rankled with Belgrade became appealing.

Italian diplomat Ugo Sola laid on the flattery with the proverbial trowel when he wrote to King Zog (as Zogu formally became on 1 September 1928, via a special legislative session). On behalf of King Vittorio Emanuele III as well as of the Duce, Sola smoothly reminded the Albanian leader about the pact which both countries had signed two years beforehand:

> The Royal Italian Government considers the establishment of the monarchical regime in Albania as a happy event which, while further strengthening the bonds existing between the two countries, will ensure the continuity of their foreign policy as laid down in the Treaty of Alliance. Italy will therefore always remain faithful to that intimate entente whose brilliant results in general policy it has pleased Your Excellency to emphasise.[38]

Not all Sola's compatriots shared his enthusiasm for unctuous ambassadorial verbosity. During a banquet where the guests (more than 200 of them) included a visiting Italian colonel and the current British Ambassador in Tirana, Sir Jocelyn Percy, sitting beside one another, the Italian assured the Englishman: 'I like the title "King of the Albanians", it sounds aggressive.'[39] The same felicitous thought doubtless occurred to Zog, who now decreed that public displays of his initials be altered from 'AZ' to 'AZ I.'

Joseph Swire, before his inconvenient revelations of Albanian bureaucratic corruption forced him to leave the country, saw much of the new monarch. In 1937 he told his readers:

> King Zog is a slight man of middle height, his hair, moustache and complexion fair, his eyes keen and alert. He dresses well but simply and wears no unnecessary baubles. When President he sometimes wore a white uniform, designed in Prince Wilhelm's time, which in those days seemed incongruous; but he wore it for effect upon his impressionable subjects and not for choice. He is courteous, with an easy grace [...] His courage is proved, so, too, his wit and foresight, and his diplomatic skill is matched by his suave evasive words when dealing with the thorny problems and tortuous minds everywhere about him.[40]

Some of the 'tortuous minds' scorned mere words. In February 1931 occurred another assassination attempt, this time near the Vienna State Opera, which staged on the relevant evening Ruggero Leoncavallo's *Pagliacci*. Two discontented Albanian exiles, Aziz Çami and Ndok Gjeloshi – both of whom carried Yugoslav passports[41] – belonged to an anti-Zog, pro-Noli group which called itself KONARE (in full, *Komiteti Nacional Revolucionar*) and received Kremlin funds. Both men, as Zog entered his car, aimed their revolvers at him. Cami's gun failed to operate, while Gjeloshi hit the wrong target: Llesh Topallaj, the King's bodyguard, whom Gjeloshi had mistaken for the monarch in the confusion, and who died immediately, with three bullets in the back of his head. (Another bullet wounded a future Albanian prime minister, Ekrem Libohova.) According to some accounts, Zog fired back at the assailants, but hit no one. The would-be murderers suffered surprisingly mild penalties: three years and six months' imprisonment in Gjeloshi's case, two years and six months in Çami's. *New York Times* coverage of the shooting contained the eminently reasonable subhead 'Albanian Monarch Reported to Be Deeply Depressed by Fourth Attempt on His Life.'[42]

By this stage Tirana was benefiting from a small but steady supply of English immigrants. Zog appointed as Inspector-General of Gendarmerie one Lieutenant-Colonel Stirling, a fellow combatant of T.E. Lawrence in Arabia. Though Stirling bore the given names Walter Francis, he insisted on being addressed as 'Michael',[43] no doubt to reinforce his credentials for authentic Lawrentian mystification. He indubitably shared Lawrence's frequent distaste for conventional diplomats, and accused Sir Harry Eyres of possessing 'the mentality of a Turk'.[44] (Eyres, in response, made uncharitable allusions to the deleterious effect on Stirling's health of Mrs Stirling's libido.)[45] The more Albania's resident Englishmen traduced one another, the more pleased Zog became. Such mutual resentment appealed to his own capacity for intrigue. Moreover, at a time when vast numbers of Continental politicians assumed that every single Englishman worked for Whitehall's Secret Service, Zog rather liked the idea of having such omniscient Englishmen around him, partly because they formed a useful counterweight to Italian influence. Stirling, although after a while he quarrelled with Zog (who later referred to Sir Jocelyn Percy as 'a far better man than Colonel Stirling'),[46] accorded the Albanian sovereign a glowing character reference in his 1955 memoir, appropriately called *Safety Last*: 'Of all the statesmen of the Middle East – and I have met most of them – I consider Zog the most brilliant, the most cultured, and the most far-seeing.'[47]

Italian dominion over Albania had steadily increased since the 1926 treaty. During the first year of the Zogu presidency, as explained by British historian Hugh Seton-Watson:

> an Albanian National Bank was founded with fifty-three per cent Italian capital. In 1926 was created a Society for the Development of the Economic Resources of Albania, controlled by the bank. In return for the loans made by this society, Albania promised for forty years to take no action which might prejudice her revenues without first consulting Italy. About the same time petrol was discovered near Valona [*Vlorë*], and, as French and British companies were not interested in an enterprise promising quite small profits, the concession was given to Italy.[48]

This constituted, in everything but name, simple colonialism. Zogu had hesitated before signing the 1926 agreement; and the British Ambassador at the time, William E. O'Reilly, had given to Albania's President 'his sincere opinion that such a pact was incompatible with Albanian independence'.[49] But after Italy had complained about O'Reilly's observation and had carefully applied pressure on O'Reilly's superiors at the British Foreign Office, Zogu gritted his teeth and signed. He reasoned that the money for his modernising programs had to be found in some place, and since Yugoslavia's government had become increasingly hostile to Albania's, he could look for no succour there.

Italy acquired its colonial status over Albania by default. Albanian trade deficits with the rest of Europe had long been almost the stuff of legend. Put simply, Albania imported practically everything and exported practically nothing. Except its own people: emigration among Albanians, especially to the USA, approached Hibernian levels. At least Italian funds produced some tangible benefits to Albanians in the form of infrastructure, though a cynical observer could not fail to notice the sheer number of Italian teachers employed in training the Albanian armed services, or the assistance which the country's newly built roads would provide to the tanks of any future Italian invading force. Thanks to such appearances (however factitious) of national prosperity, Zog managed to retain power throughout the Great Depression, an achievement beyond many other Western political leaders much more highly educated than himself.

One blessing Zog's circumstances continued to lack: marriage. Shortly after becoming President, he acquired an Austrian mistress, a dancer called Franziska Janko, 'said to sport a pair of "twinkling" legs, a slim body [...] light-chestnut-coloured hair and a pair of brown mischievous eyes'.[50] But in 1934 Fräulein Janko, her presence in Tirana having elicited from foreign newspapers unseemly comparisons with Magda Lupescu (notorious paramour of Romania's Carol II), found herself packed off to Vienna: amid comfortable circumstances, since her lover had purchased for her in that city a palace which cost him £26,000.[51]

Potential mothers-in-law regarded Zog as a less eligible bachelor than he would have hoped. Rumour announced in 1933 that one of Empress Zita's daughters, Princess Adelheid, might become Albania's queen. Anyone less enthusiastic than the redoubtable Zita about future family connections with a Muslim adventurer is difficult to imagine, and the rumour died away.

Zog's eventual choice of bride, though (a choice revealed to the public in January 1938), fell upon another Catholic: Geraldine Apponyi, then aged 22, who belonged to one of Hungary's most ancient dynasties, and whose kinsfolk included that Count Apponyi whom Horthy had defeated in the 1920 legislative election for the post of Hungarian Regent. Geraldine spoke good French and perfect English – her mother was American – while during her adolescence she had learnt to use a typewriter, a knack by no means common among the epoch's aristocrats of either sex. Her charm won over Orthodox and Muslim as well as Catholic Albanians, one Orthodox admirer being the butler to Sir Andrew Ryan (by this time Britain's Ambassador), who 'threatened to shoot anyone who questioned the beauty of the King's betrothed'.[52]

Few placed themselves at risk of the butler's weapon. As confirmed by both photographs and newsreel footage, Geraldine possessed uncommon pulchritude, which resulted in her being widely called the White Rose of Hungary. The wedding took place on 27 April 1938, in the gardens of Zog's palace: Zog thought it desirable to avoid a religious rite, given the credal gulf between bride and groom.

These nuptials attained a celebrity lasting well beyond whatever the world's cameras and photo editors generated, because George Bowling, the insurance agent whom Orwell made the protagonist of *Coming Up for Air*, refers to them. (For artistic effect, Orwell blurred the chronology involved, alluding to Zog's marriage, to a Brighton murder case from 1934, to Chiang Kai-Shek's struggle against the Japanese, and to the Spanish Civil War's early battles as if they were simultaneous.) From the following passage's concluding sentence, it will be inferred that Bowling never belonged to the ranks of the politically correct:

> I had a look at the paper, but there wasn't much news. Down in Spain and over in China they were murdering one another as usual, a woman's legs had been found in a railway waiting-room, and King Zog's wedding was wavering in the balance. [...] When I got down near Charing Cross the boys were yelling a later edition of the evening papers. There was some more drivel about the murder. LEGS. FAMOUS SURGEON'S STATEMENT. Then another poster caught my eye: KING ZOG'S WEDDING POSTPONED. King Zog! What a name! It's next door to impossible to believe a chap with a name like that isn't a jet-black Negro.[53]

Between Zog and one of Orwell's *bêtes noires*, Salvador Dalí, there existed an improbable bond pertaining to facial hair. Dalí grew his internationally celebrated moustache in homage to Zog's, and the two men resembled one another in appearance even without such growths.[54]

Guests at the wedding of Zog and Geraldine included Count Galeazzo Ciano, married since 1930 to Mussolini's daughter Edda, and in charge since 1936 of his nation's foreign policy. Ciano's boastfulness amounted, in its sheer naïveté, almost to charm. Ivy Chamberlain, wife of Sir Austen, met Ciano while she visited Rome. On being told the age at which Anthony Eden became Foreign Secretary, Ciano bragged to her: 'I was a year younger when I became Foreign Minister here.' Lady Chamberlain retorted: 'No doubt, but then Anthony's father-in-law isn't a dictator.'[55] Sir Charles Petrie, for all his kind words about both the Duce (concerning whom he had written one of the earliest English-language biographies) and Edda, acidly wrote of Ciano that 'if one bought him at one's own price and sold him at his there would be a considerable profit on the transaction'.[56]

Yet in Ciano the schemer, Zog the schemer met his match. (The two men's first face-to-face encounters had been during Ciano's April 1937 visit to Tirana.)[57] Many believed, understandably, that Ciano and his father, Admiral Costanzo Ciano – speaker of the Italian parliament's lower house – had lined their own pockets through investments in Albania's oil wells.[58] Albania became an obsession for the Foreign Minister, and not one which Mussolini shared. The Duce kept recommending caution to his son-in-law, principally because he did not want Italy's armed forces over-extended when Spain's communist-controlled government looked capable of surviving. But still Ciano plotted. He persuaded Francesco Jacomoni, the Italian Ambassador, to supply arms to anti-Zog forces in Albania. A complacent October 1938 diary entry of Ciano's refers to Jake Koci, one of Zog's cabinet ministers:

> The action begins to have a clear profile: killing of the king (it seems that Koci will be charged with it, with a payment of 10 million), riots in the streets, descent from the mountains of the bands loyal to us … appeal to Italy to intervene politically and if necessary militarily, offer of the throne to the King Emperor [Vittorio Emanuele had been Emperor of Abyssinia since 1936] and a little later annexation. Jacomoni guarantees that everything can happen regularly with a month's warning.[59]

In the assassination department, Koci proved a severe disappointment to Ciano's plans, which involved poisoning Zog's coffee. Without firm approval from Mussolini, Koci refused to act; and Mussolini gave no such approval.

Once Madrid had surrendered to Franco in March 1939, the Duce finally acceded to Ciano's demands that Italy invade. King Vittorio Emanuele, nevertheless, remained in two minds about the operation. While 'the little sardine'[60] – Mussolini's contemptuous nickname for his 5ft-tall sovereign – possessed no intrinsic objection to augmenting his realm, and viewed Zog as a vulgarian, he queried the worth of a military enterprise intended (in his own phrase) 'to capture four stones'.[61] Besides, as a crowned head himself, he worried that the habit of dethroning fellow European monarchs might become contagious. (Mussolini, afraid of a royal refusal to authorise the invasion, declared to Ciano his envy of Teutonic republican rule: 'If Hitler had had to deal with a shithead of a king he would never have been able to take Austria and Czechoslovakia.')[62] Yet Vittorio Emanuele decided – as he had so often decided before – that an open confrontation with Mussolini would imperil him too much to be attempted, and he acquiesced in his Prime Minister's call for military action against Albania.

Caught utterly off-guard, Zog received an ultimatum from the Duce on 5 April: either he agreed to renew by noon the following day the existing alliance, with terms still more favourable to Italy's interests than the 1926 treaty had been, or else popular outrage against him would force him to abdicate. Zog implored Mussolini to give him until six on the following evening before he responded. The Duce made no reply. On 7 April, very early indeed (at 0430 hours), Italian troops landed on Albania's shores.

A mere two days earlier, Geraldine had given birth to a son, Leka. The birth, by caesarean section, had been an exceptionally difficult one. She almost bled to death. Anguish about his wife's condition helped to explain Zog's failure to rally his subjects: 'No serious preparations for resistance were made, no leadership was offered. Zog behaved less than well in this final crisis.'[63] The Italians (who after their triumph systematically and tactlessly Italianised local place-names, so that Durrës turned into Durazzo, Vlorë turned into Valona, and Shkodër turned into Scutari) were astonished at how little resistance they met on the Albanian coast. Ciano's second-in-command at the Foreign Ministry, Filippo Anfuso, commented that 'If the Albanians had possessed a corps of well-trained firemen, they would have thrown us into the Adriatic.'[64]

When Italy's legislature reconvened later in the month, Ciano spoke with the utmost pride to his fellow members about the invasion, and then telephoned Giovanni Ansaldo, editor of the Livorno-based newspaper *Il Telegrafo*, which the Ciano family then owned. Unsuspected by either man, OVRA (the Duce's secret police) recorded the call. Even after one makes every cross-cultural allowance for the average young Italian male's traditional freedom from British male conversational bashfulness – his concern to cut an impressive figure in public, *fare una bella figura* – the transcript of Ciano's euphoric self-aggrandisement and of Ansaldo's obsequiousness provides distasteful reading:

CIANO	Ansaldo!
ANSALDO	Command me, Excellency!
CIANO	What did you think of it?
ANSALDO	Of what, Excellency?
CIANO	Of my speech, naturally!
ANSALDO	Ah yes, Excellency. I haven't read it. They are passing the papers to me as they are taken down by the stenographer.
CIANO	What did you think of what you have read?
ANSALDO	Magnificent!
CIANO	Just that?
ANSALDO	Well done, enthralling! It will not fail to arouse a truly worldwide reaction. The exposition is well grounded, brilliant, sublimely logical.
CIANO	Fine! I recommend that you point out all that in your comments. Rather, write an editorial about it. Note well that the reception I have had from the public has been truly extraordinary. I've never felt so moved in my life.
ANSALDO	I believe it, Excellency. Any other orders?
CIANO	Ansaldo?
ANSALDO	Command me, Excellency!
CIANO	I recommend in particular that you do not omit any of the incisions in the text of the speech.
ANSALDO	To what are you alluding, Excellency?
CIANO	To the applause, to the comments of the applauding crowd. Do I make myself clear?
ANSALDO	Without fail, Excellency!
CIANO	Especially the finale. The final applause! You will see that I have really received a lot. Make it stand out in big type! Don't be stingy with the big type![65]

Geraldine and Leka arrived at Florina, in the north of Greece, on 8 April; later that same day, Zog and many of his leading officials met them there. Although General Metaxas wanted them out of the country as soon as possible, King George II overruled him, insisting that Geraldine was by no means well enough for a further international journey. Once Geraldine's health had improved, the Albanian royals and their entourage departed by train on 2 May for Turkey. But Zog, believing that only British strength would ever be in a position to reinstate him as Albania's ruler, soon insisted that they go to live in England, where in fact they spent most of the Second World War. Julian Amery, future British Conservative cabinet minister and son of another British Conservative cabinet minister (Leo Amery), met Zog in London during 1943. The Englishman formed a very favourable impression, both of the Albanian's gravitas and of his innate astuteness:

> I had been impressed, when first involved in Albanian affairs in 1940, by the respect which the different groups of Albanian exiles seemed to share for Zog. Certainly his record as a ruler showed that he was both forceful and shrewd. He had also behaved with unusual dignity in exile. At a time when other exiled Kings patronised London's restaurants and nightclubs, Zog seldom appeared in public. He lived either in a suite in the Ritz hotel or in a house in the country. He thought it inappropriate to be seen in places of public entertainment, while his country was under enemy occupation. [...]
>
> The more Zog spoke, the more I began to realise that his gentleness of tone concealed a coiled spring of ruthless determination. Over a drink, after we had finished business, Zog told me an anecdote so improbable that it could hardly have been invented. A few days earlier he had been persuaded, much against his will, to go out with Queen Geraldine to one of the big London stores. From a prejudice against running up bills, he had put three hundred pounds in his breast pocket. The lift in the shop had been crowded and, going up to the third floor, he had developed an instinctive aversion to a little man standing just beside him. He had, however, thought no more about him until, putting his hand in his pocket to pay for one of the Queen's purchases, he found that his wallet had gone. He decided to go back to his hotel, but on the way out of the shop again saw the little man who had stood near him in the lift He stopped to watch him more closely when suddenly another man came up and proceeded to pick the little man's pocket. To Zog's astonishment what the pickpocket picked from the little man's pocket was his own wallet. At this point he walked up and took the wallet himself while the two thieves scattered in opposite directions.
>
> I came away convinced that this was a man of Odyssean proportions, brave, without illusions and of many devices. Closer acquaintance in later years would amply confirm this first impression.[66]

Zog's remaining supporters back at home – known collectively as *Lëvizja Legaliteti,* the 'Legality Movement' – struggled on his behalf, first against Italian occupation, later against both German occupation and the partly collaborationist anti-communist party of republicans, known as the *Balli Kombëtar*. The *Legaliteti* first enjoyed and then lost Allied support, being discarded late in the Second World War by Britain and America, at much the same time (and for the same reason) as were those Yugoslav Chetniks whom Marshal Josip Broz Tito outmanoeuvred. After the war, Washington and London belatedly launched Operation Valuable, whereby *Legaliteti* and other anti-communist Albanians (including *Balli Kombëtar* members) would foment counter-revolution against Hoxha's dictatorship. Operation Valuable would have stood a sizeable chance of succeeding if the personnel aware of it had not included Kim Philby. Thanks to Philby, more than 400 participants in Operation Valuable perished.[67] Richard Helms, who in 1966 would become the CIA's director, summed up Philby's handiwork: 'I don't know that the damage he did can ever be actually calculated.'[68]

The rest of Zog's tale proved a desolate anti-climax. Churchill, for all his deference to other royals, considered the Albanians little more than a nuisance. Clement Attlee's government, in November 1945, granted diplomatic recognition to Hoxha. Zog and his family made their way to Egypt, where many members of the Albanian diaspora then lived, and where King Farouk welcomed the royal family as honoured guests. This Cairo idyll abruptly ceased in July 1952 when the Egyptian army's leadership compelled Farouk himself to tread the road to exile. An August 1952 meeting near Skopje between Zog's emissaries and Tito's proved fruitless, even if – a CIA report maintained – it left the former group 'convinced that a new era is dawning in Albanian-Yugoslav relations'.[69]

By this stage Zog had fallen extremely ill with stomach cancer. (He had endured much stomach trouble, perhaps ulcers, since the early 1930s; his 1931 Austrian visit came about through the need to consult Viennese physicians.) After he moved with his family to Cannes in 1955, his physical strength slipped away. He died in Paris's Hôpital Foch on 9 April 1961, sadly aware that he had long since lost the slightest hope of seeing his country again. In 1946 the Communist regime had declared him formally deposed, and had banned him or his relatives from ever again setting foot in Albania.

For more than four decades, most of this time under the deranged totalitarianism of Hoxha (who loved to be called 'Uncle Enver' and who imposed upon school reading-lists, among other Stalinist-Maoist masterpieces, his own thirteen-volume autobiography),[70] the 'land of Albania' which moved Lord Byron to flights of poetic rapture resembled a very good imitation of hell. The *Sigurimi*, Hoxha's terrifying secret police; the deliberately induced food shortages; the public health standards so abysmal that tuberculosis afflicted three-quarters of the populace, while 'only government employees and members of the forces [got] a meat ration';[71] the vengeful show-trials of real or imaginary dissidents; the home-grown slave labour camps: these nightmares in the 'People's Socialist Republic' all made Zog's excesses seem, in retrospect, puny indeed. Future generations owe to Zog some compassionate remembrance, if not as a great man, then at least as a great monosyllable.

Epilogue

The Second World War's conclusion imperilled European monarchism almost as much as the First World War's had done. Italy, Romania, Bulgaria and Yugoslavia, all monarchies in 1945, had become republics by 1948: in Italy's case more or less peacefully via the ballot-box; in the other lands' cases, via the full gruesome panoply of show trials, firing squads, and secret police operatives chosen for their unswerving loyalty to Stalin. (Well after the Berlin Wall's collapse the last Bulgarian monarch, Simeon, achieved from 2001 to 2005 a kind of poetic justice for his dynasty by serving as prime minister of the Bulgarian Republic: his country's language rendered his surname, Saxe-Coburg-Gotha, as Sakskoburggotski.)

Even Belgium's monarchy teetered over the abyss in 1950–51, amid the national agonising over King Léopold III's ambiguous wartime role. A referendum in March 1950 showed that just over half of the Belgian electorate wanted to retain in office the sovereign, who since 1945 had been staying near Geneva; but the outcome indicated clear regional disparities, with most of Flanders voting in Léopold's favour and most of Wallonia voting against him. Taking advantage of the overall majority support, the King (represented in Brussels, during his absence, by his brother Charles as regent) announced his intention to return to Belgium, which in July he did. A general strike almost immediately broke out: in one Walloon township not far from Liège, police shot four demonstrators in the back.[1] (Three died at once. The fourth succumbed to his wounds afterwards.) For most of the next year, an uneasy stalemate held. The monarch's son, Baudouin, became acceptable as a future sovereign to all leading politicians, not least because of his extreme youth and because few outside palace circles knew anything about him. Nonetheless, only when Léopold agreed to abdicate (July 1951), with Baudouin – who had already been given the title of Prince Royal, and who turned 21 the following September – succeeding him, could normal civil society be restored. Helping the return to comparative tranquillity was the general acceptance of kingship as such. Outside local Communists' ranks, almost no one in the country wanted a republic. And even general alarm at the assassination, unsolved to this day, of the Communist Party leader Julien Lahaut in August 1950 had failed to make Belgian republicanism any more widely desired.

But what of the royal houses which, unlike Belgium's, have been discussed at length in this book? How did they fare after Yalta and Potsdam, during what America's Vice-President Henry A. Wallace – an unblushing Sovietophile even by the standards of his master FDR – euphorically dubbed 'the Century of the Common Man'?

No one since the Marquês de Pombal, who ruled from the 1750s to the 1770s, has dominated Portugal as much as did Salazar in his thirty-six-year reign. This reign ended only in 1968 when Salazar, approaching 80, suffered a stroke and had to be removed, on the orders of President Américo Tomás, from the prime ministerial role. (He lived for almost two years more, his brain functioning normally for much of that time.) The Braganças, who had once entertained hopes of preferment at Salazar's hands, remained as distant from the throne in 1968 as they had been in 1932. But they no longer had to exile themselves, because under a 1950 law, the Bragança heir Duarte Nuno – then aged 43 – received permission to dwell in Portugal, which he did until his death in 1976. He never aggressively pressed his regal claim, or aggressively pressed anything else. An American visitor described his manner as 'solitary, gentle, and kind',[2] characterised by the clinical melancholia into which the effects of his wife's death and of severe injuries in a car crash had plunged him.

Duarte Nuno's 31-year-old son, Duarte Pio, inherited the status of monarchical claimant. Courting publicity much more than his father ever did, Duarte Pio has performed the unofficial, yet very visible, function of a roving ambassador for Portugal. This function, for all his determination to transcend party politics, has been by no means a sinecure for him. Unlike numerous much more powerful Western leaders (among whom Henry Kissinger counted as merely the most egregious), Duarte Pio voiced intrepid and implacable opposition to Indonesia's 1975–99 genocide in the former Portuguese territory of East Timor. Once that land had achieved independence, its president José Ramos-Horta showed his gratitude to Duarte Pio by granting him honorary citizenship.

Hermine, stepmother of the Hohenzollerns' Crown Prince Wilhelm, maintained her unrepentant pro-Nazism. She fell into Soviet hands when the Second World War ended, and suffered a fatal heart attack in August 1947 while under house arrest. Her fellow NSDAP apologist, 'Auwi', spent three years interned by American forces at Ludwigsburg (in present-day Baden-Württemberg) and was then released; before the Soviets' warrant for his capture could reach him, he died at a Stuttgart hospital in August 1949.

Better luck attended Wilhelm's eldest surviving son, Louis Ferdinand, whom Konrad Adenauer and subsequent Chancellors allowed to live in West Berlin, quietly and unpretentiously. An affable figure, relishing his long sojourns in the United States, he told one interviewer that 'if only his grandfather, the Kaiser, had gone to America, there would have been no war because he and the Americans would have liked each other so much!'[3] (Wilhelm II's great esteem for individual Americans, whom he tended to prefer to most Europeans – he especially admired Theodore Roosevelt – is well documented.)

The Hamburg tabloid *Quick* asked its readers in a 1968 survey whom they would most want to see as West Germany's next president once the tenure of the incumbent, Heinrich Lübke, had ended. Louis Ferdinand, in spite of or because of never having held a single political office, topped the poll with almost 40 per cent of the vote, easily beating ex-Chancellor Ludwig Erhard.[4] Nothing came of this success, but the Hohenzollerns' head continued to behave with dignity and geniality until his death (September 1994) in now-unified Berlin.

Alfred Hugenberg, so loud for so long in his protestations of monarchist devotion, sold most of his newspaper empire in 1943 to the NSDAP publishing house Franz Eher Nachfolger. The handsome share portfolio that he acquired from the transaction did him no good when the British occupiers froze his assets after the war. Yet at any rate he managed to avoid being put in the defendants' dock at Nuremberg, which is more than can be said for his fellow non-Nazis Hjalmar Schacht and Franz von Papen. In March 1951 he died, aged 85, at Extertal in North Rhine-Westphalia. He had been preceded to the grave five years earlier by Gustav Noske.

Many Bavarians continue to recall the Wittelsbachs with fondness. The 86-year-old Rupprecht passed away in August 1955, and the claim to Bavaria's throne devolved to Rupprecht's son Albrecht, who in 1980 marked with elaborate celebrations the 800th anniversary of the first Wittelsbach sovereign's accession. Albrecht died, a nonagenarian, in July 1996, but his son Franz (an enthusiastic collector of paintings) remains active at a comparable age. A British journalist reported of Franz in 1991:

> he is on cordial terms with Bavaria's rulers and is invited to all sorts of official social functions where he is solemnly addressed as 'Your Royal Highness'. The family have a free box at the opera, where they are seen regularly. Foreign consuls call on them to pay respects. Their parties at Nymphenburg are the highlights of Munich's glittering social season.[5]

Admiral Horthy, defying the Great Depression which put paid to so many governments, stayed on as Regent of the 'Kingdom of Hungary' – for so his nation continued to style itself – until March 1944. Then Hitler, his patience with Horthy's vacillations exhausted, summoned the Regent to Salzburg and demanded that he start pulling his weight when it came to the Axis war effort: in particular, when it came to the killing of as many Jews as possible. (For most of the preceding decade, Jews in Hungary had suffered from legal and social discrimination but had been apt to remain alive and physically unscathed: in which comparative good fortune, they differed from their Polish, Romanian, Yugoslav, and – especially from 1942 – French counterparts.) Soon the National Socialists stripped Horthy of all power, while letting him continue to enjoy ceremonial office. From October he no longer had even that. His son in Nazi captivity would, he was assured, be murdered within twenty-four hours unless he himself resigned, vesting all authority in the Führer's chosen candidate: Ferenc Szálasi, Arrow Cross leader. Horthy obeyed this command, after which the occupiers transferred him to a Bavarian prison. American troops liberated him the following April, by which stage Szálasi's reign of pro-Nazi terror had finished and Hungary had increasingly come under communist control.

Horthy spent his last years, like the Habsburgs whom he had ill-used, under Portuguese protection. He made his home in Estoril, near Lisbon, which had the world's highest per square metre density of banished sovereigns, including Romania's Carol II and Italy's Umberto II. Fleetingly, in October-November 1956, it appeared that the Hungarians might be able to shake off Soviet oppression; the appearance proved a mirage. In February of the following year Horthy, by then 88, breathed his last. When he knew himself to be dying, he begged Otto to visit him, and asked pardon for his misdeeds against the imperial house.[6]

Not only was Otto still in the pink of health at that time, but so was his mother, Zita. That indomitable heroine reached the age of 96, surviving until March 1989, her stamina intact until a year before the end. Had Zita endured for another nine months, she would have witnessed what few had dared to imagine they would ever see: the end of the Warsaw Pact, that 'prison-house of nations' incomparably more tyrannical than anything which Lajos Kossuth in 1849 had bemoaned.

Zita bequeathed her longevity gene to Otto, who reached his ninety-ninth year, having written several books (including an admirable life of his distant ancestor, Emperor Charles V) and having served for two decades as a revered member of the European

Parliament. From 1966 the Austrian authorities granted him permission to travel to his homeland. October 2004 found him in Rome, for the beatification of his father, whom the Catholic Church now honours as 'Blessed Karl of Austria'. At Otto's funeral, in July 2011, the same time-honoured ritual occurred outside Vienna's Capuchin crypt which had marked earlier Habsburgs' final journeys. As these lines are being written, it is pleasant to be able to record that during his nineties Otto showed himself under no modish illusions concerning Vladimir Putin's power-lust. He publicly referred in 2005 to history's most over-achieving KGB boss as 'an ice-cold technocrat' (in German, '*eiskälter Tecknokrat*').[7]

L'Action Française had already ceased publication by the time de Gaulle first became French ruler, but Maurice Pujo – having served a surprisingly brief prison sentence of two years – revived it in 1947 under the bland title *Aspects de la France*, remaining in charge of it until his own death in 1955. The journal still exists, having reverted to its original name. Its parent organisation remains active too. In May 2023 Paris's Administrative Court overturned a ban, imposed by Interior Minister Gérald Darmanin, on AF conferences and protest marches. Darmanin turned out to have been in pre-ministerial days a contributor to another Maurrassian magazine, called *Politique*: which embarrassing revelation inspired the protestors to coin the slogan 'Darmanin, come back! AF needs you!'[8]

Henri, the Comte de Paris, never realised his own monarchist hopes, although from 1950 he lived in France with governmental permission. Many of his fellow French aristocrats continued to spurn him for his lineage: one lady snarled, 'Descendant of Philippe Égalité and Louis-Philippe that he is, he has never stopped courting the socialists.'[9] For years de Gaulle strung Henri along with assurances of his own monarchism, much as he contemporaneously strung along erstwhile supporters Georges Bidault, Raoul Salan, and Jacques Soustelle with assurances of his own commitment to *Algérie Française*. In 1962 he 'told Henri in strict confidence that he had arranged the direct presidential election so that the head of the royal house might succeed him as president of the Republic'.[10] Such ostensibly 'strict confidence' did not preclude dropping hints on the subject to Georges Pompidou, then Prime Minister, who informed one of his own friends: 'I know that the general has made up his mind in favour of the Count of Paris.'[11] True to form, de Gaulle underwent a change of heart, and insisted on running for presidential re-election in 1965. (He won the final electoral round, but only after his unexpected humiliation in the first round, where the combined support for five rival candidates – including François Mitterrand and the independent Jean Lecanuet – amounted to approximately 55 per cent of the votes cast.) Henri's wife, Isabelle of Orléans-Bragança, complained: 'Under de Gaulle, Henri came two fingers close to becoming king. But by 1968 it was all over, finished.'[12]

Not long before Mitterrand's 1981 election as president, a Socialist representative urged, in the august pages of *Le Monde,* that the Comte de Paris be made the Socialist Party's secretary-general.[13] Seven years later the Comte himself recommended that his followers vote to give Mitterrand a second term. By this stage his marriage to Isabelle – which had produced an awe-inspiring total of eleven children – had largely ended. From 1986 husband and wife lived apart, though as Catholics they rejected divorce. Henri died in June 1999, his widow four years later.

Another royal widow, Ena, had survived Alfonso XIII by almost three decades. After Alfonso's demise she became increasingly unwelcome in Italy (Mussolini found unpardonable her sympathies with Britain) and moved to Switzerland. There she had the bitter-sweet experience of learning that General Franco had every intention of restoring the Bourbons to Spain – which the Duke of Alba among others had implored him to do – but that the Infante Juan would be henceforth ineligible for the succession. Franco, fearing undue liberalism on Juan's part, decided to skip a generation and to make Juan's own son, Juan Carlos, the heir. This he formally did (after years of exchanging with Juan public rebukes so acidulous that no reconciliation between the two men could be contemplated) in July 1969, three months after Ena's death in Lausanne.

Juan Carlos, Franco assumed, would be more pliable than his outspoken father had been. There might even have been an element of political blackmail in the General's calculations, given how vulnerable Juan Carlos had become after a family tragedy – as if Ena had not already experienced her full meed of domestic grief – in March 1956. That month, Juan Carlos's 14-year-old brother Alfonso perished in an Estoril shooting accident. Witnesses agreed that Juan Carlos, then aged 17, had been present when the shooting took place, and that he failed to realise that the pistol was loaded; but they gave different testimonies as to whether he had fired the pistol in a spirit of horseplay or had had his arm bumped by an abruptly opened door. Clearly the boys' father suspected worse things than official sources acknowledged: Juan grabbed Juan Carlos by the scruff of the neck and shouted 'Swear to me that you didn't do it on purpose! [*¡Júrame que no lo has hecho a propósito!*]'[14] before consigning him to a military academy. In 2024 all except one of those most closely involved with the matter are dead, and it is improbable that we shall learn all the pertinent facts, unless Juan Carlos himself (who abdicated in 2014) chooses to reveal them.

The Infante Juan died at Pamplona in April 1993, by which date almost all traces of Franco's rule had faded from Spain. During November 1975 Franco, long afflicted with Parkinson's disease, fell into a coma from which he never emerged. His doctors, with a fearful symmetry, are said to have deliberately kept him alive until 20 November, the very day on which José Antonio Primo de Rivera had been shot thirty-nine years beforehand. Six months prior to Franco's death, his bitter rival Manuel Fal Conde left the scene.

Carlism continued to demonstrate its fissiparous nature well after Franco had triumphed. Those Carlists unable to forgive Alfonso Carlos for his failure to rain down constant curses upon Alfonso XIII looked, not to Prince Javier, but to a less prominent claimant: Carlos Pio, son of Habsburg Archduke Leopold Salvator. Young (27 years old when Alfonso Carlos had his fatal accident), and exceptionally handsome, Carlos Pio held off pressing his own claim until the Spanish Civil War had been over for four years. But press it he then did, with vigour if not with notable effectiveness, calling himself Carlos VIII. Prince Javier opposed Carlos Pio's activities (which attracted the name *Carloctavismo,* derived from the claimant's preferred regnal title); but others, including some of Franco's high officials, looked kindly upon them until Carlos Pio's own sudden death in 1953.

To complicate matters still more, and to underline certain Carlist branches' above-cited affinity with Monty Python's mutually antagonistic Judean warriors, there also developed a Carlist subdivision that hewed very much to the political left. Carlos Hugo, Javier's son, attracted to his cause various followers who hoped to implement in Spain the political example of Marshal Tito. Two such followers were, at a Navarre meeting in May 1976, assassinated by gunmen. In 2010 Carlos Hugo died; as of this writing (August 2023), his younger brother Sixto Enrique remains the legitimate Spanish king in the eyes of a Carlist hard-core, upon which note, the mere bewildered Anglophone historian may be allowed to bring down the Carlist drama's curtain until further notice.

When George II died in 1947, his brother Paul (who had been, it will be remembered, considered as a possible Greek sovereign back in 1920) succeeded him as monarch. Considerable ill-health belied his robust appearance, and he spent much of his reign after 1958 hospitalised. Weakened in 1963 by an operation for appendicitis, he was diagnosed the following year with stomach cancer, which claimed his life in April 1964.

Paul's own son, Constantine II, enjoyed only three-and-a-half years in the royal palace before his botched attempt in December 1967 at regaining his kingly rights, and at overthrowing Greece's newly established rule under 'the colonels', led to his banishment. Six years later the military dictatorship formally proclaimed Greece a republic, and at a referendum in 1974 (shortly after the colonels had stepped down) almost two-thirds of voters declared themselves in favour of Greece remaining republican. Constantine, permitted from 2013 to live once more in Greece, died at an Athens private clinic in January 2023, Covid-19 and cerebrovascular disorders having contributed to his death.

One of the last living links with inter-war European politics snapped in October 2002: Queen Geraldine of Albania expired, two months after her eighty-seventh birthday. She had spent much of her middle and old age in Rhodesia, then in South Africa; but shortly before her decease, the government of Prime Minister Ilir Meta had allowed her to return, for hospital treatment, to the Albanian capital which she had not seen since 1939. Until the end, she took pride in her royal status and announced that her son Leka remained Albania's true king.

Leka himself led the type of existence which, if it had not happened in real life, a hyperventilating columnist for some such bellicose periodical as *Soldier of Fortune* or *Guns & Ammo* would have needed to invent. He is alleged to have been on the CIA's payroll during the Vietnam War,[15] a theory which gains colour from his invariable failure to blend quietly into the landscape.[16] On the invitation of Franco, Leka resided near Madrid for fifteen years, only to alarm the Caudillo by the sheer size of his private arsenal. Rather than give up his cherished weaponry, he left Spain for good, chartering a jet with his spouse and sixteen adherents. 'He had hand grenades hooked on his belt, and his wife Susan toted a submachine gun.'[17]

A 1979 interviewer said of the claimant: 'Leka speaks in the tough, no-nonsense style of military spokesmen. His English is fluent and idiomatic, his accent and choice of words are those of a GI.'[18] The same interviewer, alluding to the Albanian habit of calling the country's male rulers 'Sons of the Eagle', wished Leka well, writing: 'How I would love [...] to be able to use the line: "The Eagle has landed".'[19] No such glorious aquiline descent to terra firma took place, even after Enver Hoxha astonished the world in 1978 by ending Albania's alliance with mainland China, once Deng Xiao-Ping had discarded strict Maoism.

In 1997, with Hoxha long dead and with his despotism equally belonging to an un-mourned past, the authorities allowed a referendum to occur on the issue of whether Albania should restore the crown or stick with republicanism. Leka always maintained, with considerable plausibility, that the final vote (officially reported as just under 67 per cent in favour of keeping the republic) had been rigged and that the monarchists really won. Former prime minister and president Sali Berisha, speaking at fourteen years' distance from the relevant events, admitted that much of the 1997 vote-count had been dishonest.

Following the referendum, Leka left Albania; but he returned in 2002 and attended his mother's funeral. On his arrival at Tirana he lived up to his reputation by bringing in his luggage enough grenades, hunting rifles and automatic rifles to fill eleven cases. These weapons the police first confiscated and, six years afterwards, handed back to their owner, on the quintessentially Albanian grounds that they belonged to the nation's cultural heritage. Leka died in November 2011 from, anticlimactically, heart disease.

Throughout the foregoing pages, I have forsworn prophecy, at which historians are no more talented than anyone else. That they might be *less* talented than anyone else is suggested by a passage from Richard J. Evans, the expert on Teutonic affairs. In language evocative less of scholarship than of a singularly boorish pubescent's unshackled id, Evans declared: 'Reunification [of West and East Germany] is simply not a realistic possibility, and to talk about it or to advance historical arguments in its favour is to indulge in political fantasising.'[20] That sentence appeared in December 1987. Three years afterwards, German reunification had disobligingly taken place, notwithstanding Evans' edict.

If I have forsworn the prophet's role, I have also forsworn the sycophant's. Wherever individual monarchs and monarchists damaged their own cause, I have said so. 'Nothing extenuate, nor set down aught in malice' (Othello again) has been my guiding authorial motive. While I have not concealed my respect for the monarchical principle, as a principle, I have remained aware that a historian and a hagiographer are – in the phraseology of King Charles I – two clean different things.

Seeking to draw general inferences from those monarchical campaigns which the present volume chronicles, I am forced back upon the sad realisation that 'Nice guys finish last.' Time after time my narrative confirms this bitter American aphorism. Alfonso XIII fleeing Spain in a baseless panic and in the wholly erroneous belief that republicans had won municipal elections; Emperor Karl twice trying and twice failing to effect Horthy's resignation, purely because he lacked every scintilla of Horthy's own ruthlessness; Manuel II not only neglecting to support, but openly condemning, the 1919 movement by his champions at home to bring the Braganças back; Crown Prince Wilhelm, afforded a near-perfect chance to take charge of Germany after President Ebert had died, but wholly missing this chance. These royals (like General Primo de Rivera) appear never to have comprehended Machiavelli's dictum that it is better to be feared than loved, if you cannot be both. They failed, also, to appreciate the truth given sagacious expression by Orwell: that those who virtuously 'abjure' violence can do so only because others are committing, and have committed, violence on their behalf. Alfonso's cousin, as we have seen, predicted the bloodbath which a departure by the King would precipitate.[21]

Also worth noting is the inverse correlation between inter-war monarchist movements' political success and the intellectual support on which they could draw. Not all the prodigious didactic output of a Maurras could bring the House of Orléans one millimetre closer to renewed kingship; nor could all the Carlists' philosophical firepower and advocacy of traditional regionalism move Franco (or even Primo de Rivera junior) to regard them as anything more than the hired help. In obvious contrast, inter-war monarchism achieved its two big European victories in Greece and Albania: precisely the nations least hospitable to political theorising.

Whither monarchy itself, in the countries which this book has sought to explore, and elsewhere? Whither, if it comes to that, republics perpetuated by universal adult suffrage? After all, current technological threats to the whole concept of governmental legitimacy differ in kind from anything which our ancestors knew.

On 10 January 2020, Britain's *Financial Times* published a candid indication that Artificial Intelligence and, above all, the ability of international troll-farms to manipulate elections' outcomes render the very basis of democracy obsolete. A passage from the newspaper's account of Cambridge Analytica's impact on the 2016 US presidential election (and on other contests) runs:

> Cambridge Analytica not only did this for Trump, but worked in more than 60 countries around the world, according to a trove of internal documents posted online by Brittany Kaiser, another former Cambridge Analytica employee turned whistle-blower. And as the 2019 documentary *The Great Hack* shows, these campaigns featured a host of dirty tricks: deliberate dissemination of misinformation; incitement to extremism; voter suppression tactics; the attempted blackmail of politicians. 'It may never be possible to have fair and free elections again,' says Karim Amer, co-director of *The Great Hack*.[22]

To admit that 'fair and free elections' do not exist outside Western mores is one thing. It is quite another thing to admit that online fraud has invalidated democratic procedures within Western mores as well, and has done so with such blatancy as to make any effort at defending these procedures – to quote Bismarck's famous gibe about Balkan conflicts – not worth the bones of a single Pomeranian grenadier.

But no other conclusion than this can be deduced from the *Financial Times* report concerned. Or from an exposé in 2022 (by the Tel-Aviv-based *Haaretz*) of the 'Team Jorge' enterprise. Far less celebrated than probable foreign interference in American politics, Team Jorge has been at least as effective as any Putin or Xi Jinping in guaranteeing desired electoral results abroad. It involves Israeli hackers engaging in the most systematic possible cyberspatial sabotage, through viruses, bots and social media campaigns of more than usual mendacity. Among thirty-three recent national elections around the world (primarily, to date, in Africa), Team Jorge determined the victors of twenty-seven.[23]

Amid the incandescent Hobbesianism of the USA's 2016 poll, Nikolai Tolstoy explained the merits of monarchical government in *The New York Times*. Having quoted Edmund Burke on the subject, Count Tolstoy proceeded:

> As Dr Johnson advised Boswell: 'Now, Sir, that respect for authority is much more easily granted to a man whose father had it, than to an upstart, and so society is more easily supported.' […] Edward Gibbon weighed the rival systems and came down with characteristic acerbity in favour of a hereditary sovereign. 'We may easily devise imaginary forms of government, in which the sceptre shall be constantly bestowed

on the most worthy, by the free and incorrupt suffrage of the whole community,' he wrote, but 'experience overturns these airy fabrics.'[24]

Yet almost three-quarters of a century before Count Tolstoy's article, C.S. Lewis – least ideologically warped of men – had already tried to warn the world. In a piercing and prophetic 1943 essay for *The Spectator*, he summarised monarchism's persistent appeal thus:

A man's reaction to Monarchy is a kind of test. Monarchy can easily be 'debunked'; but watch the faces, mark well the accents, of the debunkers. Those are the men whose tap-root in Eden has been cut: whom no rumour of the polyphony, the dance, can reach – men to whom pebbles laid in a row are more beautiful than an arch. Yet even if they desire mere equality they cannot reach it. Where men are forbidden to honour a king, they honour millionaires, athletes, or film stars instead; even famous prostitutes or gangsters. For spiritual nature, like bodily nature, will be served; deny it food and it will gobble poison.[25]

The late Clive James voiced similar sentiments to Lewis's, abandoning prose for heroic couplets in iambic pentameter. These sentiments marked a 1981 tribute to the future Charles III whose accession and coronation James did not live to see:

I am a Monarchist through lack of trust
In human rationality, which must
Be kept in bounds like any other force
Or else, if it's allowed to run its course,
It can and will work mischief in a fashion
Beyond the maddest daydreams of blind passion.
The two most murderous of modern nations
Had this in common – they were innovations.
Men thought them up. Time's heritage was mocked
And all the worst hobgoblins were unlocked,
Since only the collective evolution
Of custom, language, law, and institution
Can tame that impulse in the human soul
Whose awful vigour helps to make it whole. [...]
          you've still
Some room to implement your Royal will –
Your attitude will have its influence
And even when you can't much shape events
You can be sure that they'd be otherwise
Without your being there to exercise
Your foremost function, which is to deny
Anyone else the chance to deify
Himself and rule unchecked and say 'The State
Is Me' and so go mad through growing great.[26]

Endnotes

Prologue

1. Orwell compared writing in the first person to 'dosing yourself with some stimulating but very deleterious and very habit-forming drug.' George Orwell, 'Extracts from a Manuscript Note-Book', *The Collected Essays, Journalism and Letters*, ed. Sonia Orwell and Ian Angus (London: Penguin Books, 1970), Vol. 4, 572–579, at 574.
2. Edmond Taylor, *The Fall of the Dynasties* (London: Weidenfeld & Nicolson, 1963), 293–294.
3. Barbara W. Tuchman, *Practising History* (New York City: Ballantyne Books, 1982), 34.
4. A.J.P. Taylor, *The Origins of the Second World War* (London: Athenaeum, 1961), 140.
5. Quoted (without the precise source being identified) in Tuchman, 22.

Chapter I

1. Hannah Arendt, *Crises of the Republic: Lying in Politics; Civil Disobedience; On Violence; Thoughts on Politics and Revolution* (New York City: Harcourt Brace Jovanovich, 1972), 206.
2. Portuguese law, unlike English law, possessed no proviso for automatic monarchical inheritance, even via legal fiction. Accordingly the frequent statement (to be found in, for instance, Russell E. Benton, *The Downfall of a King: Dom Manuel II of Portugal* [Washington DC: University Press of America, 1977], 50) that Luís Felipe himself reigned as Portugal's king, during the interval between Carlos's death and his own, is inaccurate.
3. Anon., 'King of Portugal and His Heir Assassinated,' *The New York Times*, 2 February 1908, 1.
4. Sixtieth Congress, First Session, 'Transmission of Senate Resolution Deploring Assassination of King and Crown Prince of Portugal,' Document No. 317 (Washington DC: US Senate), 24 February 1908.
5. Sir Sidney Lee, *King Edward VII: A Biography*, Vol. 2 (London: Macmillan, 1927), 575.
6. Lee, 575.
7. V.I. Lenin, 'The Happening to the King of Portugal,' *Proletary*, 19 February 1908, reprinted in V.I. Lenin (tr. B. Isaacs), *Collected Works*, Vol. 13 (Moscow: Progress Publishers, 1972), 470–474.
8. Sir Charles Petrie, *King Alfonso XIII and His Age* (London: Chapman & Hall, 1963), 88–92; Enrique Sanabria, *Republicanism and Anticlerical Nationalism in Spain* (London: Palgrave Macmillan, 2009), 101–122. Petrie, demonstrating frankness unthinkable in a later and more fastidious era, referred to the anarchist, Mateo Morral – after whom, shortly before the Civil War, Spanish Republican cabinet ministers would rename the Madrid street where the crime took place – as 'a syphilitic pervert' (91).

9. Ernest Alfred Vizetelly, *The Anarchists: Their Faith and Their Record* (London: John Lane, 1911), 214.
10. Sir Arthur Henry Hardinge, *A Diplomatist in Europe* (London: Jonathan Cape, 1927), 226.
11. Anon., 'The Late King of Portugal as Artist: A Portrait Study of the Painter King, the Murdered Carlos of Portugal,' *Illustrated London News* 132:3590 (8 February 1908), 197; Tricia Cusack (ed.), *Art and Identity at the Water's Edge* (Farnham, Surrey: Ashgate Publishing, 2012), 91.
12. Roderick J. Barman, *Citizen Emperor: Pedro II and the Making of Brazil* (Stanford, California: Stanford University Press, 1999), 364–397.
13. James Longo, *Isabel Orléans-Bragança: The Brazilian Princess Who Freed the Slaves* (Jefferson, North Carolina: McFarland & Company, 2008).
14. Charles E. Nowell, *The Rose-Coloured Map: Portugal's Attempt to Build an African Empire from the Atlantic to the Indian Ocean* (Lisbon: Junta de Investigações Científicas do Ultramar, 1982).
15. J. M. do Espirito Santo de Almeida Correia de Sá, Marquês do Lavradio, *Portugal em África Depois de 1851: Subsídios para a História* (Lisbon: Divisão de Publicações e Biblioteca, Agência Geral das Colónias, 1936), 169–170; Maria Teresa Pinto Coelho, '"Pérfida Albion" and "Little Portugal": The Role of the Press in British and Portuguese National Perceptions of the 1890 Ultimatum,' *Portuguese Studies* 6 (1990), 173–190.
16. Sir George Young, *Portugal Old and Young: A Historical Study* (Oxford: Oxford University Press, 1917), 260.
17. F.C.C. Egerton, *Salazar: Rebuilder of Portugal* (London: Hodder & Stoughton, 1943), 91–92.
18. Douglas L. Wheeler, *Republican Portugal: A Political History 1910–1926* (Madison: University of Wisconsin Press, 1978), 32.
19. H. V. Livermore, *A New History of Portugal* (Cambridge: Cambridge University Press, 1976), 319.
20. Charles E. Nowell, *A History of Portugal* (Princeton: Van Nostrand, 1958), 210.
21. Wheeler, 35.
22. Walter C. Opello, *Portugal: From Monarchy to Pluralist Democracy* (Boulder, Colorado: Westview Press, 1991), 53. At this stage and long afterwards, Portuguese suffrage remained a masculine affair. No women in Portugal could vote till 1931. Even then, substantial property ownership qualifications limited the number of female (as well as the number of male) voters.
23. Vicente de Bragança Cunha, *Eight Centuries of Portuguese Monarchy* (New York City: John Pott, 1911), 214.
24. Stanley G. Payne, *A History of Spain and Portugal,* Vol. 2 (Madison: University of Wisconsin Press, 1973), 522.
25. Livermore, 268–279; Neill Macaulay, *Dom Pedro: The Struggle for Liberty in Brazil and Portugal, 1798–1834* (Durham, North Carolina: Duke University Press, 1986), 254–288.
26. Sir Charles Petrie, *Monarchy in the Twentieth Century* (London: Andrew Dakers, 1952), 214–215.
27. Jacinto Baptista, *O Cinco de Outubro* (Lisbon: Arcádia, 1965), 183.
28. Egerton, 94.
29. Wheeler, 26–27.
30. Bragança Cunha, *Eight Centuries*, 214–215.
31. Afonso Costa, *Correspondência política de Afonso Costa, 1896–1910* (Lisbon: Estampa, 1982), 253.

32. Abilio Manuel Guerra Junqueiro, *Horas de Combate* (Oporto: Livraria Chardron, 1924), 39–40. In relation to Carlos's corpulence, a British eyewitness called the Portuguese monarch 'the very largest sovereign that I ever saw – six feet and twenty stone.' During the 1906 Lisbon visit of Edward VII, himself inclined to bulk, Carlos (according to this same eyewitness) 'looked double the size of the English king.' Sir Charles Oman, *Things I Have Seen* (London: Methuen, 1933), 170.
33. Payne, Spain and Portugal, 554.
34. Vicente de Bragança Cunha, *Revolutionary Portugal 1910–1936* (London: James Clarke, 1937), 76; Nowell, *History,* 211.
35. Bragança Cunha, *Eight Centuries*, 225–227.
36. Jean Pailler, Charles Ier, roi de Portugal: Destin maudit d'un roi sacrifié (Biarritz: Atlantica, 2000), 118.
37. A. H. de Oliveira Marques, *History of Portugal, Vol. II: From Empire to Corporate State* (New York City: Columbia University Press, 1972), 140: 'by 1911, Portugal's total rate of illiteracy was 75.1 per cent.' Gabriel Tortella Casares (tr. V.J. Herr), *The Development of Modern Spain: An Economic History of the Nineteenth and Twentieth Centuries* (Cambridge, Massachusetts: Harvard University Press, 2000), 16: 'As late as 1911 scarcely one Portuguese in four knew how to read and write.' Nevertheless, newspaper audiences were bigger than literacy figures would suggest, to judge from a statement (unsourced) by Oliveira Marques, 145: 'In small towns and villages, the paper was often read aloud by some "intellectual," an amorphous mass of people gathering around to listen and to comment.'
38. Benton, 38.
39. Lucien Corpechot, *Memories of Queen Amélie of Portugal* (London: Eveleigh Nash, 1915), 203.
40. Corpechot, 203.
41. Augustus G. Stapleton, *George Canning and His Times* (London: J.W. Parker and Son, 1859), 25.
42. J. B. Trend, *Portugal* (London: Ernest Benn., 1957), 185.
43. Corpechot, 201.
44. Nowell, *History,* 212.
45. Manuel's first public statement after his accession included the words 'It pleases me to retain in office the present ministers.' Benton, 50.
46. Rodrigues Cavalheiro (ed.), *D. Manuel II e João Franco: Correspondência Inédita* (Lisbon: Biblioteca do Pensamento Politico, 1970).
47. *Cahiers Charles Maurras*, Issues 41–52 (1972), 25.
48. Caetano Beirão (tr. Frank R. Holliday), *A Short History of Portugal* (Lisbon: Edições Panorama, 1960), 132.
49. Pailler, 126.
50. Francis McCullagh, 'Portugal: The Republican Nightmare,' *The Nineteenth Century and After* (January 1914), 148–170, at 150.
51. Bragança Cunha, *Eight Centuries*, 240.
52. Benton, 73.
53. Dieter Nohlen and Philip Stoever, *Elections in Europe: A Data Handbook* (Baden-Baden: Nomos Publishers, 2010), 1571.
54. Benton, 75.
55. Stéphane Bern, *Eu, Amélia, Última Rainha de Portugal* (Oporto: Livraria Civilização Editora, 1999). 172.
56. Pailler, 12.

57. Barman, 255–256.
58. Hardinge, 231.
59. Bragança Cunha, *Eight Centuries,* 253.
60. Bragança Cunha, *Eight Centuries,* 253.
61. Wheeler, 45.
62. Wheeler, 49.
63. Benton, 104.
64. Jacques Rougerie, *La Commune de 1871* (Paris: Presses Universitaires de France, 2014), 118; Robert Tombs, 'Victimes et bourreaux de la Semaine Sanglante,' *1848: Révolutions et mutations du XIX siècle,* 10 (1994), 81–96. This figure of 10,000 represents a downward revision from older sources, which give a total of 20,000–25,000 dead.
65. Clive James, 'A Class Apart?,' *Times Literary Supplement* 4417 (27 November – 3 December 1987), 1327–1329, at 1327.
66. Wheeler, 32.
67. Wheeler, 62.
68. L.C.M. Simas, 'Teófilo Braga – O Grande Esquecido,' 2007, *Jardins de Epicuro,* http://www.ulisses.us/lucia-9-teofilo.htm (accessed 19 April 2023).
69. Oman, 214.
70. Susana Adelina Sinfrónio Gomes Sousa Carvalho, *Nationalism and Régime Overthrow in Early Twentieth-Century Portugal,* PhD diss., London School of Economics, 2012, esp. 188.
71. Gomes Sousa Carvalho, 189; Vasco Pulido Valente, *O Poder e o Povo: A Revolução de 1910* (Lisbon: Moraes Editores, 1982), 169.
72. António Costa Pinto, 'Muitas Crises, Poucos Compromissos: A Queda da Primeira Republica,' *Penélope* 19–20, 1998, 43–70, at 52; Gomes Sousa Carvalho, 187.
73. Though Braga would briefly occupy the presidential palace (Belém, originally built in the early eighteenth century at the behest of King João V) once again, from May to October 1915, this was no more than a coda to his long career. On 28 January 1924, he died, poor and largely forgotten.
74. Wheeler, 63.
75. Wheeler, 63.
76. Technically Henry S. Boutell, who had held a Chicago congressional constituency in the Republican interest, had been America's representative in Lisbon since 2 March 1911. But he at no stage presented his credentials to the Portuguese rulers, and (according to his entry in the *Biographical Dictionary of the United States Congress*) by May he had been sent to Switzerland instead.
77. Wheeler, 63–64.
78. Camillo Torrend, SJ, 'The Anti-Clerical Policy in Portugal and Its Results,' *Dublin Review* (January-April 1912), 128–151, at 148.
79. Oman, 165.
80. As early as 1935 future Spanish Prime Minister Francisco Largo Caballero vowed: 'A union of Iberian Soviet republics – that is our aim. The Iberian peninsula will again be one country. Portugal will come in, peaceably we hope, but by force if necessary': Edward H. Knoblaugh, *Correspondent in Spain* (London: Sheed & Ward, 1937), 16–17.
81. Twelve years earlier, Franco had put the Spanish armed forces on alert when it seemed – both to him and to the US State Department – that a barracks revolt would soon remove the septuagenarian Salazar from Portugal's prime ministry: Tom Gallagher, *Portugal: A Twentieth-Century Interpretation* (Manchester: Manchester University Press, 1983), 150. '[W]ithin six hours of the pre-dawn attack, Spanish army tanks at Mérida,

thirty-five miles inside Spain, were reported rumbling ominously toward the frontier city of Badajoz.' Benjamin Welles, 'Salazar in Trouble,' *The Atlantic Monthly* 210:2 (August 1962), 57–62, at 58.

82. Concerning Alfonso's strange childhood destiny, the temptation to quote one of the most famous among Churchill's purple passages (1931) should be sternly resisted, and therefore will not be resisted at all: 'Alfonso XIII was a posthumous child. His cradle was a throne. For a while during his mother's regency philatelists delighted in Spanish stamps which bore the image of a baby. Later came the cherubic lineaments of a child, later still the profile of a youth, and finally the head of a man.' Sir Winston Churchill, *Great Contemporaries* (London: Mandarin Paperbacks, 1990), 131–132.

83. Alexander Woollcott, *While Rome Burns* (London: Arthur Barker Ltd., 1931), 2–3.

84. Wheeler, 45, 280.

85. Oman, 169.

86. Wheeler, 281.

87. Manuel de Oliveira Gomes da Costa, *Memórias* (Lisbon: Livraria Clássica, 1930), 180.

88. Oman, 171.

89. Oman, 177.

90. Gonçalo Pereira Pimenta de Castro, *As minhas memórias, na metrópole e nas colónias,* Vol. 3 (Oporto: Livraria Progredior, 1950), 336. Colonel Pimenta de Castro spent some of the Republic's early years as governor of Portuguese Timor, and, having allied himself with Salazar, wrote in 1944 a history of that territory.

91. Francis McCullagh, 'Some Causes of the Portuguese Revolution,' *The Nineteenth Century and After*, 68 (November 1910), 931–944, at 944 and 943.

92. Wheeler, 81.

93. Bragança Cunha, *Revolutionary Portugal*, 257.

94. Francis McCullagh, 'Portugal: The Republican Nightmare,' *Nineteenth Century and After,* 75, January 1914, 148–170, at 154–55.

95. Hipolito de la Torre Gomez, *El imperio del Rey: Alfonso XIII, Portugal y los ingleses (1907–1916)* (Mérida, Spain: Editora Regional de Extremadura, 2002).

96. Artur Ferreira Coimbra, *Paiva Couceiro e a contra-revolução monárquica 1910–1919* (MA diss., University of Minho, Portugal, 2000), 102–103.

97. Sir Charles Petrie, *Alfonso XIII*, 237.

98. Robert Sencourt, *King Alfonso: A Biography* (London: Faber & Faber, 1942), 248.

99. Randolph Churchill, *Winston Spencer Churchill 1901–1914*, Vol. 2 (Boston: Houghton Mifflin, 1967), 34.

100. Hardinge, 243.

101. Nowell, *History*, 223–224.

102. Coimbra, 109.

103. Coimbra, 110; Carlos Malheiro Dias, *O Estado Actual da Causa Monarchica* (Lisbon: José Bastos, 1913), 33.

104. Sir Osbert Sitwell, *Great Morning* (London: Macmillan, 1948), 221.

105. Nowell, *History*, 226.

106. Livermore, 326.

107. Wheeler, 141.

108. Wheeler, 154.

109. For contemporary American coverage of the uprising's outbreak, see Anon., 'Proclaimed King, Manuel Resents It: Protests to Portuguese Government Against Revolt Started in His Behalf,' *The New York Times* (21 January 1919), 9.

110. Coimbra, 128– 129.
111. Coimbra, 130.
112. Wheeler, 197.
113. Anon., 'Proclaimed King,' 9.
114. Coimbra, 130.
115. Wheeler, 196.
116. Coimbra, 160.
117. McCullagh, 'Republican Nightmare,' 166.
118. Anon., 'Ex-King Manuel, Who Lost Throne for Love, Dies: Former Ruler of Portugal Choked to Death,' *Chicago Tribune* (3 July 1932), 9.
119. Franco Nogueira, *Salazar: estudo biográfico,* Vol. 4 (Coimbra: Atlántida Editora, 1980), 233.
120. Egerton, 323.
121. Egerton, 323–324.
122. António Ferro, *Salazar: Portugal and Her Leader,* tr. H. de Barros Gomes and John Gibbons (London: Faber & Faber, 1939), 129–130.
123. As late as 1944 Portugal's monarchists continued to hold their own in journalistic terms. '*A Vóz* is well known as a Catholic newspaper, but it is also very strongly and definitely a monarchist paper. As a daily paper it flourishes while supporting quite openly the monarchist cause.' David Shillan, 'Portugal Today,' *International Affairs* 20:2 (April 1944), 215–224, at 219.
124. Bernardo Putscher Pereira, *A Diplomacia de Salazar, 1932–1949* (Lisbon: Don Quixote, 2012), 59–60. The author is indebted to Jean Page for this translation.
125. McCullagh, 'Causes,' 942.

Chapter II

1. John Lukacs, *The Hitler of History* (New York City: Knopf, 1997), 50, 104.
2. Michael Balfour, *The Kaiser and His Times* (London: Cresset Press, 1964), 405.
3. Tyler Whittle, *The Last Kaiser: A Biography of William II, German Emperor and King of Prussia* (London: Heinemann, 1977), 299.
4. E. Taylor, *Dynasties,* 310.
5. Wilhelm II (tr. Thomas R. Ybarra), *The Kaiser's Memoirs* (New York City: Harper & Brothers, 1922), 290.
6. Balfour, 358–359.
7. Jonathan Boff, *Haig's Enemy: Crown Prince Rupprecht and Germany's War on the Western Front* (Oxford: Oxford University Press, 2018), 266; a slightly different wording in Balfour, 357.
8. John Terraine, 'The War Must Be Ended' (Part I), *History Today* 28:11 (November 1978), 703–711, at 709.
9. Balfour, 402–403.
10. E. Taylor, 311.
11. John Terraine, 'The War Must Be Ended' (Part II), *History Today* 28:12 (December 1978), 783–792, at 787.
12. Sir John Wheeler-Bennett, *Hindenburg: The Wooden Titan* (London: Macmillan, 1967), 197; Terraine, Part II, 789–90.
13. Whittle, 305.
14. Ben Hecht, *A Child of the Century* (New York City: Simon & Schuster, 1954), 283.

15. F.L. Carsten, *The Reichswehr and Politics, 1918 to 1933* (Oxford: Clarendon Press, 1966), 8; Jack Sweetman, *The Unforgotten Crowns: The German Monarchist Movements, 1918–1945*, PhD diss., Emory University (Atlanta), 1973, 44.

16. Richard M. Watt, *The Kings Depart: The Tragedy of Germany, Versailles and the German Revolution* (London: Weidenfeld & Nicolson, 1968), 111.

17. Sweetman, 125.

18. Anon., 'Milestones,' *Time* 19:9 (29 February 1932), 48.

19. Liam Foley, Abdication of the German Monarchies. Part I | European Royal History (wordpress.com) (accessed 1 March 2023); also Arturo E. Beéche, *The November 1918 Revolution: The Fall of the German Monarchies* (London: Eurohistory and Kensington House Books, 2021); and Jonathan Triffitt, *Twilight of the Princes: The Fall and Afterlife of Monarchy in Southern Germany, 1918–1934*, PhD diss., University of St Andrews (Scotland), 2021.

20. This term, by analogy with present-day state governments in Australia and provincial governments in Canada, can be more readily understood and is less cumbersome than the standard Teutonic nomenclature 'Minister-President'.

21. Watt, 318.

22. Howard Norman Stern, *Political Crime and Justice in the Weimar Republic*, PhD diss., John Hopkins University (Baltimore), 1966, 74.

23. Watt, 293–294.

24. Watt, 326.

25. Watt, 326.

26. Watt, 326.

27. Watt, 326.

28. Watt, 329.

29. Watt, 330.

30. Watt, 337.

31. Having fled the Third Reich in 1933, Toller – utterly disenchanted with Soviet Communism – was found hanged in his New York hotel room six years later. Whether he took his own life or was murdered by Stalin's agents is uncertain; concerning the death in 1940 of Toller's fellow apostate Willi Münzenberg, likewise found hanged, a similar doubt remains.

32. Watt, 338.

33. Watt, 266.

34. Watt, 263.

35. Walter H. Kaufmann, *Monarchism in the Weimar Republic* (New York City: Bookman Associates, 1953), 90–91.

36. J.P. Nettl, *Rosa Luxemburg* (London: Oxford University Press), Vol. 2, 779.

37. Watt, 305.

38. Watt, 305–306.

39. Watt, 308.

40. Michael Burleigh, *The Third Reich: A New History* (London: Macmillan, 2000), 40.

41. Kaufmann, 72.

42. Sir John Wheeler-Bennett, 'The End of the Weimar Republic', *Foreign Affairs* 50:2 (January 1972), 351–371, at 352.

43. Klaus W. Jonas (tr. Charles W. Bangert), *The Life of Crown Prince William* (London: Routledge & Kegan Paul, 1961), 143.

44. Anon., *The Real Crown Prince: A Record and an Indictment* (London: George Newnes, 1916), 117–118.

45. Jonas, 6–7.
46. Jonas, 44.
47. Jonas, 74.
48. Jonas, 82.
49. Anon., *Real Crown Prince*, 5.
50. Anon., *Real Crown Prince,* 195.
51. Jonas, 118.
52. Jonas, 139.
53. Erich Eyck, *A History of the Weimar Republic: From the Collapse of the Empire to Hindenburg's Election* (Cambridge, Massachusetts: Harvard University Press, 1962), 150.
54. Burleigh, 58.
55. William Manchester, *The Arms of Krupp, 1587–1968* (New York City: Bantam Books, 1970), 358.
56. Quoted in Prince Bernhard von Bülow, *The Memoirs of Prince von Bülow,* Vol. 3 (Boston: Little, Brown, & Co., 1932), 48.
57. Sweetman, 142.
58. Robert S. Garnett, *Lion, Eagle, and Swastika: Bavarian Monarchism in Weimar Germany* (New York City: Garland Publishing Inc., 1991), 66. A recent French-language essay on Bavarian regionalist movements cautiously refers to the BVP as being '*dominé par une sensibilité monarchique*': Thomas Raithel, 'Les partis régionaux en Bavière au XXe siècle,' in Hélène Miard-Delacroix, Guillaume Garner, and Béatrice von Hirschhausen (eds.), *Espaces de Pouvoir, Espaces d'Autonomie en Allemagne* (Villeneuve d'Ascq, France: Presses Universitaires du Septentrion, 2010), 131–145, at 134.
59. Garnett, 66.
60. Garnett, 73.
61. Sweetman, 131.
62. Garnett, 173.
63. Garnett, 67.
64. Bernd Widdig, *Culture and Inflation in Weimar Germany* (Berkeley: University of California Press, 2001), 46
65. Widdig, 46.
66. Roy G. Koepp, 'Gustav von Kahr and the Emergence of the Radical Right in Bavaria,' *The Historian* 77:4 (Winter 2015), 740–763, at 740.
67. Koepp, 746.
68. Sir Ian Kershaw, *Hitler, 1889–1936: Hubris* (London: Penguin, 1998), 159.
69. Burleigh, 59.
70. Harold J. Gordon, *Hitler and the Beer Hall Putsch* (Princeton: Princeton University Press, 1972), 256.
71. Burleigh, 58.
72. Burleigh, 59.
73. I. Kershaw, 205.
74. Sweetman, 159.
75. Kaufmann, 114.
76. Koepp, 761.
77. Gordon, 224.
78. Gordon, 323.
79. I. Kershaw, 209.

80. Koepp, 740.
81. Lukacs, 100. The sheer youth of so many inter-war dictators and even would-be dictators cannot fail to surprise. Hitler came to power at forty-three, Mussolini at thirty-nine; at thirty-nine, Romania's Iron Guard leader C.Z. Codreanu was murdered; Sir Oswald Mosley founded the British Union of Fascists when only thirty-six; Goebbels became Propaganda Minister at thirty-six; Béla Kun became Hungary's Communist ruler at thirty-three; Belgium's Rexist leader Léon Degrelle had already shot his political bolt before turning thirty-two. Admiral Horthy, Marshal Pilsudski, and General Primo de Rivera, all achieving office in their fifties, seem by comparison geriatric.
82. Koepp, 760.
83. Jonas, 149.
84. Rudolf Olden (tr. R.T. Clark), *Stresemann* (London: Methuen, 1930), 107.
85. Jonas, 147.
86. H.L. Mencken, 'Exile at Wieringen says he longs for day when he can assist Germany: Heir to former German throne declares he finds it "hard to stand by without taking a hand",' *Baltimore Sun* (11 October 1922), 1.
87. Jonas, 147.
88. Quoted in Jürgen Heideking, 'Das Ende der Sanktionspolitik: Die alliierten Mächte und die Rückkehr des deutschen Kronprinzen im November 1923,' *Francia* 7 (1979), 365–400, at 397.
89. Watt, 519.
90. Watt, 529.
91. Sally Marks, '"My Name Is Ozymandias": The Kaiser in Exile,' *Central European History* 16:2 (June 1983), 122–170, at 144.
92. Kaufmann, 110. Kaufmann translates *froh* as 'gay', but in view of lexical developments which have occurred with that adjective since 1953 (and which have unintentionally imparted a new relevance to the sexual orientation of Ernst Röhm), 'cheerful' appears a more suitable rendition in 2023.
93. Desmond FitzGerald, *Memoirs of Desmond FitzGerald, 1913–1916* (London: Routledge & Kegan Paul, 1968), 141.
94. Jonas, 136.
95. Jonas, 136.
96. Anon., 'Kaiser's Youngest Son, Joachim, Shoots Himself,' *The New York Times* (19 July 1920), 1 and 3. Jonas (136) wrongly gives the month of Joachim's death as June.
97. Watt, 474.
98. Andreas Dorpalen, *Hindenburg and the Weimar Republic* (Princeton: Princeton University Press, 1964), 68.
99. Dorpalen, 87.
100. Jonas, 159–160.
101. Jonas, 160.
102. Jonas, 163.
103. Kaufmann, 183.
104. Hermann Beck, *The Fateful Alliance: German Conservatives and Nazis in 1933: The* Machtergreifung *In A New Light* (Oxford: Berghahn Books, 2009), 49; James Elstone Dow, 'The German National People's Party: In the Cause of Monarchy,' *Continuity* 3 (Fall 1981), 37–50.
105. Kaufmann, 160–162.
106. Kaufmann, 163.

107. Beck, 49.
108. Frederick L. Schuman, *Hitler and the Nazi Dictatorship: A Study in Social Pathology and the Politics of Fascism* (London: Hale, 1936), 150.
109. John A. Leopold, *Alfred Hugenberg: The Radical Nationalist Campaign Against the Weimar Republic* (New Haven, Connecticut: Yale University Press, 1977), 105; Hermann Rauschning, *Makers of Destruction: Meetings and Talks in Revolutionary Germany*, tr. E.W. Dickes (London: Eyre & Spottiswode, 1942), 214.
110. Beck, 52; Leopold, 48.
111. Leopold, 21.
112. Sir John Wheeler-Bennett, *The Nemesis of Power: The German Army in Politics 1918–1945* (London: Macmillan, 1964), 208.
113. Otto Ernst (tr. H.J. Stenning), *Kings in Exile* (London: Jarrolds, 1933), 57–58.
114. G.S. Viereck, 'Ex-Kaiser Wilhelm II Breaks His Silence', *Current History* 21:2 (November 1924), 165–180, at 179–180.
115. Whittle, 358.
116. Giles MacDonogh, *The Last Kaiser: William The Impetuous* (London: Weidenfeld & Nicolson, 2000), 452.
117. Clemens von Radowitz Nei, 'Monarchy will return, but not I, says ex-Kaiser', *The New York Times* (3 July 1922), 1 and 3.
118. Kaufmann, 72.
119. Marks, 156.
120. Alan Bullock, *Hitler: A Study in Tyranny* (New York City: Bantam Books, 1961), 141, gives 108,000; T.W. Arafe, *The Development and Character of the Nazi Political Machine, 1928–1930, and the NSDAP Electoral Breakthrough*, PhD diss., Louisiana State University, Baton Rouge (1976), 93–94, gives the lower figure; the 1923 total of 55,000 comes from Andrew Brian Henson, *Before the Seizure of Power: American and British Press Coverage of National Socialism, 1922 to 1933*, MA diss., Clemson University, Clemson, Georgia (2007), 16.
121. Anon., 'Royalist Plot Misfires: Bavaria turns down scheme to crown Rupprecht', *The Manchester Guardian* (10 November 1925), 20.
122. Sweetman, 206–207.
123. Sweetman, 256.
124. Sweetman, xv.
125. Sweetman, 257.
126. H.H. Herwig, 'From Kaiser to Fuhrer: The Political Road of a German Admiral, 1923–33,' *Journal of Contemporary History* 9:2 (April 1974), 107–120, at 108. Subsequently Levetzow backed Hitler's presidential candidacy, while pouring scorn on Hugenberg, about whom he snarled: 'Germany can expect nothing from this clumsy bigwig, from this pig-skinned, dull fellow, from this crew-cut complainer, from this fusspot and pedant' (117).
127. Sweetman, 296.
128. Sweetman, 296.
129. Sweetman, 296.
130. Herwig, 113, where the first visit is wrongly attributed to 1930.
131. McDonogh, 447.
132. Herbert Vivian, *Kings In Waiting* (London: Hamish Hamilton, 1933), 44.
133. Lamar Cecil, *Wilhelm II: Emperor and Exile* (Chapel Hill: University of North Carolina Press, 1989): 338.
134. Leopold, 111.

135. Jonas, 180.
136. Leopold, 114.
137. Sweetman, 416–417.
138. Wheeler-Bennett, 'Fall of the Weimar Republic,' 362.
139. Wheeler-Bennett, 'Fall of the Weimar Republic,' 365.
140. Frank Millard, *The Palace and the Bunker: Royal Resistance to Hitler* (Stroud, Gloucestershire: The History Press, 2012), 12.
141. Wheeler-Bennett, 'Fall of the Weimar Republic,' 364.
142. Wheeler-Bennett, *Hindenburg,* 355.
143. Sean McMeekin, *The Red Millionaire: A Political Biography of Willi Münzenberg, Moscow's Secret Propaganda Tsar in the West* (New Haven, Connecticut: Yale University Press, 2003), 235.
144. Winfried Becker, 'The Nazi Seizure of Power in Bavaria and the Demise of the Bavarian People's Party,' in Hermann Beck and Larry Eugene Jones (eds.), *From Weimar to Hitler: Studies in the Dissolution of the Weimar Republic and the Establishment of the Third Reich, 1932–1934* (Oxford: Berghan Books, 2018), 111–140m at 114 and 116.
145. Becker, 116.
146. Becker, 116.
147. Kaufmann, 217–218.
148. Kaufmann, 218.
149. Kaufmann, 219.
150. Kaufmann, 219.
151. Becker, 118.
152. Kaufmann, 221, where 'one not to be discussed' is rendered in dubious English as 'indiscussible'.
153. Anon., 'Germany: Monarchist Fools?,' *Time,* 23:5 (29 January 1934), 20.
154. Kaufmann, 225.
155. Vivian, *Kings,* 61.
156. McDonogh, 452–453.
157. McDonogh, 456.
158. Balfour, 419.
159. Jonas, 180; Louis P. Lochner, *What About Germany?* (New York City: Dodd, Mead, & Co., 1942), 285.
160. Wheeler-Bennett, *Nemesis,* 502–504.
161. Gerhard Ritter (tr. R.T. Clark), *The German Resistance: Carl Goerdeler's Struggle Against Tyranny* (London: Allen & Unwin, 1958), 192.
162. Jonas, 207–209.
163. Prince Louis Ferdinand of Prussia, *The Rebel Prince: Memoirs* (Chicago: Regnery, 1952), 41.
164. Churchill, *Great Contemporaries*, 24–25.

Chapter III

1. A.J.P. Taylor, *The Italian Problem in European Diplomacy, 1847–1849* (Manchester: Manchester University Press, 1970), 13.
2. Alan Palmer, *Twilight of the Habsburgs: The Life and Times of the Emperor Francis Joseph* (London: Weidenfeld & Nicolson, 1994), 349.
3. Ilsa Barea, *Vienna: Legend and Reality* (London: Secker & Warburg, 1966), 275.
4. Jean-Paul Bled (tr. Teresa Bridgeman), *Franz Joseph* (London: Blackwell, 1992), 321.

5. Anon., 'Four Shots Were Fired in Vienna Parliament', *The Brantford Daily Expositor* [Brantford, Ontario] (5 October 1911), 1.
6. Bled, 322.
7. Eugene Bagger, *Francis Joseph: Emperor of Austria, King of Hungary* (New York City: G.P. Putnam's Sons, 1927), 555.
8. Nora Wydenbruck, *My Two Worlds: An Autobiography* (London: Longmans, Green, 1956), 18.
9. Victor von Kubinyi, *Franz Josef I, Emperor-King: A Character Sketch* (South Bend, Indiana: Hibbert Print Co., 1917), 92–93.
10. B.F. Tefft, *Hungary and Kossuth: or, An American Exposition of the Late Hungarian Revolution* (Philadelphia: John Ball, 1852), 169.
11. J.E. Edmonds, 'Military Operations France and Belgium, 1916: Sir Douglas Haig's Command to the 1st July: Battle of the Somme', *History of the Great War Based on Official Documents by Direction of the Historical Section of the Committee of Imperial Defence* (London: Macmillan, 1932), Vol. 1, 483.
12. Gordon Brook-Shepherd, *The Last Habsburg* (London: Weidenfeld & Nicolson, 1968), 89.
13. Sir Harold Nicolson, *King George the Fifth: His Life and Reign* (London: Pan Books, 1967), 410.
14. E. Taylor, 361.
15. Charles Maechling, 'The Sixtus Affair', *History Today* 23:11 (November 1973), 757–765, at 762.
16. E. Taylor, 328.
17. E. Taylor, 329.
18. Brook-Shepherd, *Habsburg*, 185.
19. Herbert Vivian, *The Life of the Emperor Charles of Austria.* (London: Grayson & Grayson, 1932), 132.
20. Béla Menczer, 'Béla Kun and the Hungarian Revolution of 1919', *History Today* 19:5 (May 1969), 299–309, at 301.
21. Gabor Vermes, 'The October Revolution in Hungary', in Ivan Volgyes (ed.), *Hungary in Revolution* (Lincoln: University of Nebraska Press, 1971), 49.
22. Brook-Shepherd, *Habsburg*, 185.
23. Brook-Shepherd, *Habsburg*, 249.
24. Menczer, 'Kun', 303.
25. Paul Lendvai (tr. Ann Major), *The Hungarians: A Thousand Years of Victory in Defeat* (Princeton, New Jersey: Princeton University Press, 2003), 368.
26. J.Z. Muller, *Capitalism and the Jews* (Princeton: Princeton University Press, 2010), 153; Colin Welch, 'The Jews of Hungary', *The Spectator* 262:8394 (27 May 1989), 27–28, at 28.
27. Laura-Louise Veress and Dalma Takács, *Clear the Line: Hungary's Struggle to Leave the Axis During the Second World War* (Cleveland: Prospero Publications, 1995), 69.
28. Menczer, 'Kun', 305.
29. Menczer, 'Kun', 306.
30. Menczer, 'Kun', 306.
31. An epigram from Lukács's *History and Class Consciousness,* 1923: 'These forms of capital are objectively subordinated, it is true, to the real life-process of capitalism, the extraction of surplus value in the course of production. They are, therefore, only to be explained in terms of the nature of industrial capitalism itself. But in the minds of people in bourgeois society they constitute the pure, authentic, unadulterated forms of

capital. In them the relations between men that lie hidden in the immediate commodity relation, as well as the relations between men and the objects that should really gratify their needs, have faded to the point where they can be neither recognised nor even perceived. For that very reason the reified mind has come to regard them as the true representatives of his societal existence. The commodity character of the commodity, the abstract, quantitative mode of calculability shows itself here in its purest form: the reified mind necessarily sees it as [...]'

32. Menczer, 'Kun', 306.
33. Menczer, 'Kun', 307.
34. Jay A. Weinstein, *Social and Cultural Change: Social Science for a Dynamic World* (Lanham, Maryland: Rowman & Littlefield, 2005), 172.
35. Menczer, 'Kun', 308.
36. Victor Serge, *Memoirs of a Revolutionist* (London: Oxford University Press, 1967), 140.
37. Edward, Duke of Windsor, *A King's Story: Memoirs of HRH the Duke of Windsor* (London: Cassell, 1951), 129.
38. Empress Zita, as quoted in Brook-Shepherd, *Habsburg*, 224.
39. John Van der Kiste, *Crowns in a Changing World: The British and European Monarchies, 1901–1936* (Stroud, Gloucestershire: Alan Sutton, 1993), 142.
40. Jacques Bainville, *Les Conséquences Politiques de la Paix* (Paris: Fayard, 1920), especially this passage: 'Let us imagine Wilhelm II driven from Berlin, while Karl I remains in Vienna, Ludwig III in Munich, the other Wilhelm, the King of Württemberg, in Stuttgart, etc. [*Imaginons Guillaume II chassé de Berlin, tandis que Charles Ier reste à Vienne, Louis III à Munich, l'autre Guillaume, roi de Wurtemberg, à Stuttgart, etc.*]' (52).
41. Kenneth Rose, *King George V* (New York City: Knopf, 1983), 385.
42. Brook-Shepherd, *Habsburg*, 250.
43. Brook-Shepherd, *Habsburg*, 224.
44. Brook-Shepherd, *Habsburg*, 242. [Emphasis added – RJS.]
45. Brook-Shepherd, *Habsburg*, 243.
46. Brook-Shepherd, *Habsburg*, 243.
47. Brook-Shepherd, *Habsburg*, 248.
48. Thomas L. Sakmyster, *Hungary's Admiral on Horseback: Miklós Horthy, 1918–1944* (Boulder, Colorado: East European Monographs, 1994), v.
49. Lendvai, 379. 'Most Jews, all respectable Jews, especially in Hungary, where they had prospered, viewed the sinister antics of Jewish Communists with fear and abhorrence. They thought and said that they would inflame anti-Semitism; and they were right.' Welch, 28.
50. Béla Menczer, 'The Habsburg Restoration: Hungary in 1921', *History Today* 22:2 (February 1972), 128–135, at 130.
51. Lendvai, 373. The names of the two Hungarian signatories were Ágost Benárd and Alfréd Drasche-Lázár.
52. Lendvai, 373.
53. Sakmyster, 384.
54. Sakmyster, 384–385.
55. Sakmyster, 86.
56. James Bogle and Joanna Bogle, *A Heart For Europe* (Leominster, Herefordshire: Gracewing Books, 1993), 124.
57. Sakmyster, 93.

58. Sakmyster, 93.
59. Bogle and Bogle, 130.
60. Sakmyster, 95.
61. Sakmyster, 95.
62. Sakmyster, 95–96.
63. Sakmyster, 96–97.
64. Sakmyster, 98.
65. Sakmyster, 101.
66. Gordon Brook-Shepherd, *The Last Empress: The Life and Times of Zita of Austria-Hungary, 1892–1989* (London: HarperCollins, 1991), 173.
67. Bogle and Bogle, 82.
68. Lendvai, 168. Because Salic Law operated in eighteenth-century Hungary (as opposed to eighteenth-century Austria), Maria Theresa was officially Hungary's king, not its queen. This was as far as her gender reassignment procedure ever went; nor had she ever been an obvious candidate for such a procedure, since she bore her husband seventeen children.
69. Vivian, *Life,* 242–243.
70. Bogle and Bogle, 132.
71. Brook-Shepherd, *Habsburg,* 281.
72. Brook-Shepherd, *Habsburg,* 285.
73. Bogle and Bogle, 134.
74. Brook-Shepherd, *Habsburg,* 291.
75. Brook-Shepherd, *Habsburg,* 287.
76. Brook-Shepherd, *Habsburg,* 292.
77. Vivian, *Life,* 257.
78. *Henry IV Part I,* Act V, Scene 1.
79. Bogle and Bogle, 135.
80. Brook-Shepherd, *Habsburg,* 297.
81. Vivian, *Life,* 249.
82. Zoltán Peterecz, 'Hungary and the League of Nations: A Forced Marriage', in Peter Becker and Natasha Wheatley (eds.), *Remaking Central Europe: The League of Nations and the Former Habsburg Lands* (Oxford: Oxford University Press, 2020), 145–166.
83. Sakmyster, 120.
84. Vivian, *Life,* 243.
85. Menczer, 'Restoration', 135.
86. Brook-Shepherd, *Habsburg,* 299.
87. Brook-Shepherd, *Habsburg,* 299.
88. Brook-Shepherd, *Habsburg,* 320.
89. Brook-Shepherd, *Habsburg,* 325.
90. Brook-Shepherd, *Habsburg,* 323.
91. Brook-Shepherd, *Habsburg,* 323.
92. Brook-Shepherd, *Habsburg,* 328.
93. Bogle and Bogle, 144.
94. Menczer, 'Restoration', 135.
95. Vivian, *Life,* 282.
96. Menczer, 'Restoration', 135.
97. Brook-Shepherd, *Empress,* 135.
98. Bogle and Bogle, 145.

99. Anon., 'Starvation Diet in Vienna', *The Western Argus* [Kalgoorlie, Western Australia] (9 March 1920), 1.
100. Benjamin M. Weissman, *Herbert Hoover and Famine Relief to Soviet Russia, 1921–1923* (Stanford, California: Hoover Institution Press, 1974), 34.
101. Lothar Höbelt, 'Nostalgic Agnostics: Austrian Aristocrats and Politics, 1918–1938', in Karina Urbach (ed.), *European Aristocracies and the Radical Right 1918–1939* (Oxford: Oxford University Press, 2007), 161–186, at 163.
102. Gordon Brook-Shepherd, *Dollfuss* (London: Macmillan, 1961), 179.
103. Herbert Vivian, *Kings in Waiting* (London: Hamish Hamilton, 1933), 107.
104. Brook-Shepherd, *Dollfuss*, 181.
105. Ernst, 79.
106. Anon., 'Austria: Double-Eagle?', *Time* 15:24 (16 June 1930), 28–29, at 29.
107. Brook-Shepherd, *Empress,* 239.
108. James Longo, *Hitler and the Habsburgs: The Führer's Vendetta Against the Austrian Royals* (New York City: Diversion Books, 2018), 81.
109. Sir Charles Petrie, *Twenty Years' Armistice – And After: British Foreign Policy Since 1918* (London: Right Book Club, 1940), 131–132.
110. Robert Self (ed.), *The Austen Chamberlain Diary Letters: The Correspondence of Sir Austen Chamberlain with His Sisters Hilda and Ida, 1916–1937* (Cambridge: Cambridge University Press, 1995), 466.
111. L.E.J. Roberts and Albert Weale, *Innovation and Environmental Risk* (Lansing: University of Michigan Press, 1991), 23.
112. Lendvai, 401.
113. Lendvai, 400.
114. Lendvai, 400.
115. Lendvai, 400.
116. Lendvai, 402.
117. Several European aristocrats, unlike Rothermere, did acquire and maintain the ability to comprehend this basic fact. Austria's Count Rudolf Hoyos, speaker of the Austrian parliament, despised Hitlerism: 'We have thoroughly broken with the democratic past and cease to take the masses seriously. Not so the Nazis. Unwittingly they cling to old liberal and democratic ways of thinking. Thus their fawning on the favour of the mob.' Höbelt, 176.
118. Lendvai, 403.
119. Lendvai, 403.
120. Lendvai, 403.
121. Anon., 'Monarchist Hopes Rise in Hungary', *Gettysburg Times* [Pennsylvania] (7 October 1936), 4.
122. Jaroslav Hašek (tr. Paul Selver), *The Good Soldier Schweik.* Harmondsworth, Middlesex: Penguin Books, 1939.
123. Edward Crankshaw, *The Fall of the House of Habsburg* (London: Sphere Books, 1970), 429, 430.

Chapter IV

1. 'Etychus and his Kin', 'Dear Slogan-Lovers', *Christianity Today* 11:21 (21 July 1967), 20.
2. Michael Curtis, *Three Against the Third Republic: Sorel, Barrès, and Maurras* (Princeton, New Jersey: Princeton University Press, 1959), 24.
3. James Harding, *The Astonishing Adventure of General Boulanger* (New York City: Scribner, 1971), xi.

4. Brian Jenkins, *Lord Lyons: A Diplomat in an Age of Nationalism and War* (Montreal: McGill-Queens University Press, 2014), 371.

5. Philippe Pétain (ed. Jacques Isorni), *Actes et Écrits* (Paris: Flammarion, 1974), 551–552; Robert Gildea, *France Since 1945* (Oxford: Oxford University Press, 1996), 65.

6. E.W. Bovill, *The Battle of Alcazar: An Account of the Defeat of Don Sebastian of Portugal at El-Ksar el-Kebir* (London: Batchworth, 1952), 157.

7. CD booklet, Gilles Servat, *A-raok mont kuit / Avant de partir* (Keltia Musique KMCD45, 1994). The author is indebted to Sophie Masson for bringing this recording to his attention.

8. Geoffrey Wheatcroft, *Churchill's Shadow: An Astonishing Life and a Dangerous Legacy* (London: The Bodley Head, 2021), 12.

9. Gildea, 70.

10. Eugen Weber, *Action Française: Royalism and Reaction in Twentieth-Century France* (Stanford, California: Stanford University Press, 1962), 529.

11. Weber, 9.

12. Charles Maurras, *Au signe de Flore: souvenirs de vie politique, l'affaire Dreyfus et l'Action Française* (Paris: B. Grasset, 1933), 55.

13. Thomas Molnar, 'Charles Maurras, Shaper of an Age', *Modern Age* 41:4 (Fall 1999), 337–342, at 338.

14. 'The first poet with whose verse he was, in his own words, madly in love, was [Alfred de] Musset [...] He was under the spell of Baudelaire when he began writing poetry himself while still in a Catholic school in Aix-en-Provence.' L.S. Roudiez, 'Amending the Record: The Early Poetic Activities of Charles Maurras', *The French Review* 24:3 (January 1951), 197–208, at 197–198.

15. Curtis, 238.

16. Edward R. Tannenbaum, *The Action Française: Die-Hard Reactionaries in Twentieth-Century France* (New York City: Wiley, 1962), 50–51.

17. Tannenbaum, 50.

18. Tannenbaum, 46–47.

19. Weber, 22.

20. Hunter Casper, *Modern Monarchy* (Philadelphia: Alpha, 2021), 32.

21. Curtis, 61.

22. Eric Arthur Blair, 'A Farthing Newspaper', *G.K.'s Weekly* 198: 8 (29 December 1928), 247–249, at 248.

23. Charles Maurras, *Enquête sur la monarchie, 1900–1909* (Paris: Nouvelle Librairie Nationale, 1910), xxxiii.

24. Francis Wheen, *Karl Marx* (New York City: Norton, 2000), 248.

25. Weber, 532.

26. Hilaire Belloc, *The House of Commons and Monarchy* (London: George Allen & Unwin, 1920), 174.

27. Charles Maurras, *Chemins de Paradis* (Paris: Calmette-Levy, 1895), xxviii-xxx; Weber, 8.

28. Charles Maurras, 'Sur le nom de socialiste', *L'Action Française* 34 (15 November 1900), 859–867, at 865.

29. Robert Stuart, *Marxism and National Identity: Socialism, Nationalism, and National Socialism during the French* Fin de Siècle (Albany: State University of New York Press, 2006), 151.

30. Maurras, *Enquête*, l.

31. Curtis, 47.

32. Curtis, 48.
33. Curtis, 214.
34. Léon Daudet, *Fantômes et vivants: souvenirs des milieux littéraires, politiques, artistiques et médicaux de 1880 à 1905* (Paris: Nouvelle Librairie Nationale, 1914), 240–241; a slightly different translation is given in Alister Kershaw, *An Introduction to Léon Daudet, with a Selection from his Memoirs* (Francestown, New Hampshire: Typographeum, 1988), 46.
35. A. Kershaw, 61.
36. A. Kershaw, 14.
37. Weber, 532.
38. A. Kershaw, 16.
39. A. Kershaw, 24.
40. A. Kershaw, 27.
41. L. Dumont-Wilden, *Le Crépuscule des Maîtres* (Brussels: La Renaissance du Livre, 1947), 173.
42. Oscar L. Amal, *Ambivalent Alliance: The Catholic Church and the Action Française, 1899–1939* (Pittsburgh: University of Pittsburgh Press, 1985), 68.
43. Henri Massis, *Maurras et notre temps* (Paris: Plon, 1964), 113; François Huguenin, *L'Action Française: Une Histoire Intellectuelle* (Paris: Éditions Perrin, 1998), 260.
44. Weber, 8.
45. Amal, 70.
46. Peter J. Bernardi SJ, 'Louis Cardinal Billot SJ (1846–1931): Thomist, Anti-Modernist, Integralist', *Journal of Jesuit Studies* 8 (2021), 585–616, at 599–600. The author is indebted to Dr Bernard Doherty for bringing to his attention this essay.
47. Francis X. Murphy, *The Papacy Today* (New York City: Macmillan, 1981), 51.
48. Huguenin, 308.
49. 'Candide', 'Doit-on le dire?', *Candide* (16 September 1926), 1; Weber, 232 (later [553] Weber incorrectly gives the year 1925 instead of 1926 for this issue).
50. Sir Shane Leslie, 'The Pope and French Royalist Protagonists', *The Catholic Advocate* [Brisbane] (17 May 1928), 27.
51. Denis Gwynn, *The Catholic Reaction in France* (New York City: Macmillan, 1924), 92.
52. Gwynn, 93.
53. Marie-Noële Harrault, 'La rupture de Bernanos avec Maurras', *La Revue des Lettres modernes* 10 (1969), 189–207.
54. Tannenbaum, 127.
55. Tannenbaum, 127–131.
56. Weber, 164, 166.
57. Weber, 166.
58. Léon Daudet and Charles Maurras, 'L'Assassinat de Philippe Daudet', *L'Action Française* 336 (2 December 1923), 1.
59. Weber, 170.
60. Anon., 'Tartarin Surrenders', *The New York Times* (15 June 1927), 26.
61. Petrie, *Historian,* 99.
62. Petrie, *Historian,* 99.
63. Petrie, *Historian,* 99.
64. Petrie, *Historian,* 99.
65. Petrie, *Historian,* 98–99.
66. Petrie, *Historian,* 100.

67. Julian Jackson, *A Certain Idea of France: The Life of Charles de Gaulle* (London: Allen Lane, 2018), 79.
68. Georges Simenon (tr. Anthea Bell), *The Late Monsieur Gallet* (London: Penguin Books, 2013), 150.
69. Simenon, 139.
70. Simenon, 140–142.
71. Weber, 365–366. Subscription income for the newspaper is given by Weber (365) as follows: in 1928, 312.760.10 francs; in 1930, 159,860.85 francs; and in 1934, only 55,787.40 francs. These figures are not automatically accurate, since Maurras's inability to delegate made AF office management much less efficient than it should have been. But they are almost certainly close to the truth.
72. Raymond Lange, 'The Right Minority in France', *The Atlantic* 158 (July 1936), 109–114, at 110.
73. Samuel M. Osgood, *French Royalism Since 1870* (The Hague: Martinus Nijhoff, 1970), 116.
74. Gildea, 87.
75. Léon Daudet, 'A French Royalist Speaks', *The Evening Standard* (1 February 1934), 7.
76. Weber, 374.
77. Weber, 374.
78. Weber, 400.
79. Osgood, 122.
80. 'Carpenter' is obviously an allusion to Christ, but 'cameleer' refers to Mohammed, and 'Maya's dreaming son' was Siddhartha Gautama, better known to the world as the Buddha.
81. Charles Maurras, 'La Politique', *L'Action Française* 137 (16 May 1936), 1.
82. Charles Maurras, 'La Politique', *L'Action Française* 99 (9 April 1935), 1.
83. Osgood, 66.
84. Anne C. Kjelling, *The Nobel Peace Prize and the Laureates: The Meaning and Acceptance of the Nobel Peace Prize in the Prize Winners' Countries* (Frankfurt: Peter Lang, 1994), 81 (where the surname of Maurras's supporter is mis-spelled 'Magellon').
85. Charles Maurras, 'Une sottise: l'hitlérisme', *L'Action Française* 84 (25 March 1938), 1.
86. Weber, 405.
87. A. Kershaw, 21.
88. Paul E. Gottfried, *Revisions and Dissents: Essays* (De Kalb: Northern Illinois University Press, 2017), 82.
89. Tannenbaum, 231.
90. Julian Jackson, *France: The Dark Years, 1940–1944* (Oxford: Oxford University Press, 2003), 140.
91. Jackson, *Dark Years*, 140.
92. Tannenbaum, 235.
93. A. Kershaw, 20.
94. Weber, 469.
95. Robert Aron, *Histoire de l'Épuration,* Vol. 2 (Paris: Fayard, 1969), 365–367.
96. Weber, 475.
97. Osgood, 184.
98. 'His [*Maurras's*] slogan "Politics first!" is perfectly comprehensible,' Salazar told interviewer António Ferro, 'and admirably sums up the dynamic of his closest

disciples. But in this expression there is a historical and sociological fallacy which is by no means without its dangers so far as the formation of the younger generation is concerned.' Egerton, 168.

99. Weber, 486.
100. Weber, 486.
101. Weber, 475.
102. Molnar, 338.
103. Weber, 469.
104. Alistair Cooke, *Six Men* (Harmondsworth, Middlesex: Penguin Books, 1978), 13.
105. Weber, 456.
106. G.K. Chesterton, *Orthodoxy* (London: Sheed & Ward, 1939), 18–19.

Chapter V

1. Jean Kerr, *Please Don't Eat the Daisies* (New York City: Doubleday, 1957), 16.
2. B.S. Erskine, *Twenty-Nine Years: The Reign of King Alfonso XIII of Spain: An Intimate and Authorized Life Story* (London: Hutchinson, 1931), 145.
3. Robert Sencourt, *King Alfonso: A Biography* (London: Faber & Faber, 1942), 135.
4. Sencourt, *Alfonso*, 135.
5. Anon., 'Tragedy in Spain: The Prime Minister Murdered', *The Advertiser* [Adelaide], 14 November 1912, 9.
6. Salvador de Madariaga, *Spain* (London: Jonathan Cape, 1942), 229–230.
7. Sencourt, *Alfonso*, 137.
8. Princess Pilar of Bavaria and Desmond Chapman-Houston, *Don Alfonso XIII: A Study of Monarchy* (London: John Murray, 1931), 156.
9. Churchill, 134.
10. William Miller Collier, *At the Court of His Catholic Majesty* (Chicago: A.C. McClurg & Co, 1912), 154–155.
11. Kenneth Rose, *King George V* (New York City: Knopf, 1984), 68.
12. Sencourt, *Alfonso*, 119–120.
13. D.M. Potts and W.T.W. Potts, *Queen Victoria's Gene* (Stroud, Gloucestershire: Alan Sutton Publishing Ltd., 1995), 128.
14. Robert Sencourt, *Spain's Uncertain Crown: The Story of the Spanish Sovereigns, 1808–1931* (London: Ernest Benn, 1932), 350.
15. Carlos H. Oberacker, *A Imperatriz Leopoldina: sua vida e sua época, ensaio de uma biografia* (Rio de Janeiro: Conselho Federal de Cultura, 1973), 46.
16. Portland, W.J.A.C.J. Cavendish-Bentinck, Sixth Duke of, *Men, Women and Things: Memories of the Duke of Portland* (London: Faber & Faber, 1938), 76.
17. Churchill, 133.
18. Hardinge, 260; quoted in H. A. Schmitt, *Neutral Europe Between War and Revolution, 1917–23* (Charlottesville, Virginia: University of Virginia Press, 1988), 13.
19. Petrie, *Alfonso*, 126.
20. Pilar and Chapman-Houston, 189.
21. Johan den Hertog and Samuël Kruizinga (eds.), *Caught in the Middle: Neutrals, Neutrality, and the First World War* (Amsterdam: Amsterdam University Press, 2011), 62.
22. Churchill, 136.
23. Sencourt, *Crown*, 379.
24. Petrie, *Alfonso*, 116. Melquíadez Álvarez was murdered by anarchists in 1936, during the Civil War's early stages.

25. Anthony Richard Ewart Rhodes, *The Vatican in the Age of the Dictators, 1922–1945* (New York City: Holt, Rinehart and Winston, 1973), 116.

26. Joaquín Mayordomo, 'Annual: horror, masacre y olvido', *El País*, 22 March 2016, 26; Juan Pando Despierto, *Historia secreta de Annual: memorias de guerra* (Barcelona: Ediciones Altaya, 2008), 335–336.

27. Pando Despierto, 336.

28. Anon., 'Spanish Premier murdered', *Evening Standard,* 9 March 1921, 1–2.

29. 'A Spanish Observer', 'Under the Spanish Dictatorship', *The Manchester Guardian,* (20 August 1924), 8.

30. Warre Bradley Wells, *The Last King: Don Alfonso XIII of Spain* (London: Frederick Muller Ltd., 1934), 174.

31. 'From time immemorial the subway at Bobadilla Junction had been used as a urinal, and when, soon after the Directory came into office, I was about to employ it for this purpose, a policeman came up with a sorrowful expression on his face and said, "You will have to go to the proper lavatory. We have a dictator now."' Sir Charles Petrie, *A Historian Looks at His World* (London: Sidgwick & Jackson, 1972), 104.

32. Ricardo Fernández de la Reguera and Susana March, *La dictadura: El régimen civil, 1926–1930* (Barcelona: Editorial Planeta, 1969), 26.

33. Erskine, 207.

34. Erskine, 207.

35. Shlomo Ben-Ami, *Fascism from Above: The Dictatorship of Primo de Rivera in Spain, 1923–1930* (Oxford: Clarendon Press, 1983), 382.

36. Ben-Ami, 388.

37. Petrie, *Alfonso,* 210.

38. Churchill, 135; Sencourt, *Crown,* 382.

39. José Ortega y Gasset, 'El error Berenguer', *El Sol,* 15 November 1930, 1.

40. Petrie, *Alfonso,* 220.

41. Churchill, 137.

42. Gerard Noel, *Ena: Spain's English Queen* (London: Constable, 1984), 219.

43. Sir Arnold Lunn, 'King Alfonso of Spain', *The Tablet* 217:6647, 14 December 1963, 12–14, at 14. The death toll which Lunn quotes has long since been abandoned. Stanley G. Payne (*The Spanish Civil* War [Cambridge: Cambridge University Press, 2012], 245) speaks of approximately 344,000 dead, including victims of war-induced famine.

44. Wells, 289.

45. Petrie, *Alfonso,* 221.

46. Noel, 212–216.

47. Theo Aronson, *Grandmama of Europe: The Crowned Descendants of Queen Victoria* (London: John Murray, 1984), 284.

48. Pilar and Chapman-Houston, 384.

49. Petrie, *Alfonso,* 227.

50. Leon Trotsky (tr. Morris Lewitt), *The Revolution in Spain* (New York City: Militant Press, 1931), 25.

51. 'The Carlist Party welcomed with great jubilation, on 14 April 1931, the overthrow of the Alfonsine monarchy and the consequent proclamation of the Second Spanish Republic [*El Partido Carlista acogió con grande jubilo, el 14 de abril de 1931, el derrocamiento de la monarquía alfonsina y la consiguiente proclamación de la II República española*].' J.C. Clemente, *El Carlismo: historia de una disidencia social, 1833–1976* (Barcelona: Editorial Ariel, 1990), 105.

52. Gerald Brenan, *The Spanish Labyrinth: An Account of the Social and Political Background of the Civil War* (Cambridge: Cambridge University Press, 1962), 204.
53. Anon., 'Death of Spanish Pretender', *Belfast Telegraph,* 3 October 1931, 6.
54. Clemente, 98. In one oration at a Madrid theatre, Vásquez de Mella 'thundered for nearly two hours against the modern Carthage, perfidious Albion': Hardinge, 258.
55. 'These burnings [...] were carried out systematically by gangs of armed men carrying cans of petrol.' Edgar Holt, *The Carlist Wars in Spain* (London: Putnam, 1967), 276.
56. Pius XI, *Dilectissima Nobis,* 3 June 1931, Dilectissima Nobis (June 3, 1933) | PIUS XI (vatican.va) (accessed 28 January 2023).'[N]either the Vatican nor its Nuncio in Madrid, Monsignor [Federico] Tedeschini, had been taken unaware by the Royal abdication and the establishment of the Republic.' Rhodes, 117.
57. Rhodes, 116.
58. John Armstrong Crow, *Spain: The Root and the Flower: An Interpretation of Spain and the Spanish People* (Berkeley: University of California Press, 1985), 310.
59. An untranslatable yet readily comprehended Italian witticism did the rounds early in Il Duce's reign when General Primo de Rivera visited Rome: '*Primo de Rivera, ma Secondo di Mussolini.*' Francesco Ricciu, *La rivoluzione spagnola* (Milan: Dall'Oglio, 1970), 94.
60. Oman, 158–159.
61. Richard Aldington*: Life for Life's Sake: A Book of Reminiscences*, 2nd edition (London: Cassell, 1968), 350–351.
62. Quoted in Scott Robert Ramsay, *Negotiating Neutrality: Anglo-Spanish Relations in the Age of Appeasement, 1931–1940*, PhD diss. (University of Leeds, 2021), 40.
63. Membership figures are hard to come by and not always reliable when available, but the Carlists are said to have 'recruited tens of thousands of Spaniards' from 1931. Martin Blinkhorn, 'Conservatism, traditionalism, and fascism in Spain, 1898–1937', in Martin Blinkhorn (ed.), *Fascists and Conservatives: The Radical Right and the Establishment in Twentieth-Century Europe* (London: Unwin Hyman, 1990), 118–137, at 126.
64. Rhodes, 119.
65. Increasingly monarchists themselves doubted Gil Robles's goodwill towards them, according to British Ambassador Sir Henry Chilton: Ramsay, 50.
66. Nine of the slain clergy – eight De La Salle brothers and one priest from the Passionist order – were canonised by John Paul II in 1999.
67. Privately some fraternisation occurred: 'in 1934 the Renovación Española leader, Goicoechea, agreed to help finance the struggling Falange [...] the understanding was that the Falange would refrain from making life difficult for the Alfonsine cause.' Blinkhorn, 130.
68. Stanley G. Payne and Jesús Palacios, *Franco: A Personal and Political Biography* (Madison: University of Wisconsin Press, 2015), 105; Roberto Villa García and Manuel Álvarez Tardío, *1936: fraude y violencia en las elecciones del Frente Popular* (Madrid: Espasa, 2017).
69. Manuel Álvarez Tardío, 'The impact of political violence during the Spanish general election of 1936', *Journal of Contemporary History* 48:3 (2013), 463–485.
70. Sir Charles Petrie, *Lords of the Inland Sea* (London: L. Dickson Ltd., 1937), 148.
71. Anon., 'Shock Police murderers: Light on Spanish assassination: four killed in a new clash', *Liverpool Daily Post*, 15 July 1936, 10. 'Dead bodies were frequently conveyed to the Municipal Cemetery by the Shock Police lorries (as was done with the body of Calvo Sotelo): the mortuary keeper was simply told that they were "dead people

found in the street". It is a strange thing that these official lorries found only the bodies of prominent people of the Right.' Luis de Fonteriz, *Red Terror in Madrid* (London: Longmans, Green and Co., 1937), 3–4.

72. Thomas Babington Macaulay, Baron Macaulay, *The History of England from the Accession of James the Second,* in *The Works of Lord Macaulay*, ed. Hannah Macaulay Trevelyan (London: Longmans, Green and Co., 1866), Vol. 2, 269.

73. Antony Beevor, *The Battle for Spain: The Spanish Civil War, 1936–1939* (London: Weidenfeld & Nicolson, 2006).

74. Burnett Bolloten, *The Spanish Civil War: Revolution and Counter-Revolution* (Chapel Hill: University of North Carolina, 1991).

75. Hugh Thomas, *The Spanish Civil War*, 3rd edition (London: Hamish Hamilton, 1977).

76. Theo Aronson, *Royal Vendetta: The Crown of Spain 1829–1965* (Indianapolis: Bobbs-Merrill Company Inc, 1966), 217.

77. Aronson, *Vendetta,* 217.

78. Aronson, *Vendetta,* 214.

79. Stanley G. Payne, *Politics and the Military in Modern Spain* (Stanford: Stanford University Press, 1967), 1.

80. Bolloten, 11.

81. Aronson, *Vendetta,* 217.

82. 'With [...] Alfonsism functioning as an admittedly influential politico-military clique, two mass parties emerged, the Carlists and the Falange. Both, in the new climate, continued their recent expansion, the Falange at a phenomenal rate.' Blinkhorn, 133.

83. Holt, 283.

84. Holt, 284.

85. Payne, *Spanish Civil War,* 191.

86. Aronson, *Vendetta,* 219.

87. Holt, 284.

88. Holt, 284–285.

89. Ignacio Romero Raizábal, *El Príncipe Requeté* (Santander, Spain: Aldus, 1965).

90. Holt, 284.

91. Georges Oudard, *Chemises noires, brunes, vertes en Espagne* (Paris: Plon, 1938), 251; Stanley G. Payne, *Falange: A History of Spanish Fascism* (Stanford, California: Stanford University Press, 1962), 191.

92. Juan Carlos Peñas Bernaldo de Quirós, *El Carlismo, la República y la Guerra Civil (1936–1937). De la conspiración a la unificación* (Madrid: Actas, 1996), 239–241.

93. Payne, *Falange,* 192.

94. Ricardo de la Cierva, *Francisco Franco: un siglo en España* (Madrid: Editora Nacional, 1973), Vol. 1, 607–611.

95. Paul Preston, 'The monarchy of Juan Carlos: from dictator's dreams to democratic realities', in Sebastian Balfour (ed.), *The Politics of Contemporary Spain* (London: Routledge, 2005), 27–38, at 29.

96. Joseph Pearce, *Bloomsbury and Beyond: The Friends and Enemies of Roy Campbell* (London: HarperCollins, 2001), 206.

97. Peter Kemp, *Mine Were of Trouble* (London: Cassell, 1957), 7.

98. Kemp, 8–9.

99. Kemp, 6.

100. Kemp, 5.

101. Kemp, 11.

102. Kemp, 31.

103. Kemp, 31.
104. Kemp, 39.
105. Kemp, 46.
106. Kemp, 46.
107. Kemp, 113.
108. Kemp, 103.
109. Kemp, 104–105.
110. Kemp, 170.
111. Kemp, 170–171.
112. Kemp, 171.
113. Kemp, 172.
114. Kemp, 173.
115. Kemp, 192.
116. Kemp, 202.
117. Kemp, 201.
118. Aronson, *Vendetta,* 216.
119. Noel, 200.
120. Rhodes, 118.
121. Noel, 255.
122. Noel, 261.
123. Noel, 260.
124. Noel, 260.
125. Sencourt, *Alfonso*, 283.
126. Anon., 'The Death of Alfonso XIII', *The Tablet* 177:5261 (18 March 1941), 184–185.
127. Viscount Templewood (Sir Samuel Hoare), *Ambassador on Special Mission* (London: Collins, 1946), 292.
128. Templewood, 293.
129. Sir Arthur Bryant, 'Our Note-Book', *Illustrated London News* 223:5982 (12 December 1953), 962.
130. Churchill noted in an April 1943 memo: 'We must not put any slight upon the Duke of Alba, who is a good friend to this country.' Quoted in Karina Urbach, 'Age of No Extremes?: The British Aristocracy Torn between the House of Lords and the Mosley Movement', in Karina Urbach (ed.), *European Aristocracies and the Radical Right, 1918–1939* (Oxford: Oxford University Press, 2007), 53–72, at 64.
131. Petrie, *Alfonso,* 70–71.
132. Churchill, 138.
133. Sir Arnold Lunn, *Spanish Rehearsal* (London: Hutchinson & Co. 1937), 43; Brian Shelmerdine, *British Representations of the Spanish Civil War* (Manchester: Manchester University Press, 2006), 177.

Chapter VI

1. William Miller, *The Ottoman Empire and Its Successors, 1801–1927* (Cambridge: Cambridge University Press, 1936), 506.
2. John Van der Kiste, *Kings of the Hellenes: The Greek Kings, 1863–1974* (Stroud, Gloucestershire: Alan Sutton, 1999), 122.
3. Van der Kiste, *Hellenes,* 123.
4. Van der Kiste, *Hellenes,* 123–124.
5. Alan Palmer, *The Royal House of Greece* (London: Weidenfeld & Nicolson, 1990), 63.

6. Petrie, *Monarchy,* 167, 171.
7. George Fyfe, 'Venizelos: A Stormy Career', *The Daily Telegraph* (12 March 1935), 12.
8. John Mavrogordato, *Modern Greece: A Chronicle and A Survey 1800–1931* (London: Macmillan, 1931), 181.
9. Slobodan G. Markovich, 'Eleftherios Venizelos, British Public Opinion and the Climax of Anglo-Hellenism (1915–1920)', *Balcanica* 49 (2018), 125–155, at 127.
10. John Nichol, *The complete poetical and dramatic works of Lord Byron, with a comprehensive outline of the life of the poet, collected from the latest and most reliable sources* (London: Macmillan, 1883), 187.
11. Markovich, 148.
12. Christopher of Greece, Prince, *Memoirs* (London: Right Book Club, 1938), 118.
13. Hugh Seton-Watson, *Eastern Europe Between the Wars 1918–1941* (Hamden, Connecticut: Archon Books, 1962), 404.
14. Sir Thomas Montgomery-Cuninghame, *Dusty Measure: A Record of Troubled Times* (London: John Murray, 1939), 186.
15. Van der Kiste, *Hellenes,* 79.
16. Van der Kiste, *Hellenes,* 114.
17. Van der Kiste, *Hellenes,* 79.
18. Van der Kiste, *Hellenes,* 99.
19. Mavrogordato, 116–117.
20. Van der Kiste, *Hellenes,* 100.
21. Palmer, *Royal House*, 60.
22. Van der Kiste, *Hellenes,* 114.
23. Van der Kiste, *Hellenes,* 114.
24. Palmer, *Royal House*, 61.
25. Christopher, 146.
26. Mavrogordato, 130.
27. Mavrogordato, 130.
28. Palmer, *Royal House,* 63.
29. Palmer, *Royal House,* 63.
30. Isaiah Friedman, *British Miscalculations: The Rise of Muslim Nationalism, 1918–1925* (New Brunswick, New Jersey: Transaction Publishers, 2012), 238.
31. Friedman, 238.
32. Richard Clogg, *A Short History of Modern Greece* (Cambridge: Cambridge University Press, 1979), 98.
33. Giles Milton, *Paradise Lost: Smyrna 1922, the Destruction of a Christian City in the Islamic World* (New York City: Basic Books, 2008), 326.
34. C.M. Woodhouse, *Modern Greece: A Short History (*London: Faber & Faber, 1986), 205, 212.
35. Anon., 'Six Greek Firing Squad Victims Go to Death Like Gentlemen', *The Buffalo News* (29 November 1922), 1.
36. John S. Koliopoulos, *Greece and the British Connection, 1935–1941* (Oxford: Clarendon Press, 1977), 7.
37. Aronson, *Grandmamma of Europe,* 247.
38. Miller, 551.
39. James Barros, 'The Greek-Bulgarian Incident of 1925: The League of Nations and the Great Powers', *Proceedings of the American Philosophical Society* 108:4 (August 1964), 354–385.
40. Miller, 553.

41. Anon., 'Dresses Nearer Ground', *The Evening News* [Harrisburg, Pennsylvania] (1 December 1925), 18; 'Our Woman Correspondent', 'Greek Premier's Decree: Imprisonment for Short Skirt Offenders', *Newcastle Daily Chronicle* (9 December 1925), 3; Myrsini Pichou and Chrysoula Kapartziani, 'Thirty centimetres above the ground: The regulation length for Greek skirts during the dictatorship of General Theodoros Pangalos, 1925–1926', *Clothing Cultures* 3:1 (January 2016), 55–74.
42. Miller, 554.
43. Anon., 'Greek Revolt Leader Still Wealthy', *The Advertiser* [Adelaide] (22 March 1935), 12.
44. Anon., *World Illiteracy At Mid-Century: A Statistical Study* (New York City: UNESCO, 1957), 42.
45. Anon., 'Greece: By The Grace of God', *Time* 21 (18 November 1935), 21–22, at 21.
46. Taki Theodoracopulos, *The Greek Upheaval: Kings, Demagogues and Bayonets* (London: Stacey International, 1976), 102.
47. Robert E. DeClerico, *Voting in America: A Reference Handbook* (Santa Barbara, California: ABC-CLIO Inc., 2004), 213.
48. Anon., 'Grace of God', 21.
49. Petrie, *Monarchy,* 174.
50. Anon., 'Sir Charles Petrie: Historian and man of letters', *The Times* (14 December 1977), 16.
51. Petrie, *Historian*, 149.
52. Christopher, 147.
53. Anon., 'Grace of God', 22.
54. Wolcott Gibbs, 'Time ... Fortune ... Life ... Luce', *The New Yorker* 12 (28 November 1936), 20–25.
55. Anon., 'Grace of God', 22.
56. Petrie, *Historian,* 148.
57. Palmer, *Royal House*, 75.
58. J.V. Kofas, *Authoritarianism in Greece: The Metaxas Regime* (Boulder, Colorado: East European Monographs, 1983), 182.
59. Palmer, *Royal House*, 75.
60. Petrie, *Monarchy,* 173.
61. Anon., 'Bomb at Cathedral: New Crime at Sofia: Many Killed and Injured', *The Daily Telegraph* (17 April 1925), 8; R.J. Crampton, *A Concise History of Bulgaria* (Cambridge: Cambridge University Press, 1997), 158.
62. Theodoracopulos, 102.
63. Clogg, 122.
64. Theodoracopulos, 103.
65. Petrie, *Historian,* 150. 'Immediately after' is an exaggeration: Condylis died on 31 January, Venizelos on 18 March.
66. Koliopoulos, 15.
67. Clogg, 134.
68. Nicholas Bethell, *The Great Betrayal: The Untold Story of Kim Philby's Biggest Coup* (London: Hodder and Stoughton, 1984), 137.
69. Charles Stuart Kennedy, 'Interview with Daniel Zachary' (The Association for Diplomatic Studies and Training Foreign Affairs Oral History Project, 3 July 1989), 70, https://tile.loc.gov/storage-services/service/mss/mfdip/2011/2011zac01/2011zac01.pdf (accessed 17 May 2023).

70. C.M. Woodhouse, *Apple of Discord: A Survey of Recent Greek Politics in Their International Setting* (London: Hutchinson, 1948), 13.
71. Anon., 'Metaxas Plans to "Discipline" All Greeks; In No Haste to Restore Civil Liberties', *The New York Times* (9 August 1936), 1; S.V. Papacosma, 'Ioannis Metaxas and the Fourth of August Dictatorship in Greece', in B.J. Fischer (ed.), *Balkan Strongmen: Dictators and Authoritarian Rulers of South-Eastern Europe* (West Lafayette, Indiana: Purdue University Press, 2007), 165–198, at 183.
72. P.J. Vatikiotis, *Popular Autocracy in Greece, 1936–41: A Political Biography of General Ioannis Metaxas* (Portland, Oregon: Frank Cass, 1998), 143.
73. Kofas, 130.
74. Clogg, 134–135.
75. Papacosma, 185.
76. Vatikiotis, 171.
77. Palmer, *Royal House*, 74.
78. Palmer, *Royal House*, 74.
79. Van der Kiste, *Hellenes*, 160–161.
80. Vatikiotis, 173.
81. Palmer, *Royal House*, 75.
82. Papacosma, 193–194.
83. Vatikiotis, 171.
84. Vatikiotis, 172.
85. Van der Kiste, *Hellenes*, 122.
86. Anon., 'Greece's King Dies, Brother Takes Throne', *Daily News* [New York] (2 April 1947), C3 and C13, at C13.
87. Van der Kiste, *Hellenes*, 158.
88. H.A.L. Fisher, *A History of Europe*, Vol. 2 (London: Eyre and Spottiswode, 1936), 734.
89. Nicholas Gage, *Eleni* (New York City: Random House, 1983), 34.
90. Andrew L. Zapantis, *Greek-Soviet Relations, 1917–1941* (Boulder, Colorado: East European Monographs, 1982), 432.
91. Zapantis, 433.
92. Zapantis, 432.
93. Papacosma, 182. Herein is another parallel with Salazar, who shared Metaxas's workaholism, and whose collapse in health during late 1946 inspired international news coverage. 'The diagnosis seems to be complete nervous and mental fatigue caused by continuous overwork. Dr Salazar used to work a regular 16-hour day. Now he has confessed to several of his closest friends that he is unable to work more than one hour a day.' Anon., 'One Man's Health Sways Portuguese Politics', *The Sydney Morning Herald* (12 October 1946), 2.
94. Vatikiotis, 214.
95. Vatikiotis, 214.
96. FDR at an electioneering speech in Boston, a month before the Electoral College rewarded him with a thumping 449–82 margin over the Republicans' Wendell Willkie: 'While I am talking to you, mothers and fathers, I give you one more assurance. I have said it before, but I shall say it again and again and again: Your boys are not going to be sent into any foreign wars.' John W. Jeffries, *A Third Term for FDR: The Election of 1940* (Lawrence: University Press of Kansas, 2017), 160.
97. Anon., 'Greece's King Dies', C3.
98. Van der Kiste, *Hellenes*, 175.
99. Van der Kiste, *Hellenes*, 175.
100. Anon., 'Greece's King Dies', C13.

Chapter VII

1. George Gordon Byron, sixth Baron Byron, *Childe Harold's Pilgrimage,* Canto 2:36 and 2:46. The 'Iskander' whom Byron's first line mentions is none other than Alexander the Great, his 'namesake' two lines later being Alexander Ypsilanti, short-lived hero of Greece's war for independence.
2. Frank Zappa and Peter Occhiogrosso, *The Real Frank Zappa Book* (New York City: Poseidon Press, 1989), 231.
3. Christopher, 146.
4. Dušan T. Bataković, 'Ahmed Bey Zogou et la Serbie: une coopération inachevée (1914–1916)', *Balcanica* 43 (2012), 169–190, at 171.
5. Joseph Swire, *King Zog's Albania* (London: Robert Hale, 1937), 202.
6. Duncan Heaton-Armstrong (ed. Gervase Belfield and Bejtullah Destani), *The Six-Month Kingdom: Albania 1914* (London: I.B. Tauris, 2005), 66–67.
7. M.W. Fodor, *Plot and Counterplot in Central Europe: Conditions South of Hitler* (Boston: Houghton Mifflin, 1937), 96.
8. Fodor, 96.
9. B.J. Fischer, *King Zog and the Struggle for Stability in Albania* (Boulder, Colorado: East European Monographs, 1984), 4.
10. Swire, 15–16.
11. Heaton-Armstrong, vi.
12. Iain Wilton, *C.B. Fry: King of Sport, England's Greatest All-Rounder, Captain of Cricket, Star Footballer and World Record Holder* (London: John Blake, 1999), 433.
13. Wilton, 303.
14. C.B. Fry, *Life Worth Living* (London: Eyre & Spottiswode, 1939), 297.
15. Wilton, 302.
16. Wilton, 320.
17. Fischer, 65.
18. Fischer, 128.
19. Faik Konitz, *Albania: The Rock Garden of Europe* (Boston: G.M. Panarity, 1957), 96.
20. Bataković, 188–189.
21. Fischer, 67.
22. Fodor, 101.
23. Eriselda Sefa, 'The Efforts of King Zog I for Nationalization of Albanian Education', *Journal of Educational and Social Research* 2:2 (May 2012), 339–346; Fischer, 62.
24. Fodor, 103.
25. Fischer, 44.
26. Fischer, 45.
27. Ramadan Marmullaku (tr. M. and B. Milosavljević), *Albania and the Albanians* (London: C. Hurst & Co., 1975), 37.
28. Fischer, 63.
29. Fischer, 129.
30. Fischer, 129.
31. Fischer, 303.
32. Fischer, 80.
33. Vandeleur Robinson, *Albania's Road to Freedom* (London: Allen & Unwin, 1941), 107.
34. Swire, 200–201.

35. Owen Pearson, *Albania and King Zog: Independence, Republic and Monarchy, 1908–1939* (London: I.B. Tauris, 2004), 216.
36. Fischer, 118.
37. Robinson, 56.
38. Fischer, 147.
39. Fischer, 144.
40. Swire, 95.
41. Miranda Vickers, *The Albanians: A Modern History* (London: I.B. Tauris, 2001), 151.
42. John McCormac, 'Blood Feud Stirred Attack on King Zog', *The New York Times* (22 February 1931), 3.
43. Jason Tomes, *King Zog: Self-Made Monarch of Albania* (Stroud, Gloucestershire: The History Press, 2003), 129.
44. Tomes, 129.
45. Tomes, 129.
46. Tomes, 131.
47. Walter Francis Stirling, *Safety Last* (London: Hollis & Carter, 1955), 157.
48. Seton-Watson, 370–371.
49. Seton-Watson, 371.
50. Fischer, 253–254.
51. Fischer, 255.
52. Fischer, 258.
53. George Orwell, *Coming Up for Air* (London: Secker & Warburg, 1948), 13, 30–31.
54. Charles Fenyvesi, *Splendor in Exile: The Ex-Majesties of Europe* (Washington DC: New Republic Books, 1979), 232.
55. Petrie, *Historian,* 142.
56. Petrie, *Historian,* 141.
57. Pearson, 386.
58. Ray Moseley, *Mussolini's Shadow: The Double Life of Count Galeazzo Ciano* (New Haven, Connecticut: Yale University Press, 1999), 51.
59. Moseley, 52.
60. Peter Neville, *Mussolini* (London: Routledge, 2004), 52.
61. Moseley, 53.
62. Moseley, 53.
63. Fischer, 280.
64. Moseley, 53.
65. Moseley, 54.
66. Julian Amery, *Approach March: A Venture in Autobiography* (London: Hutchinson, 1973), 311–312.
67. Bethell, 193; Stephen Peters, 'Kim Philby and the Albanian Mission', *The New York Times* (13 October 1985), 18.
68. Ben Macintyre, *A Spy Among Friends: Kim Philby and the Great Betrayal* (London: Bloomsbury, 2014), 281.
69. Anon., 'Information Report: Meeting of Representatives of King Zog and Marshal Tito', MEETING OF REPRESENTATIVES OF KING ZOG AND MARSHAL TITO (cia.gov) (accessed 12 May 2023).
70. Blendi Fevziu (tr. Majlinda Nishku), *Enver Hoxha: The Iron Fist of Albania* (London: I.B. Tauris, 2016), 3.
71. Bethell, 31.

Epilogue

1. Anon., 'Three Dead in Clash at Liège', *The Manchester Guardian* (31 July 1950), 5.
2. W.J.P. Curley, *Monarchs in Waiting* (London: Hutchinson, 1975), 60.
3. Curley, 35.
4. Anon., 'Unverzichtbare Kaiserkrone', *Der Spiegel* (17 November 1968), UNVERZICHTBARE KAISERKRONE – DER SPIEGEL (accessed 26 May 2023).
5. John Ardagh, *Germany and the Germans* (London: Penguin Books, 1991), 178.
6. Brook-Shepherd, *Habsburg*, 298.
7. Otto von Habsburg, 'Putin ist ein eiskälter Tecknokrat', *Suddeutsche Zeitung* (5 November 2005), Interview mit Otto von Habsburg – "Putin ist ein eiskalter Technokrat" – Politik – SZ.de (sueddeutsche.de) (accessed 26 May 2023).
8. Hélène de Lauzun, 'French Monarchists Gather in Paris After Court Reversed Ban', *The European Conservative* (16 May 2023), https://europeanconservative.com/articles/news/french-monarchists-gather-in-paris-after-court-reversed-ban/ (accessed 28 June 2023).
9. Fenyvesi, 123.
10. Fenyvesi, 128.
11. Fenyvesi, 128.
12. Fenyvesi, 128.
13. Fenyvesi, 132.
14. Cote Villar, 'Sesante años de la misterioso muerte del hermano del Rey', *El Mundo* (29 March 2016), Sesenta años de la misteriosa muerte del hermano del Rey | loc | EL MUNDO (accessed 28 June 2023).
15. Fenyvesi, 229–230.
16. An ancient joke, of unknown provenance, among spies deals with Indonesia's 1965–1966 massacres, carried out in the hope of removing from power President Sukarno. These massacres, on a conservative estimate, resulted in a death toll of 400,000. The joke runs: 'They must have been a CIA operation, because they killed almost everyone in the country except their intended target.'
17. Fenyvesi, 230. Leka's spouse Susan, *née* Cullen-Ward, was among the few Australians ever to enter a European royal house: born in Sydney, she came from a prominent family of Queensland farmers.
18. Fenyvesi, 237.
19. Fenyvesi, 244.
20. Richard J. Evans, 'The New Nationalism and the Old History: Perspective on the West German *Historikerstreit*', *Journal of Modern History*, 59 (December 1987), 761–797.
21. Lunn, 'Alfonso', 14.
22. Gillian Tett, 'Can you win an election without digital skullduggery?', *The Financial Times* (10 January 2020), Subscribe to read | Financial Times (ft.com) (accessed 7 May 2023).
23. Gur Megiddo and Omer Benjakob, 'The people who kill the truth', *Haaretz* (16 November 2022). 'The people who kill the truth' (accessed 9 May 2023).
24. Count Nikolai Tolstoy, 'Consider a Monarchy, America', *The New York Times* (6 November 2016), 11.
25. C.S. Lewis, 'Equality', *The Spectator* 171:6009 (27 August 1943), 192.
26. Clive James, *Charles Charming's Challenges on his Pathway to the Throne* (London: Jonathan Cape, 1981), 102–103.

Bibliography

Aldington: Richard, *Life for Life's Sake: A Book of Reminiscences*, 2nd edition. London: Cassell, 1968.

Amal, Oscar L., *Ambivalent Alliance: The Catholic Church and the Action Française, 1899–1939*. Pittsburgh: University of Pittsburgh Press, 1985.

Amery, Julian, *Approach March: A Venture in Autobiography*. London: Hutchinson, 1973.

Anon., 'Austria: Double-Eagle?', *Time* 15:24 (16 June 1930), 28–29.

Anon., 'Bomb at Cathedral: New Crime at Sofia: Many Killed and Injured', *The Daily Telegraph* (17 April 1925), 8.

Anon., 'Death of Spanish Pretender', *Belfast Telegraph* (3 October 1931), 6.

Anon., 'Dresses Nearer Ground', *The Evening News* [Harrisburg, Pennsylvania] (1 December 1925), 18;

Anon., 'Ex-King Manuel, Who Lost Throne for Love, Dies: Former Ruler of Portugal Choked to Death', *Chicago Tribune* (3 July 1932), 9.

Anon., 'Four Shots Were Fired in Vienna Parliament', *The Brantford Daily Expositor* [Brantford, Ontario] (5 October 1911), 1.

Anon., 'Germany: Monarchist Fools?', *Time* 23:5 (29 January 1934), 20.

Anon., 'Greece: By the Grace of God', *Time* 21 (18 November 1935), 21–22.

Anon., 'Greece's King Dies, Brother Takes Throne', *Daily News* [New York] (2 April 1947), C3 and C13.

Anon., 'Greek Revolt Leader Still Wealthy', *The Advertiser* [Adelaide] (22 March 1935), 12.

Anon., 'Information Report: Meeting of Representatives of King Zog and Marshal Tito', MEETING OF REPRESENTATIVES OF KING ZOG AND MARSHAL TITO (cia.gov) (accessed 12 May 2023).

Anon., 'Kaiser's Youngest Son, Joachim, Shoots Himself', *The New York Times* (19 July 1920), 1 and 3.

Anon., 'King of Portugal and His Heir Assassinated', *The New York Times* (2 February 1908), 1.

Anon., 'Metaxas Plans to "Discipline" All Greeks; In No Haste to Restore Civil Liberties', *The New York Times* (9 August 1936), 1.

Anon., 'Milestones', *Time* 19:9 (29 February 1932), 48.

Anon., 'Monarchist Hopes Rise in Hungary', *Gettysburg Times* [Pennsylvania] (7 October 1936), 4.

Anon., 'One Man's Health Sways Portuguese Politics', *The Sydney Morning Herald* (12 October 1946), 2.

Anon., 'Proclaimed King, Manuel Resents It: Protests to Portuguese Government Against Revolt Started in His Behalf', *The New York Times* (21 January 1919), 9.

Anon., 'Royalist plot misfires: Bavaria turns down scheme to crown Rupprecht', *The Manchester Guardian* (10 November 1925), 20.

Anon., 'Shock Police murderers: Light on Spanish assassination: four killed in a new clash', *Liverpool Daily Post* (15 July 1936), 10. '

Anon., 'Sir Charles Petrie: Historian and man of letters', *The Times* (14 December 1977), 16.

Anon., 'Six Greek Firing Squad Victims Go to Death Like Gentlemen', *The Buffalo News* (29 November 1922), 1.

Anon., 'Spanish Premier murdered', *Evening Standard* (9 March 1921), 1–2.

Anon., 'Starvation Diet in Vienna', *The Western Argus* [Kalgoorlie, Western Australia] (9 March 1920), 1.

Anon., 'Tartarin Surrenders', *The New York Times* (15 June 1927), 26.

Anon., 'The Death of Alfonso XIII', *The Tablet* 177:5261 (18 March 1941), 184–185.

Anon., 'Three Dead in Clash at Liège', *The Manchester Guardian* (31 July 1950), 5.

Anon., 'Tragedy in Spain: The Prime Minister Murdered', *The Advertiser* [Adelaide] (14 November 1912), 9.

Anon., Anon., 'The Late King of Portugal as Artist: A Portrait Study of the Painter King, the Murdered Carlos of Portugal', *Illustrated London News* 132:3590 (8 February 1908), 197.

Anon., *The Real Crown Prince: A Record and an Indictment*. London: George Newnes, 1916.

Anon., 'Unverzichtbare Kaiserkrone', *Der Spiegel* (17 November 1968), UNVERZICHTBARE KAISERKRONE – DER SPIEGEL (accessed 26 May 2023).

Anon., *World Illiteracy At Mid-Century: A Statistical Study*. New York City: UNESCO, 1957.

Arafe, T.W., *The Development and Character of the Nazi Political Machine, 1928–1930, and the NSDAP Electoral Breakthrough*, PhD diss., Louisiana State University (Baton Rouge), 1976.

Ardagh, John, *Germany and the Germans*. London: Penguin Books, 1991.

Arendt, Hannah, *Crises of the Republic: Lying in Politics; Civil Disobedience; On Violence; Thoughts on Politics and Revolution*. New York City: Harcourt Brace Jovanovich, 1972.

Aron, Robert, *Histoire de l'Épuration*, Vol. 2. Paris: Fayard, 1969.

Aronson, Theo, *Grandmama of Europe: The Crowned Descendants of Queen Victoria*. London: John Murray, 1984.

Aronson, Theo, *Royal Vendetta: The Crown of Spain 1829–1965*. Indianapolis: Bobbs-Merrill Company Inc, 1966.

Bagger, Eugene, *Francis Joseph: Emperor of Austria, King of Hungary*. New York City: G.P. Putnam's Sons, 1927.

Bainville, Jacques, *Les Conséquences Politiques de la Paix*, Paris: Fayard, 1920.

Balfour, Michael, *The Kaiser and His Times*. London: Cresset Press, 1964.

Baptista, Jacinto, *O Cinco de Outubro*. Lisbon: Arcádia, 1965.

Barea, Ilsa, *Vienna: Legend and Reality*. London: Secker & Warburg, 1966.

Barman, Roderick J., *Citizen Emperor: Pedro II and the Making of Brazil*. Stanford, California: Stanford University Press, 1999.

Barros, James, 'The Greek-Bulgarian Incident of 1925: The League of Nations and the Great Powers', *Proceedings of the American Philosophical Society* 108:4 (August 1964), 354–385.

Bataković, Dušan T., 'Ahmed Bey Zogou et la Serbie: une coopération inachevée (1914–1916)', *Balcanica* 43 (2012), 169–190.

Beck, Hermann, *The Fateful Alliance: German Conservatives and Nazis in 1933: The Machtergreifung in a New Light*. Oxford: Berghahn Books, 2009.

Becker, Winfried, 'The Nazi Seizure of Power in Bavaria and the Demise of the Bavarian People's Party', in Hermann Beck and Larry Eugene Jones (eds.), *From Weimar to Hitler: Studies in the Dissolution of the Weimar Republic and the Establishment of the Third Reich, 1932–1934*. Oxford: Berghan Books, 2018.

Beéche, Arturo E., *The November 1918 Revolution: The Fall of the German Monarchies*. London: Eurohistory and Kensington House Books, 2021.

Beevor, Antony, *The Battle for Spain: The Spanish Civil War, 1936–1939*. London: Weidenfeld & Nicolson, 2006.

Belloc, Hilaire, *The House of Commons and Monarchy*. London: George Allen & Unwin, 1920.

Ben-Ami, Shlomo, *Fascism from Above: The Dictatorship of Primo de Rivera in Spain, 1923–1930*. Oxford: Clarendon Press, 1983.

Benton, Russell E., *The Downfall of a King: Dom Manuel II of Portugal*. Washington DC: University Press of America, 1977.

Bern, Stéphane, *Eu, Amélia, Última Rainha de Portugal*. Oporto: Livraria Civilização Editora, 1999.

Bernaldo de Quirós, Juan Carlos Peñas, *El Carlismo, la República y la Guerra Civil (1936–1937). De la conspiración a la unificación*. Madrid: Actas, 1996.

Bernardi, Peter J., SJ, 'Louis Cardinal Billot SJ (1846–1931): Thomist, Anti-Modernist, Integralist', *Journal of Jesuit Studies* 8 (2021), 585–616.

Bethell, Nicholas, *The Great Betrayal: The Untold Story of Kim Philby's Biggest Coup*. London: Hodder and Stoughton, 1984.

Bierão, Caetano (tr. Frank R. Holliday), *A Short History of Portugal*. Lisbon: Edições Panorama, 1960.

Blair, Eric Arthur ('George Orwell'), 'A Farthing Newspaper', *G.K.'s Weekly* 198: 8 (29 December 1928), 247–249.

Bled, Jean-Paul (tr. Teresa Bridgeman), *Franz Joseph*. London: Blackwell, 1992.

Blinkhorn, Martin, 'Conservatism, traditionalism, and fascism in Spain, 1898–1937', in Martin Blinkhorn (ed.), *Fascists and Conservatives: The Radical Right and the Establishment in Twentieth-Century Europe*. London: Unwin Hyman, 1990.

Boff, Jonathan, *Haig's Enemy: Crown Prince Rupprecht and Germany's War on the Western Front*. Oxford: Oxford University Press, 2018.

Bogle, James, and Joanna Bogle, *A Heart For Europe* Leominster, Herefordshire: Gracewing Books, 1993.

Bolloten, Burnett, *The Spanish Civil War: Revolution and Counter-Revolution*. Chapel Hill: University of North Carolina, 1991.

Bovill, E.W., *The Battle of Alcazar: An Account of the Defeat of Don Sebastian of Portugal at El-Ksar el-Kebir*. London: Batchworth, 1952.

Bragança Cunha, Vicente de, *Eight Centuries of Portuguese Monarchy*. New York City: John Pott, 1911.

Bragança Cunha, Vicente de, *Revolutionary Portugal 1910–1936*. London: James Clarke, 1937.

Brenan, Gerald, *The Spanish Labyrinth: An Account of the Social and Political Background of the Civil War*. Cambridge: Cambridge University Press, 1962.

Brook-Shepherd, Gordon, *Dollfuss*. London: Macmillan, 1961.

Brook-Shepherd, Gordon, *The Last Empress: The Life and Times of Zita of Austria-Hungary, 1892–1989*. London: HarperCollins, 1991.

Brook-Shepherd, Gordon, *The Last Habsburg*. London: Weidenfeld & Nicolson, 1968.

Bryant, Sir Arthur, 'Our Note-Book', *Illustrated London News* 223:5982 (12 December 1953), 962.

Bullock, Alan, *Hitler: A Study in Tyranny*. New York City: Bantam Books, 1961.

Burleigh, Michael, *The Third Reich: A New History*. London: Macmillan, 2000.

'Candide', 'Doit-on le dire?', *Candide* (16 September 1926), 1.

Casper, Hunter, *Modern Monarchy*. Philadelphia: Alpha, 2021.

Carsten, F.L., *The Reichswehr and Politics, 1918 to 1933*. Oxford: Clarendon Press, 1966.

Cavalheiro, Rodrigues (ed.), *D. Manuel II e João Franco: Correspondência Inédita*. Lisbon: Biblioteca do Pensamento Politico, 1970.

Cecil, Lamar, *Wilhelm II: Emperor and Exile*. Chapel Hill: University of North Carolina Press, 1989.

Chesterton, G.K., 'King George V: "A Patriotic Ruler and a Public Servant"', *Illustrated London News* 188 (25 January 1936), 5049.

Chesterton, G.K., *Orthodoxy*. London: Sheed & Ward, 1939.

Christopher of Greece, Prince, *Memoirs*. London: Right Book Club, 1938.

Churchill, Randolph, *Winston Spencer Churchill 1901–1914*, Vol. 2. Boston: Houghton Mifflin, 1967.

Churchill, Sir Winston, *Great Contemporaries*. London: Mandarin Paperbacks, 1990.

Churchill, Sir Winston, *The Second World War: Triumph and Tragedy*. New York City: Houghton Mifflin Harcourt, 1948.

Cierva, Ricardo de la, *Francisco Franco: un siglo en España*, Vol. 1. Madrid: Editora Nacional, 1973), Vol. 1.

Clemente, J.C., *El Carlismo: historia de una disidencia social, 1833–1976*. Barcelona: Editorial Ariel, 1990.

Clogg, Richard, *A Short History of Modern Greece*. Cambridge: Cambridge University Press, 1979), 98.

Collier, William Miller, *At the Court of His Catholic Majesty*. Chicago: A.C. McClurg & Co., 1912.

Cooke, Alistair, *Six Men*. Harmondsworth, Middlesex: Penguin Books, 1978.

Corpechot, Lucien, *Memories of Queen Amélie of Portugal*. London: Eveleigh Nash, 1915.

Correia de Sá, J. M. do Espirito Santo de Almeida, Marquês do Lavradio, *Portugal em África Depois de 1851: Subsídios para a História*. Lisbon: Divisão de Publicações e Biblioteca, Agência Geral das Colónias, 1936.

Costa Pinto, António, 'Muitas Crises, Poucos Compromissos: A Queda da Primeira Republica', *Penélope* 19–20, 1998, 43–70.

Costa, Afonso, *Correspondência politica de Afonso Costa, 1896–1910*. Lisbon: Estampa, 1982.

Crampton, R.J., *A Concise History of Bulgaria*. Cambridge: Cambridge University Press, 1997.

Crankshaw, Edward, *The Fall of the House of Habsburg*. London: Sphere Books, 1970.

Crow, John Armstrong, *Spain: The Root and the Flower: An Interpretation of Spain and the Spanish People*. Berkeley: University of California Press, 1985.

Curley, W.J.P., *Monarchs in Waiting*. London: Hutchinson, 1975.

Curtis, Michael, *Three Against the Third Republic: Sorel, Barrès, and Maurras*. Princeton, New Jersey: Princeton University Press, 1959), 24.

Cusack, Tricia (ed.), *Art and Identity at the Water's Edge*. Farnham, Surrey: Ashgate Publishing, 2012.

Daudet, Léon, 'A French Royalist Speaks', *The Evening Standard* (1 February 1934), 7.

Daudet, Léon, *Fantômes et vivants: souvenirs des milieux littéraires, politiques, artistiques et médicaux de 1880 à 1905*. Paris: Nouvelle Librairie Nationale, 1914.

Daudet, Léon, and Maurras, Charles, 'L'Assassinat de Philippe Daudet', *L'Action Française* 336 (2 December 1923), 1.

de la Torre Gomez, Hipolito, *El imperio del Rey: Alfonso XIII, Portugal y los ingleses (1907–1916)*. Mérida, Spain: Editora Regional de Extremadura, 2002.

DeClerico, Robert E., *Voting in America: A Reference Handbook*. Santa Barbara, California: ABC-CLIO Inc., 2004.

Dorpalen, Andreas. *Hindenburg and the Weimar Republic*. Princeton, New Jersey: Princeton University Press, 1964.

Dow, James Elstone, 'The German National People's Party: In the Cause of Monarchy', *Continuity* 3 (Fall 1981), 37–50.

Dumont-Wilden, L., *Le Crépuscule des Maîtres*. Brussels: La Renaissance du Livre, 1947.

Edmonds, J.E., 'Military Operations France and Belgium, 1916: Sir Douglas Haig's Command to the 1st July: Battle of the Somme', *History of the Great War Based on Official Documents by Direction of the Historical Section of the Committee of Imperial Defence, Vol. 1,* London: Macmillan, 1932.

Edward, Duke of Windsor, *A King's Story: Memoirs of HRH the Duke of Windsor.* London: Cassell, 1951.

Egerton, F.C.C., *Salazar: Rebuilder of Portugal*. London: Hodder & Stoughton, 1943.

Ernst, Otto (tr. H.J. Stenning), *Kings in Exile*. London: Jarrolds, 1933.

Erskine, B.S., *Twenty-Nine Years: The Reign of King Alfonso XIII of Spain: An Intimate and Authorized Life Story.* London: Hutchinson, 1931.

'Etychus and his Kin', 'Dear Slogan-Lovers', *Christianity Today* 11:21 (21 July 1967), 20.

Evans, Richard J., 'The New Nationalism and the Old History: Perspective on the West German *Historikerstreit*', *Journal of Modern History* 59 (December 1987), 761–797.

Fenyvesi, Charles, *Splendor in Exile: The Ex-Majesties of Europe*. Washington DC: New Republic Books, 1979.

Fernández de la Reguera, Ricardo, and Susana March, *La dictadura: El régimen civil, 1926–1930*. Barcelona: Editorial Planeta, 1969.

Ferreira Coimbra, Artur, *Paiva Couceiro e a contra-revolução monárquica 1910–1919,* MA diss., University of Minho (Portugal), 2000.

Ferro, António (tr. H. de Barros Gomes and John Gibbons), *Salazar: Portugal and Her Leader.* London: Faber & Faber, 1939.

Fevziu, Blendi (tr. Majlinda Nishku), *Enver Hoxha: The Iron Fist of Albania*. London: I.B. Tauris, 2016.

Fischer, B.J., *King Zog and the Struggle for Stability in Albania*. Boulder, Colorado: East European Monographs, 1984.

Fisher, H.A.L., *A History of Europe,* Vol. 2. London: Eyre and Spottiswode, 1936.

FitzGerald, Desmond, *Memoirs of Desmond FitzGerald, 1913–1916.* London: Routledge & Kegan Paul, 1968.

Fodor, M.W., *Plot and Counterplot in Central Europe: Conditions South of Hitler*. Boston: Houghton Mifflin, 1937.

Foley, Liam, Abdication of the German Monarchies. Part I | European Royal History (wordpress.com) (accessed 1 March 2023).

Fonteriz, Luis de, *Red Terror in Madrid*. London: Longmans, Green and Co., 1937.

Friedman, Isaiah, *British Miscalculations: The Rise of Muslim Nationalism, 1918–1925*. New Brunswick, New Jersey: Transaction Publishers, 2012.

Fry, C.B., *Life Worth Living*. London: Eyre & Spottiswode, 1939.

Fyfe, George, 'Venizelos: A Stormy Career', *The Daily Telegraph* (12 March 1935), 12.

Gage, Nicholas, *Eleni*. New York City: Random House, 1983.

Gallagher, Tom, *Portugal: A Twentieth-Century Interpretation*. Manchester: Manchester University Press, 1983.

Garnett, Robert S., Jr., *Lion, Eagle, and Swastika: Bavarian Monarchism in Weimar Germany, 1918–1933*. New York City: Garland Publishing Inc., 1991.

Gibbs, Wolcott, 'Time ... Fortune ... Life ... Luce', *The New Yorker* 12 (28 November 1936), 20–25.

Gildea, Robert, *France Since 1945*. Oxford: Oxford University Press, 1996.

Gomes da Costa, Manuel de Oliveira, *Memórias*. Lisbon: Livraria Clássica, 1930.

Gomes Sousa Carvalho, Susana Adelina Sinfrónio, *Nationalism and Régime Overthrow in Early Twentieth-Century Portugal*, PhD diss., London School of Economics, 2012.

Gordon, Harold J., *Hitler and the Beer-Hall Putsch*. Princeton, New Jersey: Princeton University Press, 1972.

Gottfried, Paul E., *Revisions and Dissents: Essays*. De Kalb: Northern Illinois University Press, 2017.

Gwynn, Denis, *The Catholic Reaction in France*. New York City: Macmillan, 1924.

Habsburg, Otto von, 'Putin ist ein eiskälter Tecknokrat', *Suddeutsche Zeitung* (5 November 2005), Interview mit Otto von Habsburg – "Putin ist ein eiskalter Technokrat" – Politik – SZ.de (sueddeutsche.de) (accessed 26 May 2023).

Harding, James, *The Astonishing Adventure of General Boulanger*. New York City: Scribner, 1971), xi.

Hardinge, Sir Arthur Henry, *A Diplomatist in Europe*. London: Jonathan Cape, 1927.

Harrault, Marie-Noële, 'La rupture de Bernanos avec Maurras', *La Revue des Lettres modernes* 10 (1969), 189–207.

Hašek, Jaroslav (tr. Paul Selver), *The Good Soldier Schweik*. Harmondsworth, Middlesesx: Penguin Books, 1939.

Heaton-Armstrong, Duncan (ed. Gervase Belfield and Bejtullah Destani), *The Six-Month Kingdom: Albania 1914*. London: I.B. Tauris, 2005.

Hecht, Ben, *A Child of the Century*. New York City: Simon & Schuster, 1954.

Heideking, Jürgen, 'Das Ende der Sanktionspolitik: Die alliierten Mächte und die Rückkehr des deutschen Kronprinzen im November 1923', *Francia* 7 (1979), 365–400.

Henson, Andrew Brian, *Before the Seizure of Power: American and British Press Coverage of National Socialism, 1922 to 1933*, MA diss., Clemson University (Clemson, South Carolina), 2007.

Hertog, Johan den, and Samuël Kruizinga (eds.), *Caught in the Middle: Neutrals, Neutrality, and the First World War*. Amsterdam: Amsterdam University Press, 2012.

Höbelt, Lothar, 'Nostalgic Agnostics: Austrian Aristocrats and Politics, 1918–1938', in Karina Urbach (ed.), *European Aristocracies and the Radical Right 1918–1939* (Oxford: Oxford University Press, 2007), 161–186.

Holt, Edgar, *The Carlist Wars in Spain*. London: Putnam, 1967.

Huguenin, François, *L'Action Française: une histoire intellectuelle*. Paris: Éditions Perrin, 1998.

Jackson, Julian, *A Certain Idea of France: The Life of Charles de Gaulle*. London: Allen Lane, 2018.

Jackson, Julian, *France: The Dark Years, 1940–1944*. Oxford: Oxford University Press, 2003.

James, Clive, *Charles Charming's Challenges on his Pathway to the Throne*. London: Jonathan Cape, 1981.

James, Clive, 'A Class Apart?', *Times Literary Supplement* 4417 (27 November-3 December 1987), 1327–1329.

Jeffries, John W., *A Third Term for FDR: The Election of 1940*. Lawrence: University Press of Kansas, 2017.

Jenkins, Brian, *Lord Lyons: A Diplomat in an Age of Nationalism and War* (Montreal: McGill-Queens University Press, 2014), 371.

Jonas, Klaus W. (tr. Charles W. Bangert), *The Life of Crown Prince William*. London: Routledge & Kegan Paul, 1961.

Junqeiro, Guerra, *Horas de Combate*. Oporto: Livraria Chardron, 1924.

Kaufmann, Walter H., *Monarchism in the Weimar Republic*. New York City: Bookman Associates, 1953.

Kemp, Peter, *Mine Were Of Trouble*. London: Cassell, 1957.

Kennedy, Charles Stuart, 'Interview with Daniel Zachary' (The Association for Diplomatic Studies and Training Foreign Affairs Oral History Project, 3 July 1989), 70, https://tile.loc.gov/storage-services/service/mss/mfdip/2011/2011zac01/2011zac01.pdf (accessed 17 May 2023).

Kerr, Jean, *Please Don't Eat The Daisies*. New York City: Doubleday, 1957.

Kershaw, Alister, *An Introduction to Léon Daudet, with a Selection from his Memoirs*. Francestown, New Hampshire: Typographeum, 1988.

Kershaw, Sir Ian, *Hitler, 1889–1936: Hubris*. London: Penguin, 1998.

Kjelling, Anne C., *The Nobel Peace Prize and the Laureates: The Meaning and Acceptance of the Nobel Peace Prize in the Prize Winners' Countries*. Frankfurt: Peter Lang, 1994.

Knoblaugh, Edward H., *Correspondent in Spain*. London: Sheed & Ward, 1937.

Koepp, Roy G., 'Gustav von Kahr and the Emergence of the Radical Right in Bavaria', *The Historian* 77:4 (Winter 2015), 740–763.

Kofas, J.V., *Authoritarianism in Greece: The Metaxas Regime*. Boulder, Colorado: East European Monographs, 1983), 182.

Koliopoulos, John S., *Greece and the British Connection, 1935–1941*. Oxford: Clarendon Press, 1977.

Konitz, Faik, *Albania: The Rock Garden of Europe*. Boston: G.M. Panarity, 1957.

Kubinyi, Victor von, *Franz Josef I, Emperor-King: A Character Sketch*. South Bend, Indiana: Hibbert Print Co., 1917.

Lange, Raymond, 'The Right Minority in France', *The Atlantic* 158 (July 1936), 109–114.

Lauzun, Hélène de, 'French Monarchists Gather in Paris After Court Reversed Ban', *The European Conservative* (16 May 2023), https://europeanconservative.com/articles/news/french-monarchists-gather-in-paris-after-court-reversed-ban/ (accessed 28 June 2023).

Lee, Sir Sidney, *King Edward VII: A Biography*, Vol. 2. London: Macmillan, 1927.

Lendvai, Paul, (tr. Ann Major), *The Hungarians: A Thousand Years of Victory in Defeat*. Princeton, New Jersey: Princeton University Press, 2003.

Lenin, V.I., 'The Happening to the King of Portugal', *Proletary*, 19 February 1908, reprinted in V.I. Lenin (tr. B. Isaacs), *Collected Works*, Vol. 13 (Moscow: Progress Publishers, 1972), 470–474.

Leopold, John A., *Alfred Hugenberg: The Radical Nationalist Campaign Against the Weimar Republic*. New Haven, Connecticut: Yale University Press, 1977.

Leslie, Sir Shane, 'The Pope and French Royalist Protagonists', *The Catholic Advocate* [Brisbane] (17 May 1928), 27.

Lewis, C.S., 'Equality', *The Spectator* 171:6009 (27 August 1943), 192.

Livermore, H. V., *A New History of Portugal*. Cambridge: Cambridge University Press, 1976.

Lochner, Louis P., *What About Germany?* New York City: Dodd, Mead & Co., 1942.

Longo, James, *Hitler and the Habsburgs: The Führer's Vendetta Against the Austrian Royals*. New York City: Diversion Books, 2018.

Longo, James, *Isabel Orléans-Bragança: The Brazilian Princess Who Freed the Slaves*. Jefferson, North Carolina: McFarland & Company, 2008.

Louis Ferdinand of Prussia, Prince, *The Rebel Prince: Memoirs.* Chicago: Regnery, 1952.

Lukacs, John, *The Hitler of History.* New York City: Knopf, 1997.

Lunn, Sir Arnold, 'King Alfonso of Spain', *The Tablet* 217:6647 (14 December 1963), 12–14.

Lunn, Sir Arnold, *Spanish Rehearsal.* London: Hutchinson & Co., 1937.

Macaulay, Neill, *Dom Pedro: The Struggle for Liberty in Brazil and Portugal, 1798–1834.* Durham, North Carolina: Duke University Press, 1986.

Macaulay, Thomas Babington, Baron Macaulay, *The History of England from the Accession of James the Second,* in Hannah Macaulay Trevelyan (ed.), *The Works of Lord Macaulay.* London: Longmans, Green and Co., 1866.

MacDonogh, Giles, *The Last Kaiser: William the Impetuous.* London: Weidenfeld & Nicolson, 2000.

Macintyre, Ben, *A Spy Among Friends: Kim Philby and the Great Betrayal.* London: Bloomsbury, 2014.

Madariaga, Salvador de, *Spain.* London: Jonathan Cape, 1942.

Maechling, Charles, 'The Sixtus Affair', *History Today* 23:11 (November 1973), 757–765.

Malheiro Dias, Carlos, *O Estado Actual da Causa Monarchica.* Lisbon: José Bastos, 1913.

Manchester, William, *The Arms of Krupp 1587–1968.* New York City: Bantam Books.

Markovich, Slobodan G., 'Eleftherios Venizelos, British Public Opinion and the Climax of Anglo-Hellenism (1915–1920)', *Balcanica* 49 (2018), 125–155.

Marks, Sally, '"My Name Is Ozymandias": The Kaiser in Exile', *Central European History* 16:2 (June 1983), 122–170.

Marmullaku,.Ramadan (tr. M. and B. Milosavljević), *Albania and the Albanians.* London: C. Hurst & Co., 1975.

Massis, Henri, *Maurras et notre temps.* Paris: Plon, 1964.

Maurras, Charles, *Enquête sur la monarchie, 1900–1909.* Paris: Nouvelle Librairie Nationale, 1910.

Maurras, Charles, 'La Politique', *L'Action Française* 137 (16 May 1936), 1.

Maurras, Charles, 'La Politique', *L'Action Française* 99 (9 April 1935), 1.

Maurras, Charles, 'Sur le nom de socialiste', *L'Action Française* 34 (15 November 1900), 859–867.

Maurras, Charles, 'Une sottise: l'hitlérisme', *L'Action Française* 84 (25 March 1938), 1.

Maurras, Charles, *Au signe de Flore: souvenirs de vie politique, l'affaire Dreyfus et l'Action Française.* Paris: B. Grasset, 1933.

Maurras, Charles, *Chemins de Paradis.* Paris: Calmette-Levy, 1895.

Mavrogordato, John, *Modern Greece: A Chronicle and A Survey 1800–1931.* London: Macmillan, 1931), 181.

Mayordomo, Joaquín, 'Annual: horror, masacre y olvido', *El País* (22 March 2016), 26.

McCormac, John, 'Blood Feud Stirred Attack on King Zog', *The New York Times* (22 February 1931), 3.

McCullagh, Francis, 'Portugal: The Republican Nightmare', *The Nineteenth Century and After* (January 1914), 148–170.

McCullagh, Francis, 'Some Causes of the Portuguese Revolution', *The Nineteenth Century and After,* 68 (November 1910), 931–944.

McMeekin, Sean, *The Red Millionaire: A Political Biography of Willi Münzenberg, Moscow's Secret Propaganda Tsar in the West.* New Haven, Connecticut: Yale University Press, 2003.

Megiddo, Gur, and Omer Benjakob, 'The people who kill the truth', *Haaretz* (16 November 2022), "The people who kill the truth" (accessed 9 May 2023).

Mencken, H.L. 'Exile at Wieringen says he longs for day when he can assist Germany: Heir to former German throne declares he finds it "hard to stand by without taking a hand"', *Baltimore Sun* (11 October 1922), 1–2.

Menczer, Béla, 'Béla Kun and the Hungarian Revolution of 1919', *History Today* 19:5 (May 1969), 299–309.

Menczer, Béla, 'The Habsburg Restoration: Hungary in 1921', *History Today* 22:2 (February 1972), 128–135.

Millard, Frank, *The Palace and the Bunker: Royal Resistance to Hitler*. Stroud, Gloucestershire: The History Press, 2012,

Miller, William, *The Ottoman Empire and Its Successors, 1801–1927*. Cambridge: Cambridge University Press, 1936.

Milton, Giles, *Paradise Lost: Smyrna 1922, the Destruction of a Christian City in the Islamic World*. New York City: Basic Books, 2008.

Molnar, Thomas, 'Maurras, Charles, Shaper of an Age', *Modern Age* 41:4 (Fall 1999), 337–342.

Montgomery-Cuninghame, Sir Thomas, *Dusty Measure: A Record of Troubled Times*. London: John Murray, 1939.

Moseley, Ray, *Mussolini's Shadow: The Double Life of Count Galeazzo Ciano*. New Haven, Connecticut: Yale University Press, 1999.

Muller, J.Z., *Capitalism and the Jews*. Princeton, New Jersey: Princeton University Press, 2010.

Murphy, Francis X., *The Papacy Today*. New York City: Macmillan, 1981.

Nettl, J.D., *Rosa Luxemburg*. London: Oxford University Press, 1966.

Neville, Peter, *Mussolini*. London: Routledge, 2004.

Nichol, John, *The complete poetical and dramatic works of Lord Byron, with a comprehensive outline of the life of the poet, collected from the latest and most reliable sources*. London: Macmillan, 1883.

Nicolson, Sir Harold, *King George the Fifth: His Life and Reign*. London: Pan Books, 1967.

Noel, Gerard, *Ena: Spain's English Queen*. London: Constable, 1984.

Nogueira, Franco, *Salazar: estudo biográfico,* Vol. 4. Coimbra: Atlántida Editora, 1980.

Nohlen, Dieter, and Philip Stoever, *Elections in Europe: A Data Handbook* (Baden-Baden: Nomos Publishers, 2010.

Nowell, Charles E., *A History of Portugal*. Princeton: Van Nostrand, 1958.

Nowell, Charles E., *The Rose-Coloured Map: Portugal's Attempt to Build an African Empire from the Atlantic to the Indian Ocean*. Lisbon: Junta de Investigações Científicas do Ultramar, 1982.

Oberacker, Carlos H., *A Imperatriz Leopoldina: sua vida e sua época, ensaio de uma biografia.* Rio de Janeiro: Conselho Federal de Cultura, 1973.

Olden, Rudolf (tr. R.T. Clark), *Stresemann*. London: Methuen, 1930.

Oliveira Marques, A. H. De, *History of Portugal, Vol. II: From Empire to Corporate State*. New York City: Columbia University Press, 1972.

Oman, Sir Charles, *Things I Have Seen*. London: Methuen, 1933.

Opello, Walter C., *Portugal: From Monarchy to Pluralist Democracy*. Boulder, Colorado: Westview Press, 1991.

Ortega y Gasset, José, 'El error Berenguer', *El Sol* (15 November 1930), 1.

Orwell, George (eds. Sonia Orwell and Ian Angus), T*he Collected Essays, Journalism and Letters*, Vol. 4. London: Penguin Books, 1970.

Orwell, George, *Coming Up for Air*. London: Secker & Warburg, 1948.

Osgood, Samuel M., *French Royalism Since 1870.* The Hague: Martinus Nijhoff, 1970.

Oudard, Georges, *Chemises noires, brunes, vertes en Espagne*. Paris: Plon, 1938.

'Our Woman Correspondent', 'Greek Premier's Decree: Imprisonment for Short Skirt Offenders', *Newcastle Daily Chronicle* (9 December 1925), 3.

Pailler, Jean, *Charles Ier, roi de Portugal: Destin maudit d'un roi sacrifié*. Biarritz: Atlantica, 2000.

Palmer, Alan, *The Royal House of Greece*. London: Weidenfeld & Nicolson, 1990.

Palmer, Alan, *Twilight of the Habsburgs: The Life and Times of the Emperor Francis Joseph*. London: Weidenfeld & Nicolson, 1994.

Pando Despierto, Juan, *Historia secreta de Annual: memorias de guerra*. Barcelona: Ediciones Altaya, 2008.

Papacosma, S.V., 'Ioannis Metaxas and the Fourth of August Dictatorship in Greece', in B.J. Fischer (ed.), *Balkan Strongmen: Dictators and Authoritarian Rulers of South-Eastern Europe* (West Lafayette, Indiana: Purdue University Press, 2007), 165–198.

Payne, Stanley G., *A History of Spain and Portugal,* Vol. 2. Madison: University of Wisconsin Press, 1973.

Payne, Stanley G., and Jesús Palacios, *Franco: A Personal and Political Biography*. Madison: University of Wisconsin Press, 2015.

Payne, Stanley G., *Falange: A History of Spanish Fascism*. Stanford, California: Stanford University Press, 1962.

Payne, Stanley G., *Politics and the Military in Modern Spain*. Stanford, California: Stanford University Press, 1967.

Payne, Stanley G., *The Spanish Civil* War, Cambridge: Cambridge University Press, 2012.

Pearce, Joseph, *Bloomsbury and Beyond: The Friends and Enemies of Roy Campbell*. *London*: HarperCollins, 2001.

Pearson, Owen, *Albania and King Zog: Independence, Republic and Monarchy, 1908–1939*. London: I.B. Tauris, 2004.

Pétain, Philippe (ed. Jacques Isorni), *Actes et Écrits*. Paris: Flammarion, 1974.

Peterecz, Zoltán, 'Hungary and the League of Nations: A Forced Marriage', in Peter Becker and Natasha Wheatley (eds.), *Remaking Central Europe: The League of Nations and the Former Habsburg Lands* (Oxford: Oxford University Press, 2020), 145–166.

Peters, Stephen, 'Kim Philby and the Albanian Mission', *The New York Times* (13 October 1985), 18.

Petrie, Sir Charles, *A Historian Looks at His World*. London: Sidgwick & Jackson, 1972.

Petrie, Sir Charles, *King Alfonso XIII and His Age*. London: Chapman & Hall, 1963.

Petrie, Sir Charles, *Lords of the Inland Sea*. London: L. Dickson Ltd., 1937.

Petrie, Sir Charles, *Monarchy in the Twentieth Century*. London: Andrew Dakers, 1952.

Petrie, Sir Charles, *Twenty Years' Armistice – And After: British Foreign Policy Since 1918*. London: Right Book Club, 1940.

Pichou, Myrsini, and Chrysoula Kapartziani, 'Thirty centimetres above the ground: The regulation length for Greek skirts during the dictatorship of General Theodoros Pangalos, 1925–1926', *Clothing Cultures* 3:1 (January 2016), 55–74.

Pilar of Bavaria, Princess, and Desmond Chapman-Houston, *Don Alfonso XIII: A Study of Monarchy*. London: John Murray, 1931.

Pimenta de Castro, Gonçalo Pereira, *As minhas memórias, na metrópole e nas colónias,* Vol. 3. Oporto: Livraria Progredior, 1950.

Pinto Coelho, Maria Teresa, '"Pérfida Albion" and "Little Portugal": The Role of the Press in British and Portuguese National Perceptions of the 1890 Ultimatum', *Portuguese Studies* 6 (1990), 173–190.

Pius XI, Pope, *Dilectissima Nobis,* 3 June 1931, Dilectissima Nobis (June 3, 1933) | PIUS XI (vatican.va) (accessed 28 January 2023)

Portland, W.J.A.C.J. Cavendish-Bentinck, Sixth Duke of, *Men, Women and Things: Memories of the Duke of Portland.* London: Faber & Faber, 1938..

Potts, D.M., and W.T.W. Potts, *Queen Victoria's Gene.* Stroud, Gloucestershire: Alan Sutton Publishing Ltd., 1995.

Preston, Sir Paul, 'The monarchy of Juan Carlos: from dictator's dreams to democratic realities', in Sebastian Balfour (ed.), *The Politics of Contemporary Spain.* London: Routledge, 2005.

Pulido Valente, Vasco, *O Poder e o Povo: A Revolução de 1910.* Lisbon: Moraes Editores, 1982.

Putscher Pereira, Bernardo, *A Diplomacia de Salazar, 1932–1949.* Lisbon: Don Quixote, 2012.

Radowitz Nei, Clemens von, 'Monarchy will return, but not I, says ex-Kaiser', *The New York Times* (3 July 1922), 1 and 3.

Raithel, Thomas, 'Les partis régionaux en Bavière au XXe siècle', in Hélène Miard-Delacroix, Guillaume Garner, and Béatrice von Hirschhausen (eds.), *Espaces de Pouvoir, Espaces d'Autonomie en Allemagne* (Villeneuve d'Ascq, France: Presses Universitaires du Septentrion, 2010), 131–145.

Ramsay, Scott Robert, *Negotiating Neutrality: Anglo-Spanish Relations in the Age of Appeasement, 1931–1940*, PhD diss., University of Leeds, 2021, 40.

Rauschning, Hermann (tr. E.W. Dickes), *Makers of Destruction: Meetings and Talks in Revolutionary Germany.* London: Eyre & Spottiswode, 1942.

Rhodes, Anthony Richard Ewart, *The Vatican in the Age of the Dictators, 1922–1945.* New York City: Holt, Rinehart and Winston, 1973.

Ricciu, Francesco, *La rivoluzione spagnola.* Milan: Dall'Oglio, 1970.

Ritter, Gerhard (tr. R.T. Clark), *The German Resistance: Carl Goerdeler's Struggle Against Tyranny.* London: Allen & Unwin, 1958.

Roberts, L.E.J., and Albert Weale, *Innovation and Environmental Risk.* Lansing: University of Michigan Press, 1991.

Robinson, Vandeleur, *Albania's Road to Freedom.* London: Allen & Unwin, 1941.

Romero Raizábal, Ignacio, *El Príncipe Requeté.* Santander, Spain: Aldus, 1965.

Rose, Kenneth, *King George V.* New York City: Knopf, 1984.

Roudiez, L.S., 'Amending the Record: The Early Poetic Activities of Charles Maurras', *The French Review* 24:3 (January 1951), 197–208.

Rougerie, Jacques, *La Commune de 1871.* Paris: Presses Universitaires de France, 2014.

Sakmyster, Thomas L., *Hungary's Admiral on Horseback: Miklós Horthy, 1918–1944.* Boulder, Colorado: East European Monographs, 1994.

Sanabria, Enrique, *Republicanism and Anticlerical Nationalism in Spain.* London: Palgrave Macmillan, 2009.

Schmitt, H.A., *Neutral Europe Between War and Revolution, 1917–23.* Charlottesville, Virginia: University of Virginia Press, 1988.

Schuman, Frederick L., *Hitler and the Nazi Dictatorship: A Study in Social Pathology and the Politics of Fascism.* London: Hale, 1936.

Sefa, Eriselda, 'The Efforts of King Zog I for Nationalization of Albanian Education', *Journal of Educational and Social Research* 2:2 (May 2012), 339–346;

Self, Robert (ed.), *The Austen Chamberlain Diary Letters: The Correspondence of Sir Austen Chamberlain with His Sisters Hilda and Ida, 1916–1937.* Cambridge: Cambridge University Press, 1995.

Sencourt, Robert, *King Alfonso: A Biography.* London: Faber & Faber, 1942.

Sencourt, Robert, *Spain's Uncertain Crown: The Story of the Spanish Sovereigns, 1808–1931.* London: Ernest Benn, 1932.

Serge, Victor, *Memoirs of a Revolutionist*. London: Oxford University Press, 1967.

Seton-Watson, Hugh, *Eastern Europe Between the Wars 1918–1941*. Hamden, Connecticut: Archon Books, 1962.

Shelley, Gerard, *The Speckled Domes: Episodes of an Englishman's Life in Russia*. New York City: C. Scribner's Sons, 1925.

Shelmerdine, Brian, *British Representations of the Spanish Civil War* Manchester: Manchester University Press, 2006.

Shillan, David, 'Portugal Today', *International Affairs* 20:2 (April 1944), 215–224.

Simas, L.C.M., 'Teófilo Braga – O Grande Esquecido', 2007, *Jardins de Epicuro*, http://www.ulisses.us/lucia-9–teofilo.htm (accessed 19 April 2023).

Simenon, Georges (tr. Anthea Bell), *The Late Monsieur Gallet*. London: Penguin Books, 2013.

Sitwell, Sir Osbert, *Great Morning*. London: Macmillan, 1948.

'Spanish Observer, A', 'Under the Spanish Dictatorship', *The Manchester Guardian* (20 August 1924), 8.

Stapleton, Augustus G., *George Canning and His Times*. London: J.W. Parker and Son, 1859.

Stern, Howard Norman, *Political Crime and Justice in the Weimar Republic*. PhD diss., John Hopkins University (Baltimore), 1966.

Stirling, Walter Francis, *Safety Last*. London: Hollis & Carter, 1955.

Stuart, Robert, *Marxism and National Identity: Socialism, Nationalism, and National Socialism during the French* Fin de Siècle. Albany: State University of New York Press, 2006.

Sweetman, Jack, *The Unforgotten Crowns: The German Monarchist Movements, 1918–1945*. PhD diss., Emory University (Atlanta), 1973.

Swire, Joseph, *King Zog's Albania*. London: Robert Hale, 1937.

Tannenbaum, Edward R., *The Action Française: Die-Hard Reactionaries in Twentieth-Century France*. New York City: Wiley, 1962.

Tardío, Manuel Álvarez, 'The impact of political violence during the Spanish general election of 1936', *Journal of Contemporary History* 48:3 (2013), 463–485.

Taylor, A.J.P., *The Italian Problem in European Diplomacy, 1847–1849*. Manchester: Manchester University Press, 1970.

Taylor, A.J.P., *The Origins of the Second World War*. London: Athenaeum, 1961.

Taylor, Edmond, *The Fall of the Dynasties: The Collapse of the Old Order, 1905–1922*. London: Weidenfeld & Nicolson, 1963.

Tefft, B.F., *Hungary and Kossuth: or, An American Exposition of the Late Hungarian Revolution*. Philadelphia: John Ball, 1852.

Templewood, Viscount (Sir Samuel Hoare), *Ambassador on Special Mission*. London: Collins, 1946.

Terraine, John, 'The War Must Be Ended' (Part I), *History Today* 28:11 (November 1978), 703–711.

Terraine, John, 'The War Must Be Ended' (Part II), *History Today* 28:12 (December 1978), 783–792.

Tett, Gillian, 'Can you win an election without digital skullduggery?', *The Financial Times* (10 January 2020), Subscribe to read | Financial Times (ft.com) (accessed 7 May 2023).

Theodoracopulos, Taki, *The Greek Upheaval: Kings, Demagogues and Bayonets*. London: Stacey International, 1976.

Thomas, Hugh, *The Spanish Civil War*, 3rd edition. London: Hamish Hamilton, 1977.

Tolstoy, Nikolai, 'Consider a Monarchy, America', *The New York Times* (6 November 2016), 11.

Tombs, Robert, 'Victimes et bourreaux de la Semaine Sanglante', *1848: Révolutions et mutations du XIX siècl*e, 10 (1994), 81–96.

Tomes, Jason, *King Zog: Self-Made Monarch of Albania*. Stroud, Gloucestershire: The History Press, 2003.

Torrend, Camillo, SJ, 'The Anti-Clerical Policy in Portugal and Its Results', *Dublin Review* (January-April 1912), 128-151.

Tortella Casares, Gabriel (tr. V.J. Herr), *The Development of Modern Spain: An Economic History of the Nineteenth and Twentieth Centuries*. Cambridge, Massachusetts: Harvard University Press, 2000.

Trend, J.B., *Portugal*. London: Ernest Benn., 1957.

Triffitt, Jonathan, *Twilight of the Princes: The Fall and Afterlife of Monarchy in Southern Germany, 1918–1934.* PhD diss., University of St Andrews (Scotland), 2021.

Trotsky, Leon (tr. Morris Lewitt), *The Revolution in Spain.* New York City: Militant Press, 1931), 25.

Tuchman, Barbara W., *Practising History.* New York City: Ballantyne Books, 1982.

United States Senate, Sixtieth Congress, First Session, 'Transmission of Senate Resolution Deploring Assassination of King and Crown Prince of Portugal', Document No. 317 (Washington DC: US Government), 24 February 1908.

Urbach, Karina, 'Age of No Extremes?: The British Aristocracy Torn between the House of Lords and the Mosley Movement', in Karina Urbach (ed.), *European Aristocracies and the Radical Right, 1918–1939*. Oxford: Oxford University Press, 2007), 53–72.

Van der Kiste, John, *Crowns in a Changing World: The British and European Monarchies, 1901–1936*. Stroud, Gloucestershire: Alan Sutton, 1993.

Van der Kiste, John, *Kings of the Hellenes: The Greek Kings, 1863–1974*. Stroud, Gloucestershire: Alan Sutton, 1999.

Vatikiotis, P.J., *Popular Autocracy in Greece, 1936–41: A Political Biography of General Ioannis Metaxas* (Portland, Oregon: Frank Cass, 1998.

Veress, Laura-Louise, and Dalma Takács, *Clear the Line: Hungary's Struggle to Leave the Axis During the Second World War*. Cleveland: Prospero Publications, 1995.

Vermes, Gabor, 'The October Revolution in Hungary', in Ivan Volgyes (ed.), *Hungary in Revolution*. Lincoln: University of Nebraska Press, 1971.

Vickers, Miranda, *The Albanians: A Modern History*. London: I.B. Tauris, 2001.

Viereck, G.S., 'Ex-Kaiser Wilhelm II Breaks His Silence', *Current History* 21:2 (November 1924), 165–180.

Villa García, Roberto, and Manuel Álvarez Tardío, *1936: fraude y violencia en las elecciones del Frente Popular*. Madrid: Espasa, 2017.

Villar, Cote, 'Sesante años de la misterioso muerte del hermano del Rey', *El Mundo* (29 March 2016), Sesenta años de la misteriosa muerte del hermano del Rey | loc | EL MUNDO (accessed 28 June 2023).

Vivian, Herbert, *Kings In Waiting.* London: Hamish Hamilton, 1933.

Vivian, Herbert, *The Life of the Emperor Charles of Austria. London*: Grayson & Grayson, 1932.

Vizetelly, Ernest Alfred, *The Anarchists: Their Faith and Their Record*. London: John Lane, 1911.

Watt, Richard M., *The Kings Depart: The Tragedy of Germany, Versailles and the German Revolution.* London: Weidenfeld & Nicolson, 1968.

Weber, Eugen, *Action Française: Royalism and Reaction in Twentieth-Century France*. Stanford, California: Stanford University Press, 1962.

Weil, Simone, *The Notebooks of Simone Weil*. London: Routledge, 2014.

Weinstein, Jay A., *Social and Cultural Change: Social Science for a Dynamic World,* Lanham, Maryland: Rowman & Littlefield, 2005,

Weissman, Benjamin M. *Herbert Hoover and Famine Relief to Soviet Russia, 1921–1923.* Stanford, California: Hoover Institution Press, 1974.

Welch, Colin, 'The Jews of Hungary', *The Spectator* 262:8394 (27 May 1989), 27–28.

Welles, Benjamin, 'Salazar in Trouble', *The Atlantic Monthly* 210:2 (August 1962), 57–62.

Wells, Warre Bradley, *The Last King: Don Alfonso XIII of Spain.* London: Frederick Muller Ltd., 1934.

Wheatcroft, Geoffrey, *Churchill's Shadow: An Astonishing Life and a Dangerous Legacy.* London: The Bodley Head, 2021.

Wheeler-Bennett, Sir John, 'The End of the Weimar Republic', *Foreign Affairs* 50:2 (January 1972), 351–371.

Wheeler-Bennett, Sir John, *Hindenburg: The Wooden Titan.* London: Macmillan, 1967.

Wheeler-Bennett, Sir John, *The Nemesis of Power: The German Army in Politics 1918–1945.* London: Macmillan, 1964.

Wheeler, Douglas L., *Republican Portugal: A Political History 1910–1926.* Madison: University of Wisconsin Press, 1978.

Wheen, Francis, *Karl Marx.* New York City: Norton, 2000.

Whittle, Tyler, *The Last Kaiser: A Biography of William II, German Emperor and King of Prussia.* London: Heinemann, 1977.

Widdig, Bernd, *Culture and Inflation in Weimar Germany.* Berkeley: University of California Press, 2001.

Wilhelm II, Kaiser (tr. Thomas R. Ybarra), *The Kaiser's Memoirs.* New York City: Harper & Brothers, 1922.

Wilton, Iain, *C.B. Fry: King of Sport, England's Greatest All-Rounder, Captain of Cricket, Star Footballer and World Record Holder.* London: John Blake, 1999.

Woodhouse, C.M., *Apple of Discord: A Survey of Recent Greek Politics in Their International Setting.* London: Hutchinson, 1948.

Woodhouse, C.M., *Modern Greece: A Short History. London*: Faber & Faber, 1986.

Woollcott, Alexander, *While Rome Burns.* London: Arthur Barker Ltd., 1931.

Wydenbruck, Nora, *My Two Worlds: An Autobiography.* London: Longmans, Green, 1956.

Young, Sir George, *Portugal Old and Young: A Historical Study.* Oxford: Oxford University Press, 1917.

Zapantis, Andrew L., *Greek-Soviet Relations, 1917–1941.* Boulder, Colorado: East European Monographs, 1982.

Zappa, Frank, and Peter Occhiogrosso, *The Real Frank Zappa Book.* New York City: Poseidon Press, 1989.

Index of Names

About the Author

Historian and organist Robert James Stove is the author of *César Franck: His Life and Times* (Lanham, Maryland: Scarecrow Press, 2012), *The Unsleeping Eye: Secret Police and Their Victims* (New York City: Encounter Books, 2002), and *Prince of Music: Palestrina and His World* (Sydney: Quakers Hill Press, 1990). His articles have been frequently published in *The American Conservative* (of which he is a Contributing Editor), *Modern Age, The Musical Times, The Sydney Organ Journal, Organ Australia*, and elsewhere, while his organ-playing has been captured on five CDs (*The Gates of Vienna, Pax Britannica, French Romantic Church Music, Undertones of War,* and *Empire to Commonwealth*) all available on the Ars Organi label (www.arsorgani.com). In 2021 he was awarded his PhD in musicology from Sydney University, having devoted his doctoral thesis to Sir Charles Villiers Stanford's organ compositions. He lives in Melbourne with his beloved cat.